Praise for

WE MAKE THE ROAD BY WALKING

"This is one of the most remarkable documents in recent Christian writings... There is no evangelizing here, and no preaching, only a sinewy, but orderly and open, presentation of the faith that holds. The result is as startling as it is beautiful."

—**Phyllis Tickle**, author, *The Age of the Spirit*

"Brian McLaren has a talent for expressing theological viewpoints in a way that doesn't divide the camp. He gives everyone on the theological spectrum, from orthodox to progressive, something to chew on and contemplate. His new book, WE MAKE THE ROAD BY WALKING, doesn't disappoint."

—**Charles Toy**, co-founder of The Christian Left

"A ton of people have been waiting for this book—they just didn't know it! Brian has given us a clear and compelling guide to walking the Jesus path together, around the table, in the living room, discussing and learning and growing. This book is going to help so many people."

—**Rob Bell**, author of *What We Talk About When We Talk About God*

"It is at once inspiring and challenging, ancient and contemporary, intellectually rigorous and profoundly practical. It changed the way I engage Scripture, the way I pray, the way I experience communion, and the way I interact with my neighbors."

—**Rachel Held Evans**, author, *A Year of Biblical Womanhood*

"WE MAKE THE ROAD BY WALKING has given me the tools I needed to make sense of my friendships and weave them into something that makes our connections more meaningful; the community that I have always longed for, a community that accepts me for me, a community that faithfully lives out the gospel through its actions, treating all people with respect, value, and like they matter."

—**Romal Tune**, author, *God's Graffiti: Inspiring Stories for Teens*

"This is Brian McLaren at his best, and I think this is what so many readers want from him: Deeply rooted in scripture, yet offering fresh, even radical, readings. WE MAKE THE ROAD BY WALKING will surely be a benefit and blessing to many."

—**Tony Jones** (tonyj.net), theologian-in-residence at Solomon's Porch, author of *The Church Is Flat*

"I love this book, because through each page you will hear the whisper of Jesus echo in your heart. You will find yourself taken on a journey that will make you more alive, more loving, and with a bigger vision for changing the world. I'm buying copies for all my friends!"

—**Canon Mark Russell**, CEO, Church Army UK and Ireland

"If you're looking for a progressive, thoughtful, inspirational resource for short-term or long-term Bible exploration I highly recommend WE MAKE THE ROAD BY WALKING. I haven't seen a more adaptable model that encourages those who gather and those who lead to experiment with what's best for their particular situation or environment."

—**The Rev. Wendy Tobias**, associate priest & lead priest for Unplugged (a Fresh Expressions service), St. Joseph's Episcopal Church, Boynton Beach, FL

"WE MAKE THE ROAD BY WALKING is a refreshing and inspiring reframing of the biblical narrative, based on modern biblical scholarship. It has deeply challenged our faith community to re-imagine what it means to be followers of Jesus."

—**Christine Berghoef**, author, *Cracking the Pot: Releasing God from the Theologies that Bind Him*

"We've used this deep and thought-provoking book in our church plant in Washington DC, and each week we are invited to consider long-familiar biblical texts in a new light. Perfect for individual or group use."

—**Bryan Berghoef**, author of *Pub Theology* and pastor of Roots DC, an urban faith community in Washington, DC

"Around the table in my home, our small, diverse faith community used this book as our guide back to connection, to hope, to aliveness and ultimately to a way forward in our spiritual journeys, both individually and corporately."

—**Sarah Dammann Thomas**, leader of a faith community in her home in Santa Barbara, CA

Also by Brian D. McLaren

Why Did Jesus, Moses, the Buddha, and Mohammed Cross the Road?
The Girl with the Dove Tattoo
The Word of the Lord to Republicans
The Word of the Lord to Democrats
Naked Spirituality
A New Kind of Christianity
The Justice Project
Finding Our Way Again
Everything Must Change
The Voice of Luke
The Voice of Acts
A Search for What Makes Sense
A Search for What Is Real
The Secret Message of Jesus
The Last Word and the Word after That
A Generous Orthodoxy
The Story We Find Ourselves In
Church in the Emerging Culture: Five Perspectives
A is for Abductive
Adventures in Missing the Point
More Ready Than You Realize
A New Kind of Christian
Finding Faith
Church on the Other Side

WE MAKE THE ROAD BY WALKING

A YEAR-LONG QUEST FOR
SPIRITUAL FORMATION, REORIENTATION,
AND ACTIVATION

BRIAN D. MCLAREN

JERICHO
BOOKS

NEW YORK • BOSTON • NASHVILLE

Jericho Books
Hachette Book Group
237 Park Avenue
New York, NY 10017

www.JerichoBooks.com

This author is represented by Creative Trust, Inc.

Printed in the United States of America

RRD-C

First Edition: June 2014
10 9 8 7 6 5 4 3 2 1

Jericho Books is an imprint of Hachette Book Group, Inc.
The Jericho Books name and logo are trademarks of Hachette Book Group, Inc.

Library of Congress Cataloging-in-Publication Data

McLaren, Brian D., 1956–
We make the road by walking : a year-long quest for spiritual formation, reorientation, and activation / Brian D. McLaren. — First edition.
pages cm
Includes bibliographical references.
ISBN 978-1-4555-1400-7 (hardcover) — ISBN 978-1-4555-1398-7 (ebook) — ISBN 978-1-4789-5379-1 (audio download) 1. Spiritual formation—Meditations. 2. Bible—Reading. 3. Bible—Meditations. 4. Church year meditations. I. Title.
BV4511.M455 2014
248.4—dc23

2013047426

CONTENTS

PART II
ALIVE IN THE ADVENTURE OF JESUS

PART III
ALIVE IN A GLOBAL UPRISING

Part IV
Alive in the Spirit of God

Preface: What This Book Is about and How to Use It

You are not finished yet. You are "in the making." You have the capacity to learn, mature, think, change, and grow. You also have the freedom to stagnate, regress, constrict, and lose your way. Which road will you take?

What's true of you is also true for every community of people, including our spiritual communities. Like the individuals who constitute them, they are unfinished and "in the making." They have the capacity to move forward if they choose... and the freedom to stagnate and regress. Which road will they follow in the years ahead? Does their future depend solely on the action or inaction of officials in the headquarters of religious bureaucracies? Do the rest of us have to wait until somebody somewhere figures things out and tells the rest of us what to do?

I believe that all of us play a role in choosing and creating our futures—as individuals and as communities. We don't need to wait passively for history to happen to us. We can become protagonists in our own story. We can make the road by walking.

Growing numbers of us believe that we are in the early stages of a new moment of emergence, pulsing with danger and promise. In this catalytic period, all our spiritual traditions will be challenged and all will change—some negatively and reactively, tightening like angry fists, and others positively and constructively, opening like extended arms.[1] More and more of

1. For a variety of perspectives on this pivotal moment, see relevant works by Ewert Cousins, Phyllis Tickle, Diana Butler Bass, Philip Clayton, Leonardo Boff, Doug Pagitt, Soong-Chan Rah, Tony Jones, Harvey Cox, Robin Meyers, Marcus Borg, David Felten,

us want to participate in that positive and constructive opening. We want to explore new possibilities, to develop unfulfilled potential, to discover new resources to bless, inspire, and enliven. We don't shrink back from this moment; we feel God is calling us to walk into it with faith, hope, and love.

I've written *We Make the Road by Walking* to help individuals and groups seize this moment and walk wisely and joyfully into the future together. It is a work of Christian theology, but people of any faith tradition will find seeds of meaning they can let take root in their own spiritual soil. It is a work of *constructive* theology—offering a positive, practical, open, faithful, improvable, and fresh articulation of Christian faith suitable for people in our dynamic times. It is also a work of *public* and *practical* theology—theology that is worked out by "normal" people in daily life.

The title suggests that faith was never intended to be a destination, a status, a holding tank, or a warehouse.[2] Instead, it was to be a road, a path, a way out of old and destructive patterns into new and creative ones. As a road or way, it is always being extended into the future. If a spiritual community only points back to where it has been or if it only digs in its heels where it is now, it is a dead end or a parking lot, not a way. To be a living tradition, a living way, it must forever open itself forward and forever remain unfinished—even as it forever cherishes and learns from the growing treasury of its past.

The simplest way for you to use this book is to read it as you would any other. At the beginning of each chapter, you'll find a few Bible passages that you can read in any responsible translation such as the New Revised Standard Version or the Common English Bible. Your enjoyment of the chapter will be enriched if you take the time to read those passages. The

---

Jeff Procter-Murphy, Jack Spong, Richard Rohr, Rob Bell, Lillian Daniel, Elaine Heath, and Joan Chittister.

2. I originally heard "We make the road by walking" as a quote from one of my heroes, Brazilian educator/activist Paulo Freire. I later learned that it became the title of a book that was a dialogue between Freire and another seminal educator/activist, Myles Horton, who was an important figure in the civil rights movement in the United States. Freire may have derived the quote from the great Spanish poet Antonio Machado (1875–1939): "*Caminante, son tus huellas / el camino, y nada más; / caminante, no hay camino, / se hace camino al andar. / Al andar se hace camino, / y al volver la vista atrás / se ve la senda que nunca / se ha de volver a pisar. / Caminante, no hay camino, / sino estelas en la mar.*"

chapter itself offers a response to those passages. Of course, the line of interpretation and application I have chosen is one of many possible responses to each text. At times, it may differ from the interpretation you have heard in the past; you are asked only to give it an honest and open hearing, and you should feel free to prefer another interpretation. At the end of each chapter you'll find some *Engage* questions that you can either skip, ponder for a few minutes on your own, or perhaps respond to in a private journal or public blog.

After reading a few chapters, you may decide to recommend the book to a few friends. Then you could invite your circle of friends to gather in your living room or around your kitchen table.[3] Guided by the liturgical resources in Appendix I, your learning circle could pray together, then read the Bible passages and the chapter, then enjoy conversation using the Engage questions, and then conclude with more resources from Appendix I, including the simplified eucharistic liturgy if appropriate.[4]

Denominational leaders could encourage pastors under their care to take a year or season out of their normal church rhythms and use this book in public worship.[5] Or they could use it in adult education classes or in small groups in homes. Four or five churches from different ethnic groups, denominational backgrounds, and social classes could send two or three people from each church to form a combined multichurch learning circle. Their learning would be enriched by a diversity their home churches may

---

3. I could imagine learning circles using this book in a college dorm or church basement, in a prison or senior living community, in a high school cafeteria or coffee shop, at a retreat center or summer camp, on a hiking trail or before a yoga class, on a beach or in a video chat.

4. By *liturgy* I mean a format of a gathering—written or unwritten—that orders a series of practices, like prayer, thanksgiving, silent meditation, a sermon, and singing. By *eucharist* I mean the Christian practice of using bread and wine to remember Jesus.

5. Many churches already use the Revised Common Lectionary (RCL), a plan that assigns certain Bible passages to be read each Sunday over a four-year cycle. I appreciate and enjoy the RCL. However, it assumes significant familiarity with the Bible and with a generous Christian vision that many do not yet have. Other churches have no intentional plan for introducing people to the Bible or a generous Christian faith. For both groups of churches, *We Make the Road by Walking* offers a comprehensive orientation (or reorientation) to Christian living—a kind of on ramp, if you will, for both "new and used" Christians.

not have. They would bring this enrichment back to their home congregations, while strengthening ties among the participating congregations.

The fifty-two-plus chapters are organized in four seasonal quarters, following a simplified version of the traditional church year that is built around Advent, Epiphany, Lent, Holy Week, Easter, and Pentecost. I've chosen to begin in September with a pre-Advent overview of the Hebrew Scriptures. But a yearlong group could start at any appropriate point in the church year and work its way around the cycle. Several groups have already field-tested the book in a variety of ways, and their responses have been highly enthusiastic. You can make this book work for you by adapting it as needed.

The road of faith is not finished. There is beautiful land ahead, terra nova waiting to be explored. It will take a lot of us, journeying together, to make the road. I hope you'll be part of the adventure. The Christian faith is still learning, growing, and changing, and so are we.

Note: In addition to the resources included here in Appendices I and II, you will find a variety of resources and links at my website (www.brianmclaren.net), including commentary on each chapter, Scripture references, suggestions for using the book in weekend and weeklong formats, suggestions for daily times of prayer and reflection, and more.[6]

6. Most Bible passages quoted in the text are from the New Revised Standard. Some are the author's paraphrase. The Contemporary English Bible (CEB), New American Standard Bible (NASB), New Living Translation (NLT), Book of Common Prayer, PCUSA *Book of Common Worship*, and Episcopal *Book of Common Prayer* are cited when quoted.

Introduction: Seeking Aliveness

WHAT WE ALL WANT is pretty simple, really. We want to be alive. To feel alive. Not just to exist but to thrive, to live out loud, walk tall, breathe free. We want to be less lonely, less exhausted, less conflicted or afraid... more awake, more grateful, more energized and purposeful. We capture this kind of mindful, overbrimming life in terms like *well-being*, shalom, *blessedness*, *wholeness*, *harmony*, *life to the full*, and *aliveness*.[1]

The quest for aliveness explains so much of what we do. It's why readers read and travelers travel. It's why lovers love and thinkers think, why dancers dance and moviegoers watch. In the quest for aliveness, chefs cook, foodies eat, farmers till, drummers riff, fly fishers cast, runners run, and photographers shoot.

The quest for aliveness is the best thing about religion, I think. It's what we're hoping for when we pray. It's why we gather, celebrate, eat, abstain, attend, practice, sing, and contemplate. When people say, "I'm spiritual," what they mean, I think, is simple: "I'm seeking aliveness."

Many older religious people—Christians, Muslims, Jews, and others—are paralyzed by sadness that their children and grandchildren are far from

1. *Zoein aionian*, a Greek term in the New Testament, is often translated to English as "eternal life." Sadly, that translation suggests "life after death" to most people and is equated with going to heaven rather than hell. The term means, literally, "life of the ages" (*zoe*—as in *zoology*; *aionian*—of the *aeons*). It should be understood in contrast to "life in this present age," which could in turn be rendered "life in this economy" or "life in contemporary culture" or "life under the current regime." My suspicion is that "true aliveness" is a good contemporary translation of the term. Luke (18:18–24) uses *zoein aionian* as a synonym for *kingdom of God*, and in the Gospel of John, *kingdom of God* seems to be rendered as *life*, *eternal life*, and *life to the full*. In Paul's writings, terms like *fullness*, *freedom*, *new life*, *life in the Spirit*, and *life in Christ* seem closely related if not synonymous. All point to an excelling quality, intensity, expansiveness, meaningfulness, fruitfulness, and depth of life.

faith, religion, and God as they understand them. But on some level, they realize that religion too often shrinks, starves, cages, and freezes aliveness rather than fostering it. They are beginning to see that the only viable future for religion is to become a friend of aliveness again.

Meanwhile, aliveness itself is under threat at every turn. We have created an economic system that is not only too big to fail, it is too big to control—and perhaps too big to understand as well. This system disproportionately benefits the most powerful and privileged 1 percent of the human species, bestowing upon them unprecedented comfort, security, and luxury. To do so, it destabilizes the climate, plunders the planet, and kills off other forms of life at unprecedented rates.

The rest, especially the poorest third at the bottom, gain little and lose much as this economic pyramid grows taller and taller. One of their greatest losses is democracy, as those at the top find clever ways to buy votes, turning elected governments into their puppets. Under these circumstances, you would think that at least those at the top would experience aliveness. But they don't. They bend under constant anxiety and pressure to produce, earn, compete, maintain, protect, hoard, and consume more and more, faster and faster. They lose the connection and well-being that come from seeking the common good. This is not an economy of aliveness for anyone.

As these tensions mount, we wake up every morning wondering what fool or fiend will be the next to throw a lit match—or assault, nuclear, chemical, or biological weapon—onto the dry tinder of resentment and fear. Again, this is a formula for death, not a recipe for life.

So our world truly needs a global spiritual movement dedicated to aliveness. This movement must be *global,* because the threats we face cannot be contained by national borders. It must be *spiritual,* because the threats we face go deeper than brain-level politics and economics to the heart level of value and meaning. It must be *social,* because it can't be imposed from above; it can only spread from person to person, friend to friend, family to family, network to network. And it must be a *movement,* because by definition, movements stir and focus grassroots human desire to bring change to institutions and the societies those institutions are intended to serve.

I believe that the Spirit of God works everywhere to bring and restore aliveness—through individuals, communities, institutions, and movements. Movements play a special role. In the biblical story, for example, Moses led a movement of liberation among oppressed slaves. They left an oppressive economy, journeyed through the wilderness, and entered a promised land where they hoped to pursue aliveness in freedom and peace. Centuries after that, the Hebrew prophets launched a series of movements based on a dream of a promised time... a time of justice when swords and spears, instruments of death, would be turned into plowshares and pruning hooks, instruments of aliveness. Then came John the Baptist, a bold and nonviolent movement leader who dared to challenge the establishment of his day and call people to a movement of radical social and spiritual rethinking.

John told people he was not the leader they had been waiting for; he was simply preparing the way for someone greater than himself. When a young man named Jesus came to affiliate with John's movement through baptism, John said, "There he is! He is the one!" Under Jesus' leadership, the movement grew and expanded in unprecedented ways. When Jesus was murdered by the powers that profited from the status quo, the movement didn't die. It rose again through a new generation of leaders like James, Peter, John, and Paul, who were full of the Spirit of Jesus. They created learning circles in which activists were trained to extend the movement locally, regionally, and globally. Wherever activists in this movement went, the Spirit of Jesus was alive in them, fomenting change and inspiring true aliveness.

Sometimes institutions welcomed this nonviolent spiritual movement and were strengthened by it. Sometimes they co-opted, smothered, squelched, frustrated, corrupted, or betrayed it. If the movement slowed, receded, or weakened for a while in one place, eventually it resurged again in some new form. For example, there were the monastic movements led by the desert mothers and fathers, the Celtic movement led by St. Patrick, St. Brigid, and others, and the beautiful movements of St. Francis and St. Claire. Later reform movements grew up around people like Menno Simons, Martin Luther, John Wesley, and Walter Rauschenbusch. Over the last century, we've seen new movements being born through people like Dorothy Day, Ella Baker, Martin Luther King, Desmond Tutu, Wangari

Maathai, Óscar Romero, Rene Padilla, Richard Twiss, Joan Chittister, Jim Wallis, Tony Campolo, Richard Rohr, Phyllis Tickle, William Barber, John Dear, Steve Chalke, and Shane Claiborne.

And of course, just as the Spirit has moved among Christians, the Spirit has been at work in other communities, too. Too seldom have these diverse movements recognized their common inspiration, and too seldom have they collaborated as they should. It's surely time for that to change.

This book is a resource for this emerging spiritual movement in service of aliveness. It is written primarily for use in Christian communities, but it excludes no one. (I can imagine parallel books being written primarily for Jews, Muslims, and others.) As I explained in the Preface, you can read it as you are reading now, a personal resource for your own thinking and rethinking. But you can also use the book to form a learning circle, as Appendix I explains, creating a community for spiritual formation, reorientation, and activation.

There's an old religious word for this kind of learning experience: *catechesis* (cat-uh-*key*-sis). At first glance, catechesis hardly seems like a resource for aliveness and movement building. To most people, it evokes either nothing at all or the unpleasant aroma of dust and mold. For those of us raised in highly religious households, it may bring to mind boring classes taught by stern nuns or lay teachers where we memorized answers we didn't understand to questions we didn't care about for reasons we never knew. It suggests pacifying, indoctrinating, and domesticating people for institutional conformity.

But before Christianity was a rich and powerful religion, before it was associated with buildings, budgets, crusades, colonialism, or televangelism, it began as a revolutionary nonviolent movement promoting a new kind of aliveness on the margins of society. It dared to honor women, children, and unmarried adults in a world ruled by married men. It dared to elevate slaves to equality with those who gave them orders. It challenged slave masters to free their slaves and see them as peers. It defied religious taboos that divided people into *us* and *them*, *in* and *out*, *good* and *evil*, *clean* and *unclean*.

It claimed that everyone, not just an elite few, had God-given gifts to use for the common good. It exposed a system based on domination, privilege, and violence and proclaimed in its place a vision of mutual service, mutual responsibility, and peaceable neighborliness. It put people above profit, and made the audacious claim that the Earth belonged not to rich tycoons or powerful politicians, but to the Creator who loves every sparrow in the trees and every wildflower in the field. It was a peace movement, a love movement, a joy movement, a justice movement, an integrity movement, an aliveness movement.

It had no bank accounts, but was rich in relationships and joy. It had no elaborate hierarchy and organization, but spread like wildfire through simple practices of empowerment and self-organization. It had no seminaries or colleges, but it was constantly training new waves of courageous and committed leaders through the "each one teach one" strategy of catechesis. It had lots of problems, too, but it grappled with those problems courageously.

In this light, catechesis was a subversive practice of movement building. It was a "people's seminary," transforming any room, campfire, or shady spot beneath a tree into a movement school. It equipped the oppressed and oppressors to become partners and protagonists in their mutual liberation. Mentors (or *catechists*) would invite a student or students (*catechumens*) to meet regularly. They used a simple curriculum (or *catechesis*) of meaningful stories, healing teachings, and transformative practices. Their course of preparation traditionally culminated in a kind of oral examination based on a series of predetermined questions (a *catechism*). Those who had been mentored through this process would then be ready to pass on what they had learned. In so doing, they would learn the catechism more deeply, since teaching is surely the best way to learn.

The subversive nature of catechesis was all the more remarkable because many of the teachers and students were illiterate. It was through the personal give-and-take of face-to-face conversation and interaction that people were formed and transformed, equipped and deployed as nonviolent activists in the movement of the Spirit.

In the second century, catechesis became more formalized as a preparation for baptism. Through a rigorous and long process, catechists helped catechumens understand core teachings and adopt virtuous behavior. Catechumens would be examined and passed on from one stage, or level, of discipleship to the next before they would be accepted for baptism and full participation in the Christian community. Catechesis became less an orientation to participate in a movement and more a requirement for membership in an institution.

As churches began baptizing infants, and as persecution gave way to political and social privilege for baptized Christians, catechesis became less important. From time to time it was reinvigorated to counter spiritual lukewarmness and ignorance. During regular church services, priests would teach or remind parishioners about the basics of the faith—often centered on the Lord's Prayer, the Apostles' Creed, and the Ten Commandments. For a time in the Middle Ages, communities even developed summer drama festivals during which they acted out stories from the Bible in their historical sequence—an especially helpful practice when most people were illiterate and confused by a complex church calendar over-full of saints' days. As early as the ninth century, question-and-answer formats came into use to prepare children for their first communion.

Catechesis had a resurgence about five hundred years ago. Martin Luther designed a catechism to help a head of household train or retrain family members in the emerging Protestant faith using simple questions and answers.[2] A young leader named John Calvin also published a catechism that served as a foyer or an entryway into an intricate doctrinal system he was constructing.[3] John Wesley came along two centuries later. In many ways, he rediscovered the original power of catechesis as a movement school.

---

2. The preface to Luther's Small Catechism begins with Luther's characteristic rhetorical energy:

> "*Martin Luther* to All Faithful and Godly Pastors and Preachers: Grace, Mercy, and Peace in Jesus Christ, our Lord. The deplorable, miserable condition which I discovered lately when I, too, was a visitor, has forced and urged me to prepare [publish] this Catechism, or Christian doctrine, in this small, plain, simple form. Mercy! Good God! what manifold misery I beheld! The common people, especially in the villages, have no knowledge whatever of Christian doctrine, and, alas! many pastors are altogether incapable and incompetent to teach [so much so, that one is ashamed to speak of it]. Nevertheless, all maintain that they are Christians, have been baptized and receive the [common] holy Sacraments. Yet they [*do not* understand and] cannot [*even*] recite either the Lord's Prayer, or the Creed, or the Ten Commandments; they live like dumb brutes and irrational hogs; and yet, now that the Gospel has come, they have nicely learned to abuse all liberty like experts." (http://bookofconcord.org/smallcatechism.php#preface)

3. Calvin's first version was published in 1537, was revised in the mid-1540s, and was revised again in 1560.

He encouraged people to self-organize into small learning cohorts called classes and bands that gathered for spiritual formation, reorientation, and activation. He published his sermons to help resource these groups. And to make his movement's essential vision available to children, he published a catechism-like book called *Instructions for Children*.[4]

These examples from history have helped give shape to the fifty-two (plus a few) chapters that follow.

Based on their format, some might wonder if I'm recommending learning circles gathered around *We Make the Road by Walking* as an alternative to traditional churches.

My first answer is a firm no. Wherever possible, I would hope that these simple learning circles would be supplemental to participation in a traditional congregation and denomination (as were the early monastic and Methodist movements within Catholicism and Anglicanism). In fact, I would be thrilled for pastors in traditional congregations to use these fifty-two-plus sermons, along with the accompanying simple liturgy and Bible reading plan, as a yearlong template for spiritual formation, reorientation, and activation in traditional church settings.[5]

But this won't always be possible, so my second answer is maybe yes. I hope that *We Make the Road by Walking* will facilitate the spontaneous formation of grassroots learning circles that can bring together people who don't feel welcome or wanted in conventional churches. I would discourage these self-organizing groups from using the word *church* to describe what they're doing—at least initially. A lot of unintended pressure, baggage,

4. *Instructions for Children* was first published in 1745. Wesley also wrote a revision of the *Westminster Shorter Catechism*. The *Shorter Catechism* had been adopted by the Church of England in 1648. It was strongly Calvinistic, or deterministic, in its tone, and Wesley's revisions just over a century later (1753) show where his vision of the faith differed from the Calvinistic vision of his forbears.

5. Having spent over twenty years as a pastor, I think it's good for pastors to prepare original sermons each week. But I also know that periodically, it can be good for a pastor to use prepared sermons like the ones in this book, either for a season or a whole year. During that time, a pastor could take the time and energy normally invested in sermon preparation and use it for some other generative purpose—physical recreation, engagement with the poor, a writing project, an artistic pursuit, outreach to the community, civic engagement, interfaith work, marriage enrichment, parenting time, or good, old-fashioned fun and rest.

expectation, criticism, and complications can come along with that word.[6] Eventually, spontaneously formed learning circles may find existing congregations or denominations that will welcome them. Maybe they will eventually choose to use the word *church* to name what they have become. In the spiritual life, as in all of life, it's better to have the substance without the label than the label without the substance.[7]

If you're a seeker exploring Christian faith, or if you're new to the faith and seeking a good orientation, here you'll find the introduction I wish I had been given. If you're a long-term Christian whose current form of Christianity has stopped working and may even be causing you and others harm, here you'll find a reorientation from a fresh and healthy perspective.[8] If your faith seems to be a lot of talk without much practice, I hope this book will help you translate your faith to action. And if you're a parent trying to figure out what you should teach your kids and grandkids—knowing you want to introduce them to a kind of Christian faith, but not exactly the version you were given—I hope this book will fit the need.[9]

Right now I'm imagining each of you, gathered around a table filled with brimming glasses and plates of flavorful foods. You're all engaged in animated conversation, telling jokes, sharing stories about your experiences since you last gathered. Partway through your meal, someone says, "The Living God is with us!" and everyone else responds, "And with all creation!" And then someone begins to read.

---

6. For example, a "church" that does enormous good for five years and then shuts down is seen as a failure, whereas many congregations survive for decades while actually accomplishing little. For some reason, longevity becomes a requirement for many people when the word *church* is applied.

7. It is my hope that denominations will create special protected zones for learning circles and other innovative faith communities, zones where fresh expressions of Christian spirituality, community, and mission can experiment and flourish without being subjected to normal protocols and expectations. In a sense, denominations can understand themselves to be entering into "new lines of business" by fostering new faith communities in this experimental space.

8. For the theologically informed, I've created a resource that provides commentary on each chapter, explaining what I did and why. You can learn more about it at www.brianmclaren.net.

9. The Engage questions and liturgical resources in Appendix I encourage adults to include children in learning circles whenever possible.

I

ALIVE IN THE STORY OF CREATION

YOU ARE ENTERING A story already in process. All around you, things are happening, unfolding, ending, beginning, dying, being born. Our ancient ancestors tried to discern what was going on. They conveyed their best wisdom to future generations through stories that answered certain key questions:

Why are we here?
What's wrong with the world?
What's our role, our task, our purpose?
What is a good life?
Is there meaning and hope?
What dangers should we guard against?
What treasures should we seek?

From the Hopi to the Babylonians, from Aztecs to Australian Aboriginals, from the Vikings in Europe to the Han in China to the Yoruba in Africa to the ancient Hebrews of the Middle East—human tribes have developed, adapted, and told powerful creation narratives to convey their best answers to key questions like these. Of course, their language often sounds strange to us, their assumptions foreign, the details of their culture odd or alien. But if we listen carefully, mixing their ancient wisdom with our own, we can let their stories live on in us. We can learn to be more fully alive in our time, just as they learned in theirs. In that spirit, we turn to the creation narratives of the ancient Hebrews.

For learning circles, Part I would most naturally be used during the thirteen weeks before Advent. In the traditional church calendar, this is during Ordinary Time, the season after Pentecost. For many, it coincides with the beginning of the school year in late August or early September. Be sure to review the Five Guidelines for Learning Circles in Appendix II at your first few gatherings.

CHAPTER ONE

AWE AND WONDER

Genesis 1:1–2:3
Psalm 19:1–14
Matthew 6:25–34

BIG BANGS AREN'T BORING. Dinosaurs aren't boring. Coral reefs aren't boring. Elephants aren't boring. Hummingbirds aren't boring. And neither are little kids. Evolution isn't boring. Magnetism and electricity aren't boring. $E = MC^2$ might be hard to understand, but it certainly isn't boring. And even glaciers aren't boring, although their dramatic pace is at first quite hard for us to perceive. And God, whatever God is, must not be boring, either, because God's creation is so amazingly, wonderfully, surprisingly fascinating.

The first and greatest surprise—a miracle, really—is this: that anything exists at all, and that we get to be part of it. Ripe peach, crisp apple, tall mountain, bright leaves, sparkling water, flying flock, flickering flame, and you and me . . . here, now!

On this, the first pages of the Bible and the best thinking of today's scientists are in full agreement: it all began in the beginning, when space and time, energy and matter, gravity and light, burst or bloomed or banged into being. In light of the Genesis story, we would say that the possibility of this universe overflowed into actuality as God, the Creative Spirit, uttered the original joyful invitation: *Let it be!* And in response, what happened? Light. Time. Space. Matter. Motion. Sea. Stone. Fish. Sparrow. You. Me. Enjoying the unspeakable gift and privilege of being here, being alive.

Imagine how uncountable nucleii and electrons and sister particles danced and whirled. Imagine how space dust coalesced into clouds, and how clouds coalesced into galaxies, and how galaxies began to spin, sail, and dance through space. Imagine how in galaxy after galaxy, suns blazed, solar systems twirled, and worlds formed. Around some of those worlds, moons spun, and upon some of those worlds, storms swirled, seas formed, and waves rolled. And somewhere in between the smallest particles and the largest cosmic structures, here we are, in this galaxy, in this solar system, on this planet, in this story, around this table, at this moment—with this chance for us to breathe, think, dream, speak, and be alive together.

The Creator brought it all into being, and now some fourteen billion years later, here we find ourselves: dancers in this beautiful, mysterious choreography that expands and evolves and includes us all. We're farmers and engineers, parents and students, theologians and scientists, teachers and shopkeepers, builders and fixers, drivers and doctors, dads and moms, wise grandparents and wide-eyed infants.

Don't we all feel like poets when we try to speak of the beauty and wonder of this creation? Don't we share a common amazement about our cosmic neighborhood when we wake up to the fact that we're actually here, actually alive, right now?

Some theologians and mystics speak of the Creator withdrawing or contracting to make space for the universe to be...on its own, so to speak, so that it has its own life, its own being and history. Others imagine God creating the universe within God's self, so the universe in some way is contained "in" God, within God's presence, part of God's own life and story. Still others imagine God creating an "out there" of space and time, and then filling it with galaxies, and then inhabiting it like a song fills a forest or light fills a room or love fills a heart. Interestingly, some scholars believe the Genesis story echoes ancient Middle Eastern temple dedication texts. But in this story, the whole universe is the temple, and the Creator chooses to be represented by human beings, not a stone idol.

The romance of Creator and creation is far more wonderful and profound than anyone can ever capture in words. And yet we try, for how could we be silent in the presence of such beauty, glory, wonder, and mystery? How can we not celebrate this great gift—to be alive?

To be alive is to look up at the stars on a dark night and to feel the beyond-words awe of space in its vastness. To be alive is to look down from a mountaintop on a bright, clear day and to feel the wonder that can only be expressed in "oh" or "wow" or maybe "hallelujah." To be alive is to look out from the beach toward the horizon at sunrise or sunset and to savor the joy of it all in pregnant, saturated silence. To be alive is to gaze in delight at a single bird, tree, leaf, or friend, and to feel that they whisper of a creator or source we all share.

Genesis means "beginnings." It speaks through deep, multilayered poetry and wild, ancient stories. The poetry and stories of Genesis reveal deep truths that can help us be more fully alive today. They dare to proclaim that the universe is God's self-expression, God's speech act. That means that everything everywhere is always essentially holy, spiritual, valuable, meaningful. All matter matters.

If you ask what language the Creator speaks, the best answer is this: God's first language is full-spectrum light, clear water, deep sky, red squirrel, blue whale, gray parrot, green lizard, golden aspen, orange mango, yellow warbler, laughing child, rolling river, serene forest, churning storm, spinning planet.

A psalmist said the same thing in another way—the universe is God's work of art, God's handiwork. All created things speak or sing of the God who made them. If you want to know what the Original Artist is like, a smart place to start would be to enjoy the art of creation.

Genesis tells us that the universe is good—a truth so important it gets repeated like the theme of a song. Rocks are good. Clouds are good. Sweet corn is good. Every river or hill or valley or forest is good. Skin? Good. Bone? Good. Mating and eating and breathing and giving birth and growing old? Good, good, good. All are good. Life is good.

The best thing in Genesis is not simply human beings, but the whole creation considered and enjoyed together, as a beautiful, integrated whole, and us a part. The poetry of Genesis describes the "very goodness" that comes at the end of a long process of creation... when all the parts, including us, are working together as one whole. That harmonious whole is so good that the Creator takes a day off, as it were, just to enjoy it. That day of restful enjoyment tells us that the purpose of existence isn't money or power or fame or security or anything less than this: to participate in the goodness and beauty and aliveness of creation. And so we join the Creator in good and fruitful work... and in delightful enjoyment, play, and rest as well.

So here we are, friends. Here we are. Alive!

And this is why we walk this road: to behold the wonder and savor this aliveness. To remind ourselves who we are, where we are, what's going on here, and how beautiful, precious, holy, and meaningful it all is. It's why we pause along the journey for a simple meal, with hearts full of thankfulness, rejoicing to be part of this beautiful and good creation. This is what it means to be alive. Amen.

Engage:

1. What one thought or idea from today's lesson especially intrigued, provoked, disturbed, challenged, encouraged, warmed, warned, helped, or surprised you?
2. Share a story about a time when you most felt the humble awe and joyful wonder described in this chapter.
3. What is the most beautiful place you have ever seen? What was so special about it?
4. For children: What is your favorite animal? Why do you like it so much?
5. Activate: This week, choose one facet of creation that you love—birds, trees, weather, soil, water, light, children, sex, aging, sleep. Observe it, think about it, learn about it every chance you can, with this question in mind: if that element of creation were your only Bible, what would it tell you about God?
6. Meditate: Observe a few moments of silence. Let a silent prayer of gratitude arise from within you.

CHAPTER TWO

BEING HUMAN

Genesis 2:4–25
Psalm 8
Mark 3:1–6

TWO EYES ARE BETTER than one, because they make depth perception possible. The same goes with ears. Two ears make it possible to locate the direction of a sound. And we often say that two heads are better than one, because we know that insight from multiple perspectives adds wisdom.

The same is true with stories. We can best think of the Bible not as one tidy story with many chapters but as a wild and fascinating library with many stories told from many perspectives. On any given subject, these multiple stories challenge us to see life from a variety of angles—adding depth, a sense of direction, and wisdom. So, we're given four gospels to introduce us to Jesus. We're given dozens of parables to illustrate Jesus' message. We're given two sections or testaments in which the story of God unfolds. And right at the beginning, we're given two different creation stories to help us know who we are, where we came from, and why we're here.

According to the first creation story, you are part of creation. You are made from common soil...*dust,* Genesis says; *stardust,* astronomers tell us...soil that becomes watermelons and grain and apples and peanuts, and then they become food, and then that food becomes you. As highly organized dust, you are closely related to frogs and tortoises, lions and field mice, bison and elephants and gorillas. Together with all living things, you share the breath of life, participating in the same cycles of birth and death, reproduction and recycling and renewal. You, with them, are part of the story of creation—different branches on the tree of life. In that story, you are connected and related to everything everywhere. In fact, that is a good partial definition of God: *God is the one through whom we are related and connected to everything.*

In the first creation story, we learn two essential truths about ourselves as human beings. First, *we are good.* Along with all our fellow creatures, we were created with a primal, essential goodness that our Creator appreciates and celebrates. And second, *we all bear God's image.* Women and men, girls and boys, toddlers and seniors and teenagers, rich or poor, popular or misunderstood, powerful or vulnerable, whatever our religion or race or marital status, whatever our nationality or culture...we *all* bear God's image, no exceptions.

What is the image of God? An image is a small imitation or echo, like a reflection in a mirror. So if we bear the image of God, then like God, we experience life through relationships. Like God, we experience love through our complementary differences. Like God, we notice and enjoy and name things—starting with the animals, our companions on the Earth. Like God, we are caretakers of the garden of the Earth. And like God, we are "naked and not ashamed," meaning we can be who we are without fear.

Back in ancient times, this was a surprising message. Yes, kings and other powerful men were seen as image bearers of God. After all, since they were powerful, rich, sophisticated, and "civilized," they could reflect God's power and glory. But in Genesis, the term is applied to a couple of naked and "uncivilized" hunter-gatherers, a simple woman and man living in a garden with no pyramids or skyscrapers or economies or religions or technological inventions or even clothing to their credit! Centuries later, Jesus said something similar: the Creator loves every sparrow and every wildflower, and so how much more precious is every person—no matter how small, frail, or seemingly insignificant? Every woman, man, and child is good! Every person in every culture has value! Every person bears the image of God! It's all good!

But that's not the only story. The second creation account, which many scholars think is a much older one, describes another dimension to our identity. In that account, the possibility of "not-good" also exists. God puts the first couple in a garden that contains two special trees. The Tree of Life is theirs to enjoy, but not the Tree of the Knowledge of Good and Evil. The Tree of Life is a beautiful image—suggesting health, strength, thriving, fruitfulness, growth, vigor, and all we mean by *aliveness*. What might that second tree signify?

There are many answers, no doubt. But consider this possibility: the second tree could represent the desire to play God and judge parts of God's creation—all of which God considers good—as evil. Do you see the danger? God's judging is always wise, fair, true, merciful, and restorative. But our judging is frequently ignorant, biased, retaliatory, and devaluing. So when we judge, we inevitably *mis*judge.

If we humans start playing God and judging good and evil, how long will it take before we say this person or tribe is good and deserves to live, but that person or tribe is evil and deserves to die, or become our slaves? How long will it take before we judge this species of animal is good and deserves to survive, but that one is worthless and can be driven to extinction? How long until we judge this land is good and deserves to be preserved, but that river is without value and can be plundered, polluted, or poisoned?

If we eat from the second tree, we will soon become violent, hateful, and destructive. We will turn our blessing to name and know into a license to kill, to exploit, and to destroy both the Earth and other people. God sees everything as good, but we will accuse more and more things of being evil. In so doing, we will create in ourselves the very evil we claim to detect in others. In other words, the more we judge and accuse, the less we will reflect God... and the less we will fulfill our potential as image bearers of God.

So the second creation story presents us with our challenge as human beings. We constantly make a crucial choice: Do we eat from the Tree of Aliveness—so that we continue to see and value the goodness of creation and so reflect the image of the living God? Or do we eat from the Tree of the Knowledge of Good and Evil—constantly misjudging and playing God and as a result mistreating our fellow creatures?

It's a good and beautiful thing to be an image bearer of God. *But it's also a big responsibility.*

We can use our intelligence to be creative and generous, or to be selfish and destructive.

We can use our physical strength to be creative and generous, or to be selfish and destructive.

We can use our sexuality to be creative and generous, or to be selfish and destructive.

We can use our work, our money, our time, and our other assets to be creative and generous, or to be selfish and destructive.

Think of your hand. It can make a fist or it can extend in peace. It can wield a weapon or it can play a violin. It can point in derision or it can reach out in compassion. It can steal or it can serve. If the first creation story is about the gift of being human, the second story is about the choice all humans live with, day after day. To be alive means to bear responsibly the image of God. It means to stretch out your hand to take from the Tree of Aliveness—and to join in God's creative, healing work.

Engage:

1. What one thought or idea from today's lesson especially intrigued, provoked, disturbed, challenged, encouraged, warmed, warned, helped, or surprised you?
2. Share a story about a time when someone played god and judged you, or a time when you played god and judged someone else.
3. Tell us about a person who has reflected God to you in some special way.
4. For children: Think about your hands. What is something kind and creative you can do with your hands? What is something mean or harmful you can do with your hands? How can the same hands do both kind and mean things?
5. Activate: If part of being image bearers of God means that we represent God in caring for the Earth, it's important to learn about your corner of the Earth. You know your postal address (nation, state, city, postal code). What is your environmental address? Learn about your watershed, what makes it special, and the environmental issues it faces.
6. Meditate: Observe a few moments of silence. Let a silent prayer rise from within you.

CHAPTER THREE

A WORLD OF MEANING

Psalm 145:1–16
Proverbs 8:1–36
John 1:1–17

OK. PAY ATTENTION. (FEEL free to take a few minutes to discuss your answers.)

1, 6, 11, 16, 21, 26, 31 . . . What comes next?
1, 4, 2, 5, 3, 6, 4, 7 . . . What comes next?
1, 2, 3, 5, 8, 13, 21, 34 . . . What comes next?
I, space, L, O, V, E, space, Y, O . . . What comes next?

You know the answers because you are paying attention to the pattern.

It becomes more obvious the longer you live that all life is full of patterns. Reality is trying to tell us something. Life is speaking to us. There's lots of mystery out there, to be sure, and no shortage of chaos and unpredictability. But there's also lots of meaning . . . messages trying to find expression, music inviting us to listen and sing, patterns attracting our attention and interpretation. The chaos becomes a backdrop for the patterns, and the mysteries seem to beckon us to try to understand.

Sometimes the universe feels like this:

71, 6, 2, -48, -213, 9 . . . random numbers with no pattern. Or . . .

G, M, B, O, I, space, Q, H, Z, space, P... random letters with no meaning. Or...

1,1,1,1,1,1,1,1,1... sameness or repetition going nowhere.

But above and behind and beyond the sometimes confusing randomness of life, something is going on here. From a single molecule to a strand of DNA, from a bird in flight to an ocean current to a dancing galaxy, there's a logic, a meaning, an unfolding pattern to it all.

Like wood, reality has a grain. Like a river, it has a current. Like a story, it has characters and setting and conflict and resolution. Like poetry, it has syntax and structure, so letters are taken up in words, and words are taken up in phrases and sentences, and they're all taken up in a magnificent pattern of beauty and meaning that we can glimpse and savor, even if it's too big and deep to fully comprehend. Creation reveals wisdom through its patterns. It reveals wisdom about its source and purpose, and about our quest to be alive... if we are paying attention.

Of course, we often struggle to know how to interpret those patterns. For example, if a tornado destroys our house, an enemy army drops bombs on our village, a disease takes away someone we love, we lose our job, someone we love breaks our heart, or our best friends betray us, what does that mean? Is the logic of the universe chaos or cruelty? Does might make right? Do violence and chaos rule? Is the Creator capricious, heartless, and evil? If we had only our worst experiences in life to guide us, that might be our conclusion.

This is where the Gospel of John adds its insight to the creation stories we find in the Book of Genesis. John had a special term for the pattern of meaning God has spoken or written into the universe. He called it *Logos,* which is often translated in English as "Word." We find *logos* in words like biology, anthropology, and psychology—the logic of life, human development, or the human personality.

This Word or *Logos,* he said, was "made flesh" in a man named Jesus. In other words, if we want to know what God is like and what the universe is about, we should pay attention to the logic, meaning, wisdom, and patterns found in the life of Jesus. He communicated the *logos,* or logic, of God in his teachings. He lived the *logos*, or pattern, of God in his life. He showed the *logos*, or essence, of God in the way he treated others. From his birth to his death and beyond, John believes, Jesus translates the logic or meaning or pattern or heart of God into terms we humans can understand: skin and bone, muscle and breath, nerve and action.

So, inspired by Genesis, we are guided to look for the pattern, meaning, wisdom, and logic of God woven into galaxies, planets, forests, fields, plants, animals, you, and me. In John's gospel, we are inspired to look for the pattern in a poor man traveling across the land with a band of students and friends, telling stories, confronting injustice, helping people in need. If we learn and trust the wisdom that comes in creation and in Jesus, we will live our lives in a new way, John says. We will discover God as our loving parent, and we will encounter all other creatures as our relations, our relatives, in one family of creation.

Of course, we have other options. For example, many of us live by the logic of rivalry. Under this logic, the cosmos is a huge battlefield or coliseum in which participants can survive only by competing, defeating, deceiving, displacing, or killing their rivals. In this universe, the strongest survive, the ruthless are rewarded, the kind are killed, and the meek are crushed. You'd better fight, or you'll be trampled.

Others of us live by the logic of compliance. Under this logic, the cosmos is a big organization ruled by powerful bosses, and your job is to learn the rules and comply. Stay in your allotted place, do what you're told, curry favor in the "inner circle" of power, and the logic of compliance will work in your favor. You'd better play it safe, or you'll get in a lot of trouble.

Still others of us think of the universe as a giant machine, and live by the logic of mechanism—action, reaction; cause, effect; stimulus, response. You can use the mechanisms of the universe to seek whatever pleasure, power, and security you can during your short life. But in the end, there is no meaning to the machine, so you'd better grab whatever moments of fleeting pleasure you can. That's all there is or ever will be.

Clearly, the creation stories of Genesis and John offer us a powerful alternative to the logic of rivalry, the logic of compliance, and the logic of meaningless mechanism.

They dare us to believe that the universe runs by the logic of creativity, goodness, and love. The universe is God's creative project, filled with beauty, opportunity, challenge, and meaning. It runs on the meaning or pattern we see embodied in the life of Jesus. In this story, pregnancy abounds. Newness multiplies. Freedom grows. Meaning expands. Wisdom flows. Healing happens. Goodness runs wild.

So here we are, alive and paying attention. We discern patterns in life. We interpret those patterns and we open ourselves to the possibility of a creative *logos* of love and wisdom that runs through the universe like a current and can play in our lives like a song.

Engage:

1. What one thought or idea from today's lesson especially intrigued, provoked, disturbed, challenged, encouraged, warmed, warned, helped, or surprised you?
2. Share a story about a time when you lived by the logic of rivalry, compliance, or meaningless mechanism. How did that work out for you?
3. Imagine and describe what your life would be like if you chose to live more by the *logos* of love than you do now.
4. For children: Is there one cartoon or movie that you like to watch or hear again and again? What about it makes you want to keep enjoying it again and again?
5. Activate: Share with someone this week—a family member, a friend, a coworker, or an acquaintance—the idea that we all live by a certain *logos* or logic. Ask them which *logos* they see to be most powerful in today's world—rivalry, compliance, meaningless mechanism, or love.
6. Meditate: Observe a few moments of silence to imagine yourself living more fully in the *logos* of love.

CHAPTER FOUR

The Drama of Desire

Genesis 3:1–13
Psalm 32
Philippians 2:3–11

In the ancient wisdom of storytelling, Genesis tells us that we are part of God's good creation. It then tells us we have a special responsibility as God's reflections or image bearers. It tells us that in order to reflect God's image, we have to desire the Tree of Life, not the tree that feeds our pride so that we think we can play god and judge between good and evil.

Of course, we know what happened. The story of Adam and Eve doesn't need to be about literal historical figures in the past to tell us something very true about us, our history, and our world today. We humans have consistently chosen the wrong tree. Instead of imitating and reflecting God as good image bearers should do, we start competing with God, edging God out, playing god ourselves. We reject the Creator and choose another model instead: a snake (the story says), who seems to represent a subtle and dangerous desire to choose rivalry and violence over harmony and well-being.

In Genesis, after feeding on the Tree of Knowledge of Good and Evil, Adam and Eve suddenly feel a change come over them. Perhaps they each fear that the other will judge them for being different, so they fashion crude clothing to hide their sexual differences. When God approaches, they no longer see God as a friend, but as a rival and threat. So they hide from God in fear. When God asks what has happened, they blame one another and refuse to admit their mistake. Soon they face a harder life of pain, competition, sweat, labor, frustration, and death—East of Eden, outside the beautiful garden that was their home.

Later, their two sons repeat the pattern. The older brother—we might say he is "more advanced"—becomes an agriculturalist. His life is wrapped up in fields, fences, ownership, barns, and accumulated wealth, with all the moral complexity they bring. The younger brother—we might say he is "more vulnerable" or "less developed"—is a nomadic herdsman. He can't own land or accumulate wealth, because he moves constantly with his herds to wherever the fresh grass is growing. Their different ways of life are expressed in different forms of religious sacrifice. They soon become religious rivals, competing for a higher degree of God's favor. The perceived loser in the competition, Cain, envies and resents his brother.

Sometime later, we can imagine Abel leading his flocks into his brother's field. At that moment Cain, his resentment simmering, no longer sees a brother: he sees a trespasser, an enemy. He plays god and judges his brother as evil and therefore worthy of death. Abel soon becomes the first victim of violence, and Cain, the first murderer. So we humans quickly turn from reflecting the image of a creative, generous, life-giving God. With Adam and Eve we become graspers, hiders, blamers, and shamers. With Cain and Abel we become rivals, resenters, murderers, and destroyers—the very opposite of God's image.

What do these ancient stories mean for us today?

They help us know what's broken with our world: something in us human beings.

And they help us know what's broken in human beings: something in our desires.

And they help us know what's broken with our desires: we have stopped imitating God's good desires to create and bless and give life. Instead we've started imitating the prideful, competitive, fearful, and harmful desires we see in one another... the desire to acquire what someone else has, the desire to compete and consume, the desire to judge as evil those who get in our way, even the desire to harm or kill those who are obstacles to our desires.

Think about how much imitation runs our lives.

Somebody hits or criticizes you and what do you want to do? Hit them back! Criticize them back!

Somebody buys a new shirt or a new TV, and what do you want to do? Buy an even better shirt or bigger TV!

Somebody moves to a bigger house in a different neighborhood, and what do you desire? To get an even bigger house in an even better neighborhood!

And what happens if you can't get what you desire? You'll be tempted to cheat, steal, lie, harm, or maybe even kill to get what you desire.

Now there's nothing wrong with desire. The question is, whose desires are you imitating? To be alive is to imitate God's generous desires... to create, to bless, to help, to serve, to care for, to save, to enjoy. To make the opposite choice—to imitate one another's desires and become one another's rivals—is to choose a path of death.

If we imitate our way into that rat race, we will compete rather than create, impress rather than bless, defeat rather than protect, dominate rather than serve, and exploit rather than respect. As a result, we will turn our neighbor first into a rival, and then an enemy, and then a victim.

We all live in this drama—the drama of desire. We have the opportunity to imitate God's generous and good desires on the one hand—and we have the temptation to imitate selfish, fearful, envious human desires on the other hand.

Think of all the advertisers who are trying to influence our desires. Think of all the politicians who are eager to mold our desires so they can manipulate us for their advantage. Think of all the potential rivals who are glad to engage us in competition—their desires against ours. What's true of us as individuals can also be true of us as groups—both personally and socially, we are caught in the drama of desire.

That's another reason Jesus is so important to us: because he modeled a different way of life. He gave us a down-to-Earth example of God's creative self-giving. True, Adam and Eve grabbed for the chance to be like gods—judging others as good or evil, exploiting rather than preserving the Earth, competing with one another rather than loving and serving one another. But Jesus didn't grasp at godlike status. He humbly poured himself out for others—in service, in suffering, even to the point of death. He even gave us a way of remembering his attitude of self-giving: he said that his life was like food, like bread and wine, and he freely gave himself for us. His constant invitation—"Follow me"—could also be expressed as "Imitate me."

To be alive is to be mindful that we live in the drama of desire. We can imitate one another's competitive desires, and so be driven to fear, rivalry, judging, conflict, and killing. Or we can imitate God's generous desires... to create, bless, help, serve, care for, save, and enjoy. At this moment, let us turn toward God, not as rivals who want to play God, but as image bearers who want to imitate and reflect God. Let us humbly and fervently desire the right kind of desire.

Engage:

1. What one thought or idea from today's lesson especially intrigued, provoked, disturbed, challenged, encouraged, warmed, warned, helped, or surprised you?
2. Share a story about your interaction with someone you were jealous of or considered a rival. What did they have or desire that you desired? How did your relationship play out?
3. How do you respond to reading the Philippians 2 passage as a reversal of the Genesis 3 passage?
4. For children: How do you feel when you win or lose in a game? How do you feel when you do better or worse at something than someone else? Tell us a story about it.
5. Activate: Be especially sensitive to rivalry this week. When you feel it, ask what "desire to acquire" is driving you. And ask whom you are imitating in this "desire to acquire." In this way, seek to become more aware of the Cain and Abel struggling in your own life and heart.
6. Meditate: After a few moments of silence, let one emotion rise to the surface and express that emotion to God—and, if you'd like, to your companions, with a brief explanation.

CHAPTER FIVE

IN OVER OUR HEADS

Genesis 4:1–17; 6:5–8; 7:1–5; 8:1; 9:7–17
Psalm 51
James 4:1–8

IN THE ANCIENT GENESIS stories, our species was created in the image of God—to reflect God's character faithfully in the world, both to our fellow creatures and to one another. Soon, though, we wanted to be little gods ourselves. We wanted to judge good and evil for ourselves, to decide who would live and who would die, who would rule and who would be enslaved. Consumed by the desire to grasp what others had, we became rivals of God and our neighbors. That crisis of desire has led to great shame, pain, suffering, violence, counterviolence, and fear... in our lives, our communities, and our world. Today's headlines tell the same story in a hundred different ways.

In the Genesis story, the descendants of Cain, the first murderer, started building cities, and those cities reflected the violence of Cain. As city-states competed with each other and defeated one another, the winners created growing empires that elevated a few to godlike status and reduced most to oppression and slavery. The situation became so unbearable that in the story of Noah and the flood, God felt sorry for making the world in the first place. Eventually God decided to wipe the whole slate clean and start again. Maybe Noah's descendants would do better than Adam's had.

Although many people think of this as a cute story about animals and a boat ride, those who think more deeply find it deeply disturbing. The image of violent oppressors and innocent victims drowning together seems only to make a bad situation worse. At the very least, one would think God would have more creativity, moral finesse, and foresight than to create a good world only to destroy it because it went so bad so (relatively) quickly. Shouldn't God be better than this?

To properly understand this story—and others like it—we need to remember that ancient cultures were oral cultures. Few people were literate, and oral storytelling was to them what reading books, using the Internet, going to concerts, and watching movies and TV shows are to us today. Ancient stories had a long life as oral compositions before they were ever written down. As oral compositions, stories could evolve over time. In a sense, writing them down ended their evolution.

For ancient people in oral cultures, a story was like a hypothesis. A good and helpful story, like a tested hypothesis, would be repeated and improved and enhanced from place to place and generation to generation. Less helpful stories would be forgotten like a failed theory, or adjusted and revised until they became more helpful. Sometimes, competing stories would stand side by side like competing theories, awaiting a time when one would prevail—or both would fail, and a new story would arise with more explanatory power. In all these ways, storytelling was, like the scientific method, a way of seeking the truth, a way of grappling with profound questions, a way of passing on hard-won insights. As our ancestors deepened their understanding, their stories changed—just as our theories change.

In this light, we can reconsider the story of Noah as an adaptation of even older stories from the Middle East. In one of those earlier versions, a gang of gods unleashed a catastrophic flood as a personal vendetta against some noisy people who kept the gods awake at night. Ancient Jewish storytellers would have found that story repulsive. So they adapted it to reveal more of God's true character, replacing many vindictive gods who were irritable from lack of sleep with one Creator who unleashes a flood to flush out human violence.

That's certainly a step in the right direction, but the process doesn't need to end with the Noah story. After all, God's violence doesn't really solve anything in the Noah story, since Noah's family quickly starts cooking up more trouble so that soon, things are just as bad as they were before the flood. Again, we can't help but wonder: shouldn't God be better than that? To answer that question, we need to bring in another story. Later in Genesis, in the story of Joseph, God responds to violence in a very different way—not with more violence, but with kindness. Another big step in the right direction!

We see the same pattern in the story of the Tower of Babel. The ancient world was filled with huge structures—towers and pyramids and temples and the like—that were built with slave labor. Just about everyone in those days assumed that the gods chose a few high-echelon people to sit pretty at the top of the pyramid. The masses were destined to be slaves at the bottom, sweating to make bricks or haul stones or irrigate fields so that the elite could have a nice day. Everyone assumed that the gods supported these slave-based economies of empire, and everyone understood that the towers, pyramids, and temples both pleased and honored the gods of the status quo.

But in the Tower of Babel story, the storytellers realize that the living God must be better than that. So in their story, tower building is exposed as another form of rivalry with God. God opposes their soaring ambition of assimilation and domination. God diversifies the languages of the Babylonian empire so that its ambition of global empire fails, memorialized forever in an unfinished tower. This new version of an old story is a big step in the right direction. Later, when we come to the story of Pentecost in the Acts of the Apostles, we'll see another giant step forward, revealing God even more beautifully and fully.

As we progress through the biblical library, these stories interact with one another again and again. Together they reveal an ever-fuller and deeper vision of God. We come to know a God who consistently refuses to support a pyramid economy with a few at the top and the masses at the bottom. We come to trust a God who consistently opposes the oppressors and consistently takes the side of the humble, the vulnerable, and the poor. We eventually come to understand God as one who consistently prefers nonviolence over violence, equality over dominance, and justice over injustice. Taken together, these stories make one of the most audacious claims in all of history: the living God doesn't uphold the status quo...but repeatedly disrupts it and breaks it open so that something better can emerge and evolve.

Do you see what's happening? Generation after generation, people are telling stories that improve upon previous stories and prepare the way for even better stories to emerge. The process leaps forward in the story of Jesus. He comes proclaiming the message of the commonwealth—or kingdom, or alternative economy—of God. He shows how in God's way of arranging things, the last are first and the first are last. Leaders serve, and the humble—not the arrogant—inherit the Earth. In word and deed, in parable and miracle, Jesus shows that God is at work in history to heal what is broken—on the personal level of individual lives, and on the societal level of economics and government, too. And he proclaims God not as a reactive avenger who sweeps away the innocent with the guilty but as a forgiving, merciful, gracious parent who loves all creation with a perfect, holy, faithful, compassionate love.

No wonder he told people to "repent"—which means to "rethink everything." No wonder he was known as a brilliantly creative and original storyteller.

As with the parables of Jesus, the Adam and Eve, Cain and Abel, flood, and tower stories in Genesis don't need to be *factually* true to tell an *actual* truth about us and our civilization. Those ancient stories courageously expose how all civilizations were founded on violence and oppression, producing luxury and ease for a few but exhaustion and degradation for the many. They warn us that unjust structures are unsustainable. They advise that floods of change will sweep injustice away and internal conflicts will thwart arrogant ambitions. They promise that in the long run, justice and reconciliation will prevail over injustice and rivalry.

If we aren't careful, we can grow comfortable and complacent with a status quo of injustice, oppression, and violence. That's why we are wise to gather often and retell these ancient stories. Rather than being conformed to this world and its mixed-up priorities, we can seek together to be transformed by a different and better story so we can join with God in the healing of our world.

To be alive is to join God in caring about the oppressed, the needy, the powerless, the victims, and the vulnerable. To be alive is to believe that injustice is not sustainable and to share God's desire for a better world. To be alive is to look at our world and say, "God is better than that!"—and know that our world can be better, too. *And so can we.*

ENGAGE:

1. What one thought or idea from today's lesson especially intrigued, provoked, disturbed, challenged, encouraged, warmed, warned, helped, or surprised you?
2. Share a story where you felt like someone at the top of the pyramid, or like someone at the bottom.
3. How do you respond to the comparison between stories and scientific theories, or to the distinction between factual and actual truth?
4. For children: Have you ever known a bully, or have you ever been a bully, or have you ever been bullied? Tell us about it.
5. Activate: Look for moments this week when it might be appropriate for you to say, "God must be better than that." And look for examples this week of the powerful exploiting the vulnerable when it might be appropriate for you to say, "We can be better than that."
6. Meditate: Ask yourself, in God's presence, "What *desire to acquire* may be driving me into trouble?" After a few moments of silence, acknowledge the desires that come to mind. Then ask for other, better desires to replace the *desire to acquire.*

CHAPTER SIX

Plotting Goodness

Genesis 12:1–9
Galatians 3:6–9
Mark 11:15–19

According to the ancient stories of Genesis, God is up to something surprising and amazing in our world. While we're busy plotting evil, God is plotting goodness.

Yes, sometimes we humans try to rope God into our dark plots and use God to help us scramble to the top of the pyramid, where we can dominate over others. Yes, we sometimes try to enlist God to condemn those we want to condemn, deprive those we want to deprive, even kill those we want to kill. But God isn't willing to be domesticated into our little tribal deity on a leash who will "sic 'em" on our command. While we plot ways to use God to get blessings for ourselves, God stays focused on the big picture of blessing the world—which includes blessing us in the process.

You see this pattern unfold when God chooses a man named Abram and a woman named Sara. They are from a prominent family in a great ancient city-state known as Ur, one of the first ancient Middle Eastern civilizations. Like all civilizations, Ur has a dirty little secret: its affluence is built on violence, oppression, and exploitation. Behind its beautiful facade, its upper classes live each day in luxury, while its masses slave away in squalor.

God tells this couple to leave their life of privilege in this great civilization. He sends them out into the unknown as wanderers and adventurers. No longer will Abram and Sara have the armies and wealth and comforts of

Ur at their disposal. All they will have is a promise—that God will be with them and show them a better way. From now on, they will make a new road by walking.

God's promise comes in two parts. In the first part, Abram and Sara will be blessed. They will become a great nation, and God will bless those who bless them and curse those who curse them. That's the kind of promise we might expect. It's the second part that's surprising.

Not only will they be blessed, but they will be a blessing. Not only will their family become a great nation, but all the families on Earth will be blessed through them.

This is a unique identity indeed. It means the children of Abram and Sara will be a unique *us* in relation to all the other *thems* of the world. No, their identity will not be *us at the top* of the pyramid and *them at the bottom*, or vice versa. Nor will their identity be *us assimilated into them*, or *us assimilating them into us*. Nor will it be *us against them*, *us apart from them*, or *us in spite of them*. No, Abram and Sara's unique identity will be *us for them*, *us with them*, *us for the benefit and blessing of all*.

That "otherly" identity—*us for the common good*—wasn't intended only for Abram and Sara's clan. It is the kind of identity that is best for every individual, every culture, every nation, every religion. It says, "We're special!" But it also says, "They're special, too." It says, "God has a place for us and a plan for us." But it also says, "God has a place and plan for others, too." When we drift from that high calling and start thinking only of *me*, only of *our* clan or *our* nation or *our* religion, our sense of identity begins to go stale and sour, even toxic.

So the story of Abram and Sara's unique identity tells us something powerful about God's identity, too: God is not the tribal deity of one group of "chosen" people. God is not for us and against all others. God is for *us* and for *them*, too. God loves everyone everywhere, no exceptions.

And this story also tells us something about true faith. Faith is stepping off the map of what's known and making a new road by walking into the unknown. It's responding to God's call to adventure, stepping out on a quest for goodness, trusting that the status quo isn't as good as it gets, believing a promise that a better life is possible.

True faith isn't a deal where we use God to get the inside track or a special advantage or a secret magic formula for success. It isn't a mark of superiority or exclusion. True faith is about joining God in God's love for everyone. It's about seeking goodness with others, not at the expense of others. True faith is seeing a bigger circle in which we are all connected, all included, all loved, all blessed. True faith reverses the choice that is pictured in the story of Adam and Eve. In that story, Adam and Eve want to set themselves above everyone and everything else. True faith brings us back down to Earth, into solidarity with others and with all creation.

Sadly, for many people, faith has been reduced to a list. For some, it's a list of beliefs: ideas or statements that we have to memorize and assent to if we want to be blessed. For others, it's a list of dos and don'ts: rituals or rules that we have to perform to earn the status of being blessed. But Abram didn't have much in the way of beliefs, rules, or rituals. He had no Bibles, doctrines, temples, commandments, or ceremonies. For him, true faith was simply trusting a promise of being blessed to be a blessing. It wasn't a way of being religious: it was a way of being alive.

And so this story not only tells us something about God's true identity and about the true nature of faith, it also tells us about true aliveness. If you scramble over others to achieve your goal, that's not true aliveness. If you harm others to acquire your desire, that's not true aliveness. If you hoard your blessings while others suffer in need, that's not true aliveness. True aliveness comes when we receive blessings and become a blessing to others. It's not a blessing racket—figuring out how to plot prosperity for me and my tribe. It's a blessing economy where God plots goodness for all.

Like all of us, Abram and Sara will lose sight of this vision of aliveness sometimes. But even when they lose faith, God will remain faithful. Through their mistakes and failures, they will keep learning and growing, discovering more and more of God's desire to overflow with abundant blessing for all.

Are you ready to step out on the same journey of faith with Sara and Abram? Will you join them in the adventure of being blessed to be a blessing? Are you ready to make the road by walking?

ENGAGE:

1. What one thought or idea from today's lesson especially intrigued, provoked, disturbed, challenged, encouraged, warmed, warned, helped, or surprised you?
2. Share a story about a time when you observed or participated in a group that saw itself as blessed *to the exclusion of others* rather than *for the blessing of others.*
3. Where in today's world do you see people practicing the kind of "otherly" identity to which God called Abram—"us for the sake of others"?
4. For children: Tell us about a grown-up or another child who often asks you to help him or her. How does helping someone make you feel?
5. Activate: Look for opportunities to "be a blessing" to others this week. Come back with some stories to share.
6. Meditate: In silence, hold this truth in God's presence: *I am blessed to be a blessing.*

CHAPTER SEVEN

It's Not Too Late

Genesis 18:9–33; 22:1–14
Micah 6:6–8
Acts 17:19–34

Have you ever felt that it was too late? That things were so awful they could never get better, that you had failed so horribly and so often you could never, ever recover, that the situation was too far gone ever to be salvageable?

That was how Abram and Sara felt at one point in their lives. Like many couples, they had dreamed all of their lives of having children. But the years passed and no children came. They had received a promise from God that they would become a great family and that all people everywhere would be blessed through their descendants. But there was one problem: they had no descendants. When they were far too old to have children, you can imagine how they felt: it was just too late.

Then they received reassurance from God that they would have a child. No wonder, according to the Book of Genesis, Sara laughed when she first heard the promise!

However they felt at first, over time Abram and Sara came to believe that what seemed impossible was possible after all. When that impossible baby was born, guess what they named him? They named him Isaac, which means "laughter." And their names were changed, too, reflecting their new status as parents—from Abram and Sara to Abraham and Sarah.

You might expect a happy ending at this point, but it was not that simple. Even after embarking on the adventure of faith, and even after becoming parents when it seemed too late, Abraham and Sarah faced another huge challenge.

Put yourself in their sandals. Imagine that you and everyone you know believes that God is a severe and demanding deity who can bestow forgiveness and other blessings only after human blood has been shed. Imagine how that belief in human sacrifice will affect the way you live, the way you worship, and the way you treat others. Now imagine how hard it would be to be the first person in your society to question such a belief. Imagine how much courage it would take, especially because your blood might be the next to be sacrificed!

Questioning widely held assumptions about God can be a dangerous venture indeed. But if our assumptions aren't sometimes questioned, belief in God becomes less and less plausible. For example, biblical writers used the imagery of God sitting on a throne to express their belief that God was powerful and glorious, like an ancient king. Even though we may agree that God is powerful and glorious, does that mean we must believe that God's power and glory are exactly like those of ancient kings—who could often be insecure, capricious, vain, or vicious? Does it mean we must conclude that God has a literal gluteus maximus that rests on a really big chair floating up in the sky somewhere? Are we allowed to question or point out problems with these images and understandings that are widely held and emotionally comforting for many?

Perhaps we can agree that whoever and whatever God is, our best imagery can only point toward God like a finger. We can never capture God in our concepts like a fist. In fact, the more we know about God, the more we have to acknowledge we don't know. The bigger our understanding about God, the bigger the mystery that we must acknowledge. Our faith must always be open to correction, enhancement, and new insight. That's why humility is so essential for all who speak of God.

Science faces a similar problem, by the way. Scientists have names for gravity and light and electricity and magnetism. But even though they have names for these realities, and even though they can create models and formulas to predict how they will work, what these forces really are remains a mystery. It's pretty humbling when you think about it. That's why, in the world of science, people are constantly questioning old assumptions and creating new theories or models. Scientists test and argue about those new theories and models until they are either confirmed or replaced with something even better.

The dominant theory of God in Abraham and Sarah's day taught that the gracious God who gives human life would also demand human life as a sacrifice. So when Abraham believed God was commanding him to kill Isaac, he was being faithful to a traditional model of how God and life worked. We might wish that Abraham had argued over this theory, just as he did when he believed God was about to destroy the cities of Sodom and Gomorrah. But strangely, what Abraham did for two cities he refrained from doing for his own son.

So, one day Abraham led Isaac up a mountain. He piled stones into an altar, tied up his son, and placed him on the stones. He raised the knife, and once again, it seemed too late. But at that last possible instant, Abraham saw a ram nearby, its horns stuck in a thicket. Suddenly he realized that God had provided a ram to sacrifice in place of Isaac, his son. What a powerful new insight! Animal blood could please or appease their God as a substitute for human blood!

It was commonplace in the ancient world for a man to lead his son up a mountain to be sacrificed to his deity. It was extraordinary for a man to come down the mountain with his son still alive. Through that ancient story, Abraham's descendants explained why they had changed their theory or model of God, and why they dared to be different from their neighbors who still practiced human sacrifice. It wasn't too late to challenge widely held assumptions and change their theory of God!

But they still weren't finished. Many generations after ritualized human sacrifice was left behind forever, prophets and poets arose among Abraham's descendants who made the shocking claim that God doesn't need animal sacrifices, either. They realized that God could never need anything *from* us, since God provides everything *for* us. Not only that, but they realized God isn't the one who is angry and hostile and needs appeasement. We humans are the angry ones! Our hostile, bloodthirsty hearts are the ones that need to be changed!

So over many centuries, led along by many teachers and prophets, Abraham's descendants came to believe that God wanted one thing from humanity... not sacrifice, whether human or animal, but this: to do justice, to love kindness, and to walk humbly with God. The only sacrifice that mattered to God was the holy gift of humble hearts and lives dedicated to his way of love.

So with faith, it's not too late. It's not too late for a dream to come true, and it's not too late to learn something new.

That's true for us today as we follow in the footsteps of Abraham and Sara, walking this road together. We're still learning, rethinking, growing, discovering. In spite of long delays and many disappointments, will we dare to keep dreaming impossible dreams? In spite of the assumptions that everyone around us holds to be true, will we dare to ask new questions and make new discoveries—including lessons about God and what God really desires? It may seem as if it's too late to keep hoping, to keep trying, to keep learning, to keep growing. But to be alive in the story of creation means daring to believe it's not too late.

ENGAGE:

1. What one thought or idea from today's lesson especially intrigued, provoked, disturbed, challenged, encouraged, warmed, warned, helped, or surprised you?
2. Share a story about a time when you almost gave up, but are glad you didn't.
3. What are some critical issues in today's world—or in our personal lives—where we might say "It's too late" or "It's impossible"?
4. For children: What makes you laugh? Why do you think Sarah laughed in this story?
5. Activate: This week, try saying "It's not too late" when you're tempted to be cynical or give up. Or practice the art of "the second laugh." The first laugh comes as a reflex when we think something is impossible. The second laugh comes as a choice when we laugh at our lack of faith.
6. Meditate: After a few moments of silence, complete this sentence as your prayer: "Living God, it's not too late to change my mind about..."

CHAPTER EIGHT

Rivalry or Reconciliation?

Genesis 32:22–33:11; 50:15–21
Matthew 25:31–40
Luke 10:25–37

If you had siblings, how did you get along? The Book of Genesis is full of stories of brothers and sisters in competition and conflict. After the tragic story of Cain and Abel, we come to the story of Ishmael and Isaac. Ishmael was Abraham's first son, born not to his wife, Sarah, but to her Egyptian slave, Hagar. According to Genesis, there was a bitter rivalry between the two mothers and their two sons. Hagar and Ishmael were treated terribly, while Sarah and Isaac were given every advantage. God intervened and made it clear that even if Abraham and Sarah failed to love Hagar and Ishmael, God cared for them deeply.

Years later, Abraham's grandson Jacob was caught up in bitter sibling rivalry with his older twin brother, Esau. At the heart of their conflict was the belief that God loved Jacob and hated Esau. Based on this belief that he was uniquely favored, Jacob felt entitled to take advantage of everyone around him, especially his disfavored brother, Esau. He seemed to get away with his trickery again and again until, eventually, Esau grew so angry at Jacob that Jacob had to flee for his life. For many years, the two brothers lived far apart, maturing, but still alienated from each other. During this time, Jacob married two sisters—a favored one named Rachel and a disfavored one named Leah. Leah became the mother of six of Jacob's twelve sons, so her story had a happier ending than anyone expected.

After he became a rich and successful man, Jacob began a homeward journey. He learned that the next day he would be forced to encounter the brother he had wronged in so many ways so many years before. You can imagine how afraid he was. He had lived his whole life by trickery. Now his old tricks weren't working anymore. So all that night, he felt like he was in a wrestling match with God.

His sleepless night of inner wrestling seems like an image for the human struggle common to us all. Like Jacob, we wrestle to get our own way by trying to cheat or defeat anyone who has something we desire—including God. Like Jacob, we grapple with changing old habits, even when those habits aren't working for us anymore. Like Jacob, we agonize through the long night, held in a headlock by despair, fearing that it's too late for us to hope for a new beginning.

So hour after hour through the night, Jacob wrestled. When the new day dawned, he rose from the struggle with two signs of his emergence into maturity as a human being. First, he received the blessing of a new name, Israel, which means "God-wrestler." And he received a hip injury that required him to walk with a limp, a lifelong memento of his long night of struggle.

Jacob was now ready—limping—to face his brother. Instead of trying to trick Esau as the old Jacob would have done, he sent Esau a huge array of gifts to honor him. When Jacob finally met Esau face-to-face, Esau had his chance. Now the older twin could finally get revenge on his upstart younger twin for all Jacob's dirty tricks in the past. Esau could treat Jacob to a taste of the disdain and contempt Jacob had repeatedly poured upon him.

But Esau surprised everyone. He made it clear that he wasn't holding a grudge. He desired no revenge, nor did he require any gifts or appeasement. He simply wanted to be reconciled.

Jacob was so touched that he said these beautiful words: "Truly, to see your face is like seeing the face of God, since you have received me with such grace." The upstart trickster had finally learned to see the face of God in the face of the one he formerly tricked and despised. He discovered God's grace in the one he had always considered disgraced. In the face of the other, he rediscovered a brother. In the face of the one everyone assumed God hated…God had been revealed. What a story!

Even though Jacob learned an important lesson that day, sibling rivalry had a resurgence in the next generation. Jacob had twelve sons. One son, Joseph, was resented by his eleven brothers, because—as with Abel over Cain, Sara over Hagar, Isaac over Ishmael, Jacob over Esau, and Rachel over Leah before him—Joseph was favored over them. In fact, Joseph dreamed that one day his brothers would grovel before him. Eventually, driven by the resentment of the disfavored, they plotted to kill him. At the last minute, however, they decided to sell him as a slave to some Egyptian traders instead. Through a dramatic series of temptations, delays, setbacks, and recoveries, Joseph rose from slavery to a place of honor in the court of the Egyptian Pharaoh.

Many years later, when a famine sent the brothers to Egypt as refugees, Joseph had his chance, just as Esau did: He could get revenge on those miserable brothers who treated him so badly. He could do to them what they had done to him. But Joseph, like Esau, made a different choice—not for revenge, but for forgiveness. When his brothers groveled before him, as Joseph had dreamed they would when he was a boy, and when they offered to be treated as slaves rather than brothers, Joseph didn't gloat. He refused to play god, judge them evil, and sentence them to death or enslavement. Instead, he reinterpreted the whole story of their relationship. Their evil intent had been overshadowed by God's good intent, so that Joseph could save their lives. He had suffered and he had been blessed, he realized, for their benefit. So instead of imitating their resentful and violent example, he imitated the gracious heart of God. By refusing to play god in judging them, he imaged God in showing kindness to them.

In this way, Joseph—the victim of mistreatment by his brothers—became the hero. The one everyone cruelly rejected was the one whose kindness everyone needed. The one who was considered favored wasn't made superior so others could grovel before him; he was made strong so he could serve them.

In both of these stories of sibling rivalry, the rejected brother, the "other brother," is the one in whose face the grace of God brightly shines.

These stories pulsate with some of the most powerful and radical themes of the Bible. Blessing, power, or favor is not given for privilege over others, but for service for the benefit of others. The weaker brother or sister, the one who is deemed ugly or dull or disfavored or illegitimate, is always beloved by

God. From Abel to Ishmael to Hagar to Esau to Leah to Joseph, God keeps showing up, not in the victors who have defeated or exploited or rejected a weaker rival, but in the weaker ones who have been defeated or rejected.

These same themes are the heartbeat of two of Jesus' greatest parables. In the parable of the prodigal son, the father who runs out to welcome his runaway younger son behaves exactly as Esau did—running to him, embracing him, kissing him, showing grace rather than retaliation. And he acts just as Joseph did, as well, not making the runaway grovel as a slave, but welcoming him as a beloved member of the family. And in the parable of the good Samaritan, it is the disfavored Samaritan, not the high-status priest or Levite, who models the love of God.

As in Genesis, life today is full of rivalries and conflicts. We all experience wrongs, hurts, and injustices through the actions of others—and we all inflict wrongs, hurts, and injustices upon others. If we want to reflect the image of God, we will choose grace over hostility, reconciliation over revenge, and equality over rivalry. When we make that choice, we encounter God in the faces of our former rivals and enemies. And as we are humbled, surrendering to God and seeking to be reconciled with others, our faces, too, reflect the face of God. We come alive as God's image bearers indeed.

ENGAGE:

1. What one thought or idea from today's lesson especially intrigued, provoked, disturbed, challenged, encouraged, warmed, warned, helped, or surprised you?
2. Share a story about how a conflict or rivalry with a family member, friend, or colleague challenged you to face yourself... and God.
3. Respond to the idea that in revenge, we seek to imitate the person who has wronged us, and that in reconciliation, we imitate and reflect God.
4. For children: Tell us about someone you had a chance to forgive.
5. Activate: This week, look for opportunities for others to "see the face of God" in your face, and seek the face of God in their faces, too—especially those you may see as rivals or outcasts.
6. Meditate: In silence, ponder forgiveness, and thank God for the joy of being forgiven—and for the release of forgiving others.

CHAPTER NINE

FREEDOM!

Exodus 1:1–14; 3:1–15
John 8:1–11
Galatians 5:1, 13–15

SLAVERY WAS A SAD and common reality in the ancient world. There were at least four ways that people became slaves. First, when people suffered a terrible misfortune like sickness, accident, flood, debt, theft, or famine, they could quickly find themselves in danger of death by starvation or homelessness. In that desperate situation, they might be forced to sell themselves into slavery, under the simple reasoning that being a live slave was better than being a dead nonslave. Second, when nations won a war, they often killed off all of their vanquished enemies. But some nations decided to keep their defeated foes alive as slaves instead of killing them. Third, refugees or other vulnerable minorities might be enslaved by the dominant majority. Finally, babies born to slaves were destined to be slaves.

That was what happened to the descendants of Abraham between the end of Genesis and the beginning of Exodus in the Bible. As Genesis ended, Joseph had welcomed his brothers into Egypt as refugees to escape a famine in their land to the north. Finding refuge solved the famine problem, but refugee and minority status made them vulnerable to enslavement.

As Exodus begins, the Hebrews, as Abraham's descendants were then called, have been enslaved. And they have also grown in numbers, so much so that the Egyptians have begun to fear that they might rebel. In response, the Egyptian ruler, the Pharaoh, calls for a gradual genocide by decreeing that all the male babies born to the Israelite slaves be thrown into the Nile River to drown. You can see how this strategy would leave the next generation of Hebrew women either barren or vulnerable to sexual enslavement by Egyptian men. After one generation, no more "pure" Hebrews would be born.

Often in the Bible, when there is a big problem, God prepares a person or people to act as God's partners or agents in solving it. In other words, God gets involved by challenging us to get involved. In this case, God prepared a man named Moses.

Moses was one of the babies whom the Pharaoh required to be drowned in the Nile. His mother came up with a creative way to save his life. She placed him in the Nile River as required, but first she put baby Moses in a little raft of reeds. His raft floated downstream, where it was found by one of Pharaoh's daughters. She felt sorry for the little baby and decided to raise him as her own. So this vulnerable slave boy was adopted into the privileged household of Pharaoh—and to top it off, Moses' own mother was hired to be the wet nurse. Quite a turn of events! Now Moses could live happily ever after, right?

Not quite. The good news was that Moses survived. The bad news? Moses grew up with an identity crisis. He was an Israelite by birth but an Egyptian by culture. So a huge question was hanging over him as he matured: on whose side would he stand when he came of age? As a young man, his moment of decision came when he saw an Egyptian beating up an Israelite. He stood up for the Israelite and killed the Egyptian oppressor. Now he had made his choice. But to his surprise, his kinfolk didn't welcome him as a hero. Instead, when he tried to intervene in a quarrel between two Israelites, they distrusted him. So he went from belonging to both sides to being considered an outsider by both sides.

In disgrace, he ran away from Egypt and came to an oasis in the desert. There, he saw a group of male shepherds drive away some girls from a well. Now, sensitized to the victims of oppression, he stood up for the girls. Their father was so grateful he welcomed Moses into his family, and Moses married one of the daughters he had helped protect.

Finally Moses had a place to belong, right? Now he could settle down and be happy, right? They lived happily ever after, right? Not quite.

Imagine the scene: Moses is out tending sheep one day and something strange catches his attention: a bush is on fire, but it's not burning up. When Moses comes closer to check it out, he hears a voice calling his name. It's God—and God is telling him to go back to Egypt, confront Pharaoh about his exploitation of the Israelites, and lead them on a long road to freedom.

Moses feels he has already failed at helping the Israelites, so it takes some persuasion for him to agree to accept this mission. But finally he goes, supported by his older brother, Aaron. They confront Pharaoh with the message: "God says, 'Let my people go!'" Predictably, Pharaoh refuses. So God sends plagues as pressure on Pharaoh, as if to say, "Oppressing others may seem like the easy road to riches, power, and comfort, but there are high costs to following that road." After that cost is dramatized ten times through ten plagues, Pharaoh relents and tells the people they can leave. Now everything will be fine, right? Happily ever after, right?

Not quite. Soon after saying yes to Moses, Pharaoh has second thoughts and sends his army to pursue the Israelites and bring them back into slavery.

So Moses and the Israelites find themselves trapped between the Egyptian army and a huge body of water. At the last minute, God opens up a path through the water, and the Israelites escape. When Pharaoh's army follows, the path closes and they all drown. The fate they had planned for the Israelite babies now becomes their own fate.

Surely now there will be a happy ending for the former slaves, right? Not quite. If you're looking for a thirty-minute story with a happy ending every time, it's hard to find in the Bible—just as it is in real life. Instead, we discover the presence of God with us in our troubles, helping us deal with them, helping us discover solutions to them, helping us deal with the new problems inevitably created by those solutions, and so on. Through it all, we discover God's faithful desire to help the downtrodden, the oppressed, the exploited, and the forgotten.

We're all like Moses in a lot of ways. We all have choices to make—who we will become, whose side we'll stand on, whether we'll give up after our failures and frustrations, whether we'll have the faith to get up and keep moving forward when we sense God's call. Life may not be easy—but it sure can be an exciting path to walk, if we go through life with God!

The story of Moses and the escape, or exodus, from Egypt glows at the core of the whole biblical story. It makes one of history's most audacious and unprecedented claims: *God is on the side of slaves, not slave owners!* God doesn't uphold an unjust status quo but works to undermine it so a better future can come. That revolutionary message is still unknown or rejected in much of the world today. If you believe it, you will live one way. If you don't, you'll live another way.

Jesus, as one of the descendants of those slaves, was formed in this story of liberation. Every year he gathered around a table to remember these events and to situate his life in the ongoing march from slavery and into freedom. All who ate that Passover meal, as it was called, were demonstrating they were not part of the slave-owning economy, but were among those seeking freedom from it. They wanted God's judgment to pass over them—which is the source of the meal's name, *Passover*—so they could pass over from slavery to freedom. As part of this community, united in this meal, Jesus learned a profound way of seeing God and others. Where others used their gods to defend an unjust status quo, Jesus believed in the God of justice and liberation. Where others saw a worthless slave, an exploitable asset, a damnable sinner, a disgusting outsider, Jesus saw someone to set free.

The night before his crucifixion, Jesus and his disciples were celebrating the Passover meal. He urged his disciples to keep doing so—not just annually, but frequently, and not just in memory of Moses in ancient Egypt, but also in memory of his life and message. That's why followers of Jesus continue to gather around a simple meal of bread and wine today. By participating in that meal, we are making the same choice Moses made—and the same choice Jesus made: to join God in the ongoing struggle to be free and to set others free. That's what it means to be alive in God's story of creation and nonviolent liberation. It's a road into the wild, a road we make by walking.

ENGAGE:

1. What one thought or idea from today's lesson especially intrigued, provoked, disturbed, challenged, encouraged, warmed, warned, helped, or surprised you?

2. Share a story about a time you took the side of a vulnerable person, or the time you were the vulnerable person and others took your side... or didn't.
3. Name the Hebrew slaves of today's world. Who today is being exploited and crying out for help? Who does backbreaking work for which others reap the rewards? How can we join in solidarity with them, seeking liberation?
4. For children: What's your favorite meal and what do you like most about it? What special meaning does that meal have for you?
5. Activate: This week, seek to have "Moses eyes"—looking for people who are being oppressed or mistreated. Be open to ways God may call you to intervene.
6. Meditate: Hold this question open before God: "Loving Creator, help my small heart to join your great heart in having compassion for those most in need."

CHAPTER TEN

GETTING SLAVERY OUT OF THE PEOPLE

Exodus 20:1–21
Matthew 22:34–40
Hebrews 10:1–18

MOST OF US SPEND a lot of our lives trying to get out of something old and confining and into something new and free. That's why we so easily identify with Moses and the freed Hebrew slaves on their journey through the wild wasteland known as the wilderness.

The truth is that we're all on a wilderness journey out of some form of slavery. On a personal level, we know what it is to be enslaved to fear, alcohol, food, rage, worry, lust, shame, inferiority, or control. On a social level, in today's version of Pharaoh's economy, millions at the bottom of the pyramid work like slaves from before dawn to after dark and still never get ahead. And even those at the top of the pyramid don't feel free. They wake up each day driven by the need to acquire what others desire, and they fear the lash of their own inner slave drivers: greed, debt, competition, expectation, and a desperate, addictive craving for more, more, more.

From top to bottom, the whole system survives by plundering the planet, purchasing this generation's luxuries at the expense of future generations' necessities. Exiting from today's personal and social slavery won't be easy. It will require something like a wilderness journey into the unknown. We know who we have been: slaves. We know who we're going to be: free men and women, experiencing aliveness as God intended. And right now, we're a little bit of both, in need of the identity transformation that comes as we walk the road to freedom.

So we have much to learn from the stories of Moses and his companions. We, too, must remember that the road to freedom doesn't follow a straight line from point A to point B. Instead, it zigzags and backtracks through a discomfort zone of lack, delay, distress, and strain. In those wild places, character is formed—the personal and social character needed for people to enjoy freedom and aliveness. Like those who have walked before us, we need to know that grumbling and complaining can be more dangerous than poisonous snakes or the hot desert sun. Like them, we must be forewarned about the danger of catastrophizing the present and romanticizing the past. Like them, we must remember that going forward may be difficult, but going back is disastrous.

As they made a road through the wilderness, Moses and his fellow travelers received a mysterious food that fell from the sky each morning like dew. They called it *manna*, which in Hebrew, somewhat humorously, meant, "What is this stuff?" Like them, we will receive what we need for each day, too—often in mysterious and sometimes even humorous ways, just enough for today, provided one day at a time. And like them, we will learn that we can't survive on bread alone: we also need moral guidance, spiritual nourishment, manna for the soul.

So along with bread for their bodies, God gave the travelers inner nourishment in the form of ten commands that would become the moral basis for their lives in freedom.

1. Put the God of liberation first, not the gods of slavery.
2. Don't reduce God to the manageable size of an idol—certainly not one made of wood and stone by human hands, and not one made by human minds of rituals and words, either, and certainly not one in whose name people are enslaved, dehumanized, or killed!
3. Do not use God for your own agendas by throwing around God's holy name. If you make a vow in God's name, keep it!
4. Honor the God of liberation by taking and giving everyone a day off. Don't keep the old 24/7 slave economy going.

5. Turn from self-centeredness by honoring your parents. (After all, honor is the basis of freedom.)
6. Don't kill people, and don't do the things that frequently incite violence, including:
7. Don't cheat with others' spouses,
8. Don't steal others' possessions, and
9. Don't lie about others' behaviors or characters.
10. In fact, if you really want to avoid the violence of the old slave economy, deal with its root source—in the drama of desire. Don't let the competitive desire to acquire tempt you off the road of freedom.

Through the ten plagues, we might say, God got the people out of slavery. Through the ten commands, God got the slavery out of the people. God also gave them a set of additional practices—rituals, holidays, and so on—to help them develop and deepen the character of free people. One of those practices was setting aside a special holy place. They started with a simple "tent of meeting" that was replaced by a larger, more elaborate gathering place called the Tabernacle. That holy space in the center of their encampment reminded them that the God of liberation was journeying with them—not only above them, visualized as a cloud of smoke and fire, but among them, walking with them in the desert dust as they made the road to freedom.

In that central holy space the people offered sacrifices. Animal sacrifice had already replaced more primitive and brutal rituals of human sacrifice. But the whole idea of appeasing God through blood shedding of any kind was gradually being replaced with the idea of communing with God over a meal. So sacrifices were seen increasingly as gifts of food, as if to say, "God is calling us to gather around the family table." At certain times of the year, and at special moments when the people realized they had done something horrible, they would come to God's big tent. They would bring the makings of a feast, as if to say, "God, we're sorry for our wrongs. We want to have our family meal again—reconciling with you and with one another. So here's some food to express our desire to sit down at the table of fellowship. We won't turn back. We'll keeping walking this long road to freedom . . . together."

Of course, Jesus gathered his companions around a table one night and encouraged them to do the same. We call it a meal of communion. We could also call it a meal of liberation and reconciliation. Around this table, we remember where we've been, where we are, whom we're with, and where we're headed, as we make a new road by walking... together.

The wilderness journey is always difficult and seems to last forever. Like kids on a car ride, we keep whining, "Aren't we there yet?" But the truth is, if we arrive before we've learned the lessons of the wilderness, we won't be able to enjoy the freedom that awaits us in the promised land beyond it. There is wisdom we will need there that we can gain only right here. There is strength and skill we will need in the future that we can develop only here and now, on the wilderness road. There is moral muscle we will need then that we can exercise and strengthen only through our struggles on this road, here and now. There is a depth of connection with God that will be there when we need it in the future—if we learn to trust and follow God now, on the long, wild road to freedom.

The struggles will make us either bitter or better. The trials will lead to either breakdown or breakthrough. We will often be tempted to return to our old lives, but in that tension between a backward pull and a forward call, we will discover unexplainable sustenance (like manna) and unexpected refreshment (like springs in the desert). Against all odds, walking by faith, we will survive, and more: we will learn what it means to be alive.

There are no shortcuts. The road cannot be made by wishing, by whining, or by talking. It can be made only by walking, day after day, step by step, struggle by struggle. It's easier, it turns out, to get people out of slavery than it is to get slavery out of people. So, people, let us walk the road—right through the middle of the desert.

ENGAGE:

1. What one thought or idea from today's lesson especially intrigued, provoked, disturbed, challenged, encouraged, warmed, warned, helped, or surprised you?
2. Share a story about a significant wilderness experience in your life—either literal or figurative.

3. What do you think it means in today's world to "get the slavery out of the people"? What kinds of slavery do you think we are still stuck in?
4. For children: What's the longest trip you've ever taken? What was one of the best parts of the trip? What was one of the worst parts?
5. Activate: Each day this week, reread the Ten Commandments as worded in this chapter. (Maybe send them to yourself and others via e-mail or social media.) Look for ways this ancient moral code is relevant in today's world—and in your life.
6. Meditate: Relax for a few moments in God's presence in silence. Think of the Sabbath not as being deprived of activity, but as a day of liberation from the 24/7 workweek of a slave. Breathe deep. Let go. Thank God for rest.

CHAPTER ELEVEN

From Ugliness, A Beauty Emerges

Deuteronomy 7:1–11
Psalm 137:1–9; 149:1–9
Matthew 15:21–39

We've come a long way in our story already. We've discovered...

Creation—God brings into being this beautiful, evolving world of wonders.
Crisis—we step out of the dance and enter into rivalry with God and our fellow creatures, throwing this planet into disarray.
Calling—God calls people to join in a global conspiracy of goodness and blessing, to heal and restore whatever human evil destroys.
Captivity—the people who have joined God's global conspiracy of goodness experience the horrors of slavery, but God eventually leads them by the wilderness road out of captivity toward freedom.

And now we come to a fifth major episode. It's the story of *conquest*, as the Israelites finally reach the land their ancestors had inhabited four centuries earlier. There's just one problem: others have moved into the land and made it their home for many generations. To possess the land, the Israelites will have to displace these current residents through a war of invasion and conquest. Wars like these are the most bloody and difficult of all, but the Israelites trust that their God will give them victory.

This episode in the biblical story, more than any other, forces us to deal with one of life's most problematic questions: the question of violence. By violence, we mean an act that intends to violate the well-being of a person or people. To help some, is God willing to harm others? Is God part of the violence in the world, and is violence part of God?

Or is God the voice calling to us in our violence to move to a new place, to join God beyond violence, in kindness, reconciliation, and peace?

Today, as in the ancient world, many people sincerely believe that God loves *us* and wants peace for *us* so much that God has no trouble harming or destroying *them* for our benefit. We find a lot of that kind of thinking in the Bible, giving God credit and praise for *our* victories and *their* defeats. Before we go too far in condemning ancient people for that exclusive way of thinking, we should realize how easy it is for us to do the same—when we create a superior *us* that looks down on *them* for thinking so exclusively!

We should also notice that where we see this kind of thinking embedded in the Bible, we also find important qualifications. For example, God's favor toward *the insiders* is dependent on the insiders living good and humble lives. If the insiders become oppressors, they should not expect God's help. And God gives the freed slaves the right to conquer just enough land for themselves, just one time. They are never given a license to create an empire, expanding to enslave others as they had previously been enslaved.

Even as they prepare for war, they are told again and again that after the conquest ends, they must treat "aliens and strangers" as neighbors, with honor and respect, remembering that they once were "aliens and strangers" themselves in Egypt. Their ultimate dream is to be farmers, not warriors—so that swords can be beaten into plowshares and spears into pruning hooks, as soon as possible.

But even with these provisos in mind, we can't ignore the brutality found in many Bible passages. From Deuteronomy 7 to Leviticus 25 to 1 Samuel 15 to Psalms 137 and 149, we hear claims that "God" or "the Lord" actively commands or blesses actions that we would call crimes against humanity. Many religious scholars have assumed that because the Bible makes these claims, we must defend them as true and good. That approach, however, is morally unacceptable for growing numbers of us, and fortunately, we have another option.

We can acknowledge that in the minds of the originators of these stories, God as they understood God did indeed command these things. We can acknowledge that in their way of thinking, divine involvement in war was to be expected. We can allow that they were telling the truth as they best understood it when they found comfort and reassurance in a vision of a God who would harm or kill *them* to defend, help, or avenge *us*. We can try to empathize, remembering that when human beings suffer indignity, injustice, dehumanization, and violence, they naturally pray for revenge and dream of retribution against those who harm them. Without condoning, we can at least understand why they saw God as they did, knowing that if we had walked in their sandals, we would have been no different.

But we don't need to stop there. We can then turn to other voices in the biblical library who, in different circumstances, told competing stories to give a different—and we would say *better*—vision of God.

For example, take the passage in Deuteronomy 7 where God commands Joshua to slaughter the seven Canaanite nations. They must be shown no mercy. Even their little girls must be seen as a threat. Then we can consider a story from Matthew's gospel that offers itself as a response to the earlier passage. There, we meet a woman who is identified by Matthew as a Canaanite. This identification is significant, since Canaanites no longer existed as an identifiable culture in Jesus' day. Calling this woman a Canaanite would be like calling someone a Viking or Aztec today. She asks for the one thing that had been denied her ancestors: *mercy*... mercy for her daughter who is in great need.

Up until this point, Jesus has understood his mission only in relation to his own people. After all, they're pretty lost and they need a lot of help. So he hesitates. How can he extend himself to this Canaanite? But how can he refuse her? In her persistence, he senses genuine faith, and he hears God's call to extend mercy even to her. So he says yes to the mother, and the daughter is healed. From there, Jesus goes to an area to the northwest of the Sea of Galilee. He teaches and heals a large crowd of people there who, like the woman and her daughter, are not members of his own religion and culture. Their non-Jewish identity is clear in their response to Jesus' kindness: "And they praised the God of Israel." What was an exception yesterday is now the new rule: *Don't kill the other. Show mercy to them.*

Then, Jesus repeats a miracle for these outsiders that he had done previously for his fellow Jews, multiplying loaves and fish so they can eat. In the previous miracle, there were twelve baskets left over, suggesting the twelve tribes of Israel—the descendants, that is, of Jacob and his twelve sons. In this miracle, there are seven baskets left over—suggesting, it seems quite clear, the seven Canaanite nations that Jesus' ancestors had been commanded to destroy.

Matthew's version of this story makes a confession: *Our ancestors, led by Moses and Joshua, believed God sent them into the world in conquest, to show no mercy to their enemies, to defeat and kill them. But now, following Christ, we hear God giving us a higher mission. Now we believe God sends us into the world in compassion, to show mercy, to heal, to feed—to nurture and protect life rather than take it.*

We begin with prebiblical visions of many warring gods who are all violent and capricious. In much of the Bible, we advance to a vision of a single God who uses violence against *them* in the service of justice for *us*. Eventually, through the biblical library, we find a beautiful new vision of God being revealed. God desires justice for all, not just for *us*. God is leading both *us* and *them* out of injustice and violence into a new way of reconciliation and peace. God loves everyone, everywhere, no exceptions.

Violence, like slavery and racism, was normative in our past, and it is still all too common in the present. How will we tell the stories of our past in ways that make our future less violent? We must not defend those stories or give them the final word. Nor can we cover them up, hiding them like a loaded gun in a drawer that can be found and used to harm. Instead, we must expose these violent stories to the light of day. And then we must tell new stories beside them, stories so beautiful and good that they will turn us toward a better vision of kindness, reconciliation, and peace for our future and for our children's future.

The stories of Jesus' life and teaching, wisely told, can help us imagine and create a more peaceful future. They help us see the glory of God shining in the face of a kind, forgiving, gentle, and nonviolent man, and in the smiles and tears, words and deeds of those who radiate his love.

Engage:

1. What one thought or idea from today's lesson especially intrigued, provoked, disturbed, challenged, encouraged, warmed, warned, helped, or surprised you?
2. Share a story about a movie you've seen or a book you've read that upheld violence as the way to prosperity and peace. Can you share an alternative movie or story that pointed to a nonviolent way to peace?
3. How do you respond to Matthew's story of the Canaanite woman in conversation with the Deuteronomy story of Canaanite slaughter? Can you think of other paired stories like this?
4. For children: Who do you think is stronger—a person who can punch a bad guy and scare him away, or a person who can convince a bad guy to become good?
5. Activate: This week, listen for situations when people use God (or some other "good reason") to justify violence or unkindness. Try to understand why they would see God and violence this way. Seek to see the world through their eyes and to imagine how hard it would be for them to see God differently.
6. Meditate: Hold in silence the tension between a violent world and a God who calls us to reconciliation, mutual understanding and respect, and peace.

CHAPTER TWELVE

Stories That Shape Us

2 Kings 2:1–15
Psalm 23
Acts 1:1–11

A LITTLE GIRL ONCE asked her mother if the Bible story of Elijah flying to heaven on a chariot of fire was "real or pretend." How would you have answered her question?

You might try to explain that sometimes a "pretend" story can tell more truth and do more good than a "real" one—as Jesus' parables exemplify so powerfully. You might explain how real stories often are embellished with pretend elements. Or you might respond as that little girl's wise mother did: "That's a great question! Some stories are real, some are pretend, and some of the very best ones use a mix of both reality and make-believe to tell us something important. What do you think about the Elijah story?" The mother's answer didn't tell the little girl *what* to think. It invited her *to* think—as a bona fide member of the interpretive community.

Whenever we engage with the stories of the Bible, we become members of the interpretive community. And that's a big responsibility, especially when we remember how stories from the Bible have been used to promote both great good and great harm. We might say that good interpretation begins with three elements: science, art, and heart. First, we need *critical or scientific research* into history, language, anthropology, and sociology to wisely interpret the Bible. Second, since the Bible is a literary and therefore an artistic collection, we need an *artist's eye and ear* to wisely draw meaning from ancient stories. But at every step, we also must be guided by a *humble, teachable heart* that listens for the voice of the Spirit.

In that light, the Elijah story addresses an urgent question: *what happens when a great leader dies?* Typically, a blaze of glory surrounds the hero's departure—symbolized by the fiery chariot and horses in the story. After the leader is gone, the actual life and message of the leader are forgotten, obscured by the blaze of fame and glory. People become fans of the leader's reputation but not followers of his example. That's why the old mentor Elijah puts his young apprentice, Elisha, through many trials and warns him about the spectacle surrounding his departure. The fireworks are not the point, Elijah explains; they're a distraction, a temptation to be overcome. If the apprentice resists that distraction and remains resolutely focused on the mentor himself, a double portion of the mentor's spirit will rest on him.

We see something very similar in the story of Jesus' departure. Will his followers look up at the sky and speculate about their departed leader with their heads in the clouds? Will they be fans instead of followers? Or will they get down to work and stay focused on living and sharing Jesus' down-to-Earth way of life, empowered with his Spirit?

Like young Elisha, interpreters today must remember that it's easy to miss the point of ancient stories. Those stories didn't merely aim, like a modern textbook, to pass on factual *information*. They sought people's *formation* by engaging their interpretive *imagination*.

As a first step in wisely interpreting Bible stories with science, art, and heart, we need to put each in its intended historical context and get a sense for the big narrative in which each story is nested. Roughly speaking, we can locate the stories of Abraham and Sarah somewhere around 2000–1700 BC. We can place the stories of Moses and the exodus around 1400 BC. We can locate the conquest of the Canaanites around 1300 BC, after which they formed a loose confederacy under a series of leaders who are somewhat misleadingly called *judges* in the Bible. *Tribal leaders* or even *warlords* might be more accurate names.

Those were violent times, and some of the stories from those times are bone-chilling, especially regarding the appallingly low status of women and the appallingly violent behavior of men. For example, the Book of Judges ends with the account of a brutal gang rape, murder, and dismemberment of a young woman, followed by a horrific aftermath of intertribal retaliation and kidnapping of innocent young women. Interestingly, in the very next story in the biblical library, the Book of Ruth, we find the polar opposite—the poignant tale of two kind and courageous women, Ruth and Naomi. They forged a resilient life of dignity and beauty in the midst of brutality. Where the men failed, the women prevailed.

Around 1050 BC, pressured by aggressive nations around them and brutality among them, the twelve tribes formed a stronger alliance. They united under a king named Saul. Saul turned out to be a disappointment, but in his shadow a more heroic figure named David appeared. The story of David's gradual rise from shepherd boy to king unfolds in great detail, each episode revealing Saul as less strong and noble and David as more clever and charismatic. When Saul was killed in battle, David established his throne in Jerusalem, inaugurating what is still remembered as Israel's golden age.

David was heroic, but far from perfect, and the Bible doesn't cover up his serious failings—including those of a sexual nature. When David wanted to build a temple to honor God, God said no: a place of worship should not be associated with a man of bloodshed. David's son Solomon was not a warrior, so he was allowed to fulfill his father's dream by building a temple. But Solomon used slave labor to build that temple—a tragic irony in light of God's identity as the liberator of slaves.

After Solomon's death, around 930 BC, the kingdom split in two. Ten of the original twelve tribes who lived in the northern region broke away from the two tribes who lived to their south. From that time, the Kingdom of Israel in the north, with its capital in Samaria, was governed by its own line of kings. And the Kingdom of Judah in the south continued under the rule of David's descendants in Jerusalem. Nearly all the kings of both nations were corrupt, ineffective, and faithful only to their own agendas of gaining and maintaining power at any cost.

Those darker times made the memory of David's reign seem all the more bright. A dream was born in many hearts: that a descendant of David would one day arise and come to the throne, inaugurating a new kingdom, a new golden age, a new day. The old dream of a promised land now was replaced by a new dream—for a promised *time*, a time when the peace, unity, freedom, and prosperity of David's reign would return. This expectation kept hope alive in difficult times, but it also created a sense of pious complacency.

That was what Jesus encountered centuries later. Many were still waiting for a "son of David," a militant Messiah, to swoop in someday, fix everything, and usher in Golden Age 2.0. They expected this warrior king to raise a revolutionary army, overthrow their oppressors, and restore civil law and religious order. In anticipation of the warrior king's arrival, some were sharpening daggers and swords. But Jesus was living by a different interpretation of the old stories, so he refused to conform to their expectations. Instead of arming his followers with daggers, swords, spears, chariots, and war horses, he armed them with faith, hope, service, forgiveness, and love. When he healed people, he didn't tell them, "I will save you!" or "My faith will save you!" but "Your faith has saved you." Working from a fresh interpretation of the past, he freed them from both passive, pious complacency and desperate, violent action. His fresh interpretation empowered them for something better: faithful, peaceful action.

That's the kind of empowerment we need to face our huge challenges today. How will we deal with political and economic systems that are destroying the planet, privileging the superelite, and churning out weapons of unprecedented destruction at an unprecedented rate? How will we deal with religious systems that often have violent extremists on one wing and complacent hypocrites on the other? How will we grapple with complex forces that break down family and community cohesion and leave vulnerable people at great risk—especially women, and especially the very young and the very old? How will we face our personal demons—of greed, lust, anxiety, depression, anger, and addiction—especially when people are spending billions to stimulate those demons so we will buy their products?

These aren't pretend problems. To find real-world solutions, we need to be wise interpreters of our past. Like Elijah's apprentice, Elisha, we must stay focused on the substance at the center, undistracted by all the surrounding fireworks. Because the meaning we shape from the stories we interpret will, in turn, shape us.

Engage:

1. What one thought or idea from today's lesson especially intrigued, provoked, disturbed, challenged, encouraged, warmed, warned, helped, or surprised you?
2. Share a story about a "golden age" you learned about in your family, your school, or some other group you've been part of.
3. How do you respond to the comparison between the story of Jesus' departure in Acts and the story of Elijah's departure in 2 Kings?
4. For children: Do you have a favorite superhero? Tell us why you like him or her so much.
5. Activate: This week, try to read the gruesome story of the Levite's concubine (Judges 19–21) and then the gentle story of Ruth and Naomi (Book of Ruth). Do you see similar stories in this week's headlines?
6. Meditate: In silence, hold the phrases "passive, pious complacency," "desperate, violent action," and "faithful, peaceful action" in your mind for a few minutes. Ask God to make you an agent of faithful, peaceful action.

CHAPTER THIRTEEN

THE GREAT CONVERSATION

Isaiah 1:1–2:5
Romans 15:1–13
Matthew 9:10–17

IT WAS ABOUT 800 BC. The Israelites and Judeans had already survived so much. In addition to all the trouble within their respective borders—much of it caused by corrupt leaders—even bigger trouble was brewing outside. The two tiny nations were dwarfed by superpower neighbors, each of which had desires to expand. To the north and east were the Assyrians. To the east were the Babylonians, and to their east, the Persians. To the south were the Egyptians, and to the West, the Mediterranean Sea. How could Israel and Judah, each smaller than present-day Jamaica, Qatar, or Connecticut, hope to survive, surrounded in this way?

The northern Kingdom of Israel fell first. In 722 BC, the Assyrians invaded and deported many of the Israelites into Assyria. These displaced Israelites eventually intermarried and lost their distinct identity as children of Abraham. They're remembered today as "the ten lost tribes of Israel." The Assyrians quickly repopulated the conquered kingdom with large numbers of their own, who then intermarried with the remaining Israelites. The mixed descendants, later known as Samaritans, would experience a long-standing tension with the "pure" descendants of Abraham in Judah to the south.

Judah resisted conquest for just over another century, during which Assyrian power declined and Babylonian power increased. Finally, around

587 BC, Judah was conquered by the Babylonians. Jerusalem and its temple were destroyed. The nation's "brightest and best" were deported as exiles to the Babylonian capitol. The peasants were left to till the land and "share" their harvest with the occupying regime. For about seventy years, this sorry state of affairs continued.

Babylon, meanwhile, was being pressured by its neighbor to the east, the Persians. Soon, the Persians conquered the Babylonians. They had a more lenient policy for managing the nations under their power, so in 538, they allowed the exiled Judeans to return and rebuild their capitol city. But even with this increased freedom, the people remained under the heel of foreigners. They had survived, but they still felt defeated.

How should they interpret their plight? Some feared that God had failed or abandoned them. Others blamed themselves for displeasing God in some way. Those who felt abandoned by God expressed their devastation in heart-rending poetry. Those who felt they had displeased God tried to identify their offenses, assign blame, and call for repentance. It was during this devastating period of exile and return that much of the oral tradition known to us as the Old Testament was either written down for the first time, or reedited and compiled. No wonder, arising in such times of turmoil and tumult, the Bible is such a dynamic collection!

As the people changed and evolved, their understanding of God changed and evolved. For example, when they were nomadic wanderers in the desert, they envisioned God as a pillar of cloud and fire, cooling them by day and warming them by night. When they were involved in conquest, God was the Lord of Hosts, the commander of armies. When they were being pursued by enemies, God was pictured as a hiding place in the rocks. When they became a unified kingdom, God was their ultimate King. When they returned to their land and felt more secure, more gentle images of God took center stage—God as their Shepherd, for example. When they suffered defeat, they saw God as their avenger. When they suffered injustice, God was the judge who would convict their oppressors and restore justice. When they felt abandoned and alone in a foreign land, they imagined God as a loving mother who could never forget her nursing child.

Not only do we see their understanding of God evolve under evolving circumstances, we also see their understanding of human affairs mature. For example, to immature minds, there are two kinds of leaders: those who have been set in place by God, and those who haven't. The former deserve absolute obedience, since to disobey them would be to disobey God. But in the Bible, we see this simplistic thinking challenged. Moses, for example, was a God-anointed leader, and people were indeed urged to obey him, and they were punished when they didn't. Yet when Moses made mistakes of his own, he got no special treatment. The same with Saul, and the same even with David.

As their understanding of human affairs matured, their moral reasoning matured as well. In the Garden of Eden story, Adam and Eve wanted to grasp the fruit of knowing good and evil, as if that were a simple thing. But as the biblical story unfolded, first it became clear that the line between good and evil didn't run between groups of *us* and *them*. There were good guys among *them*—including people like Melchizedek, Abimelech, Jethro, Rahab, and Ruth. And there were plenty of bad guys among *us*—including most of the kings of Israel and Judah. It became clear that the dividing line doesn't simply run between good and bad individuals, as many people today still believe. Some of the Bible's best "good guys"—like David and Solomon—did really bad things. So the Bible presents a morally complex and dynamic world where the best of us can do wrong and the worst of us can do right. The line between good and evil runs—and moves—within each of us.

The Bible often conveys this growing moral wisdom by drawing a third option from two irreconcilable viewpoints on an issue. For example, some biblical voices interpreted the move from an alliance of tribes to a kingdom as a tragic sign that the people had rejected God as their king. Others saw the monarchy as a gift from God, a big improvement over the previous chaos. When both sets of voices are heard, it's clear that each had some of the truth: a strong central government can be both a curse and a blessing, not just one or the other.

Similarly, some biblical voices argued that God required animals to be slaughtered so their blood could be offered as a sacrifice. Without sacrifice, they believed, sins could not be forgiven, so they gave detailed instructions for sacrifice that, they claimed, were dictated by God. Other voices said no, that God never really desired bloody sacrifices, but instead wanted another kind of holy gift from humanity: contrite and compassionate hearts, and justice, kindness, and humility. When we give both sets of voices a fair hearing, we can agree that sacrifices fulfilled a necessary function for the people at one point in their development, even though ultimately sacrifices weren't an absolute and eternal necessity.

Meanwhile, many voices claimed that Abraham's descendants were God's only chosen and favored people. Others countered that God created and loves all people and has chosen and guided all nations for various purposes. If we listen to both claims, we can conclude that just as a little girl feels she is uniquely loved by her parents, even as her little brother feels the same way, each nation is intended to feel it is special to God—not to the exclusion of others, but along with others.

From Genesis to Job, the Bible is full of conversations like these—with differing viewpoints making their case, point and counterpoint, statement and counterstatement. Sadly, throughout history people have often quoted one side or the other to prove that their view alone is "biblical." That's why it's important for us to remain humble as we read the Bible, not to seek ammunition for the side of an argument we already stand on, but to seek the wisdom that comes when we listen humbly to all the different voices arising in the biblical library. Wisdom emerges from the conversation among these voices, voices we could arrange in five broad categories.

First, there are the voices of the *priests* who emphasize keeping the law, maintaining order, offering sacrifices, and faithfully maintaining traditions and taboos. Then there are the voices of the *prophets*, often in tension with the priests, who emphasize social justice, care for the poor, and the condition of the heart. Next are the *poets* who express the full range of human emotion and opinion—the good, the bad, and the ugly. Then come the *sages* who, in proverb, essay, and creative fiction, record their theories, observations, questions, and doubts. And linking them together are *storytellers*, each with varying agendas, who try to tell the stories of the people who look back to Abraham as their father, Moses as their liberator, David as their greatest king, and God as their Creator and faithful companion. To be alive is to seek wisdom in this great conversation... and to keep it going today.

Could it be that we are doing just that, here and now, walking this road in conversation together?

Engage:

1. What one thought or idea from today's lesson especially intrigued, provoked, disturbed, challenged, encouraged, warmed, warned, helped, or surprised you?
2. Share a story about an argument where both sides were partly right.
3. How do you respond to this vision of the Bible as a library full of difference of opinion, yet carrying on an essential conversation about what it means to be alive? Which set of voices do you identify with most—priests, prophets, poets, sages, or storytellers?
4. For children: What's one of your favorite stories—one that you like to hear again and again? What's your favorite thing about that story?
5. Activate: This week, listen for voices who fit in the tradition of the priests, prophets, poets, sages, and storytellers in today's culture. See if you perceive points of agreement and disagreement with their counterparts in the biblical library.
6. Meditate: In silence, imagine hearing a vigorous conversation going on. Then, let the conversation gradually fade away so that silence envelops you. In that silence, open your heart to God's wisdom.

First Quarter Queries

If possible, compose honest and heartfelt replies to these queries in a journal before gathering with one or two others to share what you have written. When you discuss your replies, you may choose to follow the Five Guidelines for Learning Circles in Appendix II. Or you may invite a trusted mentor to serve as "catechist" so he or she can listen to and respond to your replies. Make it safe for one another to speak freely, and let your conversation build conviction in each of you as individuals and among you as a community.

1. What does it mean to you to live within the story of creation?
2. What does it mean to you to live within the story of crisis?
3. What does it mean to you to live within the story of calling?
4. What does it mean to you to live in a world of captivity and conquest?
5. What does it mean to you to be a part of the great conversation? What do you learn from the priests, prophets, sages, poets, and storytellers?
6. In what ways are you integrating into your daily life your identity in God's unfolding story?
7. What are some significant changes you've experienced from being part of this learning circle?

II

ALIVE IN THE ADVENTURE OF JESUS

IN PART I, WE explored what it means to be alive in the story of creation... a story that includes crisis, calling, captivity, conquest, and conversation. Into that conversation comes a man named Jesus, a man whose character, words, and example changed history. In Part II, we will explore what it means to be alive in the adventure of Jesus.

We begin with the story of his birth (during the traditional seasons of Advent and Christmas), and then we follow him through childhood to adulthood, as the light of God shines brightly through him (during the season of Epiphany). Our exploration will lead to this life-changing choice: will we identify ourselves as honest and sincere followers of Jesus today?

You may need to rearrange the order of chapters so that Chapter 17 comes the week before Christmas. Then you can use Chapter 17A on Christmas Eve, and Chapter 18 the Sunday (or whatever day you gather) on or after Christmas. At the end of each of the first five chapters, you'll be invited to light a candle. Whether you do so alone or in a learning circle, use that simple tradition as an invitation to joyful, hopeful, reverent contemplation.

CHAPTER FOURTEEN

PROMISED LAND, PROMISED TIME

Daniel 7:9–28
Isaiah 40:9–11
Luke 1:67–79

TO BE ALIVE IS to desire, to hope, and to dream, and the Bible is a book about desires, hopes, and dreams. The story begins with God's desire for a good and beautiful world, of which we are a part. Soon, some of us desire the power to kill, enslave, or oppress others. Enslaved and oppressed people hope for liberation. Wilderness wanderers desire a promised land where they can settle. Settled people dream of a promised time when they won't be torn apart by internal factions, ruled by corrupt elites, or dominated by stronger nations nearby.

Desires, hopes, and dreams inspire action, and that's what makes them so different from a wish. Wishing is a substitute for action. Wishing creates a kind of passive optimism that can paralyze people in a happy fog of complacency: "Everything will turn out fine. Why work, struggle, sacrifice, or plan?" Guess what happens to people who never work, struggle, sacrifice, or plan? Things don't normally turn out the way they wish!

In contrast, our desires, hopes, and dreams for the future guide us in how to act now. If a girl hopes to be a doctor someday, she'll study hard and prepare for medical school. If a boy dreams of being a marine biologist someday, he'll spend time around the sea and learn to snorkel and scuba-dive. Their hope for the future guides them in how to act now. They align their lives by their hope, and in that way, their lives are shaped by hope. Without action, they would be wishing, not hoping.

Prophets in the Bible have a fascinating role as custodians of the best hopes, desires, and dreams of their society. They challenge people to act in ways consistent with those hopes, desires, and dreams. And when they see people behaving in harmful ways, they warn them by picturing the future to which that harmful behavior will lead.

One of the most important prophetic compositions was the Book of Isaiah. Most scholars today agree that at least three people contributed to the book over a long period of time, but their combined work has traditionally been attributed to one author. The first thirty-nine chapters of Isaiah were situated in the southern Kingdom of Judah, just before the northern Kingdom of Israel was invaded and colonized by the Assyrians. The prophet saw deep spiritual corruption and complacency among his people and warned them that this kind of behavior would lead to decline and defeat.

That defeat came in 587 BC at the hand of the Babylonians. After the invasion, many survivors were taken as exiles to Babylon. Chapters 40–55, often called Second Isaiah, addressed those Judean exiles, inspiring hope that they would someday return to their homeland and rebuild it. That soon happened, beginning in 538 BC under the leadership of Ezra and Nehemiah. That era of rebuilding was the setting for Third Isaiah, chapters 56–66.

For readers in later generations, ingredients from these three different settings blend into one rich recipe for hope, full of imagery that still energizes our imagination today.

They shall beat their swords into plowshares,
and their spears into pruning-hooks.
Nation shall not lift up sword against nation,
neither shall they learn war any more. (2:4)

A shoot shall come out from the stump of [David's father] Jesse,
and a branch shall grow out of his roots.
The Spirit of the Lord shall rest on him...
The wolf shall live with the lamb,

the leopard shall lie down with the kid,
the calf and the lion and the fatling together,
and a little child shall lead them. . . .
They will not hurt or destroy
on all my holy mountain;
for the Earth will be full of the knowledge of the Lord
as the waters cover the sea. (11:1–2, 6, 9)

Here is my servant, whom I uphold,
my chosen, in whom my soul delights;
I have put my spirit upon him;
he will bring forth justice to the nations.
He will not cry or lift up his voice,
or make it heard in the street;
a bruised reed he will not break,
and a dimly burning wick he will not quench;
he will faithfully bring forth justice. (42:1–3)

Isaiah's descriptions of that better day were so inspiring that Jesus and his early followers quoted Isaiah more than any other writer. But many other prophets added their own colors to this beautiful vision of hope. In Ezekiel's vision, people's hearts of stone will be replaced with hearts of flesh. For Malachi, the hearts of parents would turn to their children, and children to their parents. Joel describes the Spirit of God being poured out on all humanity—young and old, men and women, Jew and Gentile. Amos paints the vivid scene of justice rolling down like a river, filling all the lowest places. And Daniel envisioned the world's beastlike empires of violence being overcome by a simple unarmed human being, a new generation of humanity.

In the centuries between the time of the prophets and the birth of Jesus, these prophetic dreams never completely died. But they were never completely fulfilled, either. Yes, conditions for the Jews improved under the Persians, but things still weren't as good as the prophets promised. Next the Greek and Seleucid empires took control of the region, and for a time, the Jews threw off their oppressors. But their independence was brief, and the full dream of the prophets remained unfulfilled. Next the Romans seized power, subjugating and humiliating the Jews and testing their hope as never before. Yet their dream lived on. It remained alive in people like Elizabeth and Zechariah, Mary and Joseph, and Anna and Simeon, and even among humble shepherds who lived at the margins of society.

To be alive in the adventure of Jesus is to have a desire, a dream, a hope for the future. It is to translate that hope for the future into action in the present and to keep acting in light of it, no matter the disappointments, no matter the setbacks and delays. So let us begin this Advent season by lighting a candle for the prophets who proclaimed their hopes, desires, and dreams. Let us keep their flame glowing strong in our hearts, even now.

Engage:

1. What one thought or idea from today's lesson especially intrigued, provoked, disturbed, challenged, encouraged, warmed, warned, helped, or surprised you?
2. Share a story about a time when you kept hope or lost hope.
3. How do you respond to the imagery of Isaiah, and how would you translate some of that imagery from the ancient Middle East into imagery from today's world?
4. For children: What do you hope to be or do when you grow up?
5. Activate: This week, look for discouragement or cynicism in your own thinking. Challenge yourself to become cynical about your cynicism, and challenge yourself toward prophetic hope.
6. Meditate: Light a candle and choose one image from the prophets mentioned in this chapter. Simply hold that image in your heart, in God's presence. Let it inspire a simple prayer that you may wish to speak aloud.

CHAPTER FIFTEEN

WOMEN ON THE EDGE

Luke 1:5–55
Isaiah 7:14, 9:2–7
Romans 12:1–2

IMAGINE A WOMAN IN the ancient world who all her life longed to have children. She married young, maybe around the age of fifteen. At sixteen, still no pregnancy. At twenty, still no pregnancy. At twenty-five, imagine how she prayed. By thirty, imagine her anxiety as her prayers were mixed with tears of shame and disappointment—for herself, for her husband. At forty, imagine hope slipping away as she wondered if it even made sense to pray anymore. Imagine her sense of loss and regret at age fifty. Why pray now?

Of course, this was the story of Abraham's wife, Sarah, back in the book of Genesis. That ancient story was echoed in the Gospel of Luke. Luke tells us of a woman named Elizabeth who was married to a priest named Zechariah. They prayed for a child, but none came, year after year. One day as Zechariah was doing his priestly duties, he had a vision of an angelic messenger from God. Zechariah's prayers for a son would be answered, the messenger said. When Elizabeth gave birth, they should name their child John. Zechariah found this impossible to believe. "I'm an old man," he said, "and Elizabeth is past her prime as well!" The messenger told him that because of his skepticism, he would not be able to speak until the promised baby was born.

In a way, the stories of Sarah and Elizabeth are a picture of the experience of the Jewish people. The prophets had inspired them to dream of a better day. Their prophecies echoed the first promise to Abraham: that everyone everywhere would be blessed through Abraham's descendants. But those promises and prophecies had been delayed and frustrated and delayed again, until it seemed ridiculous to keep the dream alive.

All of us experience this sense of frustration, disappointment, impatience, and despair at times. We all feel that we have the capacity to give birth to something beautiful and good and needed and wonderful in the world. But our potential goes unfulfilled, or our promising hopes miscarry. So we live on one side and then on the other of the border of despair.

And then the impossible happens.

Elizabeth had a young relative named Mary. Mary was engaged but not yet married. Significantly, she was a descendant of King David, whose memory inspired the hope of a David-like king who would bring the better days long hoped for among her people. When Elizabeth was about six months pregnant, an angelic messenger—the same one who appeared to Zechariah, it turns out—now appeared to Mary. "Greetings, favored one!" he said. "The Lord is with you!" Mary felt, as any of us would, amazed and confused by this greeting.

The messenger said, "Don't be afraid, Mary. You will conceive and bear a son..." And the messenger's words echoed the promises of the prophets from centuries past—promises of a leader who would bring the people into the promised time. Mary asked, "How can this be, since I am a virgin?" The angel replied that the Holy Spirit would come upon her, so the child would be conceived by the power of God. And he added that Elizabeth, her old and barren relative, was also pregnant. "Nothing will be impossible with God," he said.

Many of us today will suspect that Luke made up this story about Mary to echo Isaiah's prophecy about a son being born to a virgin, just as he invented the story of Elizabeth conceiving in old age to echo the story of Sarah. It's tempting to quickly assign both stories to the category of primitive, prescientific legend and be done with them. After all, both stories are, to scientific minds, simply impossible.

But what if that's the point? What if their purpose is to challenge us to blur the line between what we think is possible and what we think is impossible? Could we ever come to a time when swords would be beaten into plowshares? When the predatory people in power—the lions—would lie down in peace with the vulnerable and the poor—the lambs?

When God's justice would flow like a river—to the lowest and most "god-forsaken" places on Earth? When the brokenhearted would be comforted and the poor would receive good news? If you think, *Never—it's impossible*, then maybe you need to think again. Maybe it's not too late for something beautiful to be born. Maybe it's not too soon, either. Maybe the present moment is pregnant with possibilities we can't see or even imagine.

In this light, the *actual* point of these pregnancy stories—however we interpret their *factual* status—is a challenge to us all: to dare to hope, like Elizabeth and Mary, that the seemingly impossible is possible. They challenge us to align our lives around the "impossible possibilities" hidden in this present, pregnant moment.

The image of a virgin birth has other meanings as well. The leaders of ancient empires typically presented themselves as divine-human hybrids with superpowers. Pharaohs and Caesars were "sons of gods." In them, the violent power of the gods was fused with the violent power of humans to create superhuman superviolence—which allowed them to create superpower nations. But here is God gently inviting—not coercing—a young woman to produce a child who will be known not for his violence but for his kindness. This is a different kind of leader entirely—one who doesn't rule with the masculine power of swords and spears, but with a mother's sense of justice and compassion.

In Luke's telling of the birth of Jesus, God aligns with the creative feminine power of womanhood rather than the violent masculine power of statehood. The doctrine of the virgin birth, it turns out, isn't about bypassing sex but about subverting violence. The violent power of top-down patriarchy is subverted not by counterviolence but by the creative power of pregnancy. It is through what proud men have considered "the weaker sex" that God's true power enters and changes the world. That, it turns out, is exactly what Mary understood the messenger to be saying:

> God has looked with favor on the lowliness of his servant... scattered the proud... brought down the powerful... lifted up the lowly... filled the hungry with good things, and sent the rich away empty. (Luke 1:48, 51, 52, 53)

So Mary presents herself to the Holy Spirit to receive and cooperate with God's creative power. She surrenders and receives, she nurtures and gives her all...because she dares to believe the impossible is possible. Her son Jesus will consistently model her self-surrender and receptivity to God, and he will consistently prefer the insightful kindness of motherhood to the violent blindness of statehood.

That's what it means to be alive in the adventure of Jesus. We present ourselves to God—our bodies, our stories, our futures, our possibilities, even our limitations. "Here I am," we say with Mary, "the Lord's servant. Let it be with me according to your will."

So in this Advent season—this season of awaiting and pondering the coming of God in Christ—let us light a candle for Mary. And let us, in our own hearts, dare to believe the impossible by surrendering ourselves to God, courageously cooperating with God's creative, pregnant power—in us, for us, and through us. If we do, then we, like Mary, will become pregnant with holy aliveness.

Engage:

1. What one thought or idea from today's lesson especially intrigued, provoked, disturbed, challenged, encouraged, warmed, warned, helped, or surprised you?
2. Share a story about a woman in your life who had a powerful influence.
3. How do you respond to these reflections on the meaning of the virgin birth?
4. For children: Tell us about a time you were surprised in a good and happy way.
5. Activate: Start each day this week putting Mary's prayer of commitment and surrender, "Let it be to me according to your will," into your own words. Let this be a week of presenting your life to God so that "holy aliveness" grows in you.
6. Meditate: After lighting a candle, hold the words, "Here I am, the Lord's servant," in your heart for a few minutes in silence. Try to return to those words many times in the week ahead.

CHAPTER SIXTEEN

KEEP HEROD IN CHRISTMAS

Jeremiah 32:31–35
Micah 5:2–5a
Matthew 1:18–2:15

RIGHT IN THE MIDDLE of Matthew's version of the Christmas story comes a shock. It is disturbing, terrifying, and horrific. And it is essential to understanding the adventure and mission of Jesus.

King Herod, or Herod the Great, ruled over Judea in the years leading up to Jesus' birth. Although he rebuilt the Temple in the Jerusalem—a sign of his Jewish identity—he was a puppet king who also depended on the Roman empire for his status. He was, like many biblical characters—and like many of us, too—a man with an identity crisis. Cruel and ruthless, he used slave labor for his huge building projects. He had a reputation for assassinating anyone he considered a threat—including his wife and two of his own sons. Late in his reign, he began hearing rumors... rumors that the long-awaited liberator prophesied by Isaiah and others had been born. While a pious man might have greeted this news with hope and joy, Herod only saw it as a threat—a threat to political stability and to his own status as king.

In recent years, there had been a lot of resistance, unrest, and revolt in Jerusalem, so Rome wasn't in a tolerant frame of mind. Any talk of rebellion, Herod knew, would bring crushing retaliation against the city. So Herod inquired of the religious scholars to find out if the holy texts gave any indication of where this long-anticipated child would be born. Their answer came from the Book of Micah: Bethlehem.

Herod did what any desperate, ruthless dictator would do. First, he tried to enlist some foreign mystics, known to us as "the wise men from the East." He wanted them to be his spies to help him discover the child's identity and whereabouts so he could have the child killed. But the wise men were warned of his deceit in a dream and so avoided becoming his unwitting accomplices. Realizing that his "Plan A" had failed, Herod launched "Plan B." He sent his henchmen to find and kill any young boy living in the area of Bethlehem. But the particular boy he sought had already been removed from Bethlehem and taken elsewhere.

The result? A slaughter of innocent children in Bethlehem. As is the case with many biblical stories, some scholars doubt this mass slaughter occurred, since none is recorded in other histories of the time. Others argue that Bethlehem was a small town, so the total number of casualties may have been twenty or thirty. Dictators certainly have their ways of keeping atrocities secret—just as they have their ways of making their exploits known. Whatever the infant death count in Bethlehem, we know Herod killed some of his own children when they became a threat to his agenda. So even if the story has been fictionalized to some degree, there is a deeper truth that has much to say to us today.

In his slaughter of innocent children, King Herod has now emulated the horrible behavior of Pharaoh centuries before, in the days of Moses. A descendant of the slaves has behaved like the ancient slave master. The story of Herod tells us once again that the world can't be simply divided between the good guys—*us*—and the bad guys—*them*—because like Herod, members of *us* will behave no differently from *them*, given the power and provocation. So all people face the same profound questions: *How will we manage power? How will we deal with violence?*

Herod—and Pharaoh before him—model one way: violence is simply one tool, used in varying degrees, to gain or maintain power.

The baby whom Herod seeks to kill will model another way. His tool will be service, not violence. And his goal will not be gaining and maintaining power, but using his power to heal and empower others. He will reveal a vision of God that is reflected more in the vulnerability of children than in the violence of men, more in the caring of mothers than in the cruelty of kings.

All this can sound quite abstract and theoretical unless we go one step deeper. The next war—whoever wages it—will most likely resemble every war in the past. It will be planned by powerful older men in their comfortable offices, and it will be fought on the ground by people the age of their children and grandchildren. Most of the casualties will probably be between eighteen and twenty-two years old—in some places, much younger. So the old, sad music of the ancient story of Herod and the slaughter of the children will be replayed again. And again, the tears of mothers will fall.

The sacrifice of children for the well-being and security of adults has a long history among human beings. For example, in the ancient Middle East there was a religion dedicated to an idol named Molech. Faithful adherents would sacrifice infants to Molech every year, a horrible display of twisted religiosity to appease their god's wrath and earn his favor. In contrast, beginning with the story of Abraham and Isaac, we gradually discover that the true God doesn't require appeasement at all. In fact, God exemplifies true, loving, mature parenthood... self-giving for the sake of one's children, not sacrificing children for one's own selfish interests.

This is why it matters so much for us to grapple with what we believe about God. Does God promote or demand violence? Does God favor the sacrifice of children for the well-being of adults? Is God best reflected in the image of powerful old men who send the young and vulnerable to die on their behalf? Or is God best seen in the image of a helpless baby, identifying with the victims, sharing their vulnerability, full of fragile but limitless promise?

We do not live in an ideal world. To be alive in the adventure of Jesus is to face at every turn the destructive reality of violence. To be alive in the adventure of Jesus is to side with vulnerable children in defiance of the adults who see them as expendable. To walk the road with Jesus is to withhold consent and cooperation from the powerful, and to invest it instead with the vulnerable. It is to refuse to bow to all the Herods and all their ruthless regimes—and to reserve our loyalty for a better king and a better kingdom.

Jesus has truly come, but each year during the Advent season, we acknowledge that the dream for which he gave his all has not yet fully come true. As long as elites plot violence, as long as children pay the price, and as long as mothers weep, we cannot be satisfied.

So let us light a candle for the children who suffer in our world because of greedy, power-hungry, and insecure elites. And let us light a candle for grieving mothers who weep for lost sons and daughters, throughout history and today. And let us light a candle for all people everywhere to hear their weeping. In this Advent season, we dare to believe that God feels their pain and comes near to bring comfort. If we believe that is true, then of course we must join God and come near, too. That is why we must keep Herod and the ugliness of his mass murder in the beautiful Christmas story.

Engage:

1. What one thought or idea from today's lesson especially intrigued, provoked, disturbed, challenged, encouraged, warmed, warned, helped, or surprised you?
2. Share a story about a time when you were a child and an adult other than a parent showed you great respect or kindness.
3. How do you respond to Matthew's decision to include this story that none of the other gospels recount?
4. For children: If you could ask grown-ups to do one thing to help kids, what would it be?
5. Activate: This week, try to look at personal and political situations from the vantage point of how they will affect children and their mothers.
6. Meditate: Light a candle, and hold in your mind both the image of Herod, ruthless and power-hungry, and the image of Jesus, a vulnerable baby. Observe what happens in your heart and express a prayer in response.

CHAPTER SEVENTEEN

Surprising People

Psalm 34:1–18
Matthew 1:1–17
Luke 2:8–20

AND ABRAHAM WAS THE *father of Isaac, and Isaac the father of Jacob, and Jacob*...To modern readers, the ancestor lists that are so common in the Bible seem pretty tedious and pointless. But to ancient people, they were full of meaning. They were shorthand ways of showing connections, helping people remember how they were related, and reminding them of the story that they found themselves in.

Both Matthew's and Luke's gospels give us ancestor lists for Jesus. Although they are very different lists, both agree on two essential points. First, Jesus was a descendant of Sarah and Abraham. That reminded people of God's original promise to Abraham and Sarah—that through their lineage, all nations of the world would be blessed. Second, Jesus was a descendant of King David. That brought to mind all the nostalgia for the golden age of David's reign, together with all the hope from the prophets about a promised time under the benevolent reign of a descendant of David.

Apart from these similarities, the two lists offer distinct treasures. Luke's gospel starts with the present and goes back, all the way to Abraham, and then all the way to Adam, the original human in the Genesis story: "son of Enoch, son of Jared, son of Mahalaleel, son of Cainan, son of Enos, son of Seth, son of Adam, son of God." That use of that phrase "son of God" is fascinating. It suggests a primary meaning of the term: to be *the son of* is to "find your origin in." It also suggests that Jesus, as the son of Adam, is in some way a new beginning for the human race—a new genesis, we might say. Just as Adam bore the image of God as the original human, Jesus will now reflect the image of God. We might say he is Adam 2.0.

That understanding is reinforced by what comes immediately before Luke's ancestor list: A voice comes from heaven and says, "You are my Son, the Beloved; with you I am well pleased." Just as *Son of David* prepares us to expect Jesus to model leadership, and just as *Son of Abraham* prepares us to expect Jesus to model blessing and promise for all, *Son of God* sets us up to expect Jesus to model true humanity as Adam did.

Matthew's version, which starts in the distant past and moves to the present, holds lots of treasures, too. Most surprising is his inclusion of five women. In the ancient world, people were unaware of the existence of the human egg and assumed that a man provided the only seed of a new life. So ancestor lists naturally focused on men. It's surprising enough for Matthew to include women at all, but the women he selects are quite astonishing.

First, there is Tamar. She had once posed as a prostitute in a web of sexual and family intrigue. Then there is Rahab—a Gentile of Jericho who actually was a prostitute. Then there is Ruth, another Gentile who entered into a sexual liaison with a wealthy Jew named Boaz. Then there is Bathsheba who was married to a foreigner—Uriah the Hittite—and with whom King David committed adultery. Finally there is Mary, who claims to be pregnant without the help of Joseph. These are not the kind of women whose names were typically included in ancestor lists of the past!

But that, of course, must be Matthew's point. Jesus isn't entering into a pristine story of ideal people. He is part of the story of Gentiles as well as Jews, broken and messy families as well as noble ones, normal folks as well as kings and priests and heroes. We might say that Jesus isn't entering humanity from the top with a kind of trickle-down grace, but rather from the bottom, with grace that rises from the grass roots up.

That theme is beautifully embodied in the unsung heroes of Luke's Christmas story: shepherds. They're the ones who, along with Joseph and Mary, have a front-row seat to welcome the "good news of great joy for all the people." They're the down-to-Earth people who hear the celestial announcement from angelic messengers.

Shepherds were marginal people in society—a lot like Tamar, Rahab, Ruth, Bathsheba, and Mary. They weren't normal "family men," because they lived outdoors most of the time, guarding sheep from wolves and thieves, and guiding sheep to suitable pasture. A younger son, for whom there was no hope of inheriting the family farm, might become a shepherd, as would a man who for some reason was not suitable for marriage. It was among poor men like these that Jesus' birth was first celebrated.

The poor, of course, have a special place in the Bible. The priests and prophets of Israel agreed that God had a special concern for the poor. God commanded all right-living people to be generous to them. Provision was made for the landless to be able to glean from the fields of the prosperous. According to Proverbs, those who exploited the poor—or simply didn't care about them—would not prosper, and those who were good to the poor would be blessed.

The poor were especially central to the life and ministry of Jesus. Jesus understood himself to be empowered by the Spirit to bring good news to the poor. In Jesus' parables, God cared for the poor and confronted the rich who showed the poor no compassion. Jesus taught rich people to give generously to the poor, and even though others considered the poor to be cursed, Jesus pronounced the poor and those who are in solidarity with them to be blessed. When Jesus said, "The poor you will always have with you," he was echoing Deuteronomy 15:4 (NLT), which says, "There should be no poor among you," for there is actually enough in God's world for everyone.

Although much has changed from Jesus' day to ours, this has not: a small percentage of the world's population lives in luxury, and the majority live in poverty. For example, about half the people in today's world struggle to survive on less than $2.50 per day. Those who subsist on $1.25 per day make up over a billion of the world's seven billion people. About half of the people in sub-Saharan Africa and over 35 percent of people in Southeast Asia fit in this category. They are today's shepherds, working the rice fields, streaming into slums, sleeping on sidewalks, struggling to survive.

So let us light a candle for surprising people like the women of the ancestor lists and the shepherds of the ancient world, and for their counterparts today—all who are marginalized, dispossessed, vulnerable, hungry for good nutrition, thirsty for drinkable water, desperate to know they are not forgotten. Let us join them in their vigil of hope—waiting for good news of great joy for all people, all people, all people. Amen.

ENGAGE:

1. What one thought or idea from today's lesson especially intrigued, provoked, disturbed, challenged, encouraged, warmed, warned, helped, or surprised you?
2. Share a story about a shady or colorful character from your family history.
3. How do you respond to this approach to the meaning of "son of God"?
4. For children: Imagine you are a shepherd in the time of Jesus. What do you think your life would be like?
5. Activate: This week, look for surprising people to whom you can show uncommon respect and unexpected kindness.
6. Meditate: After lighting a candle, hold the words "good news of great joy for all people" in your heart in God's presence for a few moments of silence. Break the silence with a short prayer.

CHAPTER SEVENTEEN A

The Light Has Come (Christmas Eve)

Isaiah 60:1–3
John 1:1–5, 9–10; 3:19–21; 8:12; 9:5; 12:35–36, 46

Do you remember how the whole biblical story begins? "In the..." And do you remember the first creation that is spoken into being? "Let there be..."

On Christmas Eve, we celebrate a new *beginning*. We welcome the dawning of a new *light*.

A new day begins with sunrise. A new year begins with lengthening days. A new life begins with infant eyes taking in their first view of a world bathed in light. And a new era in human history began when God's light came shining into our world through Jesus.

The Fourth Gospel tells us that what came into being through Jesus was not merely a new religion, a new theology, or a new set of principles or teachings—although all these things did indeed happen. The real point of it all, according to John, was *life*, vitality, *aliveness*—and now that Jesus has come, that radiant aliveness is here to enlighten all people everywhere.

Some people don't see it yet. Some don't want to see it. They've got some shady plans that they want to preserve undercover, in darkness. From pickpockets to corrupt politicians, from human traffickers to exploitive business sharks, from terrorists plotting in hidden cells to racists spreading messages of hate, they don't welcome the light, because transparency exposes their plans and deeds for what they are: evil. So they prefer darkness.

But others welcome the light. They receive it as a gift, and in that receiving, they let God's holy, radiant aliveness stream into their lives. They become portals of light in our world, and they start living as members of God's family—which means they're related to all of God's creation. That relatedness is the essence of enlightenment.

What do we mean when we say Jesus is the light? Just as a glow on the eastern horizon tells us that a long night is almost over, Jesus' birth signals the beginning of the end for the dark night of fear, hostility, violence, and greed that has descended on our world. Jesus' birth signals the start of a new day, a new way, a new understanding of what it means to be alive.

Aliveness, he will teach, is a gift available to all by God's grace. It flows not from taking, but giving, not from fear but from faith, not from conflict but from reconciliation, not from domination but from service. It isn't found in the outward trappings of religion—rules and rituals, controversies and scruples, temples and traditions. No, it springs up from our innermost being like a fountain of living water. It intoxicates us like the best wine ever and so turns life from a disappointment into a banquet. This new light of aliveness and love opens us up to rethink everything—to go back and become like little children again. Then we can rediscover the world with a fresh, childlike wonder—seeing the world in a new light, the light of Christ.

On Christmas Eve, then, we remember a silent, holy night long ago when Luke tells us of a young and very pregnant woman and weary man walking beside her. They had traveled over eighty miles, a journey of several days, from Nazareth in the province of Galilee to Bethlehem in the province of Judea. Mary went into labor, and because nobody could provide them with a normal bed in a normal house, she had to give birth in a stable. We can imagine oxen and donkeys and cattle filling the air with their sounds and scent as Mary wrapped the baby in rags and laid him in a manger, a food trough for farm animals. On that dark night, in such a humble place, enfleshed in a tiny, vulnerable, homeless, helpless baby... God's light began to glow.

Politicians compete for the highest offices. Business tycoons scramble for a bigger and bigger piece of the pie. Armies march and scientists study and philosophers philosophize and preachers preach and laborers sweat. But in that silent baby, lying in that humble manger, there pulses more potential power and wisdom and grace and aliveness than all the rest of us can imagine.

To be alive in the adventure of Jesus is to kneel at the manger and gaze upon that little baby who is radiant with so much promise for our world today.

So let us light a candle for the Christ child, for the infant Jesus, the Word made flesh. Let our hearts glow with that light that was in him, so that we become candles through which his light shines still. For Christmas is a process as well as an event. Your heart and mine can become the little town, the stable, the manger... even now. Let a new day, a new creation, a new you, and new me, begin. Let there be light.

ENGAGE:

The gathering can be concluded with a candle-lighting ceremony. If an Advent wreath is being used, the central Christ candle is lit at the beginning of the gathering, and at the end, the light is passed from candle to candle, person to person—in silence, or while singing an appropriate carol.

You may wish to walk together to a public place with your candles lit, in silence or while singing carols, as a visible witness to the light that has come into the world. You could also hold some small signs, lettered with simple words of peace from the Christmas story. You could even bring gifts of candy or fruit to give to people who pass by, along with a sincere "Merry Christmas."

CHAPTER EIGHTEEN

Sharing Gifts (Sunday on or after Christmas Day)

Psalm 117
Matthew 2:1–12
Luke 2:25–32

They were called Magi...we know them as wise men. They were astrologers, holy men of a foreign religion. They had observed a strange celestial phenomenon, which they interpreted to mean that a new king had been born in Judea. According to Matthew's gospel, they traveled to honor him, bringing valuable treasures of gold, frankincense, and myrrh—precious gifts indeed.

In their giving of gifts they were wiser than they realized. Gift-giving, it turns out, was at the heart of all Jesus would say and do. God is like a parent, Jesus would teach, who loves to shower sons and daughters with good gifts. The kingdom or commonwealth of God that Jesus constantly proclaimed was characterized by an abundant, gracious, extravagant economy of grace, of generosity, of gift-giving. "It is better to give than to receive," Jesus taught, and his followers came to understand Jesus himself as a gift expressing God's love to the whole world.

So, in memory of the wise men's gift-giving to Jesus, in honor of Jesus' teaching and example of giving, and as an echo of God's self-giving in Jesus, we joyfully give one another gifts when we celebrate the birth of Jesus.

Not everyone felt generosity in response to this new baby. King Herod was furious about anyone who might unsettle the status quo. When he deployed troops to the Bethlehem region with orders to kill all infant boys, Joseph was warned in a dream to escape. So the family fled south to Egypt, where Jesus spent part of his childhood as a refugee.

How meaningful it is that members of other religions—the Magi from the east and the Egyptians to the south—help save Jesus' life. Could their role in the Christmas story be a gift to us today? Could they be telling us that God has a better way for religions to relate to one another?

Through the centuries, religions have repeatedly divided people. Religions—including the Christian religion—have too often spread fear, prejudice, hate, and violence in our world. But in the Magi's offering of gifts to honor the infant Jesus, and in the Egyptians' protective hospitality for Jesus and his refugee family, we can see a better way, a way Jesus himself embodied and taught as a man. They remind us that members of Earth's religions don't need to see their counterparts as competitors or enemies. Instead, we can approach one another with the spirit of gift-giving and honor, as exemplified by the Magi. We can be there to welcome and protect one another, as exemplified by the Egyptians.

Instead of looking for faults and errors by which other religions can be discredited, insulted, and excluded, we can ask other questions: *What good can be discovered in this religion? Let us honor it. What treasures have they been given to share with us? Let us warmly welcome them. What dangers do they face? Let us protect them. What gifts do we have to share with them? Let us generously offer them.*

According to Matthew, when King Herod died, Joseph had another dream telling him it was safe to return to his homeland. But Herod's son still ruled Judea, the region around Bethlehem, so the family went farther north to another region, Galilee. They resettled in Nazareth, Galilee—which would be Jesus' address throughout the rest of his childhood and young adulthood.

So, having been protected by the Magi and the Egyptians, Jesus grew up as a Galilean Jew. The Jews were the descendants of the Judeans who had survived the Babylonian invasion over five centuries earlier. They had not lost their identity while living under exile in Babylon. Nor had they lost that identity over the following centuries, when they survived occupation and oppression by the Persians, Greeks, and Romans. Because the Jews had so courageously survived oppression and mistreatment by others, and because they believed God had given them special blessings to enjoy and share with everyone, no wonder Jewish identity was highly cherished. No wonder it was repeatedly affirmed and celebrated through holidays like Passover and rites of passage like circumcision.

Luke's gospel doesn't tell us about the Magi or the Egyptians. For Luke, the next big event after Jesus' birth came eight days later, when Jesus' parents took him to the Temple in Jerusalem to be circumcised, a primary sign of Jewish identity for every newborn son. You can imagine his parents' surprise when an old man, a perfect stranger named Simeon, came up to them in the Temple and took Jesus from their arms and began praising God. "This child will be a light for revelation to the Gentiles, and a glory to God's people, Israel," Simeon said. He was seeing in Jesus a gift for *us* and for *them* both, not one against the other or one without the other.

Old Simeon the Jew in Luke's gospel and the non-Jewish Magi from the East in Matthew's gospel agree: This child is special. He is worthy of honor. He has gifts that will bring blessing to his own people, and to all people everywhere.

To be alive in the adventure of Jesus is to know ourselves as part of a tradition and, through that tradition, to have a history and an identity to enjoy, preserve, and to share. And to be alive in the adventure of Jesus is to see others as part of their unique traditions, too, with their own history, identity, and gifts. Like the Magi, like the Egyptians, like old Simeon... we don't have to see people of other religions in terms of *us* versus *them*. We can see people of other religions as beloved neighbors, us with them, them with us, with gifts to share.

May we who follow Jesus discover the gifts of our tradition and share them generously, and may we joyfully receive the gifts that others bring as well. For every good gift and every perfect gift comes from God.

Engage:

1. What one thought or idea from today's lesson especially intrigued, provoked, disturbed, challenged, encouraged, warmed, warned, helped, or surprised you?
2. Share a story of a meaningful encounter you've had with a member of another religion. Who might be today's Magi—people from other religions (or no religion) who honor Jesus without wanting to leave the religion into which they were born?
3. How do you respond to the idea that members of different religions can see one another as neighbors with whom to exchange gifts rather than as enemies or competitors?
4. For children: What was one of your favorite Christmas presents that you received or that you gave? Why was it your favorite?
5. Activate: This week, look for someone of another faith to spend some time with. Get to know them. Learn about their tradition. Ask them what they value in their heritage, and answer any questions they ask about yours. Perhaps tell them the story of the Magi.
6. Meditate: In silence, think of the different religions in today's world. Hold in your heart the idea that each has gifts to give and each can receive gifts, too. Conclude your meditation with a prayer.

CHAPTER NINETEEN

JESUS COMING OF AGE

1 Kings 3:1–28
Luke 2:39–3:14; 3:21–22
1 Timothy 4:6–16

WHAT WERE YOU LIKE when you were twelve? In what ways are you the same today? How have you changed?

We have only this one glimpse into Jesus' childhood. Jesus was twelve, when boys came of age in ancient Jewish culture. He joined his family on their annual pilgrimage south to Jerusalem for the Passover holiday. This was a journey of over sixty miles—not a short trip on foot, maybe taking four or five days each way. This year, as at each Passover holiday, the Jewish people would celebrate the story of God liberating their ancestors from slavery in Egypt. Because the Romans now ruled over them, making them feel like slaves again, the holiday kept alive the hopes that a new Moses might arise among them and lead them to expel the Romans. Like every good holiday, then, this Passover was to be about both the past and the present.

People traveled to and from the Passover festival in large groups, so Mary and Joseph assumed that Jesus was among their fellow travelers when they began the long trek home. When Jesus couldn't be found, they rushed back to Jerusalem, where they looked for him for three long days. Finally they came to the Temple, and there Jesus sat, a twelve-year-old boy among the religious scholars and teachers. He was asking questions of them and answering questions they posed in return. Everyone was amazed at this young spiritual prodigy. He was like a modern-day Solomon, King David's son who was famous for his wisdom.

His mother pulled him aside and gave him exactly the lecture you would expect. "Child!" she began, as if to remind this young adolescent that he wasn't grown up yet. "Why have you treated us like this? Listen! Your father and I have been worried sick. We've been looking everywhere for you!" Jesus replied, "Didn't you know that it was necessary for me to be in my Father's house?"

The reply tells us a lot about Jesus. By the age of twelve, he saw God in tender, fatherly terms. He saw himself as God's child. He was already deeply curious—demonstrated by his questions to the religious scholars. And he was deeply thoughtful—demonstrated by his wise answers to their questions. Like most parents of teenagers, of course, Mary and Joseph were completely baffled by his behavior and his explanation of it. He went back to Nazareth with them, and the next eighteen years were summarized by Luke in these fourteen words: "Jesus matured in wisdom and years, and in favor with God and with people" (CEB).

As Jesus was maturing in Nazareth, his relative John, son of Elizabeth and Zechariah, was coming of age back in Jerusalem. As the son of a priest, he would have lived the comfortable, privileged life of the upper classes. We would expect him to follow in his father's footsteps at the Temple in Jerusalem, offering sacrifices, officiating at festivals, and performing ritual cleansings called baptisms.

Baptisms were essential, because pilgrims who came from distant lands to the Temple were understood to be "unclean" as a result of their contact with people of other religions and cultures. Several special baths had been constructed around the Temple so that worshipers could ceremonially wash off that contamination and present themselves to God as "clean people" again. It was another way to preserve religious identity during a time of occupation and domination by "unclean foreigners."

Can you imagine how shocking it was for Zechariah's son to burst onto the scene, preaching and performing baptisms—not in Jerusalem, but over eighty miles to the north and east? Can you imagine the disruption of him performing ritual cleansing—not in the private, holy baths near the

Temple, but in public, out in the countryside, along the banks of the Jordan River? Can you imagine the gossip about his choice to trade the luxurious robes of the priesthood for the rough garments of a beggar, and the high-class menu of Jerusalem for the subsistence fare of the wilderness? What would such actions have meant?

John's departure from both family and Temple suggested that John was protesting against the religious establishment his father faithfully served. Jerusalem's Temple was not all it was held up to be, he would have been saying. A new kind of baptism—with a radical new meaning—was needed. Traveling to a special city and an opulent building could not make people clean and holy. What they needed most was not a change in location, but a change in orientation, a change in heart. People needed a different kind of cleanness—one that couldn't come through a conventional ceremonial bath in a holy temple.

According to John, the identity that mattered most wasn't one you could inherit through tribe, nationality, or religion—as descendants of Abraham, for example. The identity that mattered most was one you created through your actions . . . by sharing your wealth, possessions, and food with those in need, by refusing to participate in the corruption so common in government and business, by treating others fairly and respectfully, and by not being driven by greed. One word summarized John's message: *repent*, which meant "rethink everything," or "question your assumptions," or "have a deep turnaround in your thinking and values." His baptism of repentance symbolized being immersed in a flowing river of love, in solidarity not just with the clean, privileged, superior *us*—but with everyone, everywhere.

Like prophets of old, John issued a powerful warning: God would soon intervene to confront wrong and set things right, and the status quo would soon come to an end. Crowds started streaming out to the countryside to be baptized by John. His protest movement grew, and with it, expectation and hope. Maybe John would be the long-awaited liberator, the people whispered—like Moses and Joshua, leading people to freedom; like David, instituting a new reign and a new golden age. John quickly squelched those expectations. "I'm not the one you're waiting for," he said. "I'm preparing the way for someone who is coming after me. He will really clean things up. He will bring the change we need."

John kept thundering out his message of warning and hope, week after week, month after month. He dared to confront the powerful and name their hypocrisy. (Herod Antipas, the son of the Herod who tried to kill Jesus, couldn't withstand the agitation of John's protest movement, so he ultimately would have John arrested and, eventually, beheaded.)

Among the crowds coming to be baptized one day was a young man about John's age. By receiving John's baptism, this young man identified himself with this growing protest movement in the Galilean countryside. As he came out of the water, people heard a sound, as if the sky was cracking open with a rumble of thunder. They saw something descending from the sky... it looked like a dove landing on his head. Some claimed to hear the voice of God saying, "You are my Son, whom I dearly love. In you I find pleasure" (Mark 1:11, author's paraphrase).

What Jesus had said about God at the age of twelve in the Temple, God now echoed about Jesus at age thirty at the riverside: they shared a special parent-child relationship, a deep connection of love and joy. And in that relationship, there was an invitation for us all, because Jesus taught that all of us could enter into that warm and secure parent-child relationship with God.

That dove is full of meaning as well. Jesus came, not under the sign of the lion or tiger, not under the sign of the bull or bear, not under the sign of the hawk or eagle or viper... but under the sign of the dove—a sign of peace and nonviolence. Similarly, when John first saw Jesus, he didn't say, "Behold the Lion of God, come to avenge our enemies," but rather "Behold the Lamb of God, who takes away the sin of the world." To remove sin rather than get revenge for it—that was an agenda of peace indeed.

So now, Jesus had come of age and stepped onto the stage: a man with a dovelike spirit, a man with the gentleness of a lamb, a man of peace whose identity was rooted in this profound reality: *God's beloved child.*

When we awaken within that deep relationship of mutual love and pleasure, we are ready to join in God's peace movement today—an adventure of protest, hope, and creative, nonviolent, world-transforming change.

Engage:

1. What one thought or idea from today's lesson especially intrigued, provoked, disturbed, challenged, encouraged, warmed, warned, helped, or surprised you?
2. Share the story of your baptism or some other initiation experience you've had.
3. How do you respond to this explanation of John the Baptist and baptism? In breaking with tradition, what kind of challenges do you think he encountered?
4. For children: When you think of a dove and a lamb, what do you think of?
5. Activate: This week, look for every chance to "grow in wisdom" by listening, learning, and asking questions.
6. Meditate: Imagine God asking you, "What one thing would you like me to do for you?" As Solomon asked for wisdom, hold one request up to God in silence. Then, receive God's message to Jesus as a message to you by saying these words, silently or aloud, one time or several times: "[Your name], you are my child, whom I dearly love. In you I find pleasure." Finally, make these words your own: "I am [my name], your child, whom you dearly love. In me you find pleasure."

CHAPTER TWENTY

Join the Adventure!

Isaiah 61:1–4
Luke 4:1–30; 5:1–11
2 Timothy 2:1–9

To never be given a chance to succeed—that's a tragedy. But in some ways it's even worse to have your chance and not be ready for it. That's why in almost every story of a great hero, there is an ordeal or a test that must be passed before the hero's adventure can begin.

That was the case with Jesus. Before he could begin his public adventure, Jesus felt the Holy Spirit leading him away from the crowds, away from the cities, and away from the fertile Jordan Valley, out into the solitude of the harsh, dry, barren Judean desert.

By saying Jesus fasted in the desert for forty days, Luke's gospel is inviting us to remember Moses who, before becoming the liberator of the Hebrew slaves, spent forty years in the wilderness, where he eventually encountered God in the burning bush. Luke's gospel is also inviting us to remember the story of the newly liberated Hebrew slaves who, after leaving Egypt, were tested for forty years in the wilderness before they were prepared to enter the promised land. Once again the gospel writers present Jesus as mirroring the experience of his ancestral people.

Luke describes Jesus' testing in the vivid language of an encounter with the devil. Some take this language literally. Others see the devil as a literary figure who developed over time among ancient storytellers to personify all that is dark, evil, and violent in human nature and human culture.

"Turn these stones into bread," the devil says in his first temptation. In other words, *Who needs the character formation and self-control that come from spiritual disciplines like fasting? That's a long, hard process. You can have it all, right now—public influence and private self-indulgence—if you just use your miraculous powers to acquire whatever you desire!* In the second temptation, Jesus is offered the chance to get on the fast track to power by acknowledging that self-seeking power, not self-giving love, reigns supreme: "You can rule over all the kingdoms of the world—if you'll simply worship me!" In the third temptation, the devil tells him, "Prove yourself as God's beloved child by throwing yourself off the Temple!" This seemingly suicidal move, with angelic intervention at the last moment before impact, would provide just the kind of public-relations spectacle that showmen love. But Jesus is not a showman, and he isn't interested in shortcuts. Besides, he doesn't need to prove he is God's beloved child. He knows that already.

So he will not use his power for personal comfort and pleasure. He will refuse unscrupulous means to achieve just and peaceful ends. He will not reach for spectacle over substance. And so Jesus sets the course for the great work before him—not driven by a human lust for pleasure, power, or prestige, but empowered by the Spirit. And of course, if we want to join Jesus in his great work, we must face our own inner demons and discover the same Spirit-empowerment.

He soon comes to his hometown, Nazareth. Like any good Jewish man, he goes to the synagogue on the Sabbath day. There is a time in the synagogue gathering where men can read a passage of Scripture and offer comment upon it. So on this day, Jesus stands and asks for the scroll of the prophet Isaiah. He unrolls the scroll until he comes to the passage that speaks of the Spirit anointing someone to bring good news to the poor, release to the captives, healing to the blind, freedom to the oppressed.

By quoting these words, Jesus stirs the hopes of his people—hopes for the time Isaiah and other prophets had urged the people to wait for, pray for, and prepare for. Then he sits—a teacher's customary posture in those days. He offers this amazing commentary—notable for its brevity and even more for its astonishing claim: "Today this Scripture has been fulfilled in your hearing."

If he had said, "Someday this Scripture will be fulfilled," everyone would have felt it was a good, comforting sermon. If he had said, "This Scripture is already fulfilled in some ways, not yet in others," that would also have been interesting and acceptable. But either commentary would postpone until the future any need for real change in his hearers' lives. For Jesus to say the promised time was here already, fulfilled, today... that was astonishing. That required deep rethinking and radical adjustment.

The same is true for us today.

Imagine if a prophet arose today in Panama, Sierra Leone, or Sri Lanka. In an interview on the BBC or Al Jazeera he says, "Now is the time! It's time to dismantle the military-industrial complex and reconcile with enemies! It's time for CEOs to slash their mammoth salaries and give generous raises to all their lowest-paid employees! It's time for criminals, militias, weapons factories, and armies to turn in their bullets and guns so they can be melted down and recast as trumpets, swing sets, and garden tools. It's time to stop plundering the Earth for quick corporate profit and to start healing the Earth for long-term universal benefit. Don't say 'someday' or 'tomorrow.' The time is today!"[1] Imagine how the talking heads would spin!

The Nazareth crowd is impressed that their hometown boy is so articulate and intelligent and bold. But Jesus won't let them simply be impressed or appreciative for long. He quickly reminds them of two stories from the Scriptures, one involving a Sidonian widow in the time of Elijah and one involving a Syrian general in the time of Elisha. God bypassed many needy people of our religion and nation, Jesus says, to help those foreigners, those Gentiles, those outsiders. You can almost hear the snap as people are jolted by this unexpected turn.

Clearly, the good news proclaimed by the hometown prophet is for *them* as well as *us*, for *all humankind* and not just for *our kind*. Somehow, that seems disloyal to the Nazarenes. That seems like a betrayal of their unique and hard-won identity. In just a few minutes, the crowd quickly flips from proud to concerned to disturbed to furious. They are transformed by their

1. This section is adapted from my book *The Secret Message of Jesus* (Nashville: W Publishing/Thomas Nelson, 2006), pp. 24–25.

fury from a congregation into a lynch mob, and they push Jesus out the door and over to the edge of a cliff. They're ready to execute this heretical traitor.

Again, imagine if a pope, a patriarch, or a famous Protestant TV preacher today were to declare that God is just as devoted to Muslims, Hindus, and atheists as to Christians. They might not be thrown off a cliff, but one can easily imagine tense brows and grave voices advocating for them to be thrown out of office or taken off the air!

No wonder Jesus needed that time of preparation in the wilderness. He needed to get his mission clear in his own heart so that he wouldn't be captivated by the expectations of adoring fans or intimidated by the threats of furious critics. If we dare to follow Jesus and proclaim the radical dimensions of God's good news as he did, we will face the same twin dangers of domestication and intimidation.

Jesus managed to avoid execution that day. But he knew it wouldn't be his last brush with hostile opposition. Soon he began inviting select individuals to become his followers. As with aspiring musicians who are invited to become the students of a master-musician, this was a momentous decision for them. To become disciples of a rabbi meant entering a rigorous program of transformation, learning a new way of life, a new set of values, a new set of skills. It meant leaving behind the comforts of home and facing a new set of dangers on the road. Once they were thoroughly apprenticed as disciples, they would then be sent out as apostles to spread the rabbi's controversial and challenging message everywhere. One did not say *yes* to discipleship lightly.

The word *Christian* is more familiar to us today than the word *disciple*. These days, *Christian* often seems to apply more to the kinds of people who would push Jesus off a cliff than it does to his true followers. Perhaps the time has come to rediscover the power and challenge of that earlier, more primary word *disciple*. The word *disciple* occurs over 250 times in the New Testament, in contrast to the word *Christian*, which occurs only three times. Maybe those statistics are trying to tell us something.

To be alive in the adventure of Jesus is to hear that challenging good news of *today*, and to receive that thrilling invitation to follow him... and to take the first intrepid step on the road as a *disciple*.

Engage:

1. What one thought or idea from today's lesson especially intrigued, provoked, disturbed, challenged, encouraged, warmed, warned, helped, or surprised you?
2. Share a story about a time you went through some hardship or temptation that prepared you for a later opportunity, or a time when you missed an opportunity because you were unprepared.
3. How do you respond to the idea that you can be captivated by the expectations of your loyal fans and intimidated by the threats of your hostile critics? Which is a greater danger for you?
4. For children: What's something you can't do right now that you hope you will be able to do someday? What will you have to learn in order to do that thing?
5. Activate: This week, write the word *disciple* in prominent places to remind yourself of Jesus' invitation to you.
6. Meditate: In silence, imagine Jesus calling your name and saying two words: *Follow me.* Allow that invitation to stir a response in you at the deepest part of your being.

CHAPTER TWENTY-ONE

SIGNIFICANT AND WONDERFUL

2 Samuel 11:26–12:15
John 2:1–12
Mark 1:21–28

YOU CAN'T GO MANY pages in the gospels without encountering a miracle. Some of us find it easy and exciting to believe in miracles. Others of us find them highly problematic.

If you find it easy to believe in miracles, the gospels are a treasure of inspiration. But you still have to deal with one big problem: the miracles in the gospels easily stir hopes that are almost always dashed in people's lives today. For example, in Matthew 9 you read about a little girl being raised from the dead, but since that time millions of faithful, praying parents have grieved lost children without miraculous happy endings. Why not? In Matthew 14, you read about fish and bread being multiplied to feed the hungry, but since that day, how many millions of faithful, praying people have slowly starved, and no miracle came? Doesn't the possibility of miracles only make our suffering worse when God could grant them but doesn't? It's all so much worse if accusatory people then blame the victim for not having enough faith.

If you are skeptical about miracles, you avoid these problems. But you have another problem, no less significant: if you're not careful, you can be left with a reduced world, a disenchanted, mechanistic world where the impossible is always and forever impossible. You may judge the miracle stories in the gospels as silly legends, childish make-believe, false advertising, or deceitful propaganda. But in banishing what you regard as superstition, you may also banish meaning and hope. If you lock out miracles, you can easily lock yourself in—into a closed mechanistic system, a small box where God's existence doesn't seem to make much difference.

There is a third alternative, a response to the question of miracles that is open to both skeptics and believers in miracles alike. Instead of "Yes, miracles actually happened," or "No, they didn't really happen," we could ask another question: *What happens to us when we imagine miracles happening?* In other words, perhaps the story of a miracle is intended to do more than inform us about an event that supposedly happened in the past, an event that if you were to believe it, might prove something else.

Perhaps a miracle story is meant to shake up our normal assumptions, inspire our imagination about the present and the future, and make it possible for us to see something we couldn't see before. Perhaps the miracle that really counts isn't one that happened to *them* back then, but one that could happen in *us* right now as we reflect upon the story.

Perhaps, by challenging us to consider impossible possibilities, these stories can stretch our imagination, and in so doing, can empower us to play a catalytic role in co-creating new possibilities for the world of tomorrow. Doesn't that sound rather... miraculous?

Consider Jesus' first miracle in the Fourth Gospel. The story begins, "On the third day there was a wedding in Cana of Galilee." Jesus' mother notices that the wedding host has run out of wine, and she nudges Jesus to do something about it. Jesus resists, but Mary doubts his resistance. She tells the servants to get ready to do whatever Jesus instructs.

Jesus points them to some nearby stone containers—six of them, used to hold water for ceremonial cleansing. These cleansings express the intention to live as "clean people," in contrast to "unclean people." The containers are huge—potentially holding twenty or thirty gallons each. But they are empty. "Fill them with water," Jesus says. So the servants get to work drawing 120–180 gallons of water and filling the huge containers. Jesus instructs them to draw out a sample to give to the banquet master. He takes a taste. He's amazed! "You've saved the best wine until last!" he says.

John says this was the first of the signs by which Jesus revealed his glory. That word *signs* is important. Signs point. They signify. They mean something. Often, the word *signs* is linked with *wonders*—which make you wonder and astonish you with awe. So having warmed up our imagination by picturing a story about a faraway place in a long-ago time, let's now apply our inspired imagination to our lives, our world, here and now. Let's consider the significance of the sign. Let's do some wondering.

In what ways are our lives—and our religions, and our cultures—like a wedding banquet that is running out of wine? What are we running out of? What are the stone containers in our day—huge but empty vessels used for religious purposes? What would it mean for those empty containers to be filled—with wine? And why so much wine? Can you imagine what 180 gallons of wine would mean in a small Galilean village? What might that superabundance signify? What might it mean for Jesus to repurpose containers used to separate the clean from the unclean? And what might it mean for God to save the best for last?

Questions like these show us a way of engaging with the miracle stories as signs and wonders, without reducing them to the level of "mere facts" on the one hand or "mere superstition" on the other. They stir us to imagine new ways of seeing, leading to new ways of acting, leading to new ways of being alive.

In Mark's gospel, the first miracle is very different. It happens in Capernaum, Jesus' home base, in the synagogue on the Sabbath day. The people have gathered and Jesus is teaching with his trademark authority. Suddenly, a man "with an unclean spirit" screams: "What do you want with us, Jesus of Nazareth? Have you come to destroy us? I know who you are—the Holy One of God!" Jesus tells the spirit to be quiet and leave the man, and the spirit shakes the man violently and leaves.

Today, we would probably diagnose the man as being mentally or emotionally unwell, anxiety-ridden, maybe even paranoid. Instead of being possessed by a demon, we would understand him to be possessed by a chemical imbalance, a psychiatric disorder, a neurological malady, or a powerful delirium. But even with our difference in diagnosing and understanding human behavior, we can imagine how we would respond to seeing Jesus return this man to mental well-being with one impromptu therapy session lasting less than ten seconds!

Again, the story stimulates us to ask questions about our own lives, our own times. What unhealthy, polluting spirits are troubling us as individuals and as a people? What fears, false beliefs, and emotional imbalances reside within us and distort our behavior? What unclean or unhealthy thought patterns, value systems, and ideologies inhabit, oppress, and possess us as a community or culture? What in us feels threatened and intimidated by the presence of a supremely "clean" or "holy" spirit or presence, like the one in Jesus? In what way might this individual symbolize our whole society? In what ways might our society lose its health, its balance, its sanity, its "clean spirit," to something unclean or unhealthy?

And what would it mean for faith in the power of God to liberate us from these unhealthy, imbalanced, self-destructive disorders? Dare we believe that we could be set free? Dare we trust that we could be restored to health? Dare we have faith that such a miracle could happen to us—today?

There is a time and place for arguments about whether this or that miracle story literally happened. But in this literary approach, we turn from arguments about history to conversations about meaning. We accept that miracle stories intentionally stand on the line between believable and dismissible. In so doing, they throw us off balance so that we see, think, imagine, and feel in a new way.

After people met Jesus, they started telling wild, inspiring stories like these... stories full of gritty detail, profound meaning, and audacious hope. They felt their emptiness being filled to overflowing. They watched as their lifelong obsession with *clean* and *unclean* was replaced with a superabundant, supercelebrative joy. They felt their anxiety and paranoia fade, and in their place faith and courage grew. They experienced their blindness ending, and they began to see everything in a new light. That was why these stories had to be told. And that's why they have to be told today. You may or may not believe in literal miracles, but faith still works wonders.

Engage:

1. What one thought or idea from today's lesson especially intrigued, provoked, disturbed, challenged, encouraged, warmed, warned, helped, or surprised you?
2. Share a story about a time when you felt you experienced a miracle, or when you prayed for a miracle that never came.
3. How do you respond to the literary approach that looks for meaning in miracle stories? Can you apply it to some other miracle stories?
4. For children: If you could have a magical power, what would it be, and why?
5. Activate: Keep these two miracle stories in mind throughout this week, and see if they bring new insights to situations you face.
6. Meditate: Hold in silence the image of an empty ceremonial stone container being filled with water that is transformed to wine. Hear the sound of water filling to the brim. See the water change in color, and taste the change in flavor as it becomes wine. Hear the sound of people celebrating in the background. Sit with the words *empty, full*, and *transformed*. See what prayer takes shape in your heart.

CHAPTER TWENTY-TWO

JESUS THE TEACHER

Proverbs 3:1–26
Jeremiah 31:31–34
Mark 4:1–34

WHO WAS JESUS? PEOPLE in his day would have given many answers—a healer, a troublemaker, a liberator, a threat to law and order, a heretic, a prophet, a community organizer. His friends and foes would have agreed on this: he was a powerful teacher. When we scan the pages of the gospels, we find Jesus teaching in many different ways.

First, he instructed through signs and wonders. By healing blindness, for example, Jesus dramatized God's desire to heal our distorted vision of life. By healing paralysis, he showed how God's reign empowers people who are weak or trapped. By calming a storm, he displayed God's desire to bring peace. And by casting out unclean spirits, he conveyed God's commitment to liberate people from occupying and oppressive forces—whether those forces were military, political, economic, social, or personal.

Second, he gave what we might call public lectures. Crowds would gather for a mass teach-in on a hillside near the Sea of Galilee. Whole neighborhoods might jam into a single house, and then spread around the open doors and windows, eager to catch even a few words. People came to hear him at weekly synagogue gatherings. Or they might catch word that he was down at the beach, sitting in a boat, his voice rising above the sounds of lapping waves and calling gulls to engage the minds and hearts of thousands standing on the sand.

Third, he taught at surprising, unplanned, impromptu moments—in transit from here to there, at a well along a road, at a dinner party when an uninvited guest showed up, in some public place when a group of his critics tried to ambush him with a "gotcha" question. You always needed to pay attention, because with Jesus, any moment could become a teaching moment.

Fourth, he saved much of his most important teaching for private retreats and field trips with his disciples. He worked hard to break away from the crowds so he could mentor those who would carry on his work. Certain places seemed the ideal setting for certain lessons.

Fifth, Jesus taught through what we might call public demonstrations. For example, he once led a protest march into Jerusalem, performing a kind of guerrilla-theater dramatization of a royal entry, while denouncing with tears the city's ignorance of what makes for peace. Once he staged an act of civil disobedience in the Temple, stopping business as usual and dramatically delivering some important words of instruction and warning. Once he demonstrated an alternative economy based on generosity rather than greed, inspired by a small boy's fish-sandwich donation.

Sixth, Jesus loved to teach through finely crafted works of short fiction called parables. He often introduced these parables with these words: "Whoever has ears to hear, let him hear." He knew that most adults quickly sort messages into either/or categories—agree/disagree, like/dislike, familiar/strange. In so doing, they react and argue without actually hearing and thinking about what is being said. His parables drew his hearers into deeper thought by engaging their imagination and by inviting interpretation instead of reaction and argument. In this way, parables put people in the position of children who are more attracted to stories than to arguments. Faced with a parable, listeners were invited to give matters a second thought. They could then ask questions, stay curious, and seek something deeper than agreement or disagreement—namely, *meaning*.

In all these overlapping ways, Jesus truly was a master-rabbi, capable of transforming people's lives with a message of unfathomed depth and unexpected imagination. But what was the substance of his message? What was his point? Sooner or later, anyone who came to listen to Jesus would hear one phrase repeated again and again: *the kingdom of God*, or *the kingdom of heaven*. Sadly, people today hear these words and frequently have no idea what they originally meant. Or even worse, they misunderstand the phrase with complete and unquestioning certainty.

For example, many think *kingdom of God* or *kingdom of heaven* means "where righteous people go when they die," or "the perfect new world God will create after destroying this hopeless mess." But for Jesus, the kingdom of heaven wasn't a place we *go up to someday*; it was a reality we pray to *come down here now*. It wasn't a distant future reality. It was *at hand*, or within reach, today. To better understand this pregnant term, we have to realize that kingdoms were the dominant social, political, and economic reality of Jesus' day. Contemporary concepts like *nation*, *state*, *government*, *society*, *economic system*, *culture*, *superpower*, *empire*, and *civilization* all resonate in that one word: *kingdom*.

The kingdom, or empire, of Rome in which Jesus lived and died was a top-down power structure in which the few on top maintained order and control over the many at the bottom. They did so with a mix of rewards and punishments. The punishments included imprisonment, banishment, torture, and execution. And the ultimate form of torture and execution, reserved for rebels who dared to challenge the authority of the regime, was crucifixion. It was through his crucifixion at the hands of the Roman empire that Jesus did his most radical teaching of all.

Yes, he taught great truths through signs and wonders, public lectures, impromptu teachings, special retreats and field trips, public demonstrations, and parables. But when he mounted Rome's most powerful weapon, he taught his most powerful lesson.

By being crucified, Jesus exposed the heartless violence and illegitimacy of the whole top-down, fear-based dictatorship that nearly everyone assumed was humanity's best or only option. He demonstrated the revolutionary truth that God's kingdom wins, not through shedding the blood of its enemies, but through gracious self-giving on behalf of its enemies. He taught that God's kingdom grows through apparent weakness rather than conquest. It expands through reconciliation rather than humiliation and intimidation. It triumphs through a willingness to suffer rather than a readiness to inflict suffering. In short, on the cross Jesus demonstrated God's nonviolent noncompliance with the world's brutal powers-that-be. He showed God to be a different kind of king, and God's kingdom to be a different kind of kingdom.

How would we translate Jesus' radical and dynamic understanding of *the kingdom of God* into our context today?

Perhaps a term like *global commonwealth of God* comes close—not a world divided up and ruled by nations, corporations, and privileged individuals, but a world with enough abundance for everyone to share. Maybe *God's regenerative economy* would work—challenging our economies based on competition, greed, and extraction. Maybe *God's beloved community* or *God's holy ecosystem* could help—suggesting a reverent connectedness in dynamic and creative harmony. Or perhaps *God's sustainable society* or *God's movement for mutual liberation* could communicate the dynamism of this radical new vision of life, freedom, and community.

Today as in Jesus' day, not everybody seems interested in the good news that Jesus taught. Some are more interested in revenge or isolation or gaining a competitive advantage over others. Some are obsessed with sex or a drug or another addiction. Many are desperate for fame or wealth. Still others can think of nothing more than relief from the pain that plagues them at the moment. But underneath even the ugliest of these desires, we can often discern a spark of something pure, something good, something holy—a primal desire for aliveness, which may well be a portal into the kingdom of God.

Interestingly, when the Gospel of John was written some years after its three counterparts, the term *kingdom of God* was usually translated into other terms: *life*, *life of the ages*, *life to the full*—clearly resonant with this word *aliveness*. However we name it—kingdom of God, life to the full, global commonwealth of God, God's sustainable society, or holy aliveness—it is the one thing most worth seeking in life, because in seeking it, we will find everything else worth having.

To be alive in the adventure of Jesus is to seek first the kingdom and justice of God . . . to become a student of the one great subject Jesus came to teach in many creative ways.

Engage:

1. What one thought or idea from today's lesson especially intrigued, provoked, disturbed, challenged, encouraged, warmed, warned, helped, or surprised you?
2. Share a story about one of the most important teachers in your life and what made him or her so significant.
3. How do you respond to the explanation of the term *kingdom of God*? How would you translate it into words or images that make sense today?
4. For children: What makes a good teacher so good? Who is one of your favorite teachers so far?
5. Activate: This week, notice where you seek and find aliveness. Relate that thirst for aliveness to the kingdom of God.
6. Meditate: Choose one of the synonyms for *kingdom of God* from this chapter and simply hold it in silence for a few moments. Conclude the silence with these words: "Let it come."

CHAPTER TWENTY-THREE

Jesus and the Multitudes

Ezekiel 34:1–31
Luke 5:17–32; 18:15–19:9

Most human societies are divided between the elites and the masses. The elites are the 1 or 3 or 5 percent at the top that have and hoard the most money, weapons, power, influence, and opportunities. They make the rules and usually rig the game to protect their interests. They forge alliances across sectors—in government, business, religion, media, the arts, science, and the military. As a result, they have loyal allies across all sectors of a society, and they reward those allies to keep them loyal.

Down at the bottom, we find the masses—commonly called "the multitude" in the gospels. They provide cheap labor in the system run by the elites. They work with little pay, little security, little prestige, and little notice. They live in geographically distant regions or in socially distant slums. So to the elites, the multitudes can remain surprisingly invisible and insignificant most of the time.

In the middle, between the elites and the multitudes, we find those loyal allies who function as mediators between the few above them and the many below them. As such, they make a little more money than the masses, and they live in hope that they or their children can climb up the pyramid, closer to the elites. But those above them generally don't want too much competition from below, so they make sure the pyramid isn't too easy to climb.

These dynamics were at work in Jesus' day, and he was well aware of them. In his parables, he constantly made heroes of people from the multitudes: day laborers, small farmers, women working in the home, slaves, and children. He captured the dilemma of what we would call middle management—the stewards, tax collectors, and their associates who extracted income from the poor and powerless below them for the sake of the rich and powerful above them. And he exposed the duplicity and greed of those at the top—especially the religious leaders who enjoyed a cozy, lucrative alliance with the rich elites.

In addressing the social realities of his day, Jesus constantly turned the normal dominance pyramid on its head, confusing even his disciples.

Take, for example, the time a group of parents brought their little children to Jesus to be blessed (Mark 10:13–16). Their great teacher had important places to go and important people to see, so the disciples tried to send them away. But Jesus rebuked them. "Let those little children come to me," he said. "For of such is God's kingdom."

Or take the time Jesus and his disciples were passing through Samaria, a region that "proper folks" hated to pass through because its inhabitants were considered religiously and culturally "unclean" (John 4:4–42). Jesus decided to wait outside the city while his companions went into town to buy lunch. When they returned, Jesus was sitting by a well, deep in a spiritual and theological conversation with a Samaritan woman...and one with a sketchy reputation at that. The sight of Jesus and this woman talking respectfully was a triple shock to the disciples: men didn't normally speak with women as peers, Jews didn't normally associate with Samaritans, and "clean" people didn't normally interact with those they considered morally stained.

Or take the time Jesus and his disciples, accompanied by a large crowd, passed a blind man along the road (Mark 10:46–52). The man seemed marginal and insignificant, just another beggar, and the people around told him to quiet down when he started crying out for mercy. But to Jesus, he mattered. The same thing happened when Jesus was on his way to heal the daughter of a synagogue official named Jairus (Mark 5:21–43). Along the way, Jesus was touched by a woman with an embarrassing "female problem" that rendered her "unclean." She didn't even think she was important enough to ask for Jesus' help. Jesus healed her, publicly affirmed her value, and then he healed the official's little girl. Little children, a Samaritan, a man who might today be classified as "disabled" and "unemployed," a frightened and "unclean" woman, a little girl...they all mattered to Jesus.

It wasn't just weak or vulnerable people whom Jesus considered important.

Even more scandalous, he saw value in those considered by everyone to be notorious and sinful. Once, for example, Jesus and his companions were invited to a formal banquet (Luke 7:36–50). Imagine their shock when a women known to be a prostitute snuck into the gathering uninvited. Imagine their disgust when she came and honored Jesus by washing his feet with her tears and drying them with her hair. When the host indulged in predictably judgmental thinking about both the woman and Jesus, Jesus turned the tables and held her up as an example for all at the banquet to follow.

That host was a member of the Pharisees, a religious reform movement in Jesus' day. The Pharisees were pious, fastidious, and religiously knowledgeable. They maintained a close association with "the scribes," or religious scholars. Today some might call them "hyperorthodox" or "fundamentalist." But back then, most would have considered them pure and faithful people, the moral backbone of society.

From the start, the Pharisees seemed strangely fascinated with Jesus. When Jesus once claimed his disciples needed a moral rightness that surpassed their own, they must have been unsettled. How could anyone possibly be more upright than they? He further troubled them by his refusal to follow their practice of monitoring every action of every person as clean or unclean, biblical or unbiblical, legal or illegal. To make matters worse, he not only associated with "unclean" people—he seemed to enjoy their company! The Pharisees just didn't know what to do with a man like this. So they kept throwing questions at him, hoping to trap him in some misstatement.

Once they criticized Jesus for healing someone on the Sabbath, their name for the seventh day of the week when no work was supposed to be done (Luke 14:1–6). Jesus asked them a question: If your son—or even your ox—falls in a hole on the Sabbath, will you wait until the next day to rescue it? By appealing to their basic humanity—kindness to their own children, if not their own beasts of burden—he implied that God must possess at least that level of "humanity." In so doing, Jesus proposed that basic human kindness and compassion are more absolute than religious rules and laws. "The Sabbath was made for human beings," Jesus said in another debate with the Pharisees (Mark 2:27). "Human beings weren't made for the Sabbath."

Jesus often turned the condemning language of the Pharisees back on them (Matthew 23). "You travel over land and sea to make a single convert," he said, "and convert him into twice the son of hell he was before you converted him! You wash the outside of the cup but leave the inside filthy and putrid. You are like those who make beautiful tombs... slapping lots of white paint on the outside, only to hide rot and death inside!"

The contrast between Jesus and the Pharisees was nowhere clearer than in their attitude toward the multitudes. The Pharisees once looked at the multitudes and said, "This crowd doesn't know the Scriptures—damn them all" (John 7:49). But when Jesus looked at the multitudes, "he had compassion for them, because they were harassed and helpless, like sheep without a shepherd" (Matthew 9:36).

With a few exceptions, the Pharisees in the gospels come out looking ugly. Their portrait in the gospels bears no resemblance to the honorable and wise Pharisees depicted in Jewish history from the historical period just after the gospels were written. Whether or not the gospel portraits were accurate, Christians in later centuries used their negative depiction of the Pharisees to stereotype and vilify all Jews. The consequences were horrible beyond words. Those Christians who did this anti-semitic stereotyping ended up resembling nobody more than the hypocritical and judgmental Pharisees as depicted in the gospels.

There are always multitudes at the bottom being marginalized, scapegoated, shunned, ignored, and forgotten by elites at the top. And there are always those in the middle torn between the two. To be alive in the adventure of Jesus is to stand with the multitudes, even if doing so means being marginalized, criticized, and misunderstood right along with them.

ENGAGE:

1. What one thought or idea from today's lesson especially intrigued, provoked, disturbed, challenged, encouraged, warmed, warned, helped, or surprised you?
2. Share a story about a time when you felt like one of the multitude, or when you behaved like one of the Pharisees.
3. How do you respond to the stories of Jesus engaging with "the multitudes" and the Pharisees in this chapter?

4. For children: Think of one of the children in your class who is the least popular or who seems to have the fewest friends. What do you think that child wishes other children would do for him or her?
5. Activate: Make an opportunity this week to spend time with some member of "the multitude."
6. Meditate: Think of some group of people you normally turn away from. Imagine them, in silence, and repeat these words: "They are harassed and helpless, like sheep without a shepherd." Notice what happens to your heart as you do so.

CHAPTER TWENTY-FOUR

Jesus and Hell

Jonah 4:1–11
Luke 16:19–31
Matthew 25:31–40

Jesus was boring, if you go by the tame and uninteresting caricature many of us were given. He was a quiet, gentle, excessively nice, somewhat fragile guy on whose lap children liked to sit. He walked around in flowing robes in pastel colors, never dirty, always freshly washed and pressed. He liked to hold a small sheep in one arm and raise the other as if hailing a taxi. Or he was like an *x* or *n*—an abstract part of a mathematical equation, not important primarily because of what he said or how he lived, but only because he filled a role in the cosmic calculus of damnation and forgiveness.

The real Jesus was far more complex and interesting than any of these caricatures. And nowhere was he more defiant, subversive, courageous, and creative than when he took the language of fire and brimstone from his greatest critics and used it for a very different purpose.

The idea of hell entered Jewish thought rather late. In Jesus' day, as in our own, more traditional Jews—especially those of a political and religious group known as the Sadducees—had little to say about the afterlife and about miracles, angels, and the like. Their focus was on this life and on how to be good and faithful human beings within it. Other Jews—especially the Pharisees, the Sadducees' great rivals—had welcomed ideas on the afterlife from neighboring cultures and religions.

To the north and east in Mesopotamia, people believed that the souls of the dead migrated to an underworld whose geography resembled an ancient walled city. Good and evil, high-born and lowly, all descended to this shadowy, scary, dark, inescapable realm. For the Egyptians to the south, the newly departed faced a ritual trial of judgment. Bad people who failed the test were then devoured by a crocodile-headed deity, and good people who passed the test settled in the land beyond the sunset.

To the West, the Greeks had a more elaborate schema. Although there were many permutations, in general, souls were sorted into four groups at death: the holy and heroic, the indeterminate, the curably evil, and the incurably evil. The incurably evil went to Tartarus where they would experience eternal conscious torment. The holy and heroic were admitted to the Elysian Fields, a place of joy and peace. Those in between might be sent back to Earth for multiple reincarnations until they could be properly sorted for shipment to Tartarus or the Elysian Fields.

Then there were the Persian Zoroastrians to the east. In Zoroastrianism, recently departed souls would be judged by two angels, Rashnu and Mithra. The worthy would be welcomed into the Zoroastrian version of heaven. The unworthy would be banished to the realm of the Satanic figure Ahriman—their version of hell.

A large number of Jews had been exiles in the Persian empire in the sixth century BC, and the Persians ruled over the Jews for about 150 years after they returned to rebuild Jerusalem. After that, the Greeks ruled and tried to impose their culture and religion. So it's not surprising that many Jews adopted a mix of Persian and Greek ideas of the afterlife. For many of them, the heaven-bound could be easily identified. They were religiously knowledgeable and observant, socially respected, economically prosperous, and healthy in body... all signs of an upright life today that would be rewarded after death. The hell-bound were just as easily identified: uninformed about religious lore, careless about religious rules, socially suspect, economically poor, and physically sick or disabled... signs of a sinful, undisciplined life now that would be further punished later.

Jesus clearly agreed that there was an afterlife. Death was not the end for Jesus. But one of the most striking facets of his life and ministry was the way he took popular understandings of the afterlife and turned them upside down.

Who was going to hell? Rich and successful people who lived in fancy houses and stepped over their destitute neighbors who slept in the gutters outside their gates. Proud people who judged, insulted, excluded, avoided, and accused others. Fastidious hypocrites who strained out gnats and swallowed camels. The condemnation that the religious elite so freely pronounced on the marginalized, Jesus turned back on them.

And who, according to Jesus, was going to heaven? The very people whom the religious elite despised, deprived, avoided, excluded, and condemned. Heaven's gates opened wide for the poor and destitute who shared in few of life's blessings; the sinners, the sick, and the homeless who felt superior to nobody and who therefore appreciated God's grace and forgiveness all the more; even the prostitutes and tax collectors. Imagine how this overturning of the conventional understanding of hell must have shocked everyone—multitudes and religious elite alike.

Again and again, Jesus took conventional language and imagery for hell and reversed it. We might say he wasn't so much teaching about hell as he was *un-teaching* about hell. In so doing, he wasn't simply arguing for a different understanding of the afterlife. He was doing something far more important and radical: proclaiming a transformative vision of God. God is not the one who punishes some with poverty and sickness, nor is God the one who favors the rich and righteous. God is the one who loves everyone, including the people the rest of us think don't count. Those fire-and-brimstone passages that countless preachers have used to scare people about hell, it turns out, weren't intended to teach us about hell: Jesus used the language of hell to teach us a radical new vision of God!

Jesus used fire-and-brimstone language in another way, as well. He used it to warn his countrymen about the catastrophe of following their current road—a wide and smooth highway leading to another violent uprising against the Romans. Violence won't produce peace, he warned; it will produce only more violence. If his countrymen persisted in their current path, Jesus warned, the Romans would get revenge on them by taking their greatest pride—the Temple—and reducing it to ashes and rubble. The

Babylonians had done it once, and the Romans could do it again. That was why he advocated a different path—a "rough and narrow path" of nonviolent social change instead of the familiar broad highway of hate and violence.

Belief in the afterlife, it turned out, provided a benefit for those who wanted to recruit people for violent revolution. They could promise heaven to those who died as martyrs in a holy war. That connection between death in battle and reward in heaven helps explain why the Pharisees joined forces with the Zealots in AD 67 to lead a revolt against the Romans. Their grand scheme succeeded for a time, but three years later, the Romans marched in and all hell broke loose. Jerusalem was devastated. The temple was reduced to ashes and rubble.

After their failed revolution, the Pharisees charted a nonviolent path of teaching and community-building. They paved the way for the development of Rabbinic Judaism, which undergirds the various traditions of Judaism today. Their story demonstrates that neither groups nor individuals should ever be stereotyped or considered incapable of learning, growth, and change.

That's the real purpose of Jesus' fire-and-brimstone language. Its purpose was not to predict the destruction of the universe or to make absolute for all eternity the insider-outsider categories of *us* and *them*. Its purpose was to wake up complacent people, to warn them of the danger of their current path, and to challenge them to change—using the strongest language and imagery available. As in the ancient story of Jonah, God's intent was not to destroy but to save. Neither a great big fish nor a great big fire gets the last word, but rather God's great big love and grace.

Sadly, many religious people still use the imagery of hell more in the conventional way Jesus sought to reverse. Like Jonah, they seem disappointed that God's grace might get the final word. If more of us would reexamine this fascinating dimension of Jesus' teaching and come to a deeper understanding of it, we would see what a courageous, subversive, and fascinating leader he was, pointing us to a radically different way of seeing God, life, and being alive.

ENGAGE:

1. What one thought or idea from today's lesson especially intrigued, provoked, disturbed, challenged, encouraged, warmed, warned, helped, or surprised you?
2. Share a story about a time someone confronted you with a mistake or fault and you didn't respond well.
3. How do you respond to the parable of the rich man and Lazarus?
4. For children: What are some of the ways that grown-ups try to keep children from doing harmful or dangerous things? What ways do you think work the best?
5. Activate: This week, look for people like Lazarus in the parable and refuse to imitate the rich man in your response to them.
6. Meditate: Imagine the rich man walking by Lazarus in the gutter. In silence, ask God if you are stepping over anyone in your life.

CHAPTER TWENTY-FIVE

Jesus, Violence, and Power

Isaiah 42:1–9; 53:1–12
Matthew 16:13–17:9

Once Jesus took his disciples on a field trip.[1] There was something he wanted them to learn, and there was a perfect place for them to learn it. So he led them on a twenty-five-mile trek north from their base in Galilee to a city called Caesarea Philippi, a regional center of the Roman empire.

The city was built beside a dramatic escarpment or cliff face. A famous spring emerged from the base of the cliff. Before Roman occupation, the spring had been known as Panias, because it was a center for worship of the Canaanite god Baal, and later for the Greek god Pan. Worshipers carved elaborate niches, still visible today, into the cliff face. There they placed statues of Pan and other Greek deities. Panias also had a reputation as the site of a devastating military defeat. At Panias, invading armies affiliated with Alexander the Great took the whole region for the Greek empire.

Eventually the Romans replaced the Greeks, and when their regional ruler Herod the Great died, his son Herod Philip was given control of the region around Panias. He changed the name to Caesarea Philippi. By the first name he honored Caesar Augustus, the Roman emperor. By the sec-

1. This chapter is adapted from my book *Everything Must Change* (Nashville: Thomas Nelson, 2007).

ond name, he honored himself and distinguished the city from another city named Caesarea Maritima—on the coast. The city was, in effect, Philip's Caesar-ville.

Imagine what it would be like to enter Caesar-ville with Jesus and his team. Today, we might imagine a Jewish leader bringing his followers to Auschwitz, a Japanese leader to Hiroshima, a Native American leader to Wounded Knee, or a Palestinian leader to the wall of separation. There, in the shadow of the cliff face with its idols set into their finely carved niches, in the presence of all these terrible associations, Jesus asks his disciples a carefully crafted question: "Who do people say the Son of Man is?"

We can imagine that an awkward silence might follow this rather strange and self-conscious question. But soon the answers flow. "Some people say you're John the Baptist raised from the dead; others say Elijah; and still others, Jeremiah or one of the prophets."

Jesus sharpens the question: "What about you? Who do you say I am?" Another silence, and then Peter, a leader among them, speaks: "You are the Christ, the Son of the living God."

It may sound like Peter is making a theological claim with these words. But in this setting, they're as much a political statement as a theological one. *Christ* is the Greek translation for the Hebrew term *Messiah*, which means "the one anointed as liberating king." To say "liberating king" anywhere in the Roman empire is dangerous, even more so in a city bearing Caesar's name. By evoking the term *Christ*, Peter is saying, "You are the liberator promised by God long ago, the one for whom we have long waited. You are King Jesus, who will liberate us from King Caesar."

Similarly, *son of the living God* takes on an incandescent glow in this setting. Caesars called themselves "sons of the gods," but Peter's confession asserts that their false, idolatrous claim is now trumped by Jesus' true identity as one with authority from the true and living God. The Greek and Roman gods in their little niches in the cliff face may be called on to support the dominating rule of the Caesars. But the true and living God stands behind the liberating authority of Jesus.

Jesus says that God has blessed Peter with this revelation. He speaks in dazzling terms of Peter's foundational role in Jesus' mission. "The gates of hell" will not prevail against their joint project, Jesus says, using a phrase that could aptly be paraphrased "the authority structures and control centers of evil." Again, imagine the impact of those words in this politically-charged setting.

Surely this Caesar-ville field trip has raised the disciples' hopes and expectations about Jesus to sky-high levels. But Jesus quickly brings them back down to Earth. Soon, he says, he will travel south to Jerusalem. There he will be captured, imprisoned, tortured, and killed by the religious and political establishment of their nation, after which, he will be raised. Peter appears not to hear the happy ending, only the horrible middle. So he responds just as we would have, with shock and denial: "Never, Lord! This shall never happen to you!" (Matt. 16:22, NIV).

Do you feel Peter's confusion? Jesus just said that Peter "gets it"—that Jesus is indeed the liberating king, the revolutionary leader anointed and authorized by the living God to set oppressed people free. If that's true, then the one thing Jesus can*not* do is be defeated. He must conquer and capture, not *be* conquered and captured. He must torture and kill his enemies, not *be* tortured and killed by them. So Peter corrects Jesus: "Stop talking this nonsense! This could never happen!"

At that moment, Jesus turns to Peter in one of the most dramatic cases of conceptual whiplash ever recorded in literature anywhere. "Get behind me, Satan!" Jesus says. It's a stunning reversal. Jesus has just identified Peter as the blessed recipient of divine revelation. Now he identifies Peter as a mouthpiece of the dark side. Jesus has just named Peter as a foundational leader in a movement that will defeat the gates of hell. Now he claims Peter is working on the side of hell. Do you feel the agony of this moment?

Like most of his countrymen, Peter knows with unquestioned certainty that God will send a Messiah to lead an armed uprising to defeat and expel the occupying Roman regime and all who collaborate with it. But no, Jesus says. That way of thinking is human, Satanic, the opposite of God's plan. Since the beginning, Jesus has taught that the nonviolent will inherit the Earth. Violence cannot defeat violence. Hate cannot defeat hate. Fear cannot defeat fear. Domination cannot defeat domination. God's way is different. God must achieve victory through defeat, glory through shame, strength through weakness, leadership through servanthood, and life through death. The finely constructed mental architecture in which Peter has lived his whole adult life is threatened by this paradoxical message. It's not the kind of change of perspective that happens quickly or easily.

But isn't that why a master-teacher takes students on a field trip? By removing students from familiar surroundings, the teacher can dislodge them from conventional thinking. By taking them to a new place, the teacher can help them see from a new vantage point, a new perspective.

It was less than a week later that Jesus took three of his disciples on another field trip, this time to the top of a mountain. There they had a vision of Jesus, shining in glory, conversing with two of the greatest leaders in Jewish history. Again, Peter was bold to speak up, offering to make three shrines to the three great men, elevating Jesus to the same elite level as the great liberator Moses and the great prophet Elijah. This time, God's own voice rebuked Peter, as if to say, "Moses and Elijah were fine for their time, but my beloved Son Jesus is on another level entirely, revealing my true heart in a unique and unprecedented way. Listen to him!"

Moses the lawgiver and Elijah the prophet, great as they were, differed from Jesus in one important way: they had both engaged in violence in God's name. But in God's name Jesus will undergo violence, and in so doing, he will overcome it. And that was why, as they came down the mountain, Jesus once again spoke of suffering, death, and resurrection—a different kind of strategy for a different kind of victory.

In many ways, we're all like Peter. We speak with great insight one minute and we make complete fools of ourselves the next. We're clueless about how many of our pious and popular assumptions are actually illusions. We don't know how little we know, and we have no idea how many of our ideas are wrong. Like Peter, we may use the right words to describe Jesus—*Christ, son of the living God.* But we still don't understand his heart, his wisdom, his way. But that's OK. Peter was still learning, and so are we. After all, life with Jesus is one big field trip that we're taking together. So let's keep walking.

Engage:

1. What one thought or idea from today's lesson especially intrigued, provoked, disturbed, challenged, encouraged, warmed, warned, helped, or surprised you?
2. Share a story about a time when you were completely certain about something, and then you realized you were completely (or at least partly) wrong.
3. How do you respond to this interpretation of the Caesar-ville field trip?
4. For children: What's one of the nicest compliments you have ever received? Why did that mean a lot to you?
5. Activate: Look for situations this week when your initial reaction should be questioned, especially in relation to power dynamics.
6. Meditate: Imagine you are Peter after he hears the words, "Get behind me, Satan!" In silence, listen for ways your thinking is out of sync with God's ways. Imagine what you would want to say to Jesus in reply.

CHAPTER TWENTY-SIX

Making It Real

Mark 2:1–19
Hebrews 11:1–8
1 John 1:1–2:6

Let's imagine ourselves visitors in a small village in Galilee, just at the time Jesus was passing through.[1] A crowd has completely filled a house. An even bigger crowd surrounds the house, with people crammed around every open window and door. We approach but can only hear a word or two. We ask a woman on the edge of the crowd about what's going on inside. She whispers that inside the house is a rabbi everyone wants to hear. We ask her who he is. She motions for us to follow her, and whispers, "I am Mary. I come from Magdala, a town not far from here. I don't want to disturb those who are trying to listen. I will be glad to tell you what I know."

When we get a stone's throw from the crowd, Mary explains that the rabbi inside is the son of a tradesman from Nazareth. He has no credentials or status, no army or weapons, no nobility or wealth. He travels from village to village with a dozen of his friends plus a substantial number of supportive women, teaching deep truths to the peasants of Galilee.

"Look around at us," she says. "We are poor. Many of us are unemployed, and some are homeless. See how many of us are disabled, and how many are, like me, women. Few of us can afford an education. But to be

1. This chapter is adapted from my book *The Secret Message of Jesus* (Nashville: Thomas Nelson, 2006).

uneducated is not the same as being stupid. Stupid people cannot survive in times like these. So we are hungry to learn. And wherever this rabbi goes, it is like a free school for everyone—even women like me. Do you see why we love him?"

We ask, "Do you think he is starting a new religion?"

She thinks for a moment and whispers, "I think Rabbi Jesus is doing something far more dangerous than starting a new religion. He says he is announcing a new kingdom."

We continue, "So he is a rebel?"

"His kingdom is not like the regimes of this world that take up daggers, swords, and spears," Mary says. "He heals the sick, teaches the unschooled, and inspires the downtrodden with hope. So no, I would not say that he is a rebel. Nor would I say that this is a revolution. I would call it an uprising, an uprising of learning and hope."

We look curious, so she continues: "According to Rabbi Jesus, you cannot point to this land or that region and say, 'The kingdom of God is located here,' because it exists in us, among us. It does not come crashing in like an army, he says. It grows slowly, quietly, under the surface, like the roots of a tree, like yeast in dough, like seeds in soil. Our faith waters the seed and makes it grow. Do you see this? When people trust it is true, they act upon it, and it becomes true. Our faith unlocks its potential. Our faith makes it real. You can see why this message is unlike anything people around here have ever heard." Mary looks concerned. She asks, "And where are you from? You aren't spies from Jerusalem, are you, looking for a reason to arrest the rabbi?"

"No, we are travelers," we reply, "passing through." We quickly turn the subject back to her: "You are one of his disciples?"

She looks down for a moment and replies, "Not yet. But I am considering it."

We wait for her to continue: "Most of my friends in Magdala are just trying to survive. Some of them are indeed dreaming about a holy war against Rome and their puppets in Jerusalem. Even little boys are sharpening their knives and talking of war. But I think that is foolish. My father was killed in the rebellion in Sepphoris, so I know. There must be another way. Another kind of uprising. An uprising of peace. If Rabbi Jesus can lead that kind of uprising, I will join it gladly."

"You seem to have a lot of faith," we observe. "Do you ever have doubts?"

She laughs. "Sometimes I think his message is the crazy dream of poets and artists, the fantasy of children at play, or old men who drink too much. But then I ask, what other message could possibly change the world? Perhaps what is truly crazy is what we are doing instead—thinking that a little more hate can conquer hate, a little more war can cure war, a little more pride can overcome pride, a little more revenge can end revenge, a little more gold can cure greed, or a little more division can create cohesion."

Mary is silent for a moment, lost in her thoughts. She turns again to us. "What about you? Are you beginning to believe in him? Do you trust him?"

That question has a peculiar power, doesn't it? "Do you trust him?" is not the same as "Do you believe he existed?" or "Do you believe certain doctrines about him?" It's a question about commitment, about confidence. For Jesus, the call to trust him was closely linked to the call to follow him. If we truly trust him, we will follow him on the road, imitate him, learn from his example, live by his way. Because his message was and is so radical on so many levels, believing and following can't be treated lightly. They are costly. They require us to rethink everything. They change the course of our lives.

This time, we have been lost in our own thoughts, so Mary asks again: "Maybe you believe he is misguided and only misleads others? That is what the religious scholars from Jerusalem think."

"We're like you," we respond. "We want to learn more. We feel our hearts being drawn toward him. Maybe we are beginning to trust him."

"So we must go back and listen," she says. We return with our new companion to the edge of the crowd. While we were away, it appears there has been some kind of commotion on the roof of the house. The crowd is buzzing about a paralyzed man being healed.

Mary leans toward us and whispers: "Often when he heals someone, he says, 'Your faith has healed you.' So there it is again. With him, faith is where it all begins. When you believe, you make it real."

"You change this"—she points to her head—"and this"—she points to her heart—"and you change all this." She gestures to indicate the whole world.

We hear in her words a summons, a challenge, a life-changing invitation. Do we dare to step out and follow Jesus, to make the road by walking, to risk everything on an uprising of peace, an uprising of generosity, an uprising of forgiveness, an uprising of love? If we believe, we will make it real.

Engage:

1. What one thought or idea from today's lesson especially intrigued, provoked, disturbed, challenged, encouraged, warmed, warned, helped, or surprised you?
2. Share a story about one of your biggest decisions—how you reached it, how it felt before and after making the choice.
3. How do you respond to the idea that *faith makes it real*?
4. For children: Who is someone you want to be like when you grow up?
5. Activate: This week, consider beginning each day with the words "I believe." If you would like, add the words, "Help my unbelief." Echo them throughout the day when they arise in your heart.
6. Meditate: Sit in silence with Jesus' words: "Your faith has made you well." What in you feels like it is being made well? End the silence with a simple prayer.

Second Quarter Queries

If possible, compose prayerful, honest, and heartfelt replies to these queries in private, and then gather to share what you have written. The Five Guidelines for Learning Circles in Appendix II may be helpful to guide your sharing. You may also find it helpful to invite a trusted spiritual leader to serve as "catechist" and ask him or her for additional guidance, feedback, and instruction. Make it safe for one another to speak freely, and let your conversation build conviction in each of you as individuals, and among you as a community.

1. Here is the meaning I find in the stories of John the Baptist, the virgin birth, Herod's slaughter of innocent children, the ancestor lists, the coming of the Magi, and Jesus in the Temple at age twelve...
2. Here is why Jesus' parables, miracles, and teaching about hell are important to me...
3. Here is how I respond to Jesus' care for the multitudes and Jesus' attitudes toward Caesar...
4. Here is my understanding of "the kingdom of God"...
5. I believe in Jesus. I have confidence in Jesus. Here is what that means to me...
6. If you have been baptized, what does that baptism mean to you? If you have not been baptized, what would it mean for you to choose to be baptized now?
7. What do you appreciate most about this learning circle?

III

ALIVE IN A GLOBAL UPRISING

JOINING THE ADVENTURE OF Jesus is a starting line, not a finish line. It leads us into a lifetime of learning and action. It challenges us to stand up against the way things have been and the way things are, to help create new possibilities for the way things can and should be. It enlists us as contemplative activists in an ongoing uprising of peace, freedom, justice, and compassion. In Part III, we focus on what it means for us to join in his adventure.

The first five chapters have been written for use in the traditional season of Lent. They are dedicated to Jesus' most concentrated teaching in the Sermon on the Mount (Matthew 5–7). Rather than having multiple Scripture readings during this season, we will read one passage multiple times to encourage deeper reflection.

Then, for Passion Week, we will imagine ourselves in and around Jerusalem. Beginning with Easter, we'll travel with the growing company of disciples as their uprising spreads across the Mediterranean world.

Because the date of Easter changes from year to year, learning circle organizers may need to adjust the order of chapters so that chapters 32 and 33 are read on Palm Sunday and Easter Sunday, respectively. Note also that Passion Week includes lessons for special gatherings on Thursday, Friday, and Saturday (chapters 32A, 32B, and 32C).

CHAPTER TWENTY-SEVEN

A New Identity

Matthew 5:1–16 (Read this passage reflectively two or three times.)

IMAGINE YOURSELF IN GALILEE, on a windswept hillside near a little fishing town called Capernaum. Flocks of birds circle and land. Wildflowers bloom among the grasses between rock outcroppings. The Sea of Galilee glistens blue below us, reflecting the clear midday sky above.

A small group of disciples circles around a young man who appears to be about thirty. He is sitting, as rabbis in this time and culture normally do. Huge crowds extend beyond the inner circle of disciples, in a sense eavesdropping on what he is teaching them. This is the day they've been waiting for. This is the day Jesus is going to pass on to them the heart of his message.

Jesus begins in a fascinating way. He uses the term *blessed* to address the question of identity, the question of who we want to be. In Jesus' day, to say "Blessed are these people" is to say "Pay attention: these are the people you should aspire to be like. This is the group you want to belong to." It's the opposite of saying "Woe to those people" or "Cursed are those people," which means, "Take note: you definitely don't want to be like those people or counted among their number." His words no doubt surprise everyone, because we normally play by these rules of the game:

Do everything you can to be rich and powerful.
Toughen up and harden yourself against all feelings of loss.
Measure your success by how much of the time you are thinking only of yourself and your own happiness.

Be independent and aggressive, hungry and thirsty for higher status in the social pecking order.
Strike back quickly when others strike you, and guard your image so you'll always be popular.

But Jesus defines success and well-being in a profoundly different way. Who are blessed? What kinds of people should we seek to be identified with?

The poor and those in solidarity with them.
Those who mourn, who feel grief and loss.
The nonviolent and gentle.
Those who hunger and thirst for the common good and aren't satisfied with the status quo.
The merciful and compassionate.
Those characterized by openness, sincerity, and unadulterated motives.
Those who work for peace and reconciliation.
Those who keep seeking justice even when they're misunderstood and misjudged.
Those who stand for justice as the prophets did, who refuse to back down or quiet down when they are slandered, mocked, misrepresented, threatened, and harmed.

Jesus has been speaking for only a matter of seconds, and he has already turned our normal status ladders and social pyramids upside down. He advocates an identity characterized by solidarity, sensitivity, and nonviolence. He celebrates those who long for justice, embody compassion, and manifest integrity and nonduplicity. He creates a new kind of hero: not warriors, corporate executives, or politicians, but brave and determined activists for preemptive peace, willing to suffer with him in the prophetic tradition of justice.

Our choice is clear from the start: If we want to be his disciples, we won't be able to simply coast along and conform to the norms of our society. We must choose a different definition of well-being, a different model of success, a new identity with a new set of values.

Jesus promises we will pay a price for making that choice. But he also promises we will discover many priceless rewards. If we seek the kind of unconventional blessedness he proposes, we will experience the true aliveness of God's kingdom, the warmth of God's comfort, the enjoyment of the gift of this Earth, the satisfaction at seeing God's restorative justice come more fully, the joy of receiving mercy, the direct experience of God's presence, the honor of association with God and of being in league with the prophets of old. That is the identity he invites us to seek.

That identity will give us a very important role in the world. As creative nonconformists, we will be difference makers, aliveness activists, catalysts for change. Like salt that brings out the best flavors in food, we will bring out the best in our community and society. Also like salt, we will have a preservative function—opposing corruption and decay. Like light that penetrates and eradicates darkness, we will radiate health, goodness, and well-being to warm and enlighten those around us. Simply by being who we are—living boldly and freely in this new identity as salt and light—we will make a difference, as long as we don't lose our "saltiness" or try to hide our light.

We'll be tempted, no doubt, to let ourselves be tamed, toned down, shut up, and glossed over. But Jesus means for us to stand *apart* from the status quo, to stand *up* for what matters, and to stand *out* as part of the solution rather than part of the problem. He means for our lives to overcome the blandness and darkness of evil with the salt and light of good works. Instead of drawing attention to ourselves, those good works will point toward God. "Wow," people will say, "when I see the goodness and kindness of your lives, I can believe there's a good and kind God out there, too."

The way Jesus phrases these memorable lines tells us something important about him. Like all great leaders, he isn't preoccupied with himself. He puts others—*us*—in the spotlight when he says, "*You* are the salt of the Earth. *You* are the light of the world." Yes, there's a place and time for him to declare who *he* is, but he begins by declaring who *we* are.

It's hot in the Galilean sunshine. Still, the crowds are hanging on Jesus' every word. They can tell something profound and life-changing is happening within them and among them. Jesus is not simply trying to restore their religion to some ideal state in the past. Nor is he agitating unrest to start a new religion to compete with the old one. No, it's abundantly clear that he's here to start something bigger, deeper, and more subversive: a global uprising that can spread to and through every religion and culture. This uprising begins not with a new strategy but with a new identity. So he spurs his hearers into reflection about who they are, who they want to be, what kind of people they will become, what they want to make of their lives.

As we consider Jesus' message today, we join those people on that hillside, grappling with the question of who we are now and who we want to become in the future. Some of us are young, with our whole lives ahead of us. Some of us are further along, with a lot of hopes left and not a lot of time to fulfill them. As we listen to Jesus, each of us knows, deep inside: *If I accept this new identity, everything will change for me. Everything will change.*

Engage:

1. What one thought or idea from today's lesson especially intrigued, provoked, disturbed, challenged, encouraged, warmed, warned, helped, or surprised you?
2. Share a story about someone who has impressed you as being the kind of salt and light Jesus spoke of.
3. How do you respond to the reversal of status ladders and social pyramids described in this chapter?
4. For children: Lots of people ask kids what they want to be when they grow up. But what kind of kid do you want to be right now?
5. Activate: This week, look for ways to be a nonconformist—resisting the pressures of your environment and conforming your life to the alternative values of the beatitudes.
6. Meditate: In silence, imagine darkness, and into that darkness, imagine light coming from a candle, a sunrise, a fire, or a flashlight. Hold these questions open before God: Which is more fragile and which is more powerful, light or darkness? How can my life become like light?

CHAPTER TWENTY-EIGHT

A New Path to Aliveness

Matthew 5:17–48 (Read this passage reflectively, two or three times.)

ANYONE PRESENT THAT DAY would have felt some tension in the air. Many in the crowd stuck to the familiar road of tradition, playing by the rules, leading conservative, conventional, and respectable lives. They were worried that Jesus was too... different, too noncompliant. Others ran on a very different road. Unfettered by tradition, they gladly bent any rule that got in their way. They were worried that Jesus wasn't different and defiant enough.

According to Jesus, neither group was on the road to true aliveness.

When Jesus said, "Do not think that I have come to abolish the law or the prophets," you can imagine the traditionalists in the crowd felt relieved, because that was just what they feared he was about to do. When he added, "I have come not to abolish but to fulfill," they must have tensed up again, wondering what he could possibly mean by "fulfill." Then, when he said, "Unless your righteousness *exceeds* that of the scribes and Pharisees, you will never enter the kingdom of heaven," the nontraditionalists would have look dismayed. How could anyone be more righteous than that fastidious crowd?

As Jesus continued, it became clear he was proposing a third way that neither the compliant nor the noncompliant had ever considered before. Aliveness won't come through unthinking conformity to tradition, he tells them. And it won't come from defying tradition, either. It will come only if we discern and fulfill the highest intent of tradition—even if doing so means breaking with the details of tradition in the process.

If tradition could be compared to a road that began in the distant past and continues to the present, Jesus dares to propose that the road isn't finished yet. To extend the road of tradition into the future—to fulfill its potential—we must first look back to discern its general direction. Then, informed by the past, we must look forward and dare to step beyond where the road currently ends, venturing off the map, so to speak, into new territory. To stop where the road of tradition currently ends, Jesus realizes, would actually end the adventure and bring the tradition to a standstill. So faithfulness doesn't simply *allow* us to extend the tradition and seek to fulfill its unexplored potential; it *requires* us to do so.

But what does it mean to fulfill the tradition? Jesus answers that question with a series of examples. Each example begins, "You have heard that it was said . . . ," which introduces what the tradition has taught. Then Jesus dares to say, "But I say . . ." This is not, as his critics will claim, an act of abolishment or destruction. His "but I say" will creatively fulfill the intent of the tradition.

The tradition said, "Don't murder." That was a good start. However, the tradition didn't want us to stop merely at the point of avoiding murder. So as a first step beyond what the tradition required, Jesus calls us to root out the anger that precedes the physical violence that leads to murder. As a second step, he calls us to deal with the verbal violence of name-calling that precedes the physical violence that leads to murder. As a third step, he urges us to engage in preemptive reconciliation. In other words, whenever we detect a breach in a relationship, we don't need to determine who is at fault. The intent of tradition isn't merely to be "in the right"; the goal is to be in a right relationship. So we are to deal with the breach quickly and proactively, seeking true reconciliation. Being in a right relationship—not merely avoiding murder—was the intent of the tradition all along.

That kind of preemptive reconciliation, Jesus teaches, will help us avoid the chain reactions of offense, revenge, and counteroffense that lead to murder, and that keep our court systems busy and our prison systems full.

After extending the road in the area of violence, Jesus moves to four more issues, each deeply important both to individuals and societies—sexuality, marriage, oaths, and revenge. In each case, conventional religious morality—which Jesus calls the righteousness of the scribes and Pharisees—focuses on *not doing external wrong*: not murdering, not committing adultery, not committing illegal divorce, not breaking sacred oaths, not getting revenge. For Jesus, true aliveness focuses on *transforming our deeper desires.*

So, regarding sexuality, the tradition requires you to avoid adultery. But Jesus says to extend the road, to go further and deeper by learning to manage your internal lustful desires. Regarding divorce, you can try to "make it legal" in the eyes of society as the tradition requires. But Jesus challenges you to go further and deeper by desiring true fidelity in your heart. Regarding oaths, you can play a lot of silly verbal games to shade the truth. Or you can go further and deeper, desiring simple, true speech, saying what you mean and meaning what you say. And regarding retaliation against injustice, you can react in ways that play right into unjust systems. Or you can go further and deeper, transcending those systems entirely.

Here Jesus gets very practical. As people living under Roman occupation, his hearers were used to getting shoved around. It was not uncommon for a Roman soldier to give one of them a backhand slap—the insulting whack of a superior to an inferior. When this happened, some would skulk away in humiliation or beg the bully not to hit them again. But that rewarded the oppressor's violence, and it made them complicit in their own diminishment.

That was why others dreamed of retaliation, of pulling out a dagger and slitting the throat of the oppressor. But that would reduce them to the same violent level as their oppressors. So Jesus offered them a creative alternative: *stand tall and courageously turn the other cheek*, he said. In so doing, they would choose nonviolence, strength, courage, and dignity... and they would model a better way of life for their oppressors, rather than mirroring the violent example they were setting.

Another problem they frequently faced: rich landowners would often take tenant farmers to court. If they hadn't paid their rent or tribute, the landowners would start suing them for their personal belongings. So, Jesus said, if someone takes you to court and they sue for your outer garment, go ahead and strip down naked and give them your underwear as well. Yes, your "generosity" leaves you exposed—but your nakedness also exposes the naked greed of your oppressor.

Often, a Roman soldier would order a civilian of an occupied nation to carry his pack for a mile. If the civilian refused to do so, he would show courage and self-respect, but he would probably end up dead or in jail. Most would comply, but once again, doing so would reinforce the oppressor's sense of superiority and their own sense of humiliation. Jesus tells his disciples to surprise their oppressors by volunteering to take the pack a second mile. The first mile may be forced upon them, but the second mile they'll walk free. The first mile, they are oppressed, but the second mile they transcend their oppression and treat their oppressor as a human being, demonstrating the very human kindness that he fails to practice.

Neither the compliant nor the defiant typically imagine such creative responses. Jesus is helping their moral and social imagination come alive.

Jesus employs his "you have heard it said... but I say..." pattern once more, perhaps the most radical example of all. Tradition always requires love and responsibility toward friends and neighbors, people we like, people like us, people "of our kind." That is a big step beyond utter selfishness and narcissism. But Jesus says that the road of tradition was never meant to end there. Love should now be extended farther than before, to outsiders as well as insiders, to *them* as well as *us*, even to our enemies. We may not have walked the road that far yet, but that is God's intent for us.

Again, using example after example, Jesus directs his disciples beyond what the tradition requires to what the Creator desires. "Be perfect, therefore, as your heavenly Father is perfect," he says. Some people might assume that by "be perfect" he means "achieve external technical perfection," which is what the scribes and Pharisees aim for. But Jesus means something far deeper and wiser. He tells them that God doesn't let rain and sunshine fall only on good people's lands, leaving bad people to starve. No, God is good to all, no exceptions. God's perfection is a compassionate and gracious perfection. It goes far beyond the traditional requirements of the scribes and Pharisees.

For us today, as for the disciples on that Galilean hillside, this is our better option—better than mere technical compliance to tradition, better than defiance of tradition. This is our third way. God is out ahead of us, calling us forward—not to stay where tradition has brought us so far, and not to defy tradition reactively, but to fulfill the highest and best intent of tradition, to make the road by walking forward together.

ENGAGE:

1. What one thought or idea from today's lesson especially intrigued, provoked, disturbed, challenged, encouraged, warmed, warned, helped, or surprised you?
2. Share a story about a time when someone knew you had done wrong but loved you anyway.
3. How do you respond to the comparison between a tradition and a road? Where do you think you are being called to move beyond where you are right now?
4. For children: Are there times when you want to do better than "good enough"? What makes you want to do your very best?
5. Activate: This week, look for opportunities to practice Jesus' teaching in regards to violence, lust, marriage, oaths, and revenge.
6. Meditate: In silence, ponder God's perfection as a compassionate perfection. Let a prayer of praise arise from your heart to break the silence.

CHAPTER TWENTY-NINE

Your Secret Life

Matthew 6:1–18 (Read this passage reflectively, two or three times.)

All of us agree: the world isn't what it should be. We all wish the world would change. But how? How can we change the world, when we can hardly change ourselves? The forces of conformity and peer pressure are so strong. We set out to change the world, and time and time again the reverse happens. Or we resist the status quo with such fury that we become bitter, cynical, angry—hardly models of a better world. That's why we aren't surprised when Jesus turns to the dynamics of change in our personal lives. He shows us how to *be* the change we want to *see* in the world.

The key concept, according to Jesus, is the opposite of what we might expect: If you want to see change in the outside world, the first step is to withdraw into your inner world. Connect with God in secret, and the results will occur "openly."

Jesus offers three specific examples of how this withdrawal process works: giving in secret, praying in secret, and fasting in secret. Giving, praying, and fasting are often called spiritual disciplines or practices: actions within our power by which we become capable of things currently beyond our power.

For example, can you run twenty miles? If you haven't trained, no matter how well-intentioned you are, you will be reduced to a quivering mass of cramps and exhaustion before you reach the finish line. But, as thousands of people have learned, you can start training. You can start running shorter distances in private, and gradually increase them. A few months from now you could cross the finish line in full public view!

If through physical practice a lazy slug can end up a lean and energetic runner, then through spiritual practice an impatient and self-obsessed egotist can become a gentle, generous, and mature human being. But Jesus makes clear that not just any practices will do: we need the right practices, employed with the right motives. "Practice makes perfect," it turns out, isn't quite accurate. It's truer to say practice makes *habit*. That's why Jesus emphasizes the importance of practicing prayer, fasting, and generosity in secret. If we don't withdraw from public view, we'll habitually turn our spiritual practices into a show for others, which will sabotage their power to bring deep change in us. So, instead of seeking to appear more holy or spiritual in public than we are in private, Jesus urges us to become more holy or spiritual in private than we appear to be in public.

When it comes to *giving to the poor*, Jesus says, don't publicize your generosity like the hypocrites do. Don't let your left hand know how generous your right hand is. By giving in secret, you'll experience the true reward of giving. A lot of us have found that a good way to make secret giving habitual is to give on a regular basis, as a percentage of our income. As our income increases over time, we can increase our standard of giving and not just our standard of living. It's kind of ironic: a lot of people do ugly things in secret—they steal, lie, cheat, and so on. Jesus reverses things, urging us to plot goodness in secret, to do good and beautiful things without getting caught.

It's the same when it comes to *prayer*, Jesus says. Prayer can either strengthen your soul in private or raise your profile in public, but not both. So don't parrot the empty phrases of those who pray as if they were being paid by the word. A few simple words, uttered in secret, make much more sense...especially since God knows what you need before you even ask. Jesus offers a model for the kind of simple, concise, private prayer that he recommends. His model prayer consists of four simple but profound moves.

First, we orient ourselves to God. We acknowledge God as the loving parent whose infinite embrace puts us in a family relationship with all people, and with all of creation. And we acknowledge God as the glorious holy mystery whom we can name but who can never be contained by our words or concepts.

Second, we align our greatest desire with God's greatest desire. We want the world to be the kind of place where God's dreams come true, where God's justice and compassion reign.

Third, we bring to God our needs and concerns—our physical needs for things like food and shelter, and our social and spiritual needs for things like forgiveness for our wrongs and reconciliation with those who have wronged us.

Finally, we prepare ourselves for the public world into which we will soon reenter. We ask to be guided away from the trials and temptations that could ruin us, and we ask to be liberated from evil.

Immediately after the model prayer, Jesus adds a reminder that God isn't interested in creating a forgiveness market where people come and acquire cheap forgiveness for themselves. God is interested in creating a whole forgiveness economy—where forgiveness is freely received and freely given, unleashing waves of reconciliation in our world that is so ravaged by waves of resentment and revenge.

Jesus takes us through the same pattern with the spiritual practice of *fasting*: "Whenever you... do not... but do," he says. Whenever you fast, don't try to look all sad and disheveled like those who make spirituality a performance. Instead, keep your hunger a secret. Let every minute when your stomach is growling be a moment where you affirm to God, "More than my body desires food, I desire you, Lord! More than my stomach craves fullness, I crave to be full of you! More than my tongue desires sweetness or salt, my soul desires your goodness!"

So, Jesus teaches, if we make our lives a show staged for others to avoid their criticism or gain their praise, we won't experience the reward of true aliveness. It's only in secret, in the presence of God alone, that we begin the journey to aliveness.

Jesus now turns to the subject of wealth. Just as we can practice giving, prayer, and fasting for social enhancement or spiritual benefit, we can build our lives around public, external, financial wealth or a higher kind of "secret" wealth. Jesus calls this higher wealth "treasure in heaven." Not only is this hidden wealth more secure, it also recenters our lives in God's presence, and that brings a shift to our whole value system so that we see everything differently. When we see and measure everything in life in terms of money, all of life falls into a kind of dismal shadow. When we seek to be rich in generosity and kindness instead, life is full of light.

Some people shame the poor, as if the only reason poor people are poor is that they're lazy or stupid. Some shame the rich, as if the only reason they're rich is that they're selfish and greedy. Jesus doesn't shame anyone, but calls everyone to a higher kind of wealth and a deeper kind of ambition. And that ambition begins, not with how we want to appear in public, but with who we want to be in secret.

The world won't change unless we change, and we won't change unless we pull away from the world's games and pressures. In secrecy, in solitude, in God's presence, a new aliveness can, like a seed, begin to take root. And if that life takes root in us, we can be sure it will bear fruit through us... fruit that can change the world.

ENGAGE:

1. What one thought or idea from today's lesson especially intrigued, provoked, disturbed, challenged, encouraged, warmed, warned, helped, or surprised you?
2. Share a story about a time you did something good—but for a less-than-ideal motive.
3. How do you respond to the four-part summary of Jesus' model prayer?
4. For children: Why do you think grown-ups think about money so much? What do you think about money? Do you get an allowance? Is that important to you? Why?
5. Activate: This week, decide whether you'd like to experiment with giving to the poor, fasting, or praying in secret. But don't tell anyone!
6. Meditate: Hold the phrase "treasure in heaven" in silence in God's presence, and notice how your heart responds.

CHAPTER THIRTY

WHY WE WORRY, WHY WE JUDGE

Matthew 6:19–7:12 (Read this passage reflectively, two or three times.)

WISE PARENTS SOON LEARN what makes their kids cranky: not getting enough sleep, too much sugar, being hungry, not getting time alone, too much time alone, lack of stimulation, too much stimulation. Have you ever wondered what makes grown-ups cranky?

In the next section of Jesus' core teaching, he strips away layer after layer until he exposes three core problems that turn us into dismal grouches and keep us from enjoying life to the full.

Our first core problem is anxiety. Driven by anxiety, we act out scripts of destruction and cruelty rather than life and creativity. We worry about things beyond our control—and in so doing, we often miss things within our control. For example, you may fear losing someone you love. As a result, driven by your anxiety, you grasp, cling, and smother, and in that way you drive away the person you love. Do you catch the irony? If you're anxious about your life, you won't enjoy or experience your life—you'll only experience your anxiety! So to be alive is to be on guard against anxiety.

Jesus names some of the things we tend to be anxious about. First, we obsess about our bodies. Are we too fat or thin, too tall or short, or too young or old, and how is our hair? Then we obsess about our food, our drink, and our clothing. Are we eating at the best restaurants, drinking the finest wines, wearing the most enviable styles? Our anxieties show us how little we trust God: *God must be either so incompetent or uncaring that we might end up miserable or starving or naked or dead!* So we worry and worry, as if anxiety will somehow make us taller, thinner, better looking, better dressed, or more healthy!

Not only are our anxieties ridiculous and counterproductive, Jesus explains, they're also unnecessary. He points to the flowers that surround his hearers on the hillside. See how beautiful they are? Then he gestures to the flock of birds flying across the sky above them. See how alive and free they are? God knows what they need, Jesus says. God cares for them. God sustains them through the natural order of things. And God does the same for us, but we are too anxious to appreciate it.

Anxiety doesn't stop its dirty work at the individual level. It makes whole communities tense and toxic. Anxiety-driven systems produce a pecking order as anxious people compete and use each other in their pursuit of more stuff to stave off their anxiety. Soon, participants in such a system feel they can't trust anybody, because everyone's out for himself or herself, driven by fear. Eventually, anxiety-driven people find a vulnerable person or group to vent their anxiety upon. The result? Bullying, scapegoating, oppression, injustice. And still they will be anxious. Before long, they'll be making threats and launching wars so they can project their internal anxiety on an external enemy. No doubt, many of Jesus' original hearers would have thought, *He's describing the Romans!* But to some degree, the diagnosis applies to us all.

Jesus advocates the opposite of an anxiety-driven system. He describes a faith-sustained system that he calls *God's kingdom and justice.* He makes this staggering promise: if we seek God's kingdom and justice first, everything that we truly need—financially, physically, or socially—will be given to us. His promise makes sense. When we each focus anxiously on our own individual well-being without concern for our neighbor, we enter into rivalry and everyone is worse off. But when we learn from the songbirds and wildflowers to live by faith in God's abundance, we collaborate and share. We watch out for each other rather than compete with each other. We bless each other rather than oppress each other. We desire what God desires—for all to be safe, for all to be truly alive—so we work for the common good. When that happens, it's easy to see how everyone will be better off. Contagious aliveness will spread across the land!

After anxiety, Jesus moves to a second core problem we all face. Anxious people are *judgmental* people. Worried that someone is judging them, they constantly judge others, which, of course, intensifies the environment of judgment for everyone. Just as anxiety quickly becomes contagious and creates an anxiety-driven system, judgment easily creates accusatory systems in which no one can rest, no one can be himself or herself, no one can feel free.

We can't help but remember the story from Genesis—the choice between two trees, the Tree of Life that nourishes us to see the goodness in everything, and the Tree whose fruit we grasp to know and judge everything and everyone around us as good or evil. When we see in these dualistic terms, we constantly judge *us* as good and condemn *them* as evil. In response, others do the same to us. In the shade of that tempting Tree, soon nobody is safe. Nobody is free. Nobody is truly and fully alive.

So Jesus calls us back to the Tree of Life where we stop creating a *them* to condemn as evil people and an *us* to privilege as good people. If Jesus' antidote to anxiety is to seek God's kingdom and justice first, his antidote to judging is self-examination. Instead of trying to take splinters out of other people's eyes—that is, focus on their faults—we should first deal with the planks in our own eyes. When we have experienced how difficult and delicate it is to deal with our own problems, we will be much more sensitive in helping others deal with theirs.

It's interesting that Jesus refers again to eyes: so much about being truly alive is about seeing in a new way.

To refrain from judging does not mean we stop discerning, as Jesus' tough words about not throwing pearls before swine make clear. Put simply, if we want to experience nonjudgmental aliveness, then in everything—with no exceptions, we will do unto all others—with no exceptions, as we would have them do to us. In these words, Jesus brings us back to the central realization that we are all connected, all children in the same family, all loved by the same Parent, all precious and beloved. In this way, Jesus leads us out of an anxiety-driven and judgment-driven system, and into a faith-sustained, grace-based system that yields aliveness.

Beneath our anxiety and judging lies an even deeper problem, according to Jesus. We do not realize how deeply we are *loved*. He invites us to imagine a child asking his mom or dad for some bread or fish. No parent would give their hungry child a stone or snake, right? If human parents, with all their faults, know how to give good gifts to their children, can't we trust the living God to be generous and compassionate to all who call out for help?

So next time you're grouchy, angry, anxious, and uptight, here is some wisdom to help you come back from being "out of your mind" to being "in your right mind" again. Try telling yourself, *My own anxiety is more dangerous to me than whatever I am anxious about. My own habit of condemning is more dangerous to me than what I condemn in others. My misery is unnecessary because I am truly, truly, truly loved.* From that wisdom, unworried, unhurried, unpressured aliveness will flow again.

ENGAGE:

1. What one thought or idea from today's lesson especially intrigued, provoked, disturbed, challenged, encouraged, warmed, warned, helped, or surprised you?
2. Share a story about a time you felt anxious, judgmental, or both.
3. How do you respond to the idea that our deepest problem is we don't know we are loved? In what ways does it help you to think of God's love as fatherly, and in what ways does it help to think of God's love as motherly? Are there ways that imagining God as a loving friend helps you in ways that parental images for God don't?
4. For children: Why do you think little children are often afraid to be left with a babysitter? What is so special about having your parents around?
5. Activate: This week, monitor yourself for anxiety and judgment. Whenever you see them arising in you, bring to mind Jesus' teaching in this lesson.
6. Meditate: In silence, ponder how the love of good parents frees their children from anxiety and the need to judge one another. Savor that feeling of being safe and secure in God's love.

CHAPTER THIRTY-ONE

THE CHOICE IS YOURS

Matthew 7:13–29 (Read this passage reflectively, two or three times.)

IMAGINE THAT HILLSIDE IN Galilee. Jesus is seated, surrounded by his disciples, a huge crowd circled around them. Perhaps it's the rhythm and tone of his voice. Maybe it's the pace of his words. Somehow they know he is building toward a climax, a moment of decision. He presents a series of vivid images, all in pairs.

First, there are two gates, opening to two roads. We can't travel both. One, he says, is broad and smooth like a Roman highway. It leads to destruction. One is narrow and rocky like a mountain path. It leads to life. "Go along with the crowd," Jesus implies, "and you'll end up in disaster. But dare to be different, dare to follow a new and different path, and you'll learn what it means to be alive."

Next, there are two vines or two trees producing two different kinds of fruit, each representing aliveness. One approach to life produces thorns, briers, and thistles; another approach produces luscious fruits. Get your inner identity straight, he tells them, and your life will be fruitful.

Next there are two groups of people, one entering Jesus' presence, the other going away. One group may boast of all its religious credentials, but Jesus isn't impressed by talk. He's looking for people he *knows*, people he recognizes—people, we might say, who "get" him and understand what he's about. We can identify them because they translate their understanding into action.

Finally there are two builders building two houses, one on sand, one on rock. They both represent people who hear Jesus' message. They both experience falling rain, rising floodwaters, and buffeting winds. The big difference? The person who builds on the solid foundation, whose structure withstands the storm, doesn't just *hear* Jesus' message; he translates it into *action*.

Each pair of images challenges us to move beyond mere interest and agreement to commitment and action. And what is the desired action? To take everything Jesus has taught us—all we have considered as we have listened to him here on this hillside—and translate it into our way of living, our way of being alive.

It makes sense, then, to go back and review the substance of Jesus' teaching:

> Be among the lowly in spirit, remain sensitive to pain and loss, live in the power of gentleness, hunger and thirst for true righteousness, show mercy to everyone rather than harshness, don't hide hypocrisy or duplicity in your heart, work for peace, be willing to joyfully suffer persecution and insult for doing what is right.
>
> Dare to be a nonconformist by being boldly different, like salt and light in the world. Demonstrate your differentness through works of generosity and beauty.
>
> Reject both mindless conformity to tradition and rebellious rejection of it. Instead, discern the true intent of tradition and pursue that intent into new territory.
>
> Never hate, hold grudges, or indulge in anger, but instead, aim to be the first to reach out a hand in reconciliation.
>
> Do not nurture secret fantasies to be sexually unfaithful to your spouse. Insure fidelity by monitoring your desires—the way you see (symbolized by the eye) and grasp (symbolized by the hand) for pleasure. And do not settle for maintaining the appearance of legality and propriety; aspire to true fidelity in your heart.
>
> Avoid "word inflation" when making vows. Instead, practice clear, straight speech, so simple words like yes and no retain their full value.
>
> Reject revenge. Instead, pursue creative and nonviolent ways to overcome wrongs done to you.

Love your enemies as well as your friends, and so imitate God's big, generous heart for all creatures.

Cultivate a hidden life of goodness by giving to the poor, praying, and fasting secretly.

Pray in secret through four movements of your heart. First, orient yourself toward a caring yet mysterious God. Second, align your desires with God's great desire for a just and compassionate world. Third, bring to God your needs and concerns—both physical and spiritual. Finally, prepare to reenter the public world of temptation and oppression, trusting God to guide you and strengthen you.

Remember that God isn't setting up a forgiveness market but is building a whole forgiveness economy.

Don't let greed cloud your outlook on life, but store up true wealth by investing in a growing portfolio of generosity and kindness.

Be especially vigilant about money becoming your slave master.

Don't let anxiety run and ruin your life, but instead trust yourself to God's gracious and parental care, and seek first and foremost to build the just and generous society that would fulfill God's best dreams for humanity.

Don't develop a sharp eye for the faults and failures of others, but instead first work on your own blindness to your own faults and failures.

Don't push on people treasures they are not yet ready for or can't yet appreciate the value of.

Go to God with all your needs, and don't be discouraged if you face long delays. Remember that God loves you as a faithful, caring parent and will come through in due time.

Do to others as you would have them do to you.

Realize that aliveness includes tough choices, and that thriving includes suffering.

Don't be misled by religious talk; what counts is actually living by Jesus' teaching.

Some may claim that God is angry and needs to be appeased through sacrifice. Some may claim that God is harsh and demanding, requiring humans to earn God's favor through scrupulous religious rule keeping. Some may claim that God scrutinizes our brains and speech for perfect doctrinal correctness. But Jesus, like the prophets before him, proclaims a different vision of God. Based on what Jesus has told us today, God is gracious and compassionate and does not need to be appeased through sacrifice. God's love is freely given and does not have to be earned. What God desires most is that we seek God's commonwealth of justice, live with generosity and kindness, and walk humbly—and secretly—with God.

If you were there that day on the Galilean hillside, what would your decision have been? No doubt you would have been impressed, but would you have said yes?

ENGAGE:

1. What one thought or idea from today's lesson especially intrigued, provoked, disturbed, challenged, encouraged, warmed, warned, helped, or surprised you?
2. Share a story about a fork in the road that you faced, where you made a life-changing choice.
3. How do you respond to the summary of Jesus' sermon?
4. For children: What do you think of this as a basic rule for life: treat other people the way you wish they would treat you?
5. Activate: Choose one of the summary statements of Jesus' teaching that you think you most need to focus on. Write it down, or e-mail it to yourself, or put it on your calendar, or in some other way make sure you will be reminded of it several times each day this week.
6. Meditate: After a few moments of holding the image of a house standing strong in a storm, ask God to help you develop this kind of strength as a disciple of Jesus.

CHAPTER THIRTY-TWO

PEACE MARCH (PALM SUNDAY)

Zechariah 9:9–10
Psalm 122
Luke 19:29–46

LET'S IMAGINE OURSELVES JUST outside Jerusalem. We are with Jesus and his band of disciples early on a Sunday morning. Jesus has walked many a mile since he taught us that day on the hillside in Galilee. He has told many a parable, answered many a question, and asked even more. Earlier this morning, he did something really strange.

He sent two of our number into a town on the Mount of Olives, which overlooks Jerusalem from the east. He said they would find a donkey's colt tied to a tree. The two disciples should untie it and bring it to him, and if anyone asked about it, they should simply say, "The master needs it." That was exactly what happened, and they brought Jesus the colt. The colt, of course, didn't have a saddle, so we took some of our coats and put them on the donkey. Then we lifted Jesus up onto it. We started down the road that led to Jerusalem.

So now we walk with him. At first it's quiet, with only the sound of the donkey's hooves clomping on the road. The wind blows through the olive trees. We don't have any idea what he has planned.

Then we hear something up ahead. What is it? A crowd is gathering. Children are shouting. Palm branches are waving. People are taking their coats and spreading them on the dusty road to make a lavish, multicolor carpet, as if Jesus were a king being welcomed to the capital. More and more people join our parade as we descend the hill. Eventually, we feel our confusion giving way to excitement. We shout and dance and praise God together as we descend the road that leads to Jerusalem. Our voices echo across the valley: "Blessings on the king who comes in the name of the Lord!" we shout. "Peace in heaven and glory in the highest heavens!"

Some Pharisees who have been part of the crowd are getting uncomfortable. They rush up to Jesus and sternly warn him that this is dangerous. He should order us all to be quiet. They're worried that proclaiming Jesus as king will be seen as a revolutionary act, the kind that might bring the Roman soldiers riding in on their horses, swords and spears in hand, to slaughter us all in the name of law and order. But Jesus refuses to silence us. "If they are silent, the rocks will start shouting!" he says.

So our parade continues. We shout louder than ever. After our long journey over these last three years, it feels as if things are finally reaching their climax. We round a bend, and there is Jerusalem spread before us in all her beauty, the Temple glistening in the sun. A reverent silence descends upon our parade. It's a sight that has choked up many a pilgrim.

But Jesus doesn't just get choked up. He begins to weep. The crowd clusters around him, and he begins to speak to Jerusalem. "If only you knew on this day of all days the things that lead to peace," he says through his tears. "But you can't see. A time will come when your enemies will surround you, and you will be crushed and this whole city leveled... all because you didn't recognize the meaning of this moment of God's visitation."

What a shock! From a shouting, celebrating crowd to the sound of Jesus weeping! From the feeling that we were about to finally win to a prediction of massive military defeat! From joyful laughter to tears!

As we continue descending the road toward Jerusalem, we also descend into the quiet of our own thoughts. We begin whispering among ourselves about what's happening. Someone reminds us of the words from the prophet Zechariah (CEB): "Rejoice greatly, Daughter Zion! Sing aloud, Daughter Jerusalem! Look, your king will come to you. He is righteous and victorious. He is humble and riding on an ass, on a colt, the offspring of a donkey." A shiver of recognition runs through us.

"What comes next?" one of us asks. "What did the prophet Zechariah say after that?" Someone else has the passage memorized: "He will cut off the chariot from Ephraim and the warhorse from Jerusalem. The bow used in battle will be cut off; he will speak peace to the nations. His rule will stretch from sea to sea, and from the river to the ends of the Earth."

Suddenly we feel the full drama of this moment. We recall another parade that frequently occurs on the other side of Jerusalem, whenever Herod rides into the city in full procession from his headquarters in Caesarea Philippi. He enters, not on a young donkey, but on a mighty warhorse. He comes in the name of Caesar, not in the name of the Lord. He isn't surrounded by a ragtag crowd holding palm branches and waving their coats. He's surrounded by chariots, accompanied by uniformed soldiers with their swords and spears and bows held high. His military procession is a show of force intended to inspire fear and compliance, not hope and joy.

And so the meaning of this day begins to become clear to us. Caesar's kingdom, the empire of Rome, rules by fear with threats of violence, demanding submission. God's kingdom, the kingdom of heaven, rules by faith with a promise of peace, inspiring joy. Jesus' tears are telling us something: he knows that our leaders aren't going to listen to him. They're going to respond to Caesar's violence with violence of their own, and that's why Jesus just made that dire prediction.

Our minds are reeling with these realizations as Jesus leads our little parade into Jerusalem and straight to the Temple. There he causes a big scene. He drives out the merchants who sell animals for sacrifice. He drives out those who exchange foreign currency for the Temple currency. Again, we know there is great meaning in his actions. He is again challenging assumptions about the necessity of sacrifice and about the need for opulent temples and all they represent. This time he links together quotes from two of our greatest prophets, Isaiah and Jeremiah. My house will be a house of prayer for all peoples, Isaiah said. But you have turned it into a hideout for crooks, Jeremiah said.

It has been quite a day, a Sunday we'll never forget, the beginning of a week we'll never forget. What a wild mix of emotions! What a collection of dramatic moments! As we fall asleep, we ponder this: to be alive is to learn what makes for peace. It's not more weapons, more threats, more fear. It's more faith, more freedom, more hope, more love, more joy. Blessed is the one who comes in the name of the Lord!

ENGAGE:

1. What one thought or idea from today's lesson especially intrigued, provoked, disturbed, challenged, encouraged, warmed, warned, helped, or surprised you?
2. Share a story about a time you were part of a public parade or demonstration.
3. How do you respond to the idea that on Palm Sunday, Jesus was intentionally echoing Zechariah's prophecy?
4. For children: What do you like about parades?
5. Activate: This week, look for moments when you, like Jesus, can see with grief that people are choosing a way of conflict or violence instead of peace. Allow yourself to feel the sadness without vilifying anyone.
6. Meditate: Hold the phrase "a house of prayer for all people" together with the phrase, "My Father's house." See what thoughts and emotions arise within you, and express them in prayer.

CHAPTER THIRTY-TWO A

A Table. A Basin. Some Food. Some Friends. (Holy Thursday)

(Selections from John 13-17 will be read to conclude this chapter.)

Let's imagine ourselves near Jerusalem. It's Thursday night, and we are walking the road with Jesus' disciples on Thursday of this climactic week. What a week it has been! It all started last Sunday as Jesus led us in that unforgettable parade into Jerusalem. And then there was that scene at the Temple. That sure stirred things up! Every night we have slept outside the city and returned the next morning for more drama. One day there were confrontations with the religious scholars and Pharisees; the next day, more controversy with the Sadducees. Jesus has issued lots of dire warnings about the fate of the Temple, which upsets many people because it's the center of their whole world. And earlier today, just as Jesus sent two of us to find that donkey for our parade last Sunday, he sent Peter and John to find a man carrying a water jar so they could prepare the Passover meal at his guest room tonight.

Every Passover all Jews remember the night before our ancestors were liberated from slavery in Egypt. We celebrate a night of great anticipation. We associate each element of the meal—bitter herbs, unleavened bread, a lamb, fruit, and more—with different meanings from the liberation story. In that meal, we feast on meaning. But tonight, at this special Passover, the focus isn't on the distant past. It's on the present and what will soon happen. Jesus draws our attention not to the lamb, but to a simple loaf of bread and a cup of wine. Near the end of the meal, Jesus lifts the bread and gives thanks for it. He says, "This is my body, given for you. Do this in remembrance of me." Then he lifts a cup of wine and says, "This cup is the new covenant by my blood, which is poured out for you for the forgiveness of sins." He adds, "Whenever you take this bread and drink from this cup, do so in memory of me."

Our first reaction is shock. To ask us to remember him suggests he will soon die. We know he has mentioned this several times, but now it hits us: he really means it, and it's coming soon. Our second reaction? To speak of his body and blood this way sounds repulsive—like cannibalism! Why would we want to eat human flesh or drink human blood! That's unkosher in our religion, and downright uncivilized! What could Jesus possibly mean by these strange words?

But before we can ponder the meaning of Jesus' strange words any more, he adds to our shock by speaking about one of us being his betrayer. That quickly gets us arguing about which one of us would do such a terrible thing. Soon, we've moved on from arguing about which of us is the worst disciple to arguing about which of us is the greatest. It's pretty pathetic, when you think about it. It says a lot about us disciples, and a lot about human nature, too. Jesus is trying to tell us he's about to suffer and die, and all we can do is think about ourselves, our egos, our status in the pecking order!

Even this becomes a teaching opportunity for Jesus. Gentiles, meaning the Romans who occupy our land and seek to dominate us in every way, play these kinds of status games, he says. They cover up their status games with all kinds of language games. "That's not the way it will be with you," Jesus says. "Instead, the greatest among you must become like a person of lower status and the leader like a servant."

Years from now, when the Fourth Gospel will tell the story, it will make this theme of service the focal point of this whole evening. It won't even include the bread and the wine and Jesus' solemn words about them. It will put center stage the dramatic moment when Jesus strips off his normal clothing and puts a towel around his waist. He pours water in a basin, stoops as a servant would, and washes the dust from our feet, one by one. When he finishes, he explains that he has set an example—of humble service, not domination—and he means us to imitate his example. Later, after the meal, he will expand "Serve one another as I have served you" to "Love one another as I have loved you."

Both ways of telling the story of this night lead us to the same meaning. The original Passover recalled one kind of liberation—liberation from slavery in Egypt. This meal suggests another kind of liberation—liberation from playing the shame games of rivalry, pecking order, domination, and competition to reach the top of the pyramid of pride. If the first Passover gets people out from under the heel of the slave master, this holy meal leads people out from the desire to be slave masters in the first place. This meal celebrates a new model of aliveness—a model of service, of self-giving, of being blessed, broken, and given for the well-being of others.

It's pretty predictable, I guess: to see how we disciples completely miss the point and turn that holy supper into an argument, a contest for who will be the greatest, who will have the most status at the table, who will be excluded. But in spite of our anxiety and rivalry...

Jesus, the patient teacher...

Jesus, the humble leader...

Jesus, the king of self-giving sets an example of service. And in that context, he asks us to remember him—not primarily for his great miracles, not primarily for his brilliant teaching, but primarily, essentially, for this: that he gives himself like food for us, and for the whole world.

Some people say that later on that unforgettable night, after the holy supper, after Jesus went to a garden to pray, after his disciples fell asleep, after Judas came to betray Jesus with a kiss, after Peter pulled out his sword and Jesus told him to put it away, after Jesus was taken into custody, after his disciples ran away, Jesus was whipped. They say he received thirty-nine lashes, one fewer than the forty lashes that constituted a death sentence. So let us conclude our time together by observing silence, extinguishing the lights, and pausing to remember thirty-nine of Jesus' sayings from this holy, horrifying night.

1. If I, your Lord and teacher, have washed your feet, you, too, must wash each other's feet.
2. I give you a new commandment: Love each other. Just as I have loved you, so you also must love each other.
3. This is how everyone will know you are my disciples, when you love each other.
4. Don't be troubled. Trust in God. Trust also in me.
5. I am the way, and the truth, and the life.
6. Whoever has seen me has seen the Father.
7. I assure you that whoever believes in me will do the works that I do. They will do even greater works than these, because I am going to the Father.
8. If you love me, you will keep my commandments.
9. I won't leave you as orphans. I will come to you.
10. Whoever has my commandments and keeps them loves me. Whoever loves me will be loved by my Father, and I will love them and reveal myself to them.
11. Whoever loves me will keep my word. My Father will love them, and we will come to them and make our home with them.
12. The Companion, or the Holy Spirit, whom the Father will send in my name, will teach you everything and will remind you of everything I told you.
13. Peace I leave with you. My peace I give you.
14. I am the true vine, and my Father is the vineyard keeper.
15. Remain in me, and I will remain in you.
16. A branch can't produce fruit by itself, but must remain in the vine.
17. I am the vine; you are the branches. If you remain in me and I in you, you will produce much fruit.
18. If you remain in me and my words remain in you, ask for whatever you want and it will be done for you.
19. As the Father has loved me, I, too, have loved you. Remain in my love.
20. This is my commandment: love each other just as I have loved you.

21. There is no greater love than to give up one's life for one's friends. You are my friends if you do what I command you.
22. I don't call you servants any longer, because servants don't know what their master is doing. Instead, I call you friends, because everything I heard from my Father I have made known to you.
23. I assure you that it is better for you that I go away. If I don't go away, the Companion won't come to you. But if I go, I will send him to you.
24. I have much more to say to you, but you can't handle it now. However, when the Spirit of Truth comes, he will guide you in all truth.
25. Soon you won't be able to see me; soon after that, you will see me.
26. Ask and you will receive, so that your joy will be complete.
27. I left the Father and came into the world. I tell you again: I am leaving the world and returning to the Father.
28. I have said these things to you so that you will have peace in me. In the world you have distress. But be encouraged! I have conquered the world.
29. This is eternal life: to know you, the only true God, and Jesus Christ whom you sent.
30. Holy Father, watch over them in your name, the name you gave me, that they will be one just as we are one.
31. Make them holy in the truth. Your word is truth.
32. As you sent me into the world, so I have sent them into the world.
33. I pray they will be one, Father, just as you are in me and I am in you. I pray that they also will be in us, so that the world will believe that you sent me.
34. I'm in them and you are in me so that they will be made perfectly one. Then the world will know that you sent me and that you have loved them just as you loved me.
35. I've made your name known to them and will continue to make it known so that your love for me will be in them, and I myself will be in them.
36. Put your sword away!

37. My kingdom doesn't originate from this world.
38. I was born and came into the world for this reason: to testify to the truth.
39. Whoever accepts the truth listens to my voice.

Amen.

Note: A hammer or wineglass may be struck, or another kind of loud noise may be used, to punctuate the thirty-nine statements as they are read slowly and reflectively. Or in a more quiet setting—a pebble may be dropped into a pool of water or a chord strummed on a guitar or a brief musical interlude played. And the room may be set up with forty candles lit around the room. As each statement is read, one candle can be extinguished, leaving the room in darkness, save for one remaining candle.

CHAPTER THIRTY-TWO B

Everything Must Change (Good Friday)

Psalm 22
Luke 22:39–23:56

Let's imagine ourselves with the disciples just before three o'clock on this Friday afternoon. A few of us have come together to talk about what has happened over the last twenty-four hours.

It all started falling apart late last night when Judas, accompanied by a band of soldiers, came for Jesus. All we could think about was saving ourselves. Only Peter and John had the courage to stay with Jesus for a while. But by the time dawn came, Peter was having an emotional breakdown and John had run away, too. The next thing we knew, about nine this morning, Jesus was carrying his cross through the streets of Jerusalem. It was obvious he had been beaten, scourged mercilessly, mocked, and tortured. He was hardly recognizable.

By noon, he was hanging on the cross.

During the last three hours, some of us have gathered at a distance to watch. We've been silent, lost in our own thoughts, but no doubt all our thoughts have been running the same circuit through the same shared memories.

We've been remembering last evening in the garden, before Judas showed up. We kept falling asleep as Jesus prayed: "My Father, if it is possible, take this cup of suffering away from me. However, not what I want but what you want." With tears and in great distress, he prayed a second and third time. But the thrust of his prayer shifted from what might be possible to what might *not* be possible: "My Father, if it is not possible that this cup be taken away unless I drink it, then let it be what you want." In the second and third prayers, he was clearly preparing to die.

But why? Why was there no other way? Why did this good man—the best we have ever known, the best we have ever imagined—have to face torture and execution as if he were some evil monster?

As the hours drag on from noon to nearly three o'clock, we imagine many reasons. Some are political. The Pharisees were right to be concerned last Sunday when Jesus came marching into the capital. First our little parade—the Romans would have called it a rebellious mob—proclaimed Jesus as king. From there, he marched into the Temple and called it a hide-out for crooks, turning over the tables and upsetting the religious economy. Only a fool would do things like these without expecting consequences. Jesus was no fool.

We think about more spiritual reasons for this to happen. Jesus has told us again and again that God is different from our assumptions. We've assumed that God was righteous and pure in a way that makes God hate the unrighteous and impure. But Jesus has told us that God is pure love, so overflowing in goodness that God pours out compassion on the pure and impure alike. He not only has told us of God's unbounded compassion—he has embodied it every day as we have walked this road with him. In the way he has sat at table with everyone, in the way he has never been afraid to be called a "friend of sinners," in the way he has touched untouchables and refused to condemn even the most notorious of sinners, he has embodied for us a very different vision of what God is like.

At dinner last night, when he knelt down and washed our feet, and later when he called us his friends, what was that supposed to mean? Was he trying to show us that God isn't a dictator high in the sky eager for us to cower in fear at his feet? Was he inviting us to think of God as the one who is down here with us, who stoops low and touches our feet—as a servant would? Was he telling us that God would rather cleanse us than condemn us? If that was the case last night, what could this horrible day be trying to show us? Could there be any meaning in this catastrophe playing out before us now?

And then we think: if Jesus is showing us something so radical about God, what is he telling us about ourselves—about human beings and our social and religious institutions? What does it mean when our political leaders and our religious leaders come together to mock and torture and kill God's messenger, God's beloved child, God's best and brightest? How misguided can our nation be? Is this the only way religions and governments maintain order—by threatening us with pain, shame, and death if we don't comply? And is this how they unify us—by turning us into a mob that comes together in its shared hatred of the latest failure, loser, rebel, criminal, outcast... or prophet? The Romans boast of their peace, and our priests boast of their holiness and justice, but today it all looks like a sham, a fraud, a con game. What kind of world have we made? What kind of people have we become?

One minute the crowds were flocking to Jesus hoping for free bread and healing. The next minute they were shouting, "Crucify him!" And we, his so-called disciples, we are no better. One minute we were eating a meal with him and he was calling us his friends. Now here we stand at a distance, unwilling to identify ourselves with him and so risk what he is going through.

It has grown strangely dark now, in the middle of the afternoon, and in the darkness, even from this distance, we can hear Jesus. "Father, forgive them!" he shouts. "For they don't know what they are doing."

Forgive them? Forgive us?

Our thoughts bring us again to the garden last night, when Jesus asked if there could be any other way. And now it seems clear. There could be no other way to show us what God is truly like. God is not revealed in killing and conquest... in violence and hate. God is revealed in this crucified man—giving of himself to the very last breath, giving and forgiving.

And there could be no other way to show us what we are truly like. We do not know what we are doing, indeed.

If God is like this, and if we are like this... everything must change. Everything must change.

ENGAGE:

1. What one thought or idea from today's lesson especially intrigued, provoked, disturbed, challenged, encouraged, warmed, warned, helped, or surprised you?
2. Share what the crucifixion of Jesus says and means to you today.
3. How do you respond to the idea that "there couldn't be any other way"?
4. For children: If a friend asked you, "Why did Jesus die?" what would you say?
5. Activate: Today, try to create or attend a "stations of the cross" service or visit a "stations of the cross" installation. Let the horror of the crucifixion story inform you about what God is like and what we are like.
6. Meditate: In silence, let scenes from the crucifixion story play in your imagination. Imagine seeing the story unfold from the vantage point of various characters in the story—Jesus' frightened disciples, the religious leaders, the Roman soldiers, the crowds, and finally, Jesus himself. Hold over all these scenes Jesus' words: "Father, forgive them, for they don't know what they're doing."

CHAPTER THIRTY-TWO C

Doubt. Darkness. Despair. (Holy Saturday)

Psalm 77
Psalm 88
Ecclesiastes 1:1–11
Job 10:1–22

Let us imagine ourselves with the disciples on that Saturday after the crucifixion. We are hiding together in a home, engaged in sober, somber conversation.

Perhaps our descendants, the disciples of the future, will call this a day of waiting. But we are not waiting. For us, there is nothing to wait for. All we know is what was lost yesterday as Jesus died on the cross. For us, it's all over. This is a day of doubt, despair, disillusionment, devastation.

Certain details of the killing yesterday are hard to shake. Jesus, carrying his cross on the road to Golgotha, surrounded by women who were weeping for him. Jesus telling them, "Don't weep for me. Weep for yourselves and your children." What did he mean? Was he telling them that the violence spilling out on him was only a trickle of the reservoir that waited behind the scenes to flood the whole region?

Then there was Peter...so full of bluster at dinner on Thursday, such a coward later that night, and invisible all of yesterday. And Judas—to think we trusted him as our treasurer! At least the women stayed true... the women, and John, who was entrusted with Mary's care as her surrogate son. None of us can imagine what yesterday must have been like for Mary. She has carried so much in her heart for so long, and now this.

Then there was that strange darkness, as if the whole world were being uncreated, and there was that strange rumor about the veil in the Temple being torn from top to bottom. Was that an image for God in agony, like a man tearing his clothes in fury over the injustice that was happening? Or was it a rejection of the priesthood for their complicity in the crime—a way of saying that God was done with the priests and the Temple, that God would welcome people into the Holiest Place without their assistance? Or maybe it could mean that God is on the loose—that God is through with being contained in a stone structure and behind a thick curtain and wants to run free through the world like the wind. That's a nice sentiment, but not likely from today's vantage point. Today it best symbolizes that no place is holy anymore. If a murder like this can take place in the so-called Holy City, supported by the so-called Holy Priesthood, then holiness is nothing but a sham. It's a torn curtain, and behind it only emptiness lies.

On top of it all, we have to come to terms with the fact that Jesus seemed to know all this was coming. True, at the last minute, just before the betrayal and arrest, he prayed that the cup might pass from him. But he had been telling us that something terrible was coming—telling us since back in Caesarea Philippi, when Peter confessed him as the Liberating King and the true Leader, telling us in many ways, even in his parables.

He loved life. Yet he did not cling to it. He loved life. Yet he was not controlled by the fear of death. In the garden Thursday night, it seemed as if to him, the fear of death was more dangerous than death itself, so he needed to deal with the fear once and for all. But look where that got him. Maybe it would have been better for him to flee back to Galilee. Lots of other people are living in communes out in the desert, waiting for Jerusalem and all it represents to crumble under its own weight. Maybe that was what we should have done. But it's too late now.

That one Roman soldier was impressed by him, but the others—all they cared about was seeing who would win a dead man's garment with a roll of the dice. True to form—playing games and obsessed with clothes and money to the very end!

Then came that moment when one of the rebels who was being crucified with Jesus started mocking him. When the other rebel spoke up to defend Jesus, Jesus said those kind words to him about being with him in Paradise. Even then he had compassion for someone else. Even in death he was kind to a neighbor. And finally there was that haunting moment when he spoke of forgiveness... for those who were crucifying him, and for us all.

Normal, sane people would have said, "God, damn them to hell forever for what they have done!" But not Jesus. "They don't understand what they're doing," he said.

What did our leaders think they were doing? Protecting law and order? Preserving the status quo? Conserving what little peace and security we have left? Silencing a heretic or blasphemer? Shutting down a rabble-rouser and his burgeoning movement?

Right up to the last minute we dared hope that God would send in some angels, stop the whole charade, and let everyone see how wrong they were and how right Jesus was. But no last-minute rescue came. Only death came. Bloody, sweaty, filthy, ugly death. Just before he died, it seemed that even he had lost faith. "My God, my God, why have you forsaken me?" he cried. Maybe some shred of hope remained, though, because his last words were "Father, into your hands I commend my spirit."

Now. Now, he is dead. Does that mean this uprising is dead, too? We feel a chill as we realize that possibility. What do we do now? Do we leave, go back home, pick up our lives where we left them before all this started for us? Do we try to carry on the teaching of a... dead, defeated, failed, and discredited leader? Do we turn cynical, disillusioned, dark, bitter? Fishing and tax collecting will seem meaningless compared to the memories of these last three years. But that's all we have left... fishing, tax collecting, and memories. The adventure of Jesus is dead and done.

Maybe we have all been fools. Maybe Pontius Pilate was right when he told Jesus that truth didn't matter, only power matters—the power of swords and spears, chariots and crosses, whips and nails. Or maybe the Sadducees and their rich friends in Jerusalem are right: Life is short, and then you die, so amass all the money you can, by any means you can. And while you can, eat the best food and drink the best wine, because that's all there is.

Wine. That brings us back to Thursday night there, around the table. "Remember me. Remember me. I will not eat of this until..." Until?

Did Jesus really believe that death wasn't the last word? Did he really believe that there was any hope of...

That's too much to believe today. Today, we sink in our doubt. Today we drown in our despair. Today we are pulled down, down, down, in our pain and disappointment. Today we allow ourselves to question everything about the story we have been told.

Creation? Maybe God made this world, or maybe it's all a cruel, meaningless joke.

Crisis? Maybe violence and hate are just the way of the world. Maybe they're not an intrusion or anomaly; maybe they're the way things are and will always, always be.

Calling? Forget about being blessed to be a blessing. Today we lie low and nurse our wounds. It is a dangerous world out there. We would be wise to stay inside and lock all doors.

Captivity? Who cares if Moses succeeded in getting our ancestors out of slavery in Egypt? Jesus failed, and there's no Moses for us now. We're still captives, worse off than we were before that crazy Galilean came and raised our hopes.

Conquest? If the most violent win and the nonviolent are killed, what kind of world is it?

Conversation? Today it seems that the skeptics and doubters were right. There's nothing to say except, "Vanity of vanities. All is vanity!" Today's lament feels like the only sure truth in all the sacred Scriptures!

Christ? What Christ? He lies in a grave, cold and dead, and with him, all our hopes for a better way to be alive. Let the women prepare to embalm his corpse, if they can find it. Probably the Romans tore it to pieces and fed the fragments to the dogs.

Engage:

1. What one thought or idea from today's lesson especially intrigued, provoked, disturbed, challenged, encouraged, warmed, warned, helped, or surprised you?
2. Share a story about a time you felt deep despair or disillusionment.
3. How do you respond to this opportunity to express your doubts so freely and honestly?
4. For children: What was a really sad or scary time in your life?
5. Activate: Today, take some time to allow yourself to feel emptiness, doubt, disappointment, and fear, and don't try to explain them away. But keep open to the possibility that God is bigger than your biggest fear, disillusionment, or sorrow.
6. Meditate: Hear Jesus crying, "My God, my God, why have you forsaken me?" And allow the parts of your own heart that feel forsaken to find a voice with Jesus.

CHAPTER THIRTY-THREE

THE UPRISING BEGINS (EASTER SUNDAY)

Ezekiel 37:1–14
Luke 24:1–32
Colossians 1:9–29

LET'S IMAGINE OURSELVES WITH the disciples on the first Easter Sunday.

Here's what we heard. At dawn, before the sun had risen, some women who are part of our movement went to the tomb to properly wash Jesus' corpse and prepare it for burial. When they arrived, they had a vision involving angels. One of the women claimed that Jesus appeared to her. The rest of us think it was just the gardener.

The gardener! What a place to be buried—a grave in a garden! A bed of death in a bed of life!

The women came and told the disciples. Peter went running back and found the tomb empty. Empty! And the burial cloths were still there, neatly folded. Who would take a naked corpse and leave the bloody cloths that it was wrapped in? Peter wondered what was going on—but he didn't have any clear theory.

We all speculated, but none of us knew what to think. We decided to go back home. That's where we are now—walking on the road back home. It's about a seven-mile walk to our little town of Emmaus. It takes a couple hours. Along the way we've been talking about all this, trying to come up with some kind of interpretation of the events that have transpired. Now we notice this other fellow walking toward us, a stranger. We lower our voices. He comes a little closer.

"What are you folks talking about?" he asks.

One of us replies, "Are you kidding? Are you the only person in this whole region who doesn't know all that's been happening around Jerusalem recently?"

"Like what?" he asks.

We tell him about Jesus, that he was clearly a prophet who said and did amazing things. We tell him how the religious and political leaders came together to arrest him. We go into some detail about the crucifixion on Friday. "We had hoped," one of us says, and pauses. "We had hoped... that this Jesus was the one who was going to turn things around for Israel, that he would set us free from the Roman occupation."

We walk on a few steps, and he adds, "And this morning was the third day since his death, and some women from our group told us that they had a vision of angels who said he was alive." It's pretty clear from the tone of his voice that none of us take the report of the women very seriously.

That's when the stranger interrupts. "You just don't get it, do you?" he says. "This is exactly what the prophets said would happen. They have been telling us all along that the Liberator would have to suffer and die like this before entering his glory." As we continue walking, he starts explaining things to us from the Scriptures. He begins with Moses, and step by step he shows us the pattern of God's work in history, culminating in what happened in Jerusalem in recent days. God calls someone to proclaim God's will. Resistance and rejection follow, often culminating in an expulsion or murder to silence the speaker. But this isn't a sign of defeat. This is the only way God's most important messages are ever heard—through someone on the verge of being rejected. God's word doesn't come in dominating, crushing force. It comes only in vulnerability, in weakness, in gentleness... just as we have seen over this last week.

At this point, we realize we've reached home already, and as we slow down, the stranger just keeps walking. We plead with him to stay here with us, since it's getting late and will soon be dark. So he comes in and we sit down at our little table for a meal. He reaches to the center of the table and takes a loaf of bread and gives thanks for it. He breaks it and hands a piece of it to each of us and...

It hits us at the same instant. This isn't a stranger... this is... it couldn't be—yes, this is Jesus! We each look down at the fragment of bread in our hands, and when we look back up to the stranger... he is gone!

And we start talking, one interrupting the other. "When he spoke about Moses and the prophets, did you feel—?" "—Inspired? Yes. It felt like my heart was glowing, hotter and hotter, until it was ready to ignite." "Did this really happen, or was it just a vision?" "*Just* a vision? Maybe a vision means seeing into what's more real than anything else." "But it wasn't just me, right? You saw him, too, right? You felt it, too, right?" "What do we do now? Shouldn't we... tell the others?" "Yes, let's do it. Let's go back to Jerusalem, even though it's late. I could never sleep after experiencing this!"

So we pack our gear and rush back to the city, excited and breathless. On our earlier journey, we were filled with one kind of perplexity—disappointment, confusion, sadness. Now we feel another kind of perplexity—wonder, awe, amazement, almost-too-good-to-be-true-ness. "Do you realize what this means?" one of us asks, and then answers his own question: "Jesus was right after all! Everything he stood for has been vindicated!"

"Yes. And something else. We never have to fear death again."

"And if that's true," another answers, "we never need to fear Caesar and his forces again, either. Their only real weapon is fear, and if we lose our fear, what power do they have left? Ha! Death has lost its sting! That means we can stand tall and speak the truth, just like Jesus did." "We never need to fear anyone again." "This changes everything." "It's not just that Jesus was resurrected. It feels like we have arisen, too. We were in a tomb of defeat and despair. But now—look at us! We're truly alive again!"

We talk as fast as we walk. We recall Jesus' words from Thursday night about his body and blood. We remember what happened on Friday when his body and his blood were separated from one another on the cross. That's what crucifixion is, we realize: the slow, excruciating, public separation of body and blood. So, we wonder, could it be that in the holy meal, when we remember Jesus, we are making space for his body and blood to be reunited and reconstituted in us? Could our remembering him actually re-member and resurrect him in our hearts, our bodies, our lives? Could his body and blood be reunited in us, so that we become his new embodiment? Is that why we saw him and then didn't see him—because the place he most wants to be seen is in our bodies, among us, in us?

It's dark when we reach Jerusalem. Between this day's sunrise and today's sunset, our world has been changed forever. Everything is new. From now on, whenever we break the bread and drink the wine, we will know that we are not alone. The risen Christ is with us, among us, and within us—just as he was today, even though we didn't recognize him. Resurrection has begun. We are part of something rare, something precious, something utterly revolutionary.

It feels like an uprising. An uprising of hope, not hate. An uprising armed with love, not weapons. An uprising that shouts a joyful promise of life and peace, not angry threats of hostility and death. It's an uprising of outstretched hands, not clenched fists. It's the "someday" we have always dreamed of, emerging in the present, rising up among us and within us. It's so different from what we expected—so much better. This is what it means to be alive, truly alive. This is what it means to be en route, walking the road to a new and better day. Let's tell the others: the Lord is risen! *He is risen indeed!* Lord is risen! *He is risen indeed!* Lord is risen! *He is risen indeed!*

ENGAGE:

1. What one thought or idea from today's lesson especially intrigued, provoked, disturbed, challenged, encouraged, warmed, warned, helped, or surprised you?
2. Share a story about a time in your life where despair was replaced with hope.
3. How do you respond to the idea that the eucharist dramatizes Jesus' body and blood being reunited in us, transforming us into a community of resurrection?

4. For children: Why do you think Jesus' friends were so happy on Easter morning?
5. Activate: This week, remember the contrast between how life looks on Friday, Saturday, and Sunday of Holy Week. Ask God to help you see with Easter eyes.
6. Meditate: Imagine the scene when the risen Christ broke the bread and suddenly disappeared. Hold that moment of disappearance in silence, and open your heart to the possibility of absence becoming fullness.

CHAPTER THIRTY-FOUR

The Uprising of Fellowship

Psalm 133
John 20:1–31
Acts 8:26–40

Matthew, Mark, and Luke tell the story of Jesus in ways similar to one another (which is why they're often called the synoptic gospels—with a similar optic, or viewpoint). Many details differ (and the differences are quite fascinating), but it's clear the three compositions share common sources. The Fourth Gospel tells the story quite differently. These differences might disturb people who don't understand that storytelling in the ancient world was driven less by a duty to convey true details accurately and more by a desire to proclaim true meaning powerfully. The ancient editors who put the New Testament together let the differences stand as they were, so each story can convey its intended meanings in its own unique ways.

One place where details differ among the gospels is in what happened right after the resurrection. Mark's gospel, which scholars agree was the earliest one to be written down, ends abruptly without any details about the days and weeks after the resurrection. In Luke's gospel and its sequel, the Book of Acts, Jesus explicitly tells the disciples to stay in Jerusalem. In contrast, in Matthew's gospel, the risen Jesus greets only some female disciples in Jerusalem. He tells these women to instruct the male disciples to go to Galilee, over sixty miles away, where he will appear to them later. In John's gospel, the risen Christ appears to the disciples in Jerusalem the evening of resurrection Sunday and then again a week later. And some time after that, the disciples leave Jerusalem and go to Galilee, where he appears to them once more.

For the next two weeks, we'll imagine ourselves with the disciples in the Fourth Gospel, this week in Jerusalem and next week in Galilee.

We were afraid that first Sunday night, just three days after Jesus died. Really afraid. We were afraid to go outside in case someone might recognize us as Jesus' friends and notify the authorities. To them, Jesus was nothing more than a troublemaker and rabble-rouser. The rumors about Jesus rising from the dead, spread by some of the women among us, only made matters worse. The authorities would know by those rumors that dreams of an uprising hadn't completely died. Which meant that we were in danger. Real danger. So we locked ourselves in a room. But even there we were afraid, because at any moment some Temple guards or Roman soldiers might bang on the door.

So there we remained, tense, jumpy, simmering with anxiety. What happened Friday had been ugly, and we didn't want it to happen to the rest of us. Every sound startled us. Suddenly, we all felt something, a presence, familiar yet... impossible. How could Jesus be among us?

"Peace be with you," he said. He showed us his scarred hands and feet. It started to dawn on us: the women's reports were not just wishful thinking—they were true, and we, too, were experiencing the risen Christ. "I give you my peace," he said again. And then he did three things that changed us forever.

First he said, "As the Father sent me, so I am sending you." Here we were, huddled in our little safe house like a bunch of cowards, and he was still interested in sending cowards like us to continue his mission!

Next he came close to us and breathed on us. "Welcome the Holy Spirit," he said. Of course, this reminded us all of the story in Genesis when God breathed life into Adam and Eve. It was a new beginning, he was telling us. It was a new Genesis, and we were to be the prototypes of a new kind of human community.

Next came the greatest shock of all. After what happened on Friday, anyone with scars like his would have been expected to say, "Go and get revenge on those evil beasts who did this to me." But Jesus said, "I'm sending you with the power to forgive."

Peace! Forgiveness! Those aren't the responses you expect from someone who had suffered what Jesus suffered. But in that brief moment when our locked hideout was filled with his presence, that was the message we all received.

All of us except Thomas, that is. Thomas wasn't with us that night. When we saw Thomas later and told him what we had experienced, he was his typical skeptical self. "I want to touch those scars with my own hands and see for myself, or I won't believe," he said. A week later, we again were all together, this time with Thomas. We still were nervous about the authorities, so we were careful to keep the doors locked.

Just as before, Jesus' presence suddenly became real among us—visible, palpable. He spoke peace to us, and then he went straight to Thomas, inviting him to see, touch, believe. He did not criticize Thomas for doubting. He wanted to help him believe.

"My Lord and my God," Thomas replied. We couldn't help but remember back on Thursday night, when Thomas asked Jesus where he was going and what was the way to get there. Jesus replied, "I am the way." Philip then asked Jesus to show us the Father, and Jesus said, "If you have seen me, you've seen the Father." Now, ten days later, it seemed as if Thomas was beginning to understand what Jesus had meant. He saw God in a scarred man whose holy aliveness is more powerful than human cruelty.

That's one thing you have to say about Thomas: even though he didn't believe at first, he stayed with us, open to the possibility that his doubt could be transformed into faith. He kept coming back. He kept showing up. If he hadn't wanted to believe, he had a week to leave and go back home. But he didn't. He stayed. Not believing, but wanting to believe.

And from that night, we learned something essential about what this uprising is going to be about.

It isn't just for brave people, but for scared folks like us who are willing to become brave. It isn't just for believers, but for doubting folks like Thomas who want to believe in spite of their skepticism. It isn't just for good people, but for normal, flawed people like you and me and Thomas and Peter.

And I should add that it isn't just for men, either. It's no secret that men in our culture often treat women as inferior. Even on resurrection morning, when Mary Magdalene breathlessly claimed that the Lord was risen, the men among us didn't offer her much in the way of respect. There were all sorts of ignorant comments about "the way women are." Now we realize the Lord was telling us something by bypassing all of the male disciples and appearing first to a woman. As we look back, we realize he's been treating women with more respect than the rest of us have right from the start.

We have a term for what we began to experience that night: *fellowship*. Fellowship is a kind of belonging that isn't based on status, achievement, or gender, but instead is based on a deep belief that everyone matters, everyone is welcome, and everyone is loved, no conditions, no exceptions. It's not the kind of belonging you find at the top of the ladder among those who think they are the best, but at the bottom among all the rest, with all the other failures and losers who have either climbed the ladder and fallen, or never gotten up enough gumption to climb in the first place.

Whatever else this uprising will become, from that night we've known it is an uprising of fellowship, a community where anyone who wants to be part of us will be welcome. Jesus showed us his scars, and we're starting to realize we don't have to hide ours.

So fellowship is for scarred people, and for scared people, and for people who want to believe but aren't sure what or how to believe. When we come together just as we are, we begin to rise again, to believe again, to hope again, to live again. Through fellowship, a little locked room becomes the biggest space in the world. In that space of fellowship, the Holy Spirit fills us like a deep breath of fresh air.

This week and in the weeks to come, a leader can introduce this concluding ritual:

> Let us lift a glass [or "Let us stand and extend our hands"] and say,
> "The Lord is risen!" *He is risen indeed!*
> We, too, are rising up! *We are rising up indeed!*
> Let us arise in fellowship. *In fellowship indeed!*

Engage:

1. What one thought or idea from today's lesson especially intrigued, provoked, disturbed, challenged, encouraged, warmed, warned, helped, or surprised you?
2. Share a story about an experience of true fellowship.
3. How do you respond to the idea that Christian fellowship is for scarred and scared people—without regard to gender, status, or achievement?
4. For children: Tell us about your best friends and why they're so special to you.
5. Activate: This week, aim to create spaces for an uprising of fellowship where people feel unconditionally welcome and included—whether in your home, in an office, on public transportation, in a restaurant, on the street, or wherever.
6. Meditate: Imagine you're Thomas at the moment Jesus shows his scarred hands, feet, and side. See where Thomas's experience from that night would resonate with your life today.

CHAPTER THIRTY-FIVE

The Uprising of Discipleship

Psalm 25
Luke 10:1–11, 17–20
John 21:1–15

Let's imagine ourselves with the disciples, a short time after the resurrection, in Galilee.

There were several of us together that day. We had left the big city of Jerusalem and gone back to Galilee, our home region to the north. Thomas was there, and so were Peter, Nathaniel, James, and John, plus a few more. Out of the blue, late in the day, Peter said he wanted to go fishing. Fishing, of all things!

We weren't sure why, but we joined him anyway. We dropped our long gill net time after time through the night, reenacting an old, familiar ritual. And time after time we hauled it in, hoping for something. But the net never struggled against us, never signaled the weight or life of a catch.

It was dawn when we saw a stranger on the shore about a hundred yards from us. Unsuccessful fishermen know the hated question: "Hey boys! Having any luck?"

"Nothing," we replied glumly.

He yelled, "Drop your net over on the other side of the boat. You'll find fish there."

There's nothing like having a stranger on the shore giving you advice after you've been fishing all night. But we did what he said.

And then it happened. We started feeling the net move. Not just a few fish, but a heavy, wriggling, squirming school! Most of us were thinking about the fish. But one thought only of that stranger on the shore. "It's the Lord!" Peter said. He immediately threw on his shirt and swam to shore while the rest of us hauled in the net. It's a wonder it didn't tear with all that weight!

When the rest of us came ashore, the stranger already had some bread laid out, with a charcoal fire glowing and some fish cooking. He invited us to add a few of our own fish to the meal, so Peter went out to pull a few from the net.

"Let's have breakfast," the stranger said.

We all had this sense of who he was, so nobody asked any questions. He broke the bread and gave it, and then the fish, to us. It seems strange to do something so normal... eat breakfast... under such extraordinary circumstances. But that was what we did. Later we remembered how Jesus had taken the role of a servant the night before the crucifixion, washing our feet. Now, he was in the same role, serving us a meal. He turned to Peter to deal with some unfinished business between them.

That night when Jesus was arrested, Peter had fallen apart. When armed guards arrived, Peter panicked, pulled out his sword, and slashed off somebody's ear. In a matter of seconds, he managed to violate half of what Jesus taught us for the better part of three years. Later, he denied that he even knew Jesus, not once but three times, and he threw in some choice language in doing so. On the morning of the resurrection, he was frantic and confused, and that was just days after he had bragged about how loyal he would be. It wasn't pretty, and we all knew this instability weighed heavy on the mind of the man Jesus had renamed "the Rock."

"Simon, son of John, do you love me more than these?" Jesus asked, using Peter's original name rather than the "Peter the Rock." We weren't sure what Jesus meant by "more than these." Did he mean more in comparison to us, his fellow disciples? Did he mean more than the fish, the boat, and the net—symbols of his old life before it was interrupted by Jesus? Peter ignored any ambiguity: "Yes, Lord. You know I love you."

"Then take care of my lambs," Jesus replied. Then, as if Peter's first reply didn't count for much, Jesus asked him again: "Simon, son of John, do you love me?" Peter replied in the same way the second time, and Jesus said, "Shepherd my sheep." Then the question came a third time, echoing in all our minds Peter's three denials. Peter replied even more strongly this time. "Lord, you know everything. Of course you know I love you!" Once again, Jesus told him to shepherd his sheep.

And that was it. It was as if all Peter's failures melted behind us in the past, like a bad night of fishing after a great morning catch. The past and its failures didn't count anymore. What counted was love... love for Jesus, love for his flock.

Like a lot of us, Peter had a way of getting it right one minute and wrong the next. Sure enough, a few minutes later, Peter had forgotten about love for the flock and was treating one of the other disciples as a rival, a competitor. Jesus responded forcefully: "Stop worrying about anyone else. You follow me!"

Those words remind us of how this whole adventure began for us, with Jesus issuing that simple, all-or-nothing invitation: *Follow me!* Three years later, it's still about that one essential thing: following him. Of course, that's what the word *disciple* has meant all along—to be a follower, a student, an apprentice, one who learns by imitating a master.

You can imagine the honor, for uneducated fishermen like us, to sit at the feet of the greatest teacher imaginable. And now, we feel it is an even greater honor to be sent out to teach others, who will in turn teach and train others in this new way of life. This revolutionary plan of discipleship means that we must first and foremost be examples. We must embody the message and values of our movement. That doesn't mean we are perfect—just look at Peter. But it does mean we are growing and learning, always humble and willing to get up again after we fall, always moving forward on the road we are walking. As Jesus modeled never-ending learning and growth for us, we will model it for others, who will model it for still others. If each new generation of disciples follows this example, centuries from now, apprentices will still be learning the way of Jesus from mentors, so they can become mentors for the following generation.

Once, a while back, Jesus sent us out on a kind of training mission, preparing us for this day. He wouldn't let us bring anything—not even a wallet, satchel, or sandals. He sent us out in complete vulnerability—like sheep among wolves, he said. In each town, we would need to find hospitable people to shelter us and feed us—"people of peace," Jesus called them. They would become our partners, and with their support we would proclaim the kingdom of God in word and deed to their neighbors. If people didn't respond, he told us to move on and not look back. We were looking for places, like fields that are ready for harvest, where the time was right and people wanted what we had to offer. We returned from that training mission full of confidence and joy.

Once again it is time for us to follow Jesus' example and teaching, even though he will not be physically present. He invited us to be his disciples, so now we will invite others to become disciples, too. And they in turn will invite still others. In this way, a worldwide movement of discipleship can begin this morning, here on this beach with this handful of tired but resilient fishermen. Small beginnings with unlikely people, given lots of time and lots of faith and lots of hope and love, can change the world.

Like Peter, if we lose our focus, we will be tempted to turn on each other—comparing, criticizing, competing. That's why, like Peter, each of us needs to hear Jesus say, "Stop worrying about anyone else! *You* follow *me*!"

I think Jesus chose fishermen like us for a good reason. To be part of his uprising, we must be willing to fail a lot, and to keep trying. We will face long, dark nights when nothing happens. But we can never give up hope. He caught us in his net of love, so now we go and spread the net for others. And so, fellow disciples, let's get moving. Let us walk the road with Jesus.

Let us lift a glass and say, "The Lord is risen!" *He is risen, indeed!*
We too are rising up! *We are rising up, indeed!*
Let us arise in fellowship. *In fellowship, indeed!*
Let us arise in discipleship. *In discipleship, indeed!*

Engage:

1. What one thought or idea from today's lesson especially intrigued, provoked, disturbed, challenged, encouraged, warmed, warned, helped, or surprised you?
2. Share a story about how you have been drawn toward discipleship through another person.
3. How do you relate to the story of Peter with its dramatic ups and downs?
4. For children: If you could help other kids learn one important thing, what would it be, and how would you teach them?
5. Activate: This week, keep your eyes open for hospitable "people of peace" who can be your allies in the uprising of peace that Jesus started.
6. Meditate: In silence, hold the image of tired fishermen at daybreak, being told to cast their nets one more time. What does this image say to you in your life right now?

CHAPTER THIRTY-SIX

The Uprising of Worship

Psalm 103
Acts 2:41–47
1 Corinthians 14:26–31
Colossians 3:12–17

Let us imagine ourselves among the early disciples in Jerusalem, a year or so after Christ's death and resurrection.

Many months have passed since the uprising began. For a short time, there were frequent reports of people seeing the risen Christ in a variety of locations. Soon, though, those reports became less frequent until they ceased entirely. A story spread that Jesus had ascended to heaven and was now sitting at God's right hand. That fueled a lot of speculation and debate about what we should expect. Some think God is going to stage a dramatic intervention any day. Some have even stopped working in anticipation of a massive change. But many of us have interpreted Jesus' ascension and enthronement to mean it is now time to get to work, living in light of what Jesus already taught us. We're convinced that what matters now is not for Christ to appear *to* us, but for Christ to appear *in* us, *among* us, and *through* us. He wants us to be his hands, his feet, his face, his smile, his voice... his embodiment on Earth.

We gather frequently as little communities that we call *ecclesia*. We borrowed this term from the Roman empire, just as we "borrowed" the cross and reversed its meaning. For the Romans, an ecclesia is an exclusive gathering that brings local citizens together to discuss the affairs of the empire. Our ecclesia brings common people together around the affairs of the kingdom of God. Whenever and wherever the Roman ecclesia gather, they honor and worship the emperor and the pantheon of gods that support him. Whenever and wherever we gather, we honor and worship the living God, revealed to us in Christ, through the power of the Holy Spirit.

Our ecclesia gather for worship wherever we can—in homes, public buildings, or outdoor settings. And we gather whenever we can—but mostly at night, since that's when nearly everyone—even the slaves among us—can assemble. We often gather on Sunday, the day Jesus rose and this uprising began, but none of us would argue about which day is best, since every day is a good day to worship God.

For us, worship includes four main functions. We begin with the teaching of the original disciples, whom we now call *apostles*. Just as an apprentice carpenter is called a master carpenter once he has learned the trade, well-trained disciples who are sent out to teach others are called *apostles*. The apostles tell us the stories of Jesus, things they saw and heard as eyewitnesses of his time among us. They read the Law and the Prophets, and explain how our sacred texts prepared the way for Jesus and his good news. The apostles and their assistants also write letters that are shared from one ecclesia to the next. Our leaders read these letters aloud to us, since many of us can't read ourselves. Whether in person or by letter, through the teaching of the apostles we learn the words of Jesus, the stories about Jesus, the parables he told, the character he embodied, so we can walk the road he walked.

Second, our worship includes breaking the bread and drinking the wine, as Jesus taught us. Usually, this is part of a meal that we call our *love feast* or *the Lord's table*. It is so unlike anything any of us have ever experienced. Everywhere in our society, we experience constant divisions between rich and poor, slave and free, male and female, Jew and Greek, city-born and country-born, and so on. But at the Lord's table, just as it was when Jesus shared a table with sinners and outcasts, we are all one, all loved, all welcome as equals. We even greet one another with a holy kiss. Nobody would ever see a high-born person greeting a slave as an equal—except at our gatherings, where those social divisions are being forgotten, and where we learn new ways of honoring one another as members of one family.

At our love feasts, we say the words Jesus said about the bread being his body given for us, and the wine being his blood shed for us and for our sins. Those words "for us" and "for our sins" are full of meaning for us. Just as we take medicine "for" an illness, we understand that Jesus' death is curing us of our old habits and ways. For example, when we ponder how he forgave those who crucified him, we are cured of our desire for revenge. When we see how he trusted God and didn't fear human threats, we are cured of our fear. When we remember how he never stopped loving, even to the point of death, we are cured of our hatred and anger. When we imagine his outstretched arms embracing the whole world, we feel our hearts opening in love for the whole world, too, curing us of our prejudice and favoritism, our grudges and selfishness.

Along with the apostles' teaching and the holy meal, our worship gatherings include fellowship or sharing. We share our experiences, our sense of what God wants to tell us, our insights from the Scriptures. We also share our fears, our tears, our failures, and our joys. There is a financial aspect to our sharing as well. At each gathering we take an offering to distribute to those who are most in need among us and around us—especially the widows and the orphans. None of us are rich, but through our sharing, none of us are in need, either.

Finally, along with gathering for teaching, the holy meal, and fellowship, our worship gatherings are for prayer. Some of our prayers are requests. We have learned it is far better to share our worries with God than to be filled with anxiety about things that are out of our control anyway. We constantly pray for boldness and wisdom so that we can spread the good news of God's love to everyone everywhere. We bring the needs and sorrows of others to God, too, joining our compassion with God's great compassion. We pray for everyone in authority—that they will turn from injustice, violence, and corruption to ways of justice, peace, and fairness. We pray especially for those who consider themselves our enemies. The more they curse and mistreat us, the more we pray for God's blessing on them, as Jesus taught us to do.

Some of our prayers are confessions. We freely confess our sins to God, because Jesus taught us that God is gracious and forgiving. God's grace frees us from hiding our wrongs or making excuses for them. We don't want to pretend to be better than we really are, and so prayers of confession help us be honest with God, ourselves, and one another.

All of our prayers lead us to thanksgiving and praise. We feel such joy to have God's Spirit rising up in our lives that we can't be silent. We sing our deep joy and longing, sometimes through the ancient psalms and also through spiritual songs that spring up in our hearts. The more we praise God, the less we fear or are intimidated by the powers of this world. And so we praise and worship God boldly, joyfully, reverently, and freely, and we aren't quiet or shy about it!

When we gather, the Holy Spirit gives each of us different gifts to be used for the common good. Someone may be gifted to teach or lead. Someone may be moved to write and sing a song. Someone may be given an inspired word of comfort or encouragement or warning for our ecclesia. Someone may be given a special message of knowledge, insight, or teaching. Someone may speak in an unknown language, and someone may pray with great faith for a healing or miracle to occur. The same Spirit who gives the gifts is teaching us to be guided by love in all we say and do, for love matters most for us. It is even greater than faith and hope!

We don't want to give anyone the impression that everything is perfect with us. We have lots of problems and a lot to learn. But somehow, our problems seem small in comparison to the joy that we feel. This is why, even when we are tired from long days of work, even when we are threatened with persecution, even when life is full of hardships and we feel discouraged or afraid, still we gather to rise up in worship. In the face of Christ, we have come to see the glory of God, the love of God, the wisdom of God, the goodness of God, the power of God, the kindness of God . . . the fullness of God. In light of that vision of God in Christ, how can we not worship?

Let us lift a glass and say, "The Lord is risen!" *He is risen, indeed!*
We too are rising up! *We are rising up, indeed!*
Let us arise in fellowship. *In fellowship, indeed!*

Let us arise in discipleship. *In discipleship, indeed!*
Let us arise in worship. *In worship, indeed!*

Engage:

1. What one thought or idea from today's lesson especially intrigued, provoked, disturbed, challenged, encouraged, warmed, warned, helped, or surprised you?
2. Share a story of a time your heart was full of worship.
3. How do you respond to the four functions of gathered worship—teaching, bread and wine, fellowship, and prayer?
4. For children: What do you like most and least about gathering for worship?
5. Activate: This week, look for opportunities to share with others what you gain from being part of an ecclesia—a gathered community of fellowship, discipleship, and worship.
6. Meditate: Choose one word that points to an attribute of God—*glory, wisdom, justice, kindness, power*, etc. Hold that word in your heart and mind, and in silence worship God. Then choose another word and hold it together with the first in silent worship. Then add a third, and so on.

CHAPTER THIRTY-SEVEN

THE UPRISING OF PARTNERSHIP

Psalm 146
Matthew 10:16–20; 11:28–30; 28:16–20
Acts 16:11–40

LET'S IMAGINE IT IS about AD 51 and we are with a group of disciples in Philippi, about halfway between Jerusalem and Rome.

For almost twenty years now the uprising has been spreading. We still remember Jesus' words about scattering seed and seeing it grow, or kneading yeast into dough so the bread will rise, or extending like fruitful branches from a central vine. We dare to believe that through tiny little seeds like us, through the yeast of our little ecclesia, through the spreading branches of this expanding movement, the world is beginning to change. Nobody knows exactly how many disciples there are, but every day, it seems, more are being added.

We've already seen uprisings of justice, peace, and joy spread across Judea and Samaria, and now, Paul, Timothy, Luke, Silas, Priscilla, Aquila, and many others travel across the empire, developing ecclesia in all its major cities. We have been invited to join them in Philippi.

Philippi is famous, because as a Roman colony, it's like a little outpost of Rome. The people of Philippi are loyal Romans—the citizens, that is.

The slaves here, just like everywhere in the empire, are not so happy with the *Pax Romana*. They do disproportionately large amounts of work and enjoy disproportionately small amounts of "pax." The same could be said for women in the empire. It was a group of women we first met here several days ago, down by the river where they gather for prayer. A businesswoman named Lydia welcomed us—and our message. She and her household were baptized, and she gave us a place to stay at her large home. It's not at all surprising that women were the first to welcome us. Luke keeps reminding us that ever since Mary, they've been leaders in the uprising.

If slaves and women are the worst-off people in the empire, young female slaves are the most vulnerable by far. It was a slave girl who next demanded our attention in Philippi. She made a lot of money for her owners by going into a trance and telling fortunes. Whenever we walked by her on the way to the riverside, she would start shouting about us: "These men are slaves of the Highest God of All. They proclaim to you the way of liberation!" You can imagine how slave owners feel when slaves shout about liberation. And you can imagine how believers in the Greek and Roman gods feel when people talk about "the Highest God of All." It sounds very threatening to their economy and their religion—their whole Roman way of life.

This went on for a couple of days until finally, yesterday, Paul got annoyed. We were not sure why, exactly. He may have been frustrated that the girl was drawing attention to us in such an inflammatory way. He may have been embarrassed that a fortune-teller was speaking up for us. Or he may have been frustrated that this outspoken girl with so much energy, intelligence, and courage was reduced to slavery. Paul constantly reminds us that all people have equal dignity in Christ, male or female, slave or free, Jew, Greek, Roman, or foreigner. Anyway, for whatever reason, yesterday he had enough. He turned to her and commanded the spirit of fortune-telling to come out of her in the name of Jesus Christ. And from that moment, no more trances. No more fortune-telling. And no more money for the men who exploited her!

The situation deteriorated rapidly. The furious slave owners grabbed Paul and another member of our group, Silas, and dragged them into the central plaza of the city where all the markets were. They told the city officials that

Paul and Silas were Jewish revolutionaries, advocating a lifestyle that good Romans could never accept. The words *Jew* and *lifestyle* were code words that the city officials picked up. We Jews, after all, derive our basic identity from the story of God liberating us from slavery in Egypt. Of all people in the empire, we Jews are considered most resistant to Roman domination. So the slave owners quickly whipped the people of the market into a frenzy. Soon, by order of the city officials, Paul and Silas were stripped naked, severely beaten, and dragged off to prison, where they were put in chains in the innermost cell.

Late last night, Paul and Silas were singing praises to God. It was as if they were saying, "You can lock us up, but you can't shut us up!" Their songs of praise demonstrated that they feared neither the whole Roman system of slavery, domination, and intimidation, nor the petty gods that upheld it. The other prisoners, as you could imagine, were quite impressed by their courage, if not their singing voices. Suddenly, around midnight, there was an earthquake. Now earthquakes aren't terribly rare in Philippi, but this kind of earthquake was completely unprecedented. It didn't cause the jail to crash in a heap of rubble. It produced no casualties. It simply shook the jail gates and chains so they came unfastened! It was an earthquake of liberation, not destruction. Imagine that!

When the jailer rushed in to check on his prisoners, he was terrified. He knew that if they escaped, he would be put into prison himself, and perhaps tortured, too. So he pulled out his sword and decided that suicide was better than being thrown into the miserable prison system that he managed. Paul shouted out to him, "Don't do it, man! We're all here!"

At this point, the poor jailer was even more shocked. Here his prisoners were concerned about his welfare! They were choosing to stay in prison voluntarily to keep him from suffering for their escape! He brought them outside the prison and fell down on his knees in front of them, trembling with emotion. "Gentlemen, what must I do to experience the liberation you have?" he asked. There was that word *liberation* again—the same word the slave girl had used.

"Have confidence in the Lord Jesus, and you will be liberated, and so will your whole household," Paul said. The jailer must have understood those words "Lord Jesus" to be in contrast to the emperor's title, "Lord Caesar." He realized that Paul was telling him to stop being intimidated by Caesar's system of threats, whips, swords, chains, locks, and prisons. He heard Paul's words as an invitation to live under a different lord or supreme leader, in a different system, a different empire, a different kingdom—the one Jesus leads, one characterized by true freedom, true grace, and true peace.

The jailer took them to his own house, washed their wounds, and gave them a good meal. He had already been transformed—from a jailer to a gracious host! And when Paul and Silas told the man, his family, and his slaves more about Jesus and the uprising, they all were baptized.

Early this morning, the city officials realized that they had violated legal protocols by playing into the wealthy businessmen's demands. So they sent police to the jail with orders to get Paul and Silas out of town as soon as possible. But Paul refused to leave. "They made a mockery of justice by publicly humiliating, beating, and imprisoning two Roman citizens without a trial, and now they want us to participate in a cover-up? No way! If they want us to leave, they need to come in person, apologize, and personally escort us from the city." When the police returned with news that the two prisoners were actually Roman citizens, the city officials were as scared as the jailer had been after the earthquake. Like him, all they could think of was how much trouble they would be in with the higher-ups! So they complied with Paul's demands and politely requested that Paul and Silas leave the city immediately.

Paul wasn't in any rush. He decided to stop and spend some time here at Lydia's house, where the rest of us have been waiting. We quickly gathered the newly forming ecclesia. Paul and Silas shared the story you just heard. Everyone is brimming with excitement, overflowing with joy. We are partners in an earthquake of liberation! As we move forward together in this partnership in mission for peace and freedom, injustice at every level of society will be confronted, and people at every level of society will be set free!

Let us lift a glass and say, "The Lord is risen!" *He is risen, indeed!*

We too are rising up! *We are rising up, indeed!*

Let us arise in fellowship. *In fellowship, indeed!*
Let us arise in discipleship. *In discipleship, indeed!*
Let us arise in worship. *In worship, indeed!*
Let us arise in partnership. *In partnership, indeed!*

Engage:

1. What one thought or idea from today's lesson especially intrigued, provoked, disturbed, challenged, encouraged, warmed, warned, helped, or surprised you?
2. Share a story about a time you felt like one character in this story.
3. How do you respond to the idea that Paul and Silas were engaged in protest and civil disobedience in Philippi? Under what circumstances would you risk arrest, imprisonment, or death?
4. For children: Have you ever been part of a really good team? Tell us about it.
5. Activate: This week, look for counterparts to the slave girl in your world. Do what you can to stand with them and stand up for them and show them you respect their dignity.
6. Meditate: Hold in your imagination the picture of jail doors shaking open. What could this image mean for your life? Listen in your deepest heart for an answer.

CHAPTER THIRTY-EIGHT

The Uprising of Stewardship

Deuteronomy 15:1–11
1 Timothy 6:3–19
2 Corinthians 8:1–15

LET US IMAGINE WE are with Paul and his team of disciples in the city of Corinth in AD 51.

We'll never forget Philippi and what we learned there about the uprising. Since leaving the Roman colony, we've visited several other cities including Thessalonica and Berea. Now we have come to a city called Corinth. It's a city with a dirty reputation, well deserved in many ways. The people here are tough. Mean. Selfish. There are all kinds of religions, lots of temple prostitution, all the worst of big-city life. But even here, an ecclesia of discipleship, fellowship, worship, and partnership is forming. It looks like Paul, Silas, and Timothy plan to settle here for a year or more. They have joined with a local couple, Priscilla and Aquila, to start a small business making tents. Together, we can produce and sell tents to make enough money that we won't be a burden on the ecclesia here.

Speaking of money, you don't have to live very long to know that money rules this world. People with money have power, and to them, what matters most is getting more of both. We see that here in Corinth, and it's obvious around the whole empire.

Paul is very suspicious of money. To him, loving money is at the root of all kinds of evil. What really counts isn't gold, but the contentment that comes from desiring God above all else.

Again and again he teaches us that the drive to accumulate money wastes our lives. Our real ambition should be to build a big account of good works—acts of generosity and kindness on behalf of those considered the last, the least, and the lost. Paul loves to quote Jesus' words that it is better to give than to receive. That's why he's got us making tents: he wants us to have enough money to provide for our own needs, plus more to share with others.

When the uprising first began in Jerusalem, people started bringing all their possessions to the apostles. Since they knew it wasn't God's will for some of us to have luxuries while others lacked necessities, those with surplus began to share freely with those in need. We held all things in common. As you might expect, that created some problems. Some old prejudices sprang up between Jews and Greeks, and some people began playing games, pretending to be more generous than they really were. In spite of the problems, holding all things in common was a beautiful thing. Some of us still practice the "all things in common" rule as they did at the beginning, and some have modified that rule.

But what hasn't changed, and what must never change, is this: we realize that the systems of this world run on one economy, and we in the commonwealth of God run on another. In our alternate economy, those who have a lot don't hoard it; they share it. Those who have been given much in terms of money and power feel not a sense of privilege and superiority but a sense of greater responsibility for their neighbors who are vulnerable and in need. We measure our well-being and holiness by the condition of the weakest and neediest among us.

Across the Roman empire, and especially here in Corinth, people exhaust themselves to get rich, and in so doing they cause much harm. Some exploit the land. You might say they are thieves who take more from the bank of creation than they put back, and in that way they steal from unborn generations. Others exploit people of this generation. They are thieves who make big profits through the sweat of their poorly paid neighbors, reducing them, if not to slavery then to something almost the same. They are often very subtle in the ways they do this, using banks, investments, and loans to enrich themselves as they impoverish others. It's a dirty economy, and those who profit by it gain the world and lose their souls.

"What's yours is mine," some people say, "and I want to steal it!" "What's mine is mine," some people say. "And I want to keep it!" "What's mine is God's," we are learning to say, "and I want to use it for the common good." We call that attitude *stewardship*.

Stewardship applies to all areas of our lives—how we use time, potential, possessions, privilege, and power. Whatever we do, we try to give it our very best, because we work for Christ and not just for money. We want no part of dishonest or harmful employment, so if necessary we change jobs, or we work for reform so we can stay in our current jobs with a clear conscience. As we are being transformed personally, we seek to transform our economic systems from corrupt to ethical, from destructive to regenerative, from cruel and dehumanizing to kind and humane. We believe this pleases God.

When it comes to how we spend our earnings, stewardship means living below our means. We do so by dividing our income into three parts. First, we determine a percentage that we will use to provide for our needs and the needs of our families. That's just basic decency. Second, we determine a percentage to save, since wisdom requires foresight. Even ants know to save some of their summer's work to get them through the winter. Third, we set aside the largest portion we can for God's work of compassion, justice, restoration, and peace.

Some of this third portion goes to people like Paul, Silas, and Timothy, who lead and serve the ecclesia springing up around the world. Some of it goes to members of the ecclesia who are in need—the sick, the widows, the orphans, the elderly, and those who have lost their homes, their land, and their work. Some of it goes to meet the needs of others near or far—as an expression of God's love and ours. That's what stewardship is, really: love in action.

Paul always reminds us that nothing has any value without love. That explains why money is so deceptive. It deceives people about what has true value. You cannot serve two masters, Jesus taught. If you love God, you will hate money, because it always gets in the way of loving God. If you love money, you will hate God, because God always gets in the way of loving money.

It is foolishness to live above your means. It is selfishness to spend all your money on yourself. It is godliness to give—to produce a surplus that is used for the commonwealth of God, which is an uprising not of greed but of joyful generosity and creative stewardship.

Let us lift a glass and say, "The Lord is risen!" *He is risen, indeed!*
We too are rising up! *We are rising up, indeed!*
Let us arise in fellowship. *In fellowship, indeed!*
Let us arise in discipleship. *In discipleship, indeed!*
Let us arise in worship. *In worship, indeed!*
Let us arise in partnership. *In partnership, indeed!*
Let us arise in stewardship. *In stewardship, indeed!*

Engage:

1. What one thought or idea from today's lesson especially intrigued, provoked, disturbed, challenged, encouraged, warmed, warned, helped, or surprised you?
2. Share a story about a time when you got mixed up about what really has value.
3. How do you respond to the idea of dividing your earnings into three parts—to spend, save, and give?
4. For children: If someone gave you a whole lot of money, what would you do with it?
5. Activate: If you've never developed a budget where you specify what percentage of your income you will spend, save, and give, do so this week. And if you have such a budget, reassess and see if you can raise your standard of giving by a percentage or two. If possible, meet with a close friend from your learning circle to speak openly of your financial lives and priorities. If you don't already do so, consider pooling your giving power through this learning circle.
6. Meditate: Quietly ponder the tension between loving God and loving money. See if any insights come to you. Ask God to help you be a wise steward or manager of the resources that are entrusted to you.

CHAPTER THIRTY-NINE

Whatever the Hardship, Keep Rising Up!

Isaiah 40:27–31
Acts 9:1–25
2 Corinthians 6:1–10; 11:22–33

Let us imagine ourselves in Rome, in about AD 64.

Over thirty years have passed since Jesus launched this uprising of faith, hope, and love in our world. Over a dozen years have passed since we traveled with Paul around the Mediterranean. Since then, the uprising has continued to spread. New leaders have arisen. People around the empire have joined us. We know the movement is gaining strength.

It is gaining strength largely because of the hardships we have faced. There have been persecutions from outsiders, betrayals by insiders, and stupid arguments that wasted time and drained our energy. There have been divisions, moral scandals, financial improprieties, all kinds of crazy teachings that confuse and distract, power struggles, sad things that in many ways show how easy it is to forget what this whole movement is supposed to be about. As we've offended each other and forgiven each other, as we've experienced rifts and then reconciliations, we've learned that God doesn't give us shortcuts around hardships, but strengthens us through them.

Speaking of hardships, we recently heard that Paul was under house arrest in Rome. Timothy told us Paul was feeling lonely and cold in the winter chill, and a little bored, too. So we joined Timothy and came to Rome to be with him. We brought him a warm coat and things to read, among other things. Since we arrived, a steady stream of visitors comes every day to talk with Paul about Jesus and the commonwealth of God, the great abiding passions of his life.

In the evenings, Paul often tells us stories about his many adventures. To our great surprise, the stories he likes to tell most are those of struggle. "If I'm going to brag like a fool," he says, "it will be about my weaknesses, limitations, sufferings, and scars."

Sometimes Paul shows us those scars—from whippings he received on five occasions, and beatings with rods that he received three times, including that unforgettable day in Philippi. He reminds us that even Jesus could only lead the way to God's new commonwealth through suffering. "Through many hardships you enter the commonwealth of God," he says. He loves to tell the story—and we love to hear it—of how he first experienced the risen Christ over a three-day period, and how from the start he knew that his path would involve suffering.

The uprising had only been under way for about three years. Saul—the name by which Paul was known back then—had been its most passionate enemy. He hated the Way, as it was called back then. He became obsessed with stamping it out. He traveled around the region arresting, imprisoning, and executing women as well as men in the name of God and the Scriptures. When he was on his way to Damascus to continue his bloody and hateful work, he was struck to the ground by a blinding light. He heard a voice saying, "Saul, Saul, why do you persecute me?" He asked who was speaking to him, and the voice said, "I am Jesus, the one you are persecuting. Now get up and go into the city and you will be shown what to do next." This shattering experience of spiritual insight left him unable to see physically. So he had to be led into Damascus by the hand. For three days he sat in darkness, unable to see. Obviously, he had a lot to think about.

A complete stranger named Ananias came to visit him. Ananias was a disciple, a follower of Jesus and the Way—exactly the kind of person Paul had come to Damascus to arrest, torture, and kill. Ananias could have killed his blind and defenseless enemy. But instead he spoke words of kindness to him. "Brother Saul," he said, "the Lord Jesus who appeared to you sent me to you so your sight could be restored and so you could be filled with the Holy Spirit." Ananias laid his hands on him and prayed for his vision to be restored.

When Paul opened his eyes, the first face he saw was that of Ananias. Ananias warned him that the road ahead would be full of hardship, and that has been the case—for Paul, and for all of us on the Way.

Of course, as followers of the Way, we face the normal hardships of life—sickness, setbacks, delays, conflict, struggle. Paul has had his share of those. Once he survived a shipwreck only to get bitten by a snake. How he laughs when he tells us that one! And there was the time he preached for so long that a young man got drowsy, dropped off to sleep, and fell out a second-story window. Paul laughs even more when he tells that one. Thankfully, it turned out OK in the end. In fact, after healing the victim of his long sermon, Paul went back and preached for several more hours!

Paul is getting older now. He is constantly plagued by eye troubles and other aches and pains. Being under house arrest means poor food, cold, restricted movement, and uncertainty about what the future holds, especially now, with Nero as emperor. Enough said about that. On a deeper level, Paul often speaks with deep regret about a break with two of his former friends, Barnabas and John Mark. He still dreams of reconciliation. And he carries constant concern for the ecclesia spread out across the empire, the way a mother carries her children in her heart even after they're grown.

In the face of all this hardship, Paul admits getting depressed at times. But he tells us that it is only through hardship, through discouragement, through exhaustion, that we learn to draw on the power of God's Spirit within us. It is only when we come to the end of our own strength, and even then refuse to give up, that we discover God's strength. "When we are weak, then we are strong," he says.

Hardships make us bitter... or better. They lead us to breakdown... or to breakthrough. If we don't give up at that breaking point when we feel we've reached the end of our own resources, we find a new aliveness, the life of the risen Christ rising within us. Paul often says it like this: "I have been crucified with Christ. So it is no longer my prideful self who lives. Now it is Christ, alive in me."

Hardships not only teach us to live in dependence upon God, but they also teach us interdependence with others. So through hardship, we move from "me" to "we." Paul reminds us that he discovered Christ not only in his vision, but also in Ananias. And after Ananias, he met Christ in the ecclesia in Damascus, the ecclesia in Antioch, and in so many individuals, too—in women like Lydia, Prisca, and Julia, in men like Timothy and Titus... and yes, even dear Barnabas and John Mark, too.

Paul isn't the least bit shy about speaking of his tenuous future. "The only thing ahead for me is imprisonment and persecution," he says. "But I don't count my life of any value to myself. My only ambition is to finish my course and fulfill the ministry the Lord Jesus has given me: to tell everyone everywhere about the good news of God's grace."

These days there's a lot of unrest. The Zealots are stirring up rebellion in Jerusalem, and if that happens, the Roman military will crush it and reduce Jerusalem to ashes and rubble. Here in Rome, Nero is utterly powerful and utterly insane. He takes sick pleasure in executing people on a whim, and any day Paul could be his next entertainment. But Paul refuses to complain—he can't stand complaining. He just keeps rejoicing and singing and being grateful for each day, each breath, each heartbeat—just as he did that night with Silas in the jail in Philippi. "For me to live is Christ," he says. "But to die will be gain." Paul has followed Jesus' example, and in so doing, he has set an example for us... an example of enduring hardship and seeing joy beyond it.

We've been enduring hardship and experiencing joy for thirty years now. Paul will soon be gone. And then it will be up to us to carry on—leading with joy through whatever hardships we will face. Who knows where the road will lead? God will be with us, and we will make the road by walking, together.

Let us lift a glass and say, "The Lord is risen!" *He is risen, indeed!*
We too are rising up! *We are rising up, indeed!*

Let us arise in fellowship. *In fellowship, indeed!*

Let us arise in discipleship. *In discipleship, indeed!*

Let us arise in worship. *In worship, indeed!*

Let us arise in partnership. *In partnership, indeed!*

Let us arise in stewardship. *In stewardship, indeed!*

And whatever the hardship, we will keep rising up. *Through hardship, indeed!*

Engage:

1. What one thought or idea from today's lesson especially intrigued, provoked, disturbed, challenged, encouraged, warmed, warned, helped, or surprised you?
2. Share a story about one of your greatest hardships.
3. How do you respond to the idea that we discover God's strength only through our weakness?
4. For children: What's something that you really don't like doing, but you make yourself do it anyway?
5. Activate: This week, when you're tempted to complain, look for a blessing that could come from enduring hardship well.
6. Meditate: In silence, ponder Paul's words, "For me to live is Christ" and "Christ lives in me." How does your heart respond?

Third Quarter Queries

If possible, compose prayerful, honest, and heartfelt replies to these queries in private, and then gather to share what you have written. The Five Guidelines for Learning Circles in Appendix II may be helpful to guide your sharing. You may also find it helpful to invite a trusted spiritual leader to serve as "catechist" and ask him or her for additional guidance, feedback, and instruction. Make it safe for one another to speak freely, and let your conversation build conviction in each of you as individuals, and among you as a community.

1. Summarize the message of the Sermon on the Mount and what it means to you.
2. Recount the events of Palm Sunday, Holy Thursday, Good Friday, and Silent Saturday, and their meaning for you today.
3. What does it mean to you to make the Easter affirmation that Christ is risen indeed?
4. What does it mean to you to be part of an uprising of fellowship and discipleship?
5. What does it mean to you to be part of an uprising of worship and partnership?
6. What does it mean to you to be part of an uprising of stewardship and hardship?
7. How has your understanding of God and yourself changed through your participation in this learning circle?

IV

ALIVE IN THE SPIRIT OF GOD

In the previous three sections of this book, we have placed ourselves in the story of creation, the adventure of Jesus, and God's peaceful uprising against the forces of fear, oppression, hostility, and violence. Jesus promised that the Holy Spirit would take the work he began and extend it across space and time, creating a global spiritual community to keep welcoming and embodying what he called the reign or kingdom or commonwealth of God.

In this final section, beginning with the season traditionally known as Pentecost, we ask this key question: how can we participate with the Spirit in this ongoing spiritual movement? That word *spiritual* means a lot of things, but for us, it will mean any experience of or response to the moving of the Spirit of God in our lives and in our world.

CHAPTER FORTY

THE SPIRIT IS MOVING! (PENTECOST SUNDAY)

John 3:1–21
Acts 2:1–41
Romans 6:1–14

FOLLOWING JESUS TODAY HAS much in common with the original disciples' experience. We are welcomed as disciples by God's grace, not by earning or status. We learn and practice Christ's teaching in the company of fellow learners. We seek to understand and imitate his example, and we commune with him around a table. But there is an obvious and major difference between our experience and theirs: they could see Jesus and we can't. Surprisingly, according to John's gospel, that gives us an advantage. "It's better that I go away so the Spirit can come," Jesus said. If he were physically present and visible, our focus would be on Christ *over there, right there, out there*... but because of his absence, we discover the Spirit of Christ *right here, in here, within.*

Jesus describes the Spirit as *another* comforter, *another* teacher, *another* guide—just like him, but available to everyone, everywhere, always. The same Spirit who had descended like a dove upon him will descend upon us, he promises. The same Spirit who filled him will fill all who open their hearts.

Take Paul, for example. He never saw Jesus in the flesh, but he did experience the Spirit of Christ. That was enough to transform him from a proud and violent agitator of hostility to a tireless activist for reconciliation. Through this experience of the Spirit, he seemed to live inside of

Christ and look out through Christ's eyes upon the world. And the opposite was equally true: through the Spirit, Christ lived inside of Paul and looked through Paul's eyes upon the world. "I in Christ" and "Christ in me"—that captures so much of Paul's vision of life.

For Paul, life in the Spirit means a threefold sharing in the death, burial, and resurrection of Jesus. First, as we turn from old habits and patterns, our "old self" with all its pride, greed, lust, anger, prejudice, and hostility dies with Christ. That former identity with all its hostilities is nailed to the cross and left behind. In this way, life in the Spirit involves a profound experience of *letting go* of what has been so far.

Then, Paul says, we join Jesus in the powerlessness and defeat of burial, symbolized by baptism. We experience that burial as a surrender to silence, stillness, powerlessness, emptiness, and rest, *a letting be.*

Then we join Jesus in the dynamic, surprising uprising of resurrection. The surrender, silence, emptiness, and rest of *letting go* and *letting be* make us receptive to something new. Like a vacuum, that receptivity welcomes infilling and activation . . . and so we experience a *letting come* of the Spirit of God.

The Bible describes the Spirit with beautiful and vivid imagery: Wind. Breath. Fire. Cloud. Water. Wine. A dove. These dynamic word pictures contrast starkly with the heavy, fixed imagery provided by, say, stone idols, imposing temples, or thick theological tomes. Through this vivid imagery, the biblical writers tell us that the Spirit invigorates, animates, purifies, holds mystery, moves and flows, foments joy, and spreads peace.

For example, in the first chapter of Genesis, God's Spirit hovers over the primal waters like *wind*, creating beauty and novelty out of chaos. The Spirit then animates living creatures like *breath.* Then, in Exodus, God's Spirit appears as *fire* in the burning bush, beckoning Moses, and then as a pillar of *cloud and fire* moving across the wilderness, cooling by day and warming by night, and leading the way to freedom. Centuries later, when John the Baptist comes on the scene, he says that just as he immerses and marks people with *water*, his successor will immerse and mark people with the Spirit. When John baptizes Jesus, bystanders see the Spirit descending like a *dove* upon him. At the beginning of his ministry, Jesus dramatizes his mission by turning water, which is kept in stone containers used for religious ceremonies, into a huge quantity of *wine* to infuse joy at a wedding banquet. Later, he promises people that if they trust him, they will experience rivers of living *water* springing up from within.

At the core of Jesus' life and message, then, was this good news: the Spirit of God, the Spirit of aliveness, the Wind-breath-fire-cloud-water-wine-dove Spirit who filled Jesus is on the move in our world. And that gives us a choice: do we dig in our heels, clench our fists, and live for our own agenda, or do we let go, let be, and let come... and so be taken up into the Spirit's movement?

That was what the disciples experienced on the day of Pentecost, according to Luke, when the Spirit manifested as wind and fire. Suddenly, the Spirit-filled disciples began speaking in languages they had never learned. This strange sign is full of significance. The Spirit of God, it tells us, is multilingual. The Spirit isn't restricted to one elite language or one superior culture, as almost everyone had assumed. Instead, the Spirit speaks to everyone everywhere in his or her native tongue.

What happened at Pentecost reverses the ancient story of the Tower of Babel, when ambitious Babylonians grasped at godlike power by unifying everyone under one imperial language and culture. At Babel, God opposed that imperial uniformity and voted for diversity by multiplying languages. Now, in the Pentecost story, we discover a third option: not unity without diversity, and not diversity without unity, but unity and diversity in harmony.

In the millennia since Christ walked with us on this Earth, we've often tried to box up the "wind" in manageable doctrines. We've exchanged the fire of the Spirit for the ice of religious pride. We've turned the wine back into water, and then let the water go stagnant and lukewarm. We've traded the gentle dove of peace for the predatory hawk or eagle of empire. When we have done so, we have ended up with just another religious system, as problematic as any other: too often petty, argumentative, judgmental, cold, hostile, bureaucratic, self-seeking, an enemy of aliveness.

In a world full of big challenges, in a time like ours, we can't settle for a heavy and fixed religion. We can't try to contain the Spirit in a box. We need to experience the mighty rushing wind of Pentecost. We need our hearts to be made incandescent by the Spirit's fire. We need the living water and new wine Jesus promised, so our hearts can become the home of dovelike peace.

Wind. Breath. Fire. Cloud. Water. Wine. A dove. When we open up space for the Spirit and let the Spirit fill that space within us, we begin to change, and we become agents of change. That's why we pause in our journey to gather together around a table of fellowship and communion. Like the disciples in the upper room at Pentecost, we present ourselves to God. We become receptive for the fullness of the Spirit to fall upon us and well up within us, to blow like wind, glow like fire, flow like a river, fill like a cloud, and descend like a dove in and among us. So let us open our hearts. Let us dare believe that the Spirit that we read about in the Scriptures can move among us today, empowering us in our times so we can become agents in a global spiritual movement of justice, peace, and joy.

So, are we ready? Are we willing to die with Christ? Are we willing to *let go*?

And are we willing to be buried with Christ? Are we willing to *let be*?

And are we willing to rise with Christ? Can we inhale, open our emptiness, unlock that inner vacuum, for the Spirit to enter and fill—like wind, breath, fire, cloud, water, wine, and a dove? Are we willing to *let come*?

Let it be so. Let it be now. Amen.

Engage:

1. What one thought or idea from today's lesson especially intrigued, provoked, disturbed, challenged, encouraged, warmed, warned, helped, or surprised you?
2. Share a story about a time you experienced the Holy Spirit in a special way.
3. How do you respond to the imagery of death, burial, and resurrection with Christ?
4. For children: What do you think it means for a person to be filled with God?
5. Activate: Make it a habit in the coming days to take a deep breath and then exhale to express *letting go.* Then remain breathless for a moment—to express *letting be.* Then inhale to express *letting the Spirit come* to fill you.
6. Meditate: In silence, hold the word "open" in God's presence. Let images of openness come to you. Direct this openness to God's Spirit as a desire to be filled.

CHAPTER FORTY-ONE

Moving with the Spirit

John 15:1–8
Galatians 3:19–4:7; 5:1, 13–26
Colossians 2:6–7; 3:1–17

THE WIND CAN BE blowing, but if your sail isn't raised, you won't go far. You can be surrounded by oxygen, but if you don't breathe, it won't do you any good. The sap can be flowing, but if a branch isn't connected to the vine, it will wither. If you don't have kindling and wood in your hearth, a lit match won't burn long. It's the same with the Spirit. We are surrounded with the aliveness of the Spirit. All that remains is for us to learn how to let the Spirit fill, flow, and glow within us.

We start in the heart—the wellspring of our desires. That's where our problems begin, and that's where our healing begins, too. When we desire to be filled with the Spirit, the Spirit begins to transform our desires so that God's desires become our own. Instead of doing the right thing because we *have* to, we do the right thing because we *want* to—because we are learning to truly desire goodness. Once our desires are being changed, a revolution is set in motion.

The New Testament gives us a simple image for how desire translates into action: *walking*. When we were newborn, we couldn't even roll over, much less crawl, much less walk and run. Eventually, a desire for movement stirred within us, and we gradually and clumsily translated that desire into action—first rolling over, then crawling, then standing and toddling, and eventually walking. Step by step, with lots of stumbles and falls, we eventually mastered the art of translating our desire into movement. And so now, with hardly a thought, we walk, we run, we jump, we dance.

This image of walking is everywhere in the Scriptures. Walk in the Spirit, we are told. Walk in the light. Walk in love. Walk in newness of life. Walk by faith. Walk in good works. Walk in truth. To be a disciple is to follow a mentor, which means walking in the mentor's footsteps. The image is simple... one step at a time, drawn by desire, leaning forward, doing the next right thing, keeping our focus on our goal, leaving the past behind. If you stumble, regain your balance and keep walking. If you fall, get up again and keep walking. If you're distracted or wander off the path, reorient yourself toward your goal and keep walking.

Jesus used another vivid image to convey the same reality: a branch abiding in a vine. If the branch were to separate itself from the vine, it would wither and die. But if it simply stays connected, the vine's aliveness flows into the branch and bears fruit through it. So if we abide or remain in vital connection to Christ, the Spirit will flow with God's aliveness in and through us, making us both beautiful and fruitful.

Paul employed several similar images. Stir up the fire in you, he said to his young protégé, Timothy. Just as fires need to be tended, our inner life needs to be tended, too. In his letter to the Colossians, he used the image of welcoming a guest, making room in our hearts so the Spirit of Christ can "dwell in us richly." In Ephesians, he made an analogy to drinking wine. Just as drinking your fill of alcoholic spirits can change your behavior for the worse, being filled with the Holy Spirit will change your behavior for the better.

If you want to gain practice walking in the Spirit or abiding in Christ or tending the inner flame, you can start when you wake up tomorrow morning. Before your feet hit the floor, open your heart to the Spirit. Ask God to help you walk in the Spirit, step by step through the day. Ask God to help you abide in the Vine so good fruit will naturally develop in your life. Ask God to keep the fire burning within you. Just starting the day this way will make a difference.

As you build that habit of yielding yourself to the Spirit morning by morning, you can build the habit of checking in with the Spirit hour by hour throughout the day. At each mealtime, you can offer a prayer of thanksgiving and you can reconnect with the Spirit. As you travel from place to place, as you wait for someone, whenever you have a free moment, you can offer yourself to God: "Here I am, Lord. Please move in and through me to bless others." Whenever an emergency or challenge arises, you can lean on the Spirit: "Give me wisdom, Spirit of God. Give me strength. Give me patience." When you sense that you've let something other than God's Spirit fill you and direct you—anger, fear, prejudice, lust, greed, anxiety, pride, inferiority, or rivalry, for example—you can stop, acknowledge your misstep, and resurrender to the Spirit. It's like breathing—exhaling an acknowledgment of your misstep and inhaling forgiveness and strength to start walking in the Spirit again.

At the end of the day, you can look back with gratitude, resting in the Spirit until a new day begins and you continue walking the journey of faith.

As we walk in the Spirit, we pass through different kinds of terrain. We walk through beautiful valleys where life is full of joy and we feel like dancing. We walk on long uphill climbs where we seem to slide back two steps for every three steps of ascent. We walk along slippery trails where it's easy to fall, and through swampy patches where we can get bogged down. We walk through dark passages where we can easily lose our way, and across flat terrain where nothing seems to change mile after mile. We walk through dangerous territory where bullets fly and it's easy to get wounded, and in peaceful places where we can breathe free. Through it all, we need patience, endurance, and perseverance so that no matter what happens, we'll keep putting one foot ahead of the other.

If we don't give up, as mile adds to mile, each of us will have some stories to tell...stories of how the Spirit guided, empowered, inspired, restrained, sustained, and trained us in the fine art of aliveness. And that's another great blessing of being part of a community of faith. Along the way, we gather around a table or campfire and share our stories about the journey so far. We share our joys and sorrows. We share mistakes we've made and falls we've taken and lessons we've learned. We share ways in which we've experienced the Spirit moving in us, among us, and through us. Through this sharing, we encourage each other. And then we get back on the road.

Sadly, lots of people get distracted and lose their way. Instead of continuing to walk in the Spirit, they slow down to look back proudly on how far they've come. They become highly impressed by all they've learned—theological concepts, Bible lore, religious history, and so on. Pretty soon, they come to a standstill and brag among themselves, comparing themselves to others who haven't walked as far or fast or cleverly as they have. They form little encampments, sitting around day after day, quarreling about this or that fine point of walking theory. Pretty soon they're so out of shape they give up walking altogether and specialize in talking about the way others walk.

That's their choice. But for us... let's keep walking. Let's keep on the road. However far we've come, there's far more ahead to explore. The Spirit is on the move, so let us keep moving, too.

Engage:

1. What one thought or idea from today's lesson especially intrigued, provoked, disturbed, challenged, encouraged, warmed, warned, helped, or surprised you?
2. Share a story about how the Spirit has encouraged you through others at this table.
3. How do you respond to the warning about losing your way and becoming a critical bystander rather than a humble walker?
4. For children: Have you ever taken a hike in the forest? Tell us about it. Did you learn anything on the trail?
5. Activate: This week, aim to "check in" with the Spirit each morning and evening, and several times throughout the day. And look for opportunities to share stories of what the Spirit is doing in your life.
6. Meditate: Hold the image of a ship raising its sail to the wind. Ponder what it would mean for you to raise your sail to the Holy Spirit. Let a prayer arise within you.

CHAPTER FORTY-TWO

Spirit of Love: Loving God

Psalm 116
Romans 8:1–17
Ephesians 3:14–21

Wherever God's Spirit is at work in the world, people are drawn more deeply to love... beginning with loving God.

Of course, we must acknowledge that the word *God* has become a big problem for a lot of people. How can they love a God who is an angry old white man with a beard, oppressing women and minorities, promoting discrimination and war, and blessing the destruction of the planet? How can they love the curator of a religious museum who seems to have a taste for all that is outdated, archaic, dour, and dusty? How can they love the host of an unending religious broadcast where everyone is always artificially smiling and excessively, unrealistically happy, desperate for you to send in your next generous financial contribution? How can they love a testy border guard who won't let new arrivals through heaven's passport control office unless they correctly answer a lot of technical doctrinal questions with a score of 100 percent?

Hot-headed religious extremists, lukewarm religious bureaucrats, and cold-hearted religious critics alike have turned the word *God* into a name for something ugly, small, boring, elitist, wacky, corrupt, or violent—the very opposite of what it should mean. Maybe God is more turned off to the word *God* than anyone else! And maybe the distaste of many for the word *God* as it is commonly used actually reveals a corresponding love that longs for what God truly is.

Whatever ember of love for goodness flickers within us, however feeble or small . . . that's what the Spirit works with, until that spark glows warmer and brighter. From the tiniest beginning, our whole lives—our whole hearts, minds, souls, and strength—can be set aflame with love for God.

Even those of us who have always believed in God's existence and never had any big problems with the word *God* . . . when it comes to actually loving God, we can feel a little intimidated. We don't know where to begin.

But really, it's not so different from loving another human being.

When we speak of loving another human being, we naturally move toward that person in a special way. We appreciate the qualities of the beloved. We respect and honor the beloved's dignity. We enjoy the beloved's company and feel curious about the beloved's personhood. We want to support the beloved's dreams and desires. And we make ourselves available for the beloved to respect, honor, enjoy, know, and support us, too, because to be "in love" is to be in a mutual relationship.

Similarly, when we learn to love God, we appreciate God's qualities. We honor and respect God's dignity. We enjoy God's presence and are curious to know more and more of God's heart. We support God's dreams coming true. And we want to be appreciated, honored, enjoyed, known, and supported as well—to surrender ourselves to God in mutuality.

It all begins with moving toward God, taking a first step by simply showing up, becoming aware of God's presence and presenting ourselves to God. It's as simple as saying, "God, here I am," or "God, here you are," or even better, "God, here we are, together."

A second step is appreciation. Sometimes we take a spouse, child, parent, or friend for granted. Then some shock or threat occurs—an accident, a disease, or an argument through which they are nearly taken from us. Suddenly, we appreciate afresh this precious person we've been taking for granted. If we don't want to take God for granted, we can express gratitude and appreciation for what it means to have God in our lives. That's why many of us try to begin each day and each meal with a prayer of thankful appreciation—it's a way of being sure we don't take God and God's blessings for granted. If the simple word *here* helps us show up, the simple word *thanks* can help us with appreciation.

A third step is to cultivate honor and respect for God—not just gratitude for what God does for us or gives us, but respect for God's dignity, honor for God's character. That's why many of us try to begin each week with a time of gathered worship and to begin and end each day with a few moments of praise. A single simple word like *Hallelujah* might help us, or even *Wow!* or *O!*

We all know that we do the opposite of loving God sometimes. We remain aloof or preoccupied, we complain instead of appreciate, and we ignore or disrespect rather than honor God. That's where a fourth step comes in: learning to say we're sorry and to express to God our regrets. When we say and mean a simple sentence like "I'm sorry" or "Lord, have mercy," we move toward God again, receiving forgiveness and renewing our loving connection.

If love means supporting the beloved's dreams and plans, we love God by expressing our support for what God desires. We express this support whenever we pray, "May your kingdom come. May your will be done on Earth as it is in heaven." We do so whenever we come to God in empathetic concern for others, joining our compassion with God's compassion for those in need, sorrow, or pain. By refusing to allow numbness or hardness of heart to gain a foothold in our lives, we keep our hearts aligned with God's heart, and in this way, express love for God. Sometimes, holding up the name or face of a person in God's presence, simply breathing the words "please help him" or "please bless her" can be a way of loving God by loving those God loves.

If love is about mutuality, love also means opening ourselves for God to support our dreams and desires. In that way, every time we cry out, "Help me, Lord!" we are expressing love for God. Why that is the case becomes obvious when we consider the opposite. Imagine shutting out a friend, parent, or spouse from our need, sorrow, or pain. Imagine never asking for help. That would be a sign of indifference and distrust, not love. So, opening ourselves to God when we're in need says that we trust God and want God to accompany us, support us, and befriend us in every way.

We trust those we love most with our deepest fears, doubts, emptiness, and disillusionment. So we love God when we share those vulnerable aspects of our lives with God. Just as a little child in the middle of a temper tantrum can shout "I hate you, Mommy!" only because he knows his outburst will not end their relationship, we can express to God our deep doubts, anger, or frustrations only because we possess an even deeper trust in God's love. At times, then, our hearts cry out, "When, Lord? How long, Lord?" or "Why?" or even "No!" But the fact that we share this pain with God rather than withhold it turns out to be an expression of love.

Imagine an elderly couple who have loved one another through a long lifetime, or an adult child sitting at the bedside of a dying parent. Often, their love is expressed most powerfully by presence and touch, not by words. Simply being together, holding hands, smiling, sitting close in mutual enjoyment—these are profound expressions of love, beyond words. Something like this develops over time in our relationship with God.

Like one tuning fork that resonates effortlessly with another, we release our whole being to resonate with the love, grace, and joy of God. We feel a habitual attentiveness to God that spontaneously smiles or reaches out in an affectionate touch—without obligation, without trying, without even thinking. No words are necessary as we simply and deeply enjoy being together here and now. We are not alone. We are loved. We love.

Remembering our true identity in the family of creation, being rooted and grounded in love, we experience the multidimensional love of Christ that surpasses all knowledge, and we are filled with the very fullness of God. In that fullness, we simply breathe, be, and let be. This is life in the Spirit, being in love, with God—true aliveness indeed.

Engage:

1. What one thought or idea from today's lesson especially intrigued, provoked, disturbed, challenged, encouraged, warmed, warned, helped, or surprised you?
2. Share a story about a time when you felt most "in love" with God.
3. How do you respond to the comparison between human love and loving God?

4. For children: The Bible says, "God is love." What do you think that means?
5. Activate: Use some of the simple words from this chapter—*here*, *thanks*, *O*, *sorry*, and so on—to practice postures of love for God.
6. Meditate: Invest a few minutes to practice simply being with God, in silence, in love. When your mind distracts you and wanders off, simply acknowledge that has happened and turn your attention back to God, being aware of God's constant loving attention toward you.

CHAPTER FORTY-THREE

SPIRIT OF LOVE: LOVING NEIGHBOR

Acts 10:1–48
1 Corinthians 13:1–13

WHERE THE SPIRIT IS moving, love for God always, always, always overflows in love for neighbor. And according to Jesus, our neighbor isn't just the person who is like us, the person who likes us, or the person we like. Our neighbor is anyone and everyone—like us or different from us, friend or stranger—even enemy. As Peter learned in his encounter with Cornelius, the Spirit wants to break down walls of prejudice and hostility so that we stop judging *us* as clean and *them* as unclean, opening the way for strangers and enemies to become neighbors, friends, family.

That comes as a shock to many of us who were taught that *same is safe* and *different is dangerous.* That belief probably served our ancestors well at certain points in our history. Their survival often depended on maintaining trust in "our" tribe and fear of other tribes. That's why they used paint, feathers, clothing, language, and even religion as markers, so everyone would know who was same and safe and *us*, and who was different and dangerous and *them*.

Driven by that belief, our ancestors spread out across the world, each tribe staking out its own territory, each guarding its borders from an invasion by others, each trying to expand its territory whenever possible, each driving others farther and farther away. No wonder our history is written in blood: wars, conquests, invasions, occupations, revolutions, and counter-revolutions. The winners take all, and the losers, if they aren't killed or enslaved, escape to begin again somewhere else.

Eventually, because the Earth is a sphere, our dispersing tribes had to come full circle and encounter one another again. That is our challenge today. We must find a way to live together on a crowded planet. We have to graduate from thinking in terms of "our kind versus their kind" to thinking in terms of "humankind." We must turn from the ways of our ancestors and stop trying to kill off, subjugate, or fend off everyone we judge different and dangerous. We must find a new approach, make a new road, pioneer a new way of living as neighbors in one human community, as brothers and sisters in one family of creation.

That's why the apostle Paul repeatedly describes how in Christ we see humanity as one body and our differences as gifts, not threats, to one another. In Christ, Paul came to realize that people aren't different because they're trying to be difficult or evil—they're different because the Spirit has given them differing gifts. Just as a foot needs an eye to tell it where to step, and just as a nose needs a hand to grasp the food it smells, and just as feet, eyes, noses, and hands all need kidneys and bones and skin... we humans need other humans who are different from ourselves. The Spirit of God, we learn, is a team spirit, and in the holy team Spirit, we experience a unity that is energized by diversity.

That doesn't mean all our tribes need to wear the same paint and feathers, speak the same language, cook with the same spices, and celebrate the same religious holidays. But it means all our human tribes—nations, religions, cultures, parties—need to convert from what we might call dirty energy to clean energy to fuel our tribal life. True, the dirty energy of fear, prejudice, supremacy, inferiority, resentment, isolation, and hostility is cheap, abundant, and familiar. That's why our societies run on it, even though it's destroying us. More than ever before in our history, we need a new kind of personal and social fuel. Not fear, but love. Not prejudice, but openness. Not supremacy, but service. Not inferiority, but equality. Not resentment, but reconciliation. Not isolation, but connection. Not the spirit of hostility, but the holy Spirit of hospitality.

So the "most excellent way," Paul said, is the way of love. Old markers of gender, religion, culture, and class must recede: "There is neither Jew nor Gentile, slave nor free, male nor female, for you are all one in Christ Jesus." Old tribal indicators, he says, count for nothing: "the only thing that counts is faith working through love." Where the Spirit is, love is. Where the Spirit teaches, people learn love. Faith communities at their best are Spirit-schools of love, engaging everyone, from little children to great-grandparents, in lifelong learning. In the school of the Spirit, everyone majors in love.

Of course, if love remains a generality, it's just a word. That's why the New Testament is serious about translating love into practical, specific, concrete, down-to-Earth action. Because each of us has something to give and much to receive, the term *one another* keeps popping up on page after page of the New Testament. These "one-anothers" tell us what the prime directive—*love one another*—looks like in action:

1. "**Love one another** as I have loved you." (John 13:34; John 15:12, 17; Rom. 13:8; 1 Thess. 4:9; Heb. 13:1; 1 Pet. 1:22, 1 Pet. 3:8, 1 Pet. 4:8; 1 John 3:11, 23; 1 John 4:7, 11; 2 John 1:5)
2. "**Wash one another's feet... serve one another in love.**" (John 13:14, Gal. 5:13)
3. "**Be at peace with each other.**" (Mark 9:50, 1 Thess. 5:13, 1 Pet. 3:8)
4. "**Be devoted to one another** with mutual affection." (Rom. 12:10)
5. "**Honor one another above yourselves.**" (Rom. 12:10)
6. "**Live in harmony with one another.**" (Rom. 12:16)
7. "**Stop passing judgment on one another.**" (Rom. 14:13)
8. "**Accept one another** as Christ accepted you." (Rom. 15:7)
9. "**Greet one another with a holy kiss.**" (Rom. 16:16, 1 Cor. 16:20, 2 Cor. 13:12, 1 Pet. 5:14)
10. "**Agree with one another** so that there may be no divisions among you and that you may be perfectly united in mind and thought." (1 Cor. 1:10)
11. "When you come together to eat, **wait for each other.**" (1 Cor. 11:33)

12. "But God has combined the members of the body and has given greater honor to the parts that lacked it, so that there should be no division in the body, but that its parts should **have equal concern for each other**." (1 Cor. 12:24–25)
13. "**Let us not become conceited, provoking and envying each other.**" (Gal. 5:26)
14. "**Carry each other's burdens**, and in this way you will fulfill the law of Christ." (Gal. 6:2)
15. "Be completely humble and gentle; be patient, **bearing with one another** in love." (Eph. 4:2, Col. 3:13)
16. "**Be kind and compassionate to one another, forgiving each other**, just as in Christ God forgave you." (Eph. 4:32, Col. 3:13, 1 Thess. 5:15)
17. "**Submit to one another** out of reverence for Christ." (Eph. 5:21)
18. "**Do not lie to each other.**" (Col. 3:9)
19. "Let the word of Christ dwell in you richly as you **teach and admonish one another** with all wisdom, and as you sing psalms, hymns, and spiritual songs with gratitude in your hearts to God." (Eph. 5:19, Col. 3:16)
20. "Therefore **encourage one another** and **build each other up**." (1 Thess. 5:11, Heb. 3:13)
21. "And let us consider how we may **spur one another on toward love and good deeds**. Let us not give up meeting together... but let us **encourage one another.**" (Heb. 10:24–25)
22. "Brothers and sisters, **do not slander one another**." (James 4:11)
23. "**Don't grumble against each other.**" (James 5:9)
24. "Therefore **confess your sins to each other** and **pray for each other** so that you may be healed." (James 5:16)
25. "**Offer hospitality to one another without grumbling.**" (1 Pet. 4:9)
26. "**Clothe yourselves with humility toward one another.**" (1 Pet. 5:5)

For all of us who want to be part of the movement of God's Spirit in our world, there is no more important and essential pursuit than love. That's why we walk this road. That's why we seek to improve our fluency and grace in "one-anothering"—especially with people who seem very different from us. For in the story of creation, in the adventure and uprising of Jesus, and in the movement of the Spirit, to love is to live.

ENGAGE:

1. What one thought or idea from today's lesson especially intrigued, provoked, disturbed, challenged, encouraged, warmed, warned, helped, or surprised you?
2. Share a story about a time when someone affirmed one of your unique gifts or abilities, and when you appreciated the unique gifts or abilities of someone else.
3. How do you respond to the list of one-another's?
4. For children: What's something you're really good at, and something you're not so good at?
5. Activate: Take a few minutes with each person around your table to identify and affirm some gifts or virtues you see in them. Have someone place a hand on that person's head or shoulder and pray for the Spirit to fill and empower that person in love.
6. Meditate: In silence, simply hold the term "one another" before God. Open yourself to the depths of meaning in this beautiful term.

CHAPTER FORTY-FOUR

SPIRIT OF LOVE: LOVING SELF

Proverbs 4:1–27
Romans 12:3–21
James 1:2–8; 3:13–18

IF LOVE FOR GOD is always linked with love for others, and if we are to love others *as we love ourselves*, what does it mean to love ourselves? Could the Spirit of God teach us a holy and healthy kind of self-love?

Of course, advertisers and politicians often tempt us to become more *selfish* or *self-centered*—our doing so is often in their *self-interest*. But the Spirit teaches us a profoundly different way of loving ourselves—a way of maturity that involves self-examination, self-control, self-development, and self-giving. These practices of mature self-care enable us to love God and others more fully and joyfully.

Now our struggles with self are often struggles with pleasure, for the self is, among other things, a pleasure-seeking entity. When it comes to pleasure, if you listen to some people, you might conclude that God is a divine killjoy, sitting in heaven with a sourpuss glare, eyes roaming to and fro across the Earth to find anyone who is having fun—especially sexual fun—and *stop it immediately*! If the pleasures of life were compared to the awe of looking into the Grand Canyon, these anxious people worry so much about someone falling over the edge that they erect fences farther and farther back... so far, in fact, that you can no longer enjoy the view!

Pleasure, of course, was originally the Creator's idea. By giving us taste, smell, sound, sight, and touch, God was making possible an amazing array of pleasures: from eating to sex, from music to sport, from painting to gardening, from dance to travel. Human pleasure is a good and beautiful creation, mirroring, it would seem, a great capacity for enjoyment that exists in God. We are told that God takes pleasure in creation and in us, something all parents, teachers, and artists understand in relation to their children, students, and works of art. So again and again in the Bible, we are reminded that our Creator has given us all things to enjoy richly, and that in God's presence is fullness of joy. The Creator is definitely pro-pleasure.

If that's the case, why do we find so many warnings and rules about pleasure in the Bible? Those rules make sense when you realize how easily all life's great pleasures—food, drink, sex, owning, winning, resting, playing, working—can become addictive and destructive. When we indulge in pleasures without self-examination or self-control, great pleasure can quickly lead to great pain—for the addicts themselves and for those whose lives are touched by their addiction.

So rules about pleasures have an important place. The desire center within us that demands "what I want, when I want it, as much as I want" can all too easily become an addictive dictator. We all need to learn to say "No, that's not right," or "No, this isn't the right time," or "No, that's enough for now." Without wise rules and that basic level of self-control to follow them, we'll all be stuck in childish, selfish, self-destructive, and even suicidal immaturity. But the Spirit never gives rules the final word. Living by rules—"law" in the Bible—is at most like primary school.

Primary school has its place, but if we're never allowed to graduate to secondary school, it feels like a prison. So when we're ready, the Spirit always leads us to graduate from rule-oriented primary school to secondary school with its new emphasis: wisdom. From basic questions like *Is this right or wrong, legal or illegal?* we graduate to questions of wisdom: *Will this help or hinder me in reaching my highest goals? Where will this lead short-, medium-, and long-term? What unintended consequences might it entail? Who might be hurt by this? Are there better alternatives? Is now the best time? Should I seek wise counsel before moving forward?*

Wisdom helps us see how a hasty purchase of a desired indulgence can lead to the long-term pressure of debt. Wisdom reminds us that a one-night sexual liaison can lead to lasting tragic consequences for both parties, plus their spouses, children, parents, and many others—literally, for generations to come. Wisdom knows that a single ill-advised business shortcut to increase profits can ruin a reputation earned over decades—as can one careless sentence spoken in anger or dishonesty. Wisdom remembers that habitual overindulgence in alcohol, drugs, tobacco, or even food can greatly shorten your life. And wisdom warns that even one night of drunkenness or one outburst of anger can end your life and the lives of others. Wisdom guides us to see beyond life's immediate pleasures to potential consequences that are less obvious and less pleasant.

Wisdom also helps us see how excessively denying ourselves pleasure can itself become unwise. For example, if a mom and dad are so exhausted from the work of parenting that they forget to keep their romance alive, they can drift apart even though they're sleeping under the same roof. Wisdom guides them to nurture their romance and sexuality so they'll be less vulnerable to infidelity—and so their family will stay in a sustainable, healthy, life-giving balance. The same goes for someone who loves his work and gets great pleasure from it. If he works too much, his life will fall out of balance...and soon he will hate his work. So, a wise person learns that he must find pleasures outside of work so that his work will remain pleasurable rather than addictive. A wise person in this way practices self-care, sometimes stepping on the brakes and sometimes stepping on the accelerator of pleasure.

We all need wisdom to know our limits and keep our balance, to know when to say yes and when to say "That's enough" or "That's unwise" or "This isn't the right time." We need wisdom to know when to ask for help—from a friend or professional—when we are in over our heads. We need wisdom to monitor the difference between legitimate desires and dangerous temptations. We even need wisdom to keep different kinds of pleasure in a healthy and sustainable balance. As a wise teacher said, "Watch over your heart with all diligence, for from it flow the springs of life" (Proverbs 4:23, NASB).

After all, nobody is more likely to ruin your life than you. By pursuing wisdom, you get out of your own way. You learn to be a friend to yourself instead of your own worst enemy. You learn self-examination, self-control, self-development, and self-care—so you can better practice true self-giving toward God and others. Rules are good, wisdom is better, and love is best of all.

Could this be a central purpose of the universe—to provide an environment in which self-control, wisdom, and love can emerge and evolve? Could this be a central purpose in our lives—to mature in self-control, wisdom, and love? And could this be a central purpose of religion and spirituality—to multiply contagious examples of maturity, to create communities where the more mature can mentor others, to build a global Spirit movement toward individual and collective maturity?

So. You have this self. What you do with it matters a lot. You can be self-absorbed, self-contained, self-centered, selfish, self-consumed—and your closed-in self will stagnate, spoil, and deteriorate over time. Or you can engage in Spirit-guided self-examination, self-control, self-development, and self-giving—and your self will open and mature into a person of great beauty and Christ-like maturity.

God, it turns out, isn't a divine killjoy. God wants you to love you the way God loves you, so you can join God in the one self-giving love that upholds you and all creation. If you trust your self to that love, you will become the best self you can be, thriving in aliveness, full of deep joy, part of the beautiful whole. That's the kind of self-care and love of self that is good, right, wise, and necessary. And that's one more reason we walk this road together: to journey ever deeper into the beautiful mystery of the Spirit's love. There we find God. There we find our neighbor. And there we find ourselves.

Engage:

1. What one thought or idea from today's lesson especially intrigued, provoked, disturbed, challenged, encouraged, warmed, warned, helped, or surprised you?
2. Share a story about how a rule, a wise saying, and a mentor have helped you.

3. How do you respond to the idea that if we love ourselves, we will practice self-examination, self-control, self-development, self-care, and self-giving rather than self-indulgence?
4. For children: What are some things that usually make you feel sad, grouchy, happy, and superhappy?
5. Activate: This week, pair up with someone else from this circle and meet privately to talk honestly and confidentially about how you're doing in the areas of self-examination, self-control, self-development, self-care, and self-giving.
6. Meditate: Imagine those who love you most—parents, a spouse, friends, children, and God. Now imagine standing with them as they see and love you. In silence and in God's presence, hold yourself in that kind of love.

CHAPTER FORTY-FIVE

SPIRIT OF UNITY AND DIVERSITY

Proverbs 8:1–36
John 17:1–23
Ephesians 4:1–16

IN THE CENTURIES AFTER Jesus walked this Earth, theologians and mystics who reflected on Jesus' life and teaching were faced with a paradox. They agreed there was only one God as their tradition had taught. But the oneness of the Creator wasn't as flat or static as they had assumed. In Christ and through the Spirit, they came to see that God's unity was so deep and dynamic that it included diversity. And this diversity didn't compromise God's unity but made it more beautiful and wonderful. Over time, they tried to describe this mysterious paradox. After much dialogue and debate, a radically new understanding and teaching about God emerged. They had to create a whole new term to convey it: *Trinity.* There were, naturally, three parts to the teaching.

First, through Jesus and his good news they had come to know and relate to God in a parental way. Like a parent, God was the source of all creation, the giver of all life and existence. God's parental love held all creation in a family relationship. This parental givingness, this reproductive creativity and fertility, this primal motherly and fatherly generosity, they called *God the Father.* There were reasons they only rarely used *motherhood* to describe God back then. Were they here today, they would probably include both *motherhood* and *fatherhood* and speak of *God's parental love.*

Second, in Jesus they came to see a childness in God, a givenness of the child-life corresponding to the givingness of the parent-life. If God the Father gave of God's self, the self-gift was simultaneously God and an offspring, or self-gift, of God. If God the Creator was self-expressive, the self-expression, or Word, was simultaneously God and the Word, or expression, of God. This primal givenness, self-outpouring, or expressivity they called *God the Son*, or *God the Word*.

Through Jesus and his good news, they had also experienced a third reality: the loving, harmonious Spirit that flowed in and between and out from the first and the second. This loving and unifying presence, this primal harmony, this deep, joyful, contagious communion they called *God the Spirit*.

This all sounds highly speculative, but it was a sincere attempt to put into words the radical way they were rethinking and freshly experiencing God in the aftermath of their experience of Jesus. By God's parental love, through Christ's beautiful life, death, and resurrection, and through the Holy Spirit, they felt that they had been caught up into this divine communion themselves. God could never again be for them a distant, isolated One to whom they were "the other." Now they knew God as a dynamic and hospitable one-another in whom they lived, moved, and had their being. The Trinity described how they experienced God "from the inside."

Because they had been trained in Greek philosophy as well as in the Bible, of course they used philosophical language in their deliberations. Sometimes they overestimated the capacity of their philosophical terms to capture God's unfathomable depths. When they erred in this way, they grew proud and used the new teaching of the Trinity as a weapon. But at their best, they remained humble and awestruck by the realization that God was a mystery so big and deep and beautiful that human words could never fully contain it. Like fingers, words could point up and out and in to God, but they could never grasp God like a flipped coin caught in a clenched fist. When they spoke from this humility and awe, the teaching of the Trinity brought healing—reminding us that the word *doctrine* and the word *doctor* share a common root.

This healing teaching began unleashing a revolution that is still unfolding today in at least five distinct but related ways.

First, the teaching of the Trinity leads us beyond *violent* understandings of God. The many Greek and Roman gods of ancient tradition were, truth be told, a gang of overgrown adolescents who had more power than moral maturity. They were competitive and egotistical projections of human nature, glorious and gracious one minute, vindictive and cruel the next. But now, imagine the shift when we understand our source and destiny not as a rivalrous gang but as a loving, nonviolent community.

This insight was revolutionary, because even the Supreme Being of monotheism was often seen as the violent patron of one nation, religion, and culture. Such a Supreme Being typically ruled by instilling fear, making threats, and crushing the noncompliant. But again, imagine the change when our vision of God shifts from a violent dictator to a kind and caring father who loves all and wants the best for all. And imagine how in the Son, or Word, we see God as one who identifies, serves, and suffers with creation as Christ did, who would rather be tortured and killed than torture or kill. And then, imagine how the image of a violent commander sending us into the world to wage war is eclipsed by the image of a gentle, healing, reconciling, purifying, empowering Spirit who descends upon us like a dove. A healing teaching indeed!

Similarly, this healing teaching leads us beyond *fixed* or *frozen* understandings of God. After all, if God in Christ surprised us once, showing us we had a lot left to learn, shouldn't we expect more surprises? And if Jesus told us the Spirit would guide us into more truth when we were ready to bear it, shouldn't we expect to learn more whenever we can bear more? And so the old image fades of God as a removed and unmoved mover, static, fixed, and frozen. In its place, we see God as a whirling, intimate, glorious dance of eternal, creative, joyful movement. What a revolution!

Third, through the Trinity we transcend *us-them, in-out thinking.* Imprisoned in our old familiar dualistic thinking, we were always dividing the world into *mine* and *yours, one* and *other, same* and *different, better* and *worse.* In the Trinity, we move beyond that dualism so that *mine* and *yours* are reconciled into *ours. One* and *other* are transformed into *one another. Same* and *different* are harmonized without being homogenized or colonized. *Us* and *them* are united without loss of identity and without dividing walls of hostility. To put it in philosophical terms, dualism doesn't regress to monism. It is transcended.

The healing teaching of Trinity also helps us transcend *top-down* or *hierarchical* understandings of God. If God's Father-ness elevates and includes Son-ness in full equality, do you see what that means? If God's Son-ness doesn't grasp at equality, but rather mirrors the Father's self-giving and self-emptying love, do you see what that means? If the Spirit is not subordinated as inferior but is honored and welcomed as equal, do you see what that means? God is characterized by equality, empathy, and generosity rather than subordination, patriarchy, and hierarchy.

These four shifts in our understanding predictably lead to a fifth. Our ancestors assumed that God's holiness would be polluted by any contact with imperfection. So in their minds, God was *exclusive* and unwilling to associate with any imperfection. But Jesus, in his habit of eating with "sinners," gave us a new vision of God. God's holiness is drawn to unholiness the way a doctor is drawn to disease. Rather than catching disease, God's holiness "infects" the sick with a chronic case of regenerating health. Rather than being polluted by association with imperfection, God's holiness perfects imperfection. In this way, the healing teaching of Trinity undermines *exclusivist* understandings of God, presenting us with a God who doesn't reject imperfection but embraces it, and in so doing, perfects it and makes it holy.

Sadly, too often our forbears wielded a warped and jagged understanding of the Trinity as a weapon. In so doing, they reinforced violent, static, dualist, hierarchical, and exclusive understandings of God. But it's still not too late. If we open our hearts, we can feel the Spirit guiding us now to let the healing teaching of the Trinity continue its joyful revolution. Perhaps we are now ready to bear it...and to dare to practice it. Because if God is not violent, static, dualist, hierarchical, or exclusive, neither should we be.

To join the movement of the Spirit is to let our Trinitarian tradition continue to live, learn, and grow...so the hostile one-versus-otherness of Earth can become more like the hospitable one-anotherness of heaven. From beginning to end, the Spirit leads us into vibrant diversity and joyful unity in beautiful harmony.

Engage:

1. What one thought or idea from today's lesson especially intrigued, provoked, disturbed, challenged, encouraged, warmed, warned, helped, or surprised you?
2. Share a story about how your understanding of God changed—suddenly or gradually—at some point in your life.
3. How do you respond to the proposal that a deep appreciation of the Trinity can move us beyond violent, static, dualist, hierarchical, and exclusive understandings of God?
4. For children: What do you like about music? What makes music so special?
5. Activate: If the Trinity isn't just a concept to be believed but is a way of life to be practiced, this week, try moving toward the other whenever you can—seeking to show others the honor, love, and respect that are shared among Father, Son, and Spirit.
6. Meditate: Ponder these words from John 17:21: "As you, Father, are in me and I am in you, may they also be in us." Then simply hold the word *us* in reverence before God.

CHAPTER FORTY-SIX

Spirit of Service

Matthew 23:1–12
John 13:1–15
Philippians 2:1–11

The Spirit leads us downward.

That may come as a surprise to people who are raised in a culture that is obsessed with upward mobility. We climb social ladders. We rise to a higher standard of living. We reach for a higher position. We want to be on top. Some use drugs so that whatever their actual circumstances, they will at least feel high. Even our religious communities often have an "up, up, and away" mentality—flying away to heaven, leaving this old Earth below and behind.

But the Spirit leads us downward. To the bottom, to the place of humility, to the position and posture of service... that's where the Spirit, like water, flows.

Jesus modeled this for us. Before Jesus, and even after him, most people assumed that God was at a great distance above us. To approach God meant to leave this world. But Jesus modeled a profoundly different vision. God comes down. God meets us where we are, in our neighborhood, on our level, where we need God most. God descends to the pit of need, suffering, and abandonment. God is not distant from us, aloof, across a chasm, far above looking down. No, God is with us. Here. Now. In reach.

While we race to get to the head of the table, Jesus shocks everyone and takes the role of a servant, washing their feet. While we push and squeeze into the inner circle, Jesus shocks everyone and walks out to the margins to hang out with the outcasts and outsiders. While we struggle to make ourselves rich—often at the expense of others—Jesus shocks everyone. He pours out everything he is and has. While we fight to seize power over others, Jesus empowers others by standing with them in solidarity, by listening to them with respect, by seeking to make them successful, even at great cost to himself.

If you listen to the Spirit, here is what will happen to you. You'll be at a party and you'll notice on one side of the room all the beautiful people laughing and having fun together. In a far corner, you'll notice a person who is alone, feeling awkward, not knowing anyone. The Spirit will draw you to the person in need. You may become the bridge that connects the outsider to the insiders—and in that connection, both will be better off.

If you listen to the Spirit, here is what will happen to you. You'll be in a voting booth or in a position of power. People more powerful than you will appeal to you for your vote, your support, your cooperation. They will have a lot to offer you if you comply. But the Spirit will draw you to use your vote and your power for those who aren't at the table of privilege—the homeless, the sick or infirm in body or mind, the poor, the unemployed, those with special needs, the refugee, the immigrant, the alien, the minority, the different, the odd, the last, the least, the lonely, and the lost. The Spirit will invite you to hear their concerns, take them to heart, and join your heart with theirs.

Here's what will happen to you if you listen to the Spirit. You will realize that someone is angry at you or resentful toward you. You will hear that someone has spread false information about you or worked behind your back to do you harm. Everything in you will want you to write them off or get them back. But the Spirit will draw you toward them in humility. "I have a problem and need your help," you will say. "I feel there may be some tension or distance between us. I want to close the gap and be sure things between us are good." Your opponent may be too angry or insecure to respond well, but whatever happens, know this: the Spirit is at work in you.

Here's what will happen if you listen to the Spirit. You will make a mistake and you will be tempted to cover it up, minimize it, make an excuse for it, hide it from view. But the Spirit will draw you to admit it, first to yourself and to God, and then to those who deserve to know. You will say, "Here's what I did...I was wrong. Will you forgive me?" In that acknowledgment, God will be real. In your humility, God will be present. For the Spirit moves downward.

Here's what will happen if you listen to the Spirit. You will see a person or a group being vilified or scapegoated. Everyone is blaming them, shaming them, gossiping about them, feeling superior to them, venting their anxieties on them. If you join in, you'll feel part of the group. If you are silent, they'll assume you're with them. But the Spirit will draw you to differ courageously and graciously. "I'm sorry," you'll say, "but I see things very differently. I know this person. He is my friend. She is a good person. They are human beings just like us." You will risk your reputation in defending the person or people being scapegoated. And in that risk, both you and they will know that God's Spirit is alive and at work in your midst.

If you listen to the Spirit, here's what will happen to you. It will be late. You will be tired. There will be dishes to do or clothes to pick up or trash to empty. *Someone else should have done this*, you will think with anger. You will rehearse in your mind the speech you will give them. And then you will think, *But I guess they're just as tired and overworked as I am. So maybe I can help.* You won't do this as a manipulative ploy but as a simple act of service. Or maybe, if their negligence is habitual, you won't step in, but you will find a way to gently, kindly, wisely speak to them and help them better fulfill their responsibilities. Either way, as you serve, you will know that God is real, for God is alive in you.

Here's what will happen to you if you listen to the Spirit. You will be in a public place. You will see a person who, by their dress or language or mannerisms, is clearly from another religion, another culture, another social class. That person will be uncomfortable or in need. And you will feel the Spirit inspiring a question within you. "If I were in their shoes—in an unfamiliar or uncomfortable environment, what would I want someone to do for me?" And you will move toward them. You will overcome differences in language or culture. Your kind eyes and warm smile and gentle presence will speak a universal language of neighborliness. And in that moment, they will feel that God is real, for God's Spirit is alive in you.

There is a prison near you. A hospital. A park or a bridge or an alley where homeless people sleep. A playground or shopping center where teenagers hang out and get into trouble. Or there's a country in great need or a social problem that few people notice. If you listen to the Spirit, you will be drawn toward an opportunity to serve. At first, the thought will frighten or repel you. But when you let the Spirit guide you, it will be a source of great joy—one of the richest blessings of your life.

One more thing. There will be times in your life when you will need to be served—not to be the one serving. But even then, you will have the opportunity to appreciate, bless, and thank those who serve you, and in so doing, you and they will experience mutual service, one of life's greatest joys.

The Spirit of God leads downward. Downward in humility. Downward in service. Downward in solidarity. Downward in risk and grace. You used to strive to be cool, but the Spirit makes you warm. You used to strive to climb over others, but the Spirit leads you to wash their feet. You used to strive to fit in among the inner circle, but the Spirit dares you to be different on behalf of the outcasts and outsiders. You don't find God at the top of the ladder. No, you find God through descent. There is a trapdoor at the bottom, and when you fall through it, you fall into God.

It happened to Jesus. It will happen to you, too, if you follow the Spirit's lead.

Engage:

1. What one thought or idea from today's lesson especially intrigued, provoked, disturbed, challenged, encouraged, warmed, warned, helped, or surprised you?
2. Share a story about a time when you served someone else, and about a time when you were served.
3. How do you respond to the specific scenarios presented in the lesson, including the last one about being served?
4. For children: Some people think getting your own way is the greatest thing in life. Other people think helping others is the greatest thing in life. Some people think both are true. What do you think?
5. Activate: This week, be open to the Spirit leading you downward. Come to the next learning circle ready to share your experiences.
6. Meditate: Imagine yourself among the original learning circle of disciples. Jesus comes to wash your feet. Simply let that experience play out in your imagination in silence.

CHAPTER FORTY-SEVEN

THE SPIRIT CONSPIRACY

Ephesians 5:15–6:9
Philemon 1:8–19
Hebrews 13:1–8
James 5:1–6

THERE ARE CIRCLES OF people that the Spirit of God wants to touch and bless, and you are the person through whom the Spirit wants to work. Your mission, should you choose to accept it, is to conspire with the Spirit to bring blessing to others.

Let's start with your family. Nobody is better positioned to wound and harm your spouse than you, and nobody better to love and enhance your spouse's thriving than you. The same goes for your parents, your children, your siblings. The Spirit wants to conspire with you in making their lives rich, full, free, good, and fruitful.

When Jesus wanted to confront religious hypocrisy in his day, he pointed out the way hypocrites served their religion at the expense of their families. Paul picked up this theme in his letters to the early churches, calling such behavior worse than unbelief. So Paul urged husbands and wives to submit to one another and show one another true love and respect. Although his writings may strike us as chauvinistic by today's standards, they were progressive by the standards of his time, because they promoted mutual responsibility, not merely top-down privilege. Similarly, he told children to obey and honor their parents, and parents to nurture their children and raise them without frustrating them—presumably by excessively high or unclear demands. And Paul repeatedly showed special consideration for widows—which today might mean an elderly aunt, uncle, or grandparent, or any family member who is alone and vulnerable.

Paul quickly moved out from the circle of family to what we would call the circle of work. In his day, slavery was a social norm. Where he had the opportunity—as he did with a church leader named Philemon—he urged slave owners to release their slaves and accept them as equals. Where that couldn't be done, he urged slave owners to transcend the normal master-slave relationship and dare to treat their slaves with kindness—to mirror the kindness of God.

Similarly, he urged slaves to transcend social norms by doing their work with pride and dignity. Before, they might have given the least required by a human master. But now in the Spirit, they would work for and with God. They would do whatever was required and even more, giving their best.

James took Paul's concern for a Spirit-led work ethic to the level of business management and economic policy. In strong language, he warned rich employers not to underpay their workers. What employers might call "keeping labor costs low," James called wage theft, and he reminded employers that God hears the cries of every underpaid laborer.

Our economic behavior will change greatly when we stop asking typical questions like "How little will the market or the law allow me to pay this person?" Instead, the Spirit leads people to conspire around new questions like "What would God consider fair and generous pay to this person? How can we expand the bottom line from economic profit to something deeper and broader—economic, social, and ecological benefit? How could our business and economic systems and policies become less harmful and more beneficial to aliveness on planet Earth—for us and for future generations? Could we measure success not by how much we consume and how fast we consume it, but by how well we live, care, and serve?" Just imagine how the business world would change if more and more of us went to work conspiring goodness in the Spirit.

In the next circle out beyond family and work relationships, the Spirit activates our concern for people in our neighborhoods, including strangers we meet on the street. Whatever their race, class, religion, political party, or sexual identity, they, too, are our neighbors, and the Spirit will constantly awaken us to opportunities to serve and care. Biblical writers constantly emphasize the importance of hospitality—especially to strangers. "As you have done for the least of these, you have done for me," Jesus said. So the Spirit is looking for conspirators who are interested in plotting goodness in their communities. "What would our community look like if God's dreams for it were coming true?" we ask. The answer gives us a vision to work toward.

From the circles of family, work, and neighborhood, the Spirit moves us to another sphere of concern: vulnerable people who would normally be forgotten. According to James, our religion is nothing but hot air if we don't translate our faith into action in regards to the vulnerable and easily forgotten around us. So the Spirit invites us to conspire for the well-being of orphans, widows, undocumented aliens, refugees, prisoners, people with special needs, the sick, the poor, the homeless, the uneducated, the unskilled, the unemployed, and the underpaid.

Then there's the still larger circle of our civic and community life. We're told in the New Testament to pray for and show due respect for our political leaders. We're told to avoid debt—except the perpetual debt of love that we owe to every human being. In today's world, that means everyone on the planet, because as never before our world is bound together in one global ecology, one global economy, and one global military-industrial complex. To be in tune with the Spirit is to transcend all smaller boundaries and to conspire in terms of the planetary whole.

There's another circle that we can't dare forget: the circle that includes our critics, opponents, and enemies—the people who annoy us and those we annoy, the people who don't understand us and those we don't understand, the people who try our patience and those whose patience we try. Rather than write them off as unimportant and unwanted, we need to rediscover them as some of the most important people we know. If we ignore them, our growth in the Spirit will be stunted. If we let the Spirit guide us in what we say to their faces and behind their backs, we will become more Christ-like.

Speaking of our words, one of the most important ways the Spirit moves us to care for people in all these circles is by training us to control the tongue. Words can wound, sometimes deeply: careless words, critical words, condemning words, harsh words, insulting words, dehumanizing words, words of gossip or deception. If your life were a ship, your words would be its rudder, James implies (3:1–12). So if you want to be a mature agent in the movement of the Spirit in our world, conspire with the Spirit in your choice of every single word.

You'll never regret forgoing an unkind word. And you'll never regret uttering a kind and encouraging word. An overworked person doing customer service, a housekeeper in a hotel, a landscaper or janitor, a harried mother on a plane with a cranky child, the cashier at a busy fast food joint, your child's third-grade teacher, the nurse in the emergency room—how much could they be encouraged today by a kind word from you, not to mention by a card, a gift, a large tip, a written note? If you're a part of the Spirit's conspiracy, you can be God's secret agent of blessing to anyone in any of these circles.

There's one other circle we haven't mentioned: the circle of your community of faith. It's the learning circle that forms whenever we encourage each other to let the Spirit keep flowing and moving in one another's lives. It's important to keep showing up and to show up with a good attitude. It's especially important to be a channel of blessing to those who lead in your community of faith... being sure they don't have to worry about money, for example, and being sure they feel truly appreciated. Their work is so important and surprisingly hard. Your encouragement could make the difference in whether they give up or keep giving their best.

The largest circle of all extends beyond humans and includes all living things and the physical structures on which we all depend: air, rain, soil, wind, climate. You can't claim to love your neighbor and pollute the environment on which he depends. You can't claim to love the Creator and abuse the climate of this beautiful, beloved planet. The Spirit that moves among us is the same Spirit that moves in and through all creation. If we are attuned to the Spirit, we will see all creatures as our companions... even as our relatives in the family of God, for in the Spirit we are all related.

In all these circles, you can be part of the Spirit conspiracy that is spreading quietly across our world. Your mission, should you choose to accept it, is to be a secret agent of God's commonwealth, conspiring with others behind the scenes to plot goodness and foment kindness wherever you may be.

ENGAGE:

1. What one thought or idea from today's lesson especially intrigued, provoked, disturbed, challenged, encouraged, warmed, warned, helped, or surprised you?
2. Share a story about a time when you felt the Spirit guided you to go above and beyond your normal way of responding to a situation.
3. How do you respond to the idea that our words are a rudder that steers our lives?
4. For children: Could you share a story about a time someone used words that hurt your feelings? And could you share a story about a time someone used words that made you feel wonderful?
5. Activate: Choose one of the circles from this lesson and make it your focus in the week ahead.
6. Meditate: In your imagination, walk through a typical day, from waking up to going to bed at night. Imagine yourself as a portal of blessing in each circle of influence. Simply pray, "Let it be so."

CHAPTER FORTY-EIGHT

SPIRIT OF POWER

Acts 4:1–31
1 Thessalonians 5:1–11
2 Timothy 1:1–14
Ephesians 6:10–20

SOONER OR LATER, EVERYONE should be arrested and imprisoned for a good cause. Or if not arrested and imprisoned, put in a position of suffering and sacrifice. Or if not that, at least be criticized or inconvenienced a little. Because if we're coconspirators with the Spirit of God to bring blessing to our world, sooner or later it's going to cost us something and get us in trouble.

Jesus told his followers to "count the cost." He promised that those who walk his road would experience push-back, even persecution. And he often described that push-back as demonic or Satanic in nature. Some people today believe Satan and demons to be literal, objective realities. Others believe they are outmoded superstitions. Still others interpret Satan and demons as powerful and insightful images by which our ancestors sought to describe shadowy realities that are still at work today. In today's terminology, we might call them social, political, structural, ideological, and psychological forces. These forces take control of individuals, groups, and even whole civilizations, driving them toward destruction.

Think of it like this: You can have a crowd of normal, happy people dancing in a popular night club. Suddenly someone shouts, "Fire!" and people panic. Within seconds, everyone stampedes towards the exits. Soon, some people are being trampled—even killed—in the chaos, which means that others are doing the trampling and killing. None of the happy dancers in that club would have been seen as heartless killers before the scare. But we might say "the spirit of panic" possessed them and drove them to violence. That spirit had a will of its own, as it were, turning peaceful, decent individuals into a ruthless, dangerous mob that became every bit as dangerous as the threat it feared.

Now, imagine a similar spirit of racism, revenge, religious supremacy, nationalism, political partisanship, greed, or fear getting a foothold in a community. You can imagine previously decent people being possessed, controlled, and driven by these forces, mind-sets, or ideologies. Soon, individuals aren't thinking or feeling for themselves anymore. They gradually allow the spirit of the group to possess them. If nobody can break out of this frenzy, it's easy to imagine tragic outcomes: vandalism, riots, beatings, lynchings, gang rapes, house demolitions, plundered land, exploited or enslaved workers, terrorism, dictatorship, genocide. Bullets can fly, bombs explode, and death tolls soar—among people who seemed so decent, normal, and peace loving just minutes or months before.

You don't need to believe in literal demons and devils to agree with Jesus and the apostles: there are real and mysterious forces in our world that must be confronted. But how? If we respond to violence with violence, anger with anger, hate with hate, or fear with fear, we'll soon be driven by the same unhealthy and unholy forces that we detest and are trying to resist. To make matters worse, we'll be the last to know what's driving us, because we'll feel so pure and justified in our opposition. "We must be good and holy," we will say to ourselves, "because what we're fighting against is so evil!"

We can see in this light why ancient people described Satan as a deceiver, an accuser, and a liar. When we allow ourselves to come under the spell of an ideology or a similar force, we feel utterly convinced that evil is over there among *them*, and only moral rightness is here among *us*. In this accusatory state of mind, focused so exclusively on the faults of our counterparts, we become utterly blind to our own deteriorating innocence and disintegrating morality. Even when we begin to inflict harm on those we accuse, we are unable to see our actions as harmful. Self-deceived in this way, we lie to ourselves and live in denial about what we have become.

That's why Paul had so much to say about "spiritual warfare" against "the principalities and powers" that rule the world. He kept reminding the disciples that they weren't struggling against flesh-and-blood people. They were struggling against invisible systems and structures of evil that possess and control flesh-and-blood people. The real enemies back then and now are invisible realities like racism, greed, fear, ambition, nationalism, religious supremacy, and the like—forces that capture decent people and pull their strings as if they were puppets to make them do terrible things.

In that light, being filled with and guided by the Holy Spirit takes on profound meaning—and practical importance. Where unholy, unhealthy spirits or value systems judge and accuse, the Holy Spirit inspires compassion and understanding. Where unholy, unhealthy spirits or movements drive people toward harming others, the Holy Spirit leads us to boldly and compassionately stand up for those being harmed. Where unholy, unhealthy spirits or ideologies spread propaganda and misinformation, the Holy Spirit boldly speaks the simple truth. Where unholy, unhealthy spirits or mind-sets spread theft, death, and destruction, God's Holy Spirit spreads true aliveness.

How do we resist being "possessed" by the unholy, unhealthy systems that are so prevalent and powerful in today's world? Sometimes it's as simple—and difficult—as responding to harsh words with a kind, disarming spirit. When a website vilifies a group, for example, you might add a gentle, vulnerable comment: "You're talking about people I count among my closest friends." When a religious group, overly confident in its own purity or rightness, condemns others, you might humbly and unargumentatively quote a relevant Scripture: "Whoever thinks he stands should take care, lest he fall," or "Knowledge puffs up, but love builds up." When powerful forces organize to do harm, you may need to form or join some sort of collective, nonviolent action—a march, a boycott or buy-cott, a protest, even nonviolent civil disobedience. Whether in small, quiet ways or big, dramatic ones, if we join the Spirit in the ongoing mission of Jesus, we won't be overcome by evil; we will overcome evil with good.

But don't expect overcoming evil with good to be popular, easy, convenient, or safe, as Paul's words to his young protégé, Timothy, make clear:

"God has not given us a spirit of cowardice but of power, love, and a sound mind." When people are threatening you, hating you, and calling you a heretic, an infidel, or worse—a bold and courageous spirit of empowerment, love, and a sound mind is exactly what you need!

Paul, of course, spoke from personal experience. He had once been a confident, accusatory, violent persecutor of those he considered evil—utterly sure of himself, utterly convinced of his moral rightness in all he did. When he encountered Jesus and was filled with the Holy Spirit, he soon became the one being persecuted. The Spirit gave him nonviolent boldness to face repeated arrests, beatings, imprisonments, and ultimately, according to tradition, beheading by Nero in Rome. Clearly, for Paul, being a leader in the Spirit's movement wasn't a boring desk job!

No wonder one of their most oft-repeated themes in the New Testament is to *suffer graciously*, echoing Jesus' words about turning the other cheek. In 1 Peter 2:21 and 23 (CEB), for example, we read, "Christ left you an example so that you might follow in his footsteps... When he was insulted, he did not reply with insults. When he suffered, he did not threaten revenge. Instead, he entrusted himself to the one who judges justly." To do that takes courage and power. It takes love. And it takes a sound—or nonreactive—mind. In other words, it takes the Holy Spirit.

As we walk this road together, we are being prepared and strengthened for struggle. We're learning to cut the strings of "unholy spirits" that have been our puppet masters in the past. We're learning to be filled, led, and guided, not by a spirit of fear but by the Holy Spirit instead... a spirit of power, love, and a sound mind to face with courage whatever crises may come.

When a crisis hits, unprepared people may be paralyzed with fear, but we'll set an example of confidence and peace. Unprepared people may not know where to turn, but we'll have this circle of peace in which to welcome them. Unprepared people may turn on one another and pull apart, but we'll turn toward one another and pull together. Unprepared people may withdraw into survival mode, but we'll have strength enough to survive, and more to share. Through the Spirit, we will have unintimidated power, unfailing love, and a sound, nonreactive mind. When necessary, we will suffer graciously. For we will know that for us, whatever happens, even the end of the world… isn't really the end of the world.

Engage:

1. What one thought or idea from today's lesson especially intrigued, provoked, disturbed, challenged, encouraged, warmed, warned, helped, or surprised you?
2. Share a story about a time where you suffered in some way for standing up for what was right, or when someone else paid a price for standing up for you.
3. How do you respond to the idea that racism, revenge, religious supremacy, tribalism, political partisanship, fear, or economic greed can "possess" people?
4. For children: What would you do to help a child who is being bothered by a bully?
5. Activate: All of us can't do everything or fight every injustice everywhere. But we all should have "some skin in the game" on a handful of issues about which we feel a special call to action. Identify some of your issues and look for ways to stand up for them this week.
6. Meditate: Imagine your life as a tree in a storm. Imagine deep roots, a strong trunk, and flexible branches. After holding this image for a few moments, ask God for the strength to stand bold and strong against whatever adversity may come.

CHAPTER FORTY-NINE

SPIRIT OF HOLINESS

Psalm 98
John 14:15–18, 25–27; 15:26–27; 16:33
1 Corinthians 3:9–15; 15:20–28

JESUS PROMISED HIS FOLLOWERS three things. First, their lives would not be easy. Second, they would never be alone. Third, in the end, all will be well.

But all is not well now, and that raises the question of how...how does God get us from here to there? How does God put things right?

The word in the Bible for putting things right is *judgment.* Unfortunately, many today, drawing from the concept of a judge in today's court system, understand *judgment* to mean nothing more than condemnation and punishment. In contrast, in biblical times, good judges did more than condemn or punish. They worked to set things right, to restore balance, harmony, and well-being. Their justice was restorative, not just punitive. The final goal of judgment was to curtail or convert all that was evil so that good would be free to run wild.

It's obvious to everyone that this kind of justice doesn't always happen in a satisfying way in this life. So people of faith have trusted that God can continue to set things right on the other side of the threshold of death. Through the idea of final judgment, we have dared to hope that somehow, beyond what we see in history, restorative justice could have the last word.

Final judgment, or final restoration, means that God's universe arcs toward universal repentance, universal reconciliation, universal purification, universal "putting wrong things right." That means more than saying that everything that can be punished will be punished: it means that everything that can be restored will be restored. It means the disease will be treated and healed, not just diagnosed. It means everything will, in God's ultimate justice, not only be evaluated: it will be given new value.

So when we say, with the writer of Hebrews (Hebrews 9:27), that "it is appointed for mortals to die once, and after that the judgment," we are not saying, "and after this, the condemnation." We are saying, "after this, the setting right." With John, we dare to believe that to "see God as God is," to be in God's unspeakable light, will purge us of all darkness:

> How great is the love the Father has lavished on us, that we should be called children of God! And that is what we are!... Dear friends, now we are children of God, and what we will be has not yet been made known. But we know that when he appears, we shall be like him, for we shall see him as he is. All who have this hope in them purify themselves, just as God is pure. (1 John 3:1–3)

Since "what we will be has not yet been made known," it is hard to say anything more, except this: in the end, God will be all in all, and all will be well.

Does that mean there will be no cost, no loss, no regret, no mourning? This is where the so-often misused image of fire comes in. Many a hellfire-and-brimstone preacher has depicted fire as an instrument of torture, but it is far better understood as an instrument of purification. Paul describes it this way: God's purifying fire can't consume "gold, silver, and precious stones," because in so doing, God would be destroying something good, which would render God evil. The cleansing or refining fire of God must destroy only the "wood, hay, and stubble" of hypocrisy, evil, and sin.

So if some of us have constructed our lives like a shoddy builder, using worthless building materials, there won't be much of our life's story left. We will experience the purification of judgment as loss, regret, remorse.

We thought we were pretty smart, powerful, superior, or successful, but the purifying fire will surprise us with the bitter truth. In contrast, others of us who thought ourselves nothing special will be surprised in a positive way. Thousands of deeds of kindness that we had long forgotten will have been remembered by God, and we will feel the reward of God saying, "Welcome into my joy!"

This understanding of God's restorative judgment changes the way you live before death. It makes you eager to use your wealth to make others rich, not to hoard it. It inspires you to use your power to empower others, not to advance yourself. It liberates you to give and give so that you will finish this life having given more than you received. It encourages you to try to be secretive about your good deeds because you would rather defer the return on your investment to the future. In fact, this hope makes you willing to give up this life, if necessary, for things that matter more than survival.

And this hope also changes the way we see trials and difficulties in this life. If we see trials and difficulties not as a punishment for our wrongs, but as a refining fire to strengthen and purify us, trials become our friends, not our enemies. So, in this light, delay is like a fire that burns away our impatience. Annoyances are like flames that burn away our selfishness. The demands of duty are like degrees of heat that burn away our laziness. The unkind words and deeds of others are like a furnace in which our character is tempered, until we learn to bless, not curse, in response. It's not even worth comparing our short-term trials, Paul said, to the long-term glory that comes from enduring them. Whatever we face—ease or struggle, life or death, Paul's encouragement is the same: "Therefore, my beloved, be steadfast, immovable, always excelling in the work of the Lord, because you know that in the Lord your labor is not in vain."

If we believe in judgment—in God's great "setting things right," we won't live in fear. We'll keep standing strong with a steadfast, immovable determination, and we'll keep excelling in God's good work in our world. If we believe the universe moves toward purification, justice, and peace, we'll keep seeking to be pure, just, and peaceable now. If we believe God is pure light and goodness, we'll keep moving toward the light each day in this life. Then, someday, when our time comes to close our eyes in death, we will trust ourselves to the loving Light in which we will awaken, purified, beloved, forever.

Until then, the Spirit leads us along in that arc toward restoration and healing. Like a mother in childbirth, groaning with pain and anticipation, the Spirit groans within us. She will not rest until all is made whole, and all is made holy, and all is made well.

Life will not be easy. We will never be alone. In the end all will be well. That is all we know, and all we need to know. Amen.

Engage:

1. What one thought or idea from today's lesson especially intrigued, provoked, disturbed, challenged, encouraged, warmed, warned, helped, or surprised you?
2. Share a story about a time when what seemed impossible became possible and then actual for you.
3. How do you respond to the idea that life's troubles are like a refining or purifying fire?
4. For children: What are some of the places where you feel most peaceful and safe? What makes those places so special?
5. Activate: This week, hold on to the hope that God is setting things right. Notice what effect this hope has in your inner life and outer behavior.
6. Meditate: Imagine a refiner's fire. As you picture that image of heat and purification, ask yourself what areas of your life are being purified these days. Hold those areas up to God.

CHAPTER FIFTY

SPIRIT OF LIFE

Psalm 90
Luke 20:27–38
Philippians 1:20–30

WE ALL WILL DIE someday. Mortality rates remain at 100 percent, and nobody among us is getting any younger. Among the Spirit's many essential movements in our lives is this: to prepare us for the end of our lives, without fear.

So many us are afraid to even think about death, much less speak of it. That fear can enslave us and can rob us of so much aliveness. The Spirit moves within us to help us face death with hope, not fear... with quiet confidence, not anxiety. "The law of the Spirit of life in Christ Jesus," Paul said (Romans 8:2), "has set you free from the law of sin and of death."

Here's a way to think about death. We often speak of God as the one who was, who is, and who is to come. The God who *was* holds all our past. The God who *is* surrounds us now. And the God who *is to come* will be there for us beyond this life as we know it. With that realization in mind, death could never mean leaving God, because there is nowhere we can escape from God's presence, as the psalmist said (139:7). Instead, death simply means leaving the presence of God in this little neighborhood of history called the present. Through death, we join God in the vast, forever-expanding future, into which both past and present are forever taken up.

Some religious scholars tried to trap Jesus once by bringing up a conflict between moral sense and belief in the afterlife. If there is life after death, they asked, does that mean that a woman who was widowed seven times in this life will have seven husbands in the next? You can almost see them smirking, thinking themselves very clever for stumping the rabbi. In response, Jesus said that to God, all who ever lived are alive (Luke 20:38). In that light, death is merely a doorway, a passage from one way of living in God's presence in the present to another way of living in God's presence—in the open space of unseized possibility we call the future.

We've all heard the cliché about someone being "so heavenly minded he's no earthly good," and maybe we've met people on whom the cliché fits like an old bedroom slipper. But there is also a way of being so earthly minded that you're no earthly good. And there's a way of being heavenly minded so that you are more earthly good than you ever could have been any other way. To be liberated from the fear of death—think of how that would change your values, perspectives, and actions. To believe that no good thing is lost, but that all goodness will be taken up and consummated in God—think of how that frees you to do good without reservation. To participate in a network of relationships that isn't limited by death in the slightest degree—think of how that would make every person matter and how it would free you to live with boundless, loving aliveness.

So what might we expect to happen when we die? Nobody knows for sure, but in light of Jesus' death and resurrection, we can expect to experience death as a passage, like birth, the end of one life stage and the beginning of another. We don't know how that passing will come... like a slow slipping away in disease, like a sudden jolt or shock in an accident. However it happens, we can expect to discover that we're not falling out of life, but deeper into it.

On the other side, we can expect to experience as never before the unimaginable light or energy of God's presence. We will enter into a goodness so good, a richness so rich, a holiness so holy, a mercy and love so strong and true that all of our evil, pride, lust, greed, resentment, and fear will be instantly melted out of us. We will at that moment more fully understand how much we have been forgiven, and so we will more than ever be filled with love... love for God who forgives, and with God, love for everyone and everything that has like us been forgiven.

We can expect to feel a sense of reunion—yes, with loved ones who have died, but also with our great-great-great-great-grandparents and our thirty-second cousins a thousand times removed whose names we've never known but to whom we are in fact related. That sense of relatedness that we now feel with closest of kin will somehow be expanded to every person who has ever lived. And that sense of relatedness won't stop with human beings, but will expand infinitely outward to all of God's creation. We can expect to feel the fullest, most exquisite sense of oneness and interrelatedness and harmony—a sense of belonging and connection that we approached only vaguely or clumsily in our most ecstatic moments in this life.

We can expect to feel differently about our sufferings. We will see not the short-term pain that so preoccupied us on the past side of death but instead the enduring virtue, courage, and compassion that have been forged in us through each fall of the hammer on the anvil of pain. So we will bless our sufferings and feel about them as we feel about our pleasures now. What has been suffered or lost will feel weightless compared to the substance that has been gained.

We can expect to feel a limitless sense of "Ah yes, now I see." What we longed for, reached for, touched but couldn't grasp, and knew in part will then be so clear. And all of our unfulfilled longing on this side of death will, we can expect, enrich and fulfill the having on that side of death. We can expect to feel as if we're waking up from being half asleep, waking into an explosion of pure, utter gratitude as we suddenly and fully realize all we've had and taken for granted all along.

You may imagine that dying will be like diving or falling or stepping into a big wave at the beach. You will feel yourself lifted off your feet and taken up into a swirl and curl and spin more powerful than you can now imagine. But there will be no fear, because the motion and flow will be the dance of Father, Son, and Holy Spirit. The rising tide will be life and joy. The undertow will be love, and you will be drawn deeper and deeper in.

We normally don't look forward to the process of dying, and most of us would be happy if the dying process is as short and painless as possible. But if we allow the Spirit to prepare us for dying by contemplating it in these ways, we can begin to understand the dual pull that Paul wrote about: "For me to live is Christ but to die is gain." On the one hand, we feel a pull to stay here in this life, enjoying the light and love and goodness of God with so many people who are dear to us, with so much good work left to be done. On the other hand, we feel an equal and opposite pull toward the light and love and goodness of God experienced more directly beyond this life.

Many of us remember the experience as children of "waiting your turn." Maybe it was waiting your turn to ride a pony at the county fair, or waiting your turn to play a game, or waiting your turn to ride a sled down a hill in winter snow. Imagine the feeling of having had your turn on this Earth and having enjoyed it thoroughly. Now, you are ready to step aside to let someone else have their turn. In that way, even dying can be an act of love and generosity: vacating space to make room for others, especially generations as yet unborn, just as others vacated their space so you could have your turn in this life. Perhaps the act of letting others have their turn will be one of our most mature and generous actions, a fitting end to our adventure in this life. At that moment, it will be our turn to graduate into a new adventure, beyond all imagining.

As we walk this road, we not only remember the past, we also anticipate the future, which is described as a great banquet around God's table of joy. When you pass from this life, do not be afraid. You will not pass into death. You will pass through death into a greater aliveness still—the banquet of God. Trust God, and live.

Engage:

1. What one thought or idea from today's lesson especially intrigued, provoked, disturbed, challenged, encouraged, warmed, warned, helped, or surprised you?
2. Share a story about one of your significant encounters with death.
3. How do you respond to the idea that people are enslaved by the fear of death?
4. For children: Tell us about someone in your family who died. What do you remember about them, or what have you learned about them from people who knew them?

5. Activate: Set a time this week to meet with another member of your learning circle in private. Create space to listen to one another talk freely about your own deaths, in light of this lesson.
6. Meditate: Take one of the images of death from this lesson—being caught up in a wave, falling through this life into deeper life, waking up, birth, passing through a doorway—and hold it in God's presence until you feel death can be your friend, not your enemy.

CHAPTER FIFTY-ONE

SPIRIT OF HOPE

Psalm 126
Revelation 1:9–19; 19:11–16; 21:1–8; 22:16–21

THE LAST BOOK IN the Bible is the Book of Revelation, also known as the Apocalypse (or unveiling). Some people ignore it, wondering why such an odd composition was even included in the biblical library. Other people seem obsessed by it. They are certain that it is a coded "history of the future," telling us how the world will someday end.

That way of reading Revelation is based on a lot of assumptions that deserve to be questioned. For example, did God create a closed and predetermined universe, or a free and participatory one? Is the future a movie that has already been shot, so to speak, and we are just watching it play? Or is the future open, inviting us not simply to resign ourselves and adapt, but to be protagonists who invent, improvise, and help create the outcome as God's coworkers and fellow actors?

Having left behind the "roadmap of the future" way of reading Revelation, more and more of us are rediscovering it in a fresh way. The first step in this fresh approach is to put the text back in its historical context. Our best scholars agree it was composed during the bloody reign of either Nero in the AD 60s or Domitian in the AD 90s. Life was always hard in the Roman empire for poor people, as it was for most of the followers of Jesus. But life was extremely precarious when the man at the helm of the empire was vicious, paranoid, and insane, as both Nero and Domitian were. Life got even tougher when the madman on the throne demanded to be worshiped as a god, something followers of Jesus would never do.

Under these circumstances, you can imagine the followers of Christ thinking something like this: *Jesus has been gone now for decades. The world doesn't seem to be getting better. If anything, with a mad dictator in Rome, it's getting worse. Maybe Jesus was wrong... maybe it's time for us to forget about this "turn the other cheek and love your enemies" business. Maybe we need to take matters into our own hands and strap on a sword to fight for our future. Or maybe we should just eat, drink, make a buck, and be merry, because tomorrow we might all be dead.*

In this light, Revelation was the very opposite of a codebook that mapped out the end of the world in the distant future. It addressed the crisis at hand. Even if the emperor is mad, Revelation claimed, it's not the end of the world. Even if wars rage, it's not the end of the world. Even if peace-loving disciples face martyrdom, it's not the end of the world. Even if the world as we know it comes to an end, that ending is also a new beginning. Whatever happens, God will be faithful and the way of Christ—a way of love, non-violence, compassion, and sustained fervency—will triumph.

Along with its historical context, we would be wise to understand the literary context for Revelation, which is *literature of the oppressed*. Literature of the oppressed arises among people living under dictatorships who have no freedom of speech. If they dare to criticize the dictator, they'll be "disappeared" and never seen again. Before being executed, they may be brutally tortured so their oppressors can extract names of others they should go arrest, torture, and elicit still more names from. No wonder people learn to be silent in a dictatorship.

But being silent in the presence of injustice feels like a way of cooperating with it.

As literature of the oppressed, the Book of Revelation provided early disciples with a clever way of giving voice to the truth—when freedom of speech was dangerous in one way, and remaining silent was dangerous in another. Instead of saying, "The Emperor is a fraud and his violent regime cannot stand," which would get them arrested, Revelation tells a strange story about a monster who comes out of the sea and is defeated. Instead of saying, "The religious establishment is corrupt," it tells a story about a whore. Instead of naming today's Roman empire as being doomed, they talk about a past empire—Babylon—that collapsed in failure.

If we keep reading Revelation as a road map of a predetermined future, the consequences can be disastrous. For example, we may read the vision of Jesus coming on a white horse (Rev. 19:11 ff.) and think that's about a Jesus completely different from the one we met in the gospels. This Jesus won't be a peace-and-love guy anymore but a violence-and-revenge guy. What might happen if we leave the peace-and-love Jesus in the past and follow a violence-and-revenge Jesus into the future?

We may read about people being thrown into a lake of fire at the end of Revelation (20:7 ff.), and if we take it literally, we may see God as some kind of a sadistic torturer. If God tortures for eternity, might it be OK for us to do the same in our next war or political upheaval? Or if we interpret literally the passage in Revelation (21:1) that makes it sound like the Earth will be destroyed, might we think, *Hey, why worry about overconsumption, environmental destruction, or climate change? God is going to destroy the world soon anyway, so we might as well pitch in!* There is a high cost to reading Revelation outside its historical and literary context.

People who read Revelation without understanding that context tend to miss some telling details. For example, when Jesus rides in on the white horse, his robes are bloodstained and he carries a sword. Many have interpreted this scene as a repudiation of Jesus' nonviolence in the gospels. But they miss the fact that he carries his sword in his mouth, not his hand. Instead of predicting the return of a killer Messiah in the future, Revelation recalls the day in the past when Jesus rode into Jerusalem on a donkey. His humble words of peace, love, and justice will, Revelation promises, prove more powerful than the bloody swords of violent emperors. In addition, we notice his robe is bloodstained before the battle begins, suggesting that the blood on his robe is not the blood of his enemies, but is his own, shed in self-giving love. In that light, Revelation reinforces rather than overturns the picture we have of Jesus in Matthew, Mark, Luke, and John.

There's a beautiful visionary scene at the end of the Book of Revelation that is as relevant today as it was in the first century. It doesn't picture us being evacuated from Earth to heaven as many assume. It pictures a New Jerusalem descending from heaven to Earth. This new city doesn't need a temple because God's presence is felt everywhere. It doesn't need sun or moon because the light of Christ illuminates it from within. Its gates are never shut, and it welcomes people from around the world to receive the treasures it offers and bring the treasures they can offer. From the center of the city, from God's own throne, a river flows—a river of life or aliveness. Along its banks grows the Tree of Life. All of this, of course, evokes the original creation story and echoes God's own words in Revelation: "Behold! I'm making all things new!"

Rather than giving its original readers and hearers a coded blueprint of the future, Revelation gave them visionary insight into their present situation. It told them that the story of God's work in history has never been about escaping Earth and going up to heaven. It has always been about God descending to dwell among us. Faithfulness wasn't waiting passively for a future that had already been determined. Faithfulness meant participating with God in God's unfolding story. God wasn't a distant, terrifying monster waiting for vengeance at the end of the universe. God was descending among us here and now, making the tree of true aliveness available for all.

What was true for Revelation's original audience is true for us today. Whatever madman is in power, whatever chaos is breaking out, whatever danger threatens, the river of life is flowing now. The Tree of Life is bearing fruit now. True aliveness is available now. That's why Revelation ends with the sound of a single word echoing through the universe. That word is not *Wait!* Nor is it *Not Yet!* or *Someday!* It is a word of invitation, welcome, reception, hospitality, and possibility. It is a word not of ending, but of new beginning. That one word is *Come!* The Spirit says it to us. We echo it back. Together with the Spirit, we say it to everyone who is willing. *Come!*

ENGAGE:

1. What one thought or idea from today's lesson especially intrigued, provoked, disturbed, challenged, encouraged, warmed, warned, helped, or surprised you?

2. Share a story about an invitation that changed your life.
3. How do you respond to the idea of Revelation being literature of the oppressed?
4. For children: What is something you are looking forward to, and why?
5. Activate: Whenever you think of the future this week, listen for the Spirit's invitation to enter the future with hope: *Come!*
6. Meditate: Imagine creation inviting God, and God inviting creation, through that powerful word *Come!* Hold that mutual invitation in your heart.

CHAPTER FIFTY-TWO

God in the End

Luke 15:11–32
Romans 8:31–39
1 Corinthians 15:50–58

Astronomers tell us that in a little less than eight billion years, our sun will turn into a red dwarf and Earth will be incinerated. Before that time, they offer a number of other scenarios that could wipe out human civilization on our planet—a massive comet or asteroid, a black hole, or a hypernova elsewhere in our galaxy, not to mention likely fruits of human stupidity in the form of nuclear or biological warfare, climate catastrophe, and environmental collapse.

Somewhere between science and science fiction is the possibility of escaping Earth and populating other planets elsewhere in the universe if we ruin this one. But even if we manage a "Plan B," scientists suspect that the entire universe is winding down. It will eventually end either in a Big Freeze or a Big Crunch, after which there will be nobody left to remember that any of this ever existed. If this prediction is the whole truth, our unremembered lives and their illusory meaning will be reduced to nothing, gone forever—utterly, absolutely, infinitely gone.

In the biblical library, in contrast, neither Big Freeze nor Big Crunch gets the last annihilating word. Instead, we are given an ultimate vision of a Big Celebration. From Genesis to Revelation we find the story of an infant universe into which is born an infant humanity that grows, comes of age, makes mistakes, learns lessons, and finally reaches maturity. Like most coming-of-age stories, this one ends with a wedding, as humanity welcomes God into its heart.

What could such a story mean? What could it mean to us right now? Jesus gave us a clue in one of his best-known but least-understood parables. In it, human history can be seen as the story of a family, a father and two sons. The family experiences conflict. The rebellious younger son runs away and for a while forgets his true identity. The dutiful older son stays home but also forgets his true identity. The younger son reaches a crisis and comes home. He is welcomed by the father, which then creates a crisis for the older son. Of course, the story isn't only about the identity crises of the sons. It also reveals the true identity of the father, whose heart goes out to both brothers, who graciously loves them even when they don't know it, and even when they don't love each other. The story ends with a celebration—a welcome-home party, a reunion party.

Like many of our best stories, it doesn't have to be factual to tell the truth, and its ending is left unresolved. Will the older brother remain outside, nursing his petty resentments? Or will he come inside to join the Big Celebration and rediscover his true identity in the family? We find ourselves cheering for him: "Come inside, man! Come on! Don't hold back! Come in!" That word *come*, interestingly, is the same word we find echoing at the end of the last book in the biblical library.

If we enter this story and let it do its work on us, we can look out from within it and see ourselves and all creation held in the parental love of God. We can empathize with God, who wants all to come, all to enjoy the feast, all to discover or rediscover their true identity in God's family, in God's love.

This short parable is one of the best mirrors of humanity ever composed. In it, both the rebellious and the religious can see themselves. But more important, it is one of the best windows into God ever composed, because it shows a gracious and spacious heart that welcomes all to the table.

Can you see why it is so good and right for us to pause as we walk this road to gather around a table to celebrate God's love? At this table, we look *back* to Jesus, remembering all he said and did to help us see and enter God's great feast. And at this table, we look *around* at one another, seeing one another—and being seen—with God's eyes of love, as sisters and brothers, part of one human family.

And no less important, at this table we look *forward* to a festive celebration that beckons us from the future. The story began in God's creative love, and it ends in God's creative love, too... if such an ending can even be called an ending. Perhaps it is most true to say that any story with God in it is a story that never, ever ends.

The Big Freeze or Big Crunch predictions of the astronomers may be accurate on some limited level, but they don't have the right instruments to detect the widest, deepest dimensions of reality. It takes stories like the ones we have been exploring to help us imagine those deeper and bigger dimensions.

Imagine a moment before the Big Bang banged. Imagine a creativity, brilliance, fertility, delight, energy, power, glory, wisdom, wonder, greatness, and goodness sufficient to express itself in what we know as the universe. Try to imagine it, even though you know you cannot: a creative imagination and energy so great that it would produce light, gravity, time, and space... galaxies, stars, planets, and oceans... mountains, valleys, deserts, and forests... cobia, bison, dragonflies, and meadowlarks... gorillas, dolphins, golden retrievers, and us.

And then dare to imagine that this is the great, big, beautiful, mysterious goodness, wholeness, and aliveness that surrounds us and upholds us even now.

Finally, try to imagine that this is also the great, big, beautiful, mysterious goodness, wholeness, and aliveness into which all of us and all creation will be taken up—in a marriage, in a homecoming, in a reunion, in a celebration.

We inherited various words to name this ultimate mystery. In English, *God.* In Spanish, *Dios.* In French, *Dieu.* In Russian, *Bog.* In Mandarin, *Thianzhu. Mungu* in Swahili. *Allah* in Arabic. *Edoda* in Cherokee. *Elohim* and *Adonai* and many others in Hebrew. *Wakan Tanka* in Sioux, and so on. So many books have been written to describe and define this mystery. And sadly, so many arguments and inquisitions have been launched and wars waged over it, too. But here in Jesus' parable, as in the closing chapters of Revelation, we get a window into its true heart, its intention, its flow. The whole story flows toward reconciliation, not in human creeds or constitutions, but in love, the love of the One who gave us being and life. We can boast of knowing the "right" name and still have the wrong understanding. But if we have eyes to see and ears to hear, the great, big, beautiful, wonderful, holy, mysterious, reconciling heart of God waits to be discovered and experienced.

So our journey in the story of creation, the adventure of Jesus, and the global uprising of the Spirit has come full circle. It all came from God in the beginning, and now it all comes back to God in the end.

Big Bang to Big Death? Or Big Bang to Big Celebration? If the biblical story is true, it is the latter. In the end as Paul envisioned it, death is swallowed up in a great big victory, as if death were a tiny drop in comparison to God's huge ocean of aliveness. A contemporary writer put the same insight like this: "All the death that ever was, set next to life, would scarcely fill a cup."

Human speculation—whether religious or scientific—does the best it can, like a little boat that ventures out on the surface of a deep, deep ocean, under the dome of a fathomless sky. Our eyes cannot see beyond the rim. Our ears cannot hear the music beneath the silence. Our hearts cannot imagine the meaning above us, below us, around us, within us. But the Spirit blows like wind. And so this mystery humbles us even as it dignifies us. This mystery impresses us with our smallness even as it inspires us with our ultimate value. This mystery dislodges us from lesser attachments so we sail on in hope. This mystery dares us to believe that the big love of God is big enough to swallow all death and overflow with aliveness for us all.

"Do not fear," the Spirit whispers. "All shall be well." That is why we walk this road, from the known into the unknown, deeper into mystery, deeper into light, deeper into love, deeper into joy.

Engage:

1. What one thought or idea from today's lesson especially intrigued, provoked, disturbed, challenged, encouraged, warmed, warned, helped, or surprised you?
2. Share a story about a moment in your life when everything came together and, for at least a moment, "all was well."

3. How do you respond to the image of the end as a great homecoming celebration, or a great marriage banquet?
4. For children: If someone said, "Tell me the five best things about being part of your family," what would you say?
5. Activate: This week, keep the words "this mystery" with you . . . and contrast the deep ocean of "this mystery" with the little boats of human speculation.
6. Meditate: Imagine being on a small boat, buoyed up by depths that you cannot fathom. Feel what it means to be upheld by mystery. Let the peace of God uphold you.

Fourth Quarter Queries

If possible, compose prayerful, honest, and heartfelt replies to these queries in private, and then gather to share what you have written. The Five Guidelines for Learning Circles in Appendix II may be helpful to guide your sharing. You may also find it helpful to invite a trusted spiritual leader to serve as "catechist" and ask him or her for additional guidance, feedback, and instruction. Make it safe for one another to speak freely, and let your conversation build conviction in each of you as individuals, and among you as a community.

1. How have you experienced the Spirit through letting go, letting be, and letting come?
2. Recount a history of your experience with the Holy Spirit. What are some of your most significant spiritual experiences?
3. How would you explain to sincere spiritual seekers ways to increase their experience of the Spirit's transforming power in their lives?
4. How are you learning to love God, self, neighbor, and enemy?
5. Share your understanding of how the mystery of the Trinity can be a healing (rather than harmful) teaching.
6. How have you experienced the Spirit working through you to serve and bless others, and to confront evil forces in our world?
7. How does the Holy Spirit help you face the future, including your own death?
8. How do you feel about forming and leading a new group to teach others what you have learned through *We Make the Road by Walking*?

Appendix I: Liturgical Resources

Liturgy means "an order plan or format for gathering." Not every learning circle that works with *We Make the Road by Walking* will want to use the following liturgical resources, but many will find them helpful. They have been kept simple enough that participants can easily learn the responses by heart. Ideally, only the leader or leaders will need print or digital versions in front of them, since the goal is for the liturgy to be a shared social and spiritual experience rather than a script that is read. (A downloadable version is available at www.brianmclaren.net.)

The prayers and other resources in this liturgy are derived from traditional sources, but they are simplified here and adapted for use by a wide range of people from a wide range of religious backgrounds. If you wish that more traditional material were included, of course you can add it. If you wish things were stated differently, of course you can revise them, in keeping with your convictions and commitments. These resources avoid masculine or feminine pronouns for God. They frequently use the direct address *Living God*, but you may wish to substitute other direct addresses as well, such as *Holy One, Living Creator, Spirit of Life*, and so on.

Many groups won't be able to make a one-year commitment. For them, one quarter will be more doable. Church membership classes will find chapters 34–39 on church life especially helpful. At www.brianmclaren.net, you'll find suggestions for using the lessons in a weekend retreat setting, and it's easy to imagine groups using a chapter a day to complete the book in less than two months.

Whenever possible, leadership should be shared widely among group participants so all can develop leadership skills. Whenever school-aged children are present, encourage them to participate to the degree they are able and willing; show them uncommon respect as fellow learners. The group convener or host can assign responsibilities in advance or spontaneously.

For churches using this liturgy for public worship, appropriate music—vocal or instrumental—can be added before, during, or after any of the elements. Care should be taken to avoid songs that are contrary to the spirit or content of the lessons. At www.brianmclaren.net, you will find links to suggested musical resources.

For many groups, a shorter liturgy is recommended: Opening (5 minutes), Scripture Readings (5–7 minutes), Lesson (10–12 minutes), Engagement (20–40 minutes), Benediction (5 minutes). If a group tries the shorter format and is hungry for more, they can experiment with the longer liturgy: Opening, Prayer (5–10 minutes), Scripture Readings, Lesson, Engagement, Offering (2–3 minutes), Eucharist (15 minutes), Benediction.

The context for these liturgical resources may be a meal, worship service, class, home group, choir rehearsal, hike (where the hikers pause periodically along the journey), sports event, drum circle, yoga session, vespers, or some other shared activity. Whatever the context, the tone should be joyful, reverent, energetic, and personal.

During a meal or informal gathering time, people can use queries like these to invite one another into meaningful conversation:

How is your life? How is your work? How is your soul?
How have you experienced God at work in you or through you this week?
What was your experience in applying last week's Activate prompt (#5 in the Engage section)?
What have been some of your joys and sorrows (or high points and low points) since we last met?

At the beginning of a meal, the following prayer of thanksgiving can be used. The response (in italics) can be signaled by a pause or gesture.

Let us give thanks for this meal, saying, *We thank you, Living God.*
For this breath, for this heartbeat, for the gift of these companions, *we thank you, Living God.*
For this nourishment and flavor, for soil and sunlight, air and rainfall, *we thank you, Living God.*

For all to whom this food connects us, from field to farm and store to table, *we thank you, Living God.*
As we share this meal together, may our thirst for peace be strengthened and our hunger for justice deepened, until all are fed, and safe, and well.
We thank you, Living God. Amen.

OPENING

Whenever it is time to move from the meal or other activity to the lesson and conversation, the convener or host can begin with these words, spoken with joy and energy, never in a dull or mechanical monotone:

One: The Living God is with us!
All: *And with all creation!*

Then, each line of an invocation like the following can be preceded by a bell, a singing bowl, the lighting of a candle, or another simple action that helps participants focus their attention and open their hearts. (Responses are in italics.)

Let us awaken our hearts to the presence of God, saying, *We praise you for your glory.*
God before us, behind us, above us, upholding us... *We praise you for your glory.*
God with us, among us, beside us, befriending us... *We praise you for your glory.*
God within us, flowing through us, animating, harmonizing... *We praise you for your glory. Amen.*

The following invocation may be read—again, with sincerity and joy (adapted from the *Book of Common Prayer*, 355):

Almighty God, to you all hearts are open, all desires known, and from you no secrets are hid. Purify and unify the thoughts of our hearts by the inspiration of your Holy Spirit, that we may more perfectly love you and more worthily magnify your holy Name, through Christ our Lord. *Amen.*

PRAYER

If one of the following forms of prayer is used each week, over the course of a month, groups can move from thanksgiving (perhaps with hands raised high, palms up) to intercession (perhaps with hands raised shoulder height, palms out in blessing) to confession (perhaps with hands placed over the heart or chest) to contemplation (with hands lowered, palms open). Responses should be spoken with energy and sincerity.

Week 1. A prayer of thanksgiving (adapted from the **Book of Common Prayer,** *836–837).*

Let us give thanks to the living God for all the gifts that we enjoy, saying, *We thank you, living God.*

For the beauty and wonder of your creation, in earth and sky and sea, *We thank you, Living God.*

For all that is gracious in the lives of men and women, revealing the image of Christ, *We thank you, Living God.*

For our daily food and drink, our homes and families, and our friends, *We thank you, Living God.*

For minds to think, hearts to love, and hands to serve, *We thank you, Living God.*

For health and strength to work, and leisure to rest and play, *We thank you, Living God.*

For challenges that call forth new strength, for failures that teach greater humility, and for encouragement to persevere when life is hard, *We thank you, Living God.*

For all who have gone before us, for all who walk beside us, and for all children, who are precious to us and to you, *We thank you, Living God.*

And for the great wisdom and hope that you reveal to us through Jesus, our leader, example, teacher, liberator, and friend, *We thank you, Living God.*

Week 2. A prayer of intercession: after each request, pause for a moment of silent prayer.

With all our heart and with all our mind and with all our strength, let us pray to the living God: *Lord, hear our prayer.*

For this good earth, this holy creation, and for the wisdom and will to cherish, understand, reverence, rightly use, and conserve it, we pray to the living God: *Lord, hear our prayer.*

For all in danger, hunger, or sorrow, for the aged and infirm, the widowed and orphaned, the sick and suffering in body or mind, for prisoners and refugees, the poor and oppressed, the unemployed and destitute, the bereaved and alone, the war-torn and wounded, and for all who care for them, we pray to the living God: *Lord, hear our prayer.*

For all who hold positions of trust in the worlds of religion, education, government, business, community, culture, and family, that they may promote the well-being of all creation, we pray to the living God: *Lord, hear our prayer.*

For any who have caused us pain, for those we struggle to understand and strain to love, for all who do not love us or who consider themselves our enemies, that they may be truly blessed and that we may be fully reconciled, we pray to the living God: *Lord, hear our prayer.*

For ourselves and our circles of family and friends, for the grace to learn, desire, and do your will humbly in our daily life and work, we pray to the living God: *Lord, hear our prayer.*

Week 3. A prayer of confession: one of the following can be used, read line by line by a leader and repeated by the group, followed by a few moments of silence.

Gracious God, we have hurt others, and we have been hurt./ We have presumed upon others, and we have been presumed upon./ We have taken others for granted, and we have been taken for granted./ We have dishonored others, and we have been dishonored./ As we receive Your forgiveness for our wrongs,/ we extend forgiveness to others who have wronged us./ Have mercy upon us all. Amen.

Gracious God, our sins are too heavy to carry,/ too real to hide,/ and too deep to undo./ Forgive what our lips tremble to name/ and what our hearts can no longer bear./ Set us free from a past that we cannot change;/ open to us a future in which we can be changed;/ and grant us grace to grow more and more in your likeness and image,/ through Jesus Christ, the light of the world. Amen. (Adapted from the *PCUSA Book of Common Worship*)

Most merciful God,/ we confess that we have sinned against you/ in thought, word, and deed,/ by what we have done, and by what we have left undone./ We have not loved you with our whole heart;/ we have not loved our neighbors as ourselves./ We are truly sorry and we humbly repent./ For the sake of your Son Jesus Christ,/ have mercy on us and forgive us;/ that we may delight in your will,/ and walk in your ways,/ to the glory of your Name. Amen./ (From the *Episcopal Book of Common Prayer*)

After the prayer, a member of the group may offer an assurance of pardon, perhaps using words like this: *Whatever is wrong, God forgives. Whatever is wounded, God heals. Whatever is partial, God completes. Whatever is weak, God makes strong. You are forgiven and loved, my brothers and sisters. Now, as you have received grace and peace from God, share a greeting of grace and peace with one another, saying, "The grace of God is upon you," or "The peace of Christ is with you."*

Week 4. Contemplative prayer can be introduced with words like these:

Let us in stillness hold our hearts open to God. When thoughts and worries come, let us release them and return to restful openness, enjoying the companionship of God, who is closer to us than we are to ourselves. We trust that in quietness and surrender, as we breathe out trust and breathe in grace, the deepest part of us will find our home more deeply in the gracious heart of God.

SCRIPTURE READINGS

Most of the Bible was an oral composition before it was a written text, and most of the written texts were meant to be heard aloud and "live." In that spirit, whenever possible, participants can learn passages by heart and share them as a form of performance art.[1] Where that isn't possible, each passage

1. For training to appreciate and present the biblical text in this way, see the Network of Biblical Storytellers website (www.nbsint.org).

should be read by a child or adult who has had time to become familiar with it in advance so it can be read naturally and with feeling. Or participants can take turns reading the passages aloud around the circle. Your group should agree on which Bible translation(s) you will use in your gatherings, such as the New Revised Standard Version or the Contemporary English Bible. The passages may be introduced like this:

One: The Living God is with us!
All: *And with all creation!*
One: A passage from [the first passage is presented]. May we be equipped by these words to walk in love for God, ourselves, our neighbors, all people, and all God's creation.
All: *Thanks be to God.*
One: A passage from [additional passages are presented]. May we be enlivened by these words to do justice, love kindness, and walk humbly with God. [Or:] Through these words, may we see God more clearly, love God more dearly, and follow God more nearly, day by day.
All: *Thanks be to God.*

LESSON/ENGAGEMENT

The chapter can be presented aloud by one person as a short sermon or homily. Or it may be presented by several people reading a few paragraphs each. It should be read with feeling and energy, not in a wooden or mechanical way. If there are Scripture references in parentheses (e.g., John 3:16), don't read them aloud. After the chapter is presented, a facilitator should introduce the Engage time. For large groups, it will be best to break into smaller groups of four people to engage with the questions. (In a church service, people can easily stand and form groups of two or three.) Depending on available time, the leader may need to select which questions will be used and how much time can be allotted to each question.

Engagement should initially be introduced with the Five Guidelines for Learning Circles (Appendix II).[2] After a few weeks, when everyone is familiar with these five guidelines, the leader can simply use a reminder like this to begin the interaction time: "Let's recall our five guidelines as we begin:

2. Some groups may prefer to replace the Engage time with a Create time, in which they respond creatively to the lesson through poetry, drawing, painting, music, or other artistic media.

mutual participation, honor, silence, understanding, and brevity." When new people join the group, the five guidelines can be reviewed.

Whenever possible, children should be included in the Engage time, and when that's the case, adults should avoid language that would be inappropriate for children. Some groups may find it helpful to use a talking stick or some other physical object for a person to hold as he or she responds to a question. The speaker then hands off the talking stick to the next person who will share. Anyone is free to pass the stick on to someone else if they would rather not speak.

The Engage questions follow this pattern:

1. *What one thought or idea from today's lesson especially intrigued, provoked, disturbed, challenged, encouraged, warmed, warned, helped, or surprised you?* This question invites simple self-reporting and gives a lot of freedom—including the freedom to question, disagree with, or object to anything in the Scripture reading or reflection/sermon. The response should begin like this: "I was intrigued [or disturbed, etc.] by…," followed by an explanation of why the person felt this response.

2. *Share a story about…* This question invites the sharing of personal experience. Not everyone will have a response to every question, but often, after a few moments of silence, stories will come to mind and begin to flow.

3. *How do you respond to…* These questions invite personal response to an idea, an image, or a proposal from the lesson. When people respond in different ways to the same prompt, it's an excellent opportunity for learning and growth. There's no need to validate or invalidate any response as long as it is expressed in line with the Five Guidelines for Learning Circles.

4. *For children…* These questions are fine for adults, too, but they're intended to invite school-aged kids to have a voice in the group as equals. It's important for adults not to respond to kids' sharing in ways that kids will experience as dismissive or demeaning. The goal should be for adults and children alike to be taken seriously, to be drawn into honest thinking and free speech, and to learn together.

5. *Activate…* These questions invite participants to move from reflection to action.

6. *Meditate…* These prompts create space for participants to open deeper parts of themselves to God.

OFFERING

This is a good time to include a financial offering as an expression of worship, discipleship, and stewardship. Someone can lead in a prayer like this to introduce the offering:

> Our gracious and generous Creator,/ you have blessed us with abundance:/ This beautiful earth and all we enjoy,/ health and strength, family and friends;/ work and rest; home and belongings./ We are blessed indeed./ To support this community and provide for those who serve us,/ To help those in need and extend our mission,/ In proportion to what we have earned and saved,/ In gratitude we now joyfully give./ Amen.

A basket may be passed or people may come forward to give, accompanied by joyful music, if possible, to demonstrate that it is indeed more blessed to give than receive. Be sure to handle finances transparently and ethically.

EUCHARIST

If your tradition and convictions allow you to do so, you may use or adapt the words below to celebrate the eucharist. Many faith communities require an authorized person to preside in the blessing or consecration of bread and wine. In that case, you may invite that authorized person to join your group and serve in this way. Some traditions allow for previously consecrated bread and wine to be brought to the homebound, prisoners, and so on. A representative from your group may be able to arrange for your group to receive in this way.

The first few weeks of a gathering, these words may be shared on paper or digitally, or, better, the leader can coach people in the responses. After even a few weeks, the responses are easy enough that they will flow from memory.

> *The Living God is with us!*
> And with all creation!
> *Lift up your hearts!*
> We lift them to the living God.
> *Let us give thanks to the Creator of all.*
> It is right to give our thanks and praise.

It is right, and a good and joyful thing, always and everywhere to give thanks to you, Living God, who loves us with the faithful care of a father and mother. For this reason, we join with all creation to proclaim your glory:

Holy, Holy, Holy One, God of power, God of love.
Earth, sea, and sky are full of your glory.
With joy we praise you! With joy we praise you! Amen!

We praise you and we bless you, holy and gracious Creator, source of life. Your Spirit has always been with creation, guiding its development, calling forth life, infusing beauty, inspiring joy and love. In your infinite love you created us in your image and allowed us to share in the precious gift of life. You gave us a home in this beautiful world to live in harmony with you, with one another, and with all your creatures.

But we have so often turned from your love and wisdom. We have chosen our own way and broken faith with you, our neighbors, and our fellow creatures. Now all around us we see the tragic harvest of the bitter seed we have sown.

Yet through it all, you have remained faithful to us. You graciously called us to turn from our destructive ways and return to you. You sent us prophets, priests, sages, storytellers, and poets to lead us to repentance and wisdom. In the fullness of time, through Mary, a humble woman full of faith, you sent Jesus into the world.

Living among us, Jesus loved us. In word and deed, he proclaimed the good news of your reign. He broke bread with outcasts and sinners, and in imitation of your perfect love, he taught us to love neighbor, stranger, outsider, and enemy. He redirected us from violence to peace, from fear to faith, from rivalry to mutual service, and from worry and greed to generosity and joy. He taught us to pray:

A version of the Lord's prayer may be said or sung here. For groups unfamiliar with the version that is being used, it can be read by the leader and echoed by the group, line by line. Eventually it can be spoken by heart.

The following version of the prayer can be chanted to a scale of five ascending and descending notes (see www.brianmclaren.net for a sample):

1. O God, whose love makes us one family,
2. May your unspeakable name be revered.
3. Now, here on earth, may your commonwealth come,
4. On earth as in heaven, may your dreams come true.
5. Give us today our bread for today.
4. Forgive us our wrongs as we forgive.
3. Lead us away from the perilous trial.
2. Liberate us from the evil.
1. For the kingdom is yours and yours alone.
2. The power is yours and yours alone.
3. The glory is yours and yours alone.
4. Now and forever, amen.
5. Alleluia... 4. Alleluia... 3. Alleluia... 2. Alleluia... 1. Amen.

On the night before he showed us the full extent of his love, Jesus took a loaf of bread, gave thanks, broke it, gave it to his friends, and said, "Take, eat. This is my body which is given for you. Do this in remembrance of me." As supper was ending, he took a cup of wine. Again he gave thanks and gave it to his friends, saying, "Drink from this, all of you, for this is my blood of the New Covenant, which is poured out for you and for many for the forgiveness of sins. Whenever you drink this cup, remember me."

Now, gathered as one family around this table of joyful reconciliation and fellowship, united in your Spirit, we receive these gifts, and we gratefully offer you our lives as a living sacrifice. As Christ stretched out his arms upon the cross to welcome the whole world into your gracious embrace, we rejoice to enter that embrace and with you, extend it to all. Through Christ and with Christ and in Christ, in the unity of the Holy Spirit, to the living God be honor, glory, and praise, forever and ever. Amen.

The group should decide in advance how the eucharist will be observed. If the group is small, the elements can easily be shared around a table. In larger groups, people can come forward and be served. Intinction (where the bread is dipped into the wine) is often advisable for larger groups. Those serving others can say words like these:

The body of Christ, broken for you. *Amen.* (or *Hallelujah*, or *Thanks be to God*, etc.)
The cup of liberation, poured out for you. *Amen.* (or *Hallelujah*, or *Thanks be to God*, etc.)

Or these:

Take this bread in remembrance of Christ's great love for you, and for all.
Drink this cup in remembrance of Christ's great love for you, and for all.

When everyone has participated, the leader may close with words like these:

As Christ's body and blood were separated on the cross, so now they have been rejoined in us. Let us, then, by faith, now arise, filled with the Spirit, to be the embodiment of Christ in our world.
[Or:] As we have been fed around God's table of grace, let us go forth in grace and hospitality to others.

Some people may be prohibited by conscience or tradition from including the eucharist in their gathering. In that case, the following words may be used at some point during a shared meal—not as a formal eucharist, but as a spontaneous "toast to Jesus and the kingdom* of God."

One: Let us celebrate Jesus and the kingdom* of God: we lift our bread in memory of Jesus.
All: *To Jesus and the kingdom* of God.*
(A moment of reverent silence is observed before and after eating.)
One: We lift our glasses in honor of Jesus.
All: *To Jesus and the kingdom* of God.*
(A moment of reverent silence is observed before and after drinking.)
One: Amen.
(*Amen*, *Hallelujah*, or other joyful expressions follow.)

*You may substitute *commonwealth*, *reign*, *dream*, or another suitable word for *kingdom*.

BENEDICTION

There are many ways to conclude the gathering. The Lord's Prayer may be recited, if it hasn't been already. A special theme song may be sung, such as the doxology, an amen or a hallelujah, or a benediction song. Each member of the group may be asked to share a single word that describes their response to the time together, or a single sentence of gratitude to God or the group. An individual could recite a benediction (see www.brianmclaren.net for links), or your group could compose its own benediction to learn and say by heart in unison as a special way of concluding your time together. The following can be spoken by a leader and echoed by all:

We are a circle/ Of learners and seekers/ Alive in God's story of creation.
We are disciples/ who follow our leader/ Alive in the adventure of Jesus.
We are uprising/ in a new way of living/ Transformed by the Spirit of God.
Let us go forth in joy and peace/ To love and serve God and our neighbors./ Amen.

APPENDIX II: FIVE GUIDELINES FOR LEARNING CIRCLES

A LEARNING CIRCLE THAT gathers to use *We Make the Road by Walking* is on a quest for spiritual formation, reorientation, and activation. We aren't seeking to impress each other, to convince each other to agree with us, or to fix each other. We desire everyone to gain deeper understanding from and with one another, and to practice gracious ways of relating to one another. To keep our space safe and open for deeper understanding and growth to occur, we will observe these five guidelines:

1. *The guideline of participation:* Our goal is for all to share and all to learn, so all should feel encouraged but not pressured to participate. Before and after you have made a contribution, welcome others to contribute by listening from the heart with uncommon interest and kindness. In so doing, you will "listen one another into free speech." Avoid dominating, and gently seek to draw out those who may be less confident than you. Be sure to express appreciation when others share honestly and from the heart.

2. *The guideline of honor:* We honor one another for having the courage to share honestly and from the heart. It is important to freely express your own views without insulting the views of others. Advising, silencing, fixing, upstaging, correcting, or interrupting others often leaves them feeling dishonored, so these responses are not appropriate among the learners in this circle. Often, using "I" language helps in this regard—for example, "I see that differently" instead of "You are wrong." Trust that a safe, honoring environment will make space for the "inner teacher," God's Spirit, to guide others better than you can.

3. *The guideline of silence:* Silence is an important part of every good conversation. Don't rush to fill silence. Expect that important insights will arise through silence. Often, right after a silence has become a little uncomfortable, it becomes generative and holy.

4. *The guideline of understanding:* Each question or prompt is designed to promote something more important than agreement or argument: understanding—of ourselves and one another. So see differing views as a gift and an opportunity for greater understanding, not argument. Our full acceptance of one another does not infer full agreement with every opinion that is expressed. Assured of mutual honor, in the presence of differing views, we will all experience greater understanding.

5. *The guideline of brevity:* It's important to feel free to think out loud and speak at some length at times. But in general, err on the side of being too brief and having people ask to hear more, rather than on the side of taking more than your share of the group's time.

Each participant should verbally agree to these guidelines, or another set of guidelines the group prefers. Leaders can help the learning circle address problems as they arise, always keeping the goals of spiritual formation, reorientation, and activation in mind.

DEDICATION AND ACKNOWLEDGMENTS

I RECENTLY RECEIVED AN e-mail from a young man whom I admire a lot. He started a wonderful organization that does immense good for children in some of the world's most dangerous places. His Christian faith played a formative role in his development, yet he feels pain about his religious heritage:

> There are a number of my friends, including myself, who feel like we had to let almost everything go to follow Jesus or at least truth and what made sense to us... Because things are shifting so much in the world and in our thinking, this process can feel like we are "on the way out" of the faith. The disorientation creates confusion and leaves us asking what to still believe in. When we let so many things go, what do we know we need to hold on to? We believe deeply in truth but feel like the milieus we grew up with were strategically designed to make us feel like we were losing our souls when we opened our minds.
>
> But even though we have realized that is not the case and have begun to find freedom, we are still left wondering exactly what our convictions actually are... I keep feeling like you would be a good person to talk to about it, perhaps even in a room with a few other of these people from my generation... **the believers who still want to believe but aren't sure what is left to believe in.**

This book is dedicated to people like this gifted young man and his friends. It is my hope that it will help them find something worth believing in again... something to sustain them in their good and meaningful work, something better than what they've left behind.

This book is also dedicated to the memory of Richard Twiss, a friend, colleague, and mentor. He died of a heart attack while I was writing this book. A Lakota Sioux who spent many years in more traditional Christian company, in recent years he pioneered a new way of following the path of Jesus in an indigenous way—in bare feet, so to speak, leaving the heavy, steel-toed boots of industrial-era, Euro-American Christianity behind. This beloved *ikce wicasa* was a true trailblazer who made the road by walking. I and thousands of others feel a deep hole in our hearts since he left. I pray that this book will contribute to the fulfillment of his dreams.

Finally, this book is dedicated to the churches and fellowship groups that have nourished my faith through the years. I learned so much about worship and the Bible at New Hampshire Avenue Gospel Chapel where I grew up, a Plymouth Brethren congregation in Silver Spring, Maryland. That learning continued at the Fellowship in Rockville in its various forms in my high school and college years, along with the Cornerstone community in College Park. Then I learned so much about discipleship, evangelism, fellowship, and leadership at Cedar Ridge Community Church, now in Spencerville, Maryland, the interdenominational congregation in which I had the privilege of serving as a pastor for over twenty years.

For the last five years, I have been a quiet but grateful participant in the life of St. Mark's Episcopal in Marco Island, Florida, led by Kyle Bennett, John Ineson, Sue Price, and their colleagues, where I have experienced needed rest and recuperation. I have also been blessed, in my travels and speaking, through literally thousands of other churches of many denominations, from Southern Baptist to Greek Orthodox, from Pentecostal to Presbyterian, from Quaker to Roman Catholic to Adventist to Unitarian. I thank God for them all.

As always, I'm grateful to my agent and friend, Kathryn Helmers; along with my publisher, Wendy Grisham; along with Chelsea Apple, Katherine Venn, and all the good people of Jericho Books in the US and Hodder and Stoughton in the UK. Rachel Held Evans, Tony Jones, Joel Costa, and Charles Toy also deserve great thanks for reading the manuscript and offering needed feedback, as do Sarah Thomas, Bryan and Christy Berghoef, and Wendy Tobias, who field-tested the book in groups they lead.

About the Author

Brian D. McLaren is an author, a speaker, an activist, and a public theologian. After teaching college English, Brian was a church planter and pastor in the Baltimore–Washington, D.C., area for over twenty years. He is a popular conference speaker and a frequent guest lecturer for denominational and ecumenical leadership gatherings in the United States and internationally, and is theologian-in-residence at Life in the Trinity Ministry.

Brian's writing spans over a dozen books, including *Why Did Jesus, Moses, the Buddha, and Mohammed Cross the Road?*, his acclaimed A New Kind of Christian trilogy, *A Generous Orthodoxy*, and *Naked Spirituality*. A frequent guest on television, radio, and news media programs, Brian is also an active and popular blogger, a musician, and an avid outdoor enthusiast. Brian is married to Grace, and they have four adult children and four grandchildren. Learn more at his website, www.brianmclaren.net.

For more information on Brian, and for a commentary and other resources related to this book, visit www.brianmclaren.net.

MAKING A DIFFERENCE

Also by Milton Viorst

Hostile Allies: FDR & Charles de Gaulle

The Great Documents of Western Civilization

Fall from Grace: The Republican Party and the Puritan Ethic

Hustlers and Heroes: An American Political Panorama

Fire in the Streets: America in the 1960s

MAKING A DIFFERENCE

The Peace Corps at Twenty-Five

Edited by MILTON VIORST

with a Foreword by President Ronald Reagan

Weidenfeld & Nicolson
New York

Published by Weidenfeld & Nicolson, New York
A Division of Wheatland Corporation
10 East 53rd Street
New York, NY 10022

Library of Congress Cataloging-in-Publication Data

Making a difference.

1. Peace Corps (U.S.) I. Viorst, Milton.
HC60.5.M26 1986 361.2'6'06073 86-9055
ISBN 1-55584-010-8

Manufactured in the United States of America

Designed by Irving Perkins Associates, Inc.

First Edition

10 9 8 7 6 5 4 3 2 1

Contents

And so, my fellow Americans, ask not what your country can do for you; ask what you can do for your country.

My fellow citizens of the world, ask not what America can do for you, but together what we can do for the freedom of man.

John F. Kennedy
Inaugural Address, January 20, 1961

Acknowledgment

The Peace Corps' twenty-fifth anniversary year has provided the opportunity to increase American understanding of the developing world and the unique partnership that has resulted from people taking time to help one another. As the Peace Corps looks to the next twenty-five years, it is fitting that a book should be published about the Peace Corps' past, present, and potential for the future.

In all matters of substance, someone works behind the scenes with a creative spirit that gives birth to an idea. Ailene Goodman is the person who in this instance provided the inspiration for what you are about to read. We are thankful for her pioneer efforts, which are reflected in the pages that follow.

Milton Viorst has done more than one could have imagined possible in pulling together this collection of thoughts and reflections by and about those who have really made a difference, for the Peace Corps and for the nations they served. To each of them and to Milton, we at the Peace Corps are profoundly grateful.

And, of course, the book would not have been possible in the first place were it not for the more than 120,000 Americans who have served in more than ninety countries around the globe. Each has begun the process of laying a firm foundation upon which a real lasting peace can be built.

Loret Miller Ruppe
Director of the Peace Corps

Foreword

by President Ronald Reagan

For a quarter of a century, Peace Corps volunteers have been offering their time, their talent, and their training to help people in developing countries around the world make a better life for themselves and their children.

In a troubled world, the Peace Corps is waging peace. Every day in Africa, Asia, and Latin America, they answer the cries of hunger, disease, poverty, and illiteracy by showing America at its best.

Peace Corps workers save lives by helping those who suffer from malnutrition and starvation. They improve the quality of life by teaching mothers how to prevent disease. And they have helped create new avenues to prosperity by showing farmers and fishermen new ways to produce and market their products.

Each one of us is responsible for building the society we want. Peace Corps volunteers do that with people-to-people exchanges, using their energy, their spirit, and their creativity to help solve problems.

In the South Pacific island country of Tonga, the Peace Corps helped an agricultural cooperative increase its volume nearly twelve-fold in a single year. In Swaziland, the Peace Corps designed water systems that will reach 37 percent of the population. In Costa Rica, a major nursery was established to market forest and fruit trees that thrive in that climate. And Peace Corps volunteers, working as educators, have taught more than five million people in classrooms across Africa.

This is the American way. Once we see a need, we want to serve—even when the neighbor we reach out to help is halfway around the world.

More than 120,000 Peace Corps volunteers have helped people throughout the world gain a better understanding of Americans, and in turn have helped Americans understand the people of the world. Our colleges and universities have been enriched by their knowledge and experience.

Giving, learning, and sharing is what the Peace Corps is all about. Our volunteers make us proud to be Americans.

THE IDEAL

The Vision

by Sargent Shriver

Oscar Wilde is said to have observed that America really was discovered by a dozen people before Columbus but that the discovery remained a secret. I am tempted to feel that way about the Peace Corps. A national effort of this type had been proposed many times in previous years, but only in 1961 did it become reality.

In *quantitative* terms, the Peace Corps has never been a big idea. It started the first year with a few thousand Americans being dispatched to serve in the underdeveloped world, and, though the number has gone up and down, the concept has remained essentially the same. Compared to the millions in uniform who have served America abroad, the ambition was modest—perhaps too modest. Compared to the funds our government transmits in foreign aid to countries less affluent than ours, the budget was barely visible. Still, those of us who were present at the creation nurtured the notion that the Peace Corps had a huge potential for promoting the peace of the world and the well-being of humanity. After twenty-five years, though poverty and war remain with us, I think I see some evidence that we were right. *Qualitatively,* the Peace Corps has succeeded.

My own interest in the Peace Corps idea had started quite a few years before, when I was a part of and, later, leader for Experiment in International Living groups in Europe in the 1930s. In the 1950s I visited several Asian countries—Japan, Korea, Vietnam, Cambodia, Thailand—and, when I returned, I proposed sending three-man political action teams to Asia, Africa, and Latin America. These teams were to consist of vigorous and imaginative young labor leaders, businessmen, and politicians. They would offer their services at a grass-roots level and work

---

Sargent Shriver, a senior partner at Fried, Frank, Harris, Shriver & Jacobson in Washington, D.C., was the first director of the Peace Corps.

directly with the people, contributing to the growth of the economies, to the democratic organization of the societies, and to the peaceful outcome of the social revolutions under way. When the idea of the Peace Corps emerged during the presidential campaign of 1960, it seemed to offer the possibility of realizing, in a new form, this old objective, which seemed to me more important than ever.

A month or so after President Kennedy took office, he asked me to report to him on how the Peace Corps could be organized, and then to organize it. John Kennedy believed Americans had decent ideals that were going untapped, and a physical and spiritual resilience that was being unused. He told me to make the Peace Corps a tough agency, to prove wrong those who were skeptical about the willingness of Americans, especially young Americans, to make the kind of sacrifices that the Peace Corps would require. "Go ahead," he said, "you can do it," and to do it we assembled the best people we could find from the professions, from our universities and foundations, from our corporations and unions, from private agencies and the civil service. We knew the Peace Corps would have only one chance to work. We felt like parachute jumpers: the chute had to open the first time, or we were sure to come to an abrupt end.

Within the team I had assembled, we wrestled with a hundred questions of policy, debating around the clock, in those early days of 1961. Not the least of the questions was the name we would give to the undertaking. For a while, "Peace Corps," which Kennedy had used during the election campaign, was not the first choice. Some of the President's advisers scoffed at it, arguing for a solid bureaucratic title like "Agency for Overseas Voluntary Service." Conservatives, furthermore, said the word "peace" sounded soft, vague, and weak. They insisted Communists had corrupted it by applying it to every political initiative and even to every war they were involved in. Not to be outdone, many liberals disliked the word "corps." They said it sounded militaristic.

But I thought we should try to recapture the term "peace," to liberate it, so to speak. I thought we should be able to use it without its sounding like propaganda, metaphor, or corn. As for "corps," I was not uncomfortable with conveying the militance of our purpose, at least a quiet militance. The fact was that I could not visualize the elimination of war except through the kind of effort in which the Peace Corps was to engage. Peace was our goal, and we were not embarrassed to envisage this effort as a genuine way station along the road.

We knew there were misgivings about the new Peace Corps. I was disappointed when some very distinguished Americans made fun of our conviction that volunteers could do a serious job in the developing world.

Congressmen and columnists called it a range of invidious names, but Americans were not alone. U Nu, who was then prime minister of Burma, asked me during a visit to Rangoon, "Do you think you can send me a young man from Kokomo, Indiana, who will have the dedication, determination, and sense of mission of someone from Communist China? Make no mistake about the kind of person you will be competing with." We were not so sure ourselves how well Peace Corps volunteers would work, nor were we sure that our idea would catch on, either overseas or at home. I recalled with some apprehension an African proverb I had heard, which went, "Until you have crossed the river, don't insult the crocodile's mouth."

Our Peace Corps task force worked literally day and night for weeks, readying recommendations for the President. John Kennedy had set the theme of the new administration with his inaugural statement, "Ask not what your country can do for you, ask what you can do for your country." Those were inspiring words, and at that point, many were asking, "All right, what *can* we do for our country?" We considered speed essential in order to maintain the momentum of the Kennedy theme.

By March 1, 1961, we were ready with a detailed report, which recommended to President Kennedy the Peace Corps' immediate, full-scale establishment. We rejected proposals for pilot programs or small, experimental initiatives. We asked for an independent agency, not answerable to the Agency of International Development, and we turned down suggestions to limit the mission of the Peace Corps to supplementing efforts of the Junior Red Cross, the Chamber of Commerce, or other American groups working abroad. We rejected uniforms, badges, medals, and any other distinctive clothing, along with rankings and grades. We said we wanted no special housing, food, schools, or anything else, except health services: we decided to send our own doctors to care for the volunteers. We even promised to discourage vacations in the "fleshpot" cities of the world, though many were accessible.

Yet we did not stake the Peace Corps gamble on the power of a few thousand Americans to accomplish a physical transformation of the underdeveloped world. We based our gamble on a conviction that it was not muscle power but idea power that changed the world. We did, after all, have some precedent. Religious movements have long demonstrated how ideas transform societies. Ideas were the driving force behind the Renaissance and the Enlightenment, even the Industrial Revolution, movements that gave the West a new, a more dynamic social character. The idea of the American Revolution, born more than two hundred years ago, continues to resound with explosive force throughout the world.

I shall always remember a visit I received in India in early 1961, while

I was exploring the prospects of sending one of our first contingents for service there. Ashadevi Aryanayakam, an extraordinary woman who had been an associate of Mahatma Gandhi, traveled three days and nights on a train to see me in New Delhi. "Yours was the first revolution," she reminded me. "Do you think young Americans possess the spiritual values they must have to bring the spirit of that revolution to our country? India should not boast of any spiritual superiority. There is a great valuelessness spreading around the world. Your Peace Corps volunteers must bring more than science and technology. They must touch the idealism of America and bring that to us, too. Can they do it?" I was stunned by the question, but inspired, too. Later, in describing the experience before the Senate Foreign Relations Committee, I said, "Our answer, based on faith, was yes."

It reminded me, of course, that an idea, to conquer, must fuse with the will of men and women who are prepared to dedicate their lives to its realization. We had a sense twenty-five years ago that there were such men and women in America waiting to be called, impatient to carry the idea of service to mankind. As it turned out, I think we underestimated both their numbers and their dedication. Thousands responded when we first raised the Peace Corps banner, and thousands have been responding in every succeeding year. Therein lies the true grandeur of our country.

Since 1961, the Peace Corps has sent more than 120,000 Americans to serve overseas. They are patriots, committed to the special vision upon which the Peace Corps was founded, and they have helped to disseminate this vision far and wide. As Americans in service abroad, they have gone beyond Cold War competition, beyond careerism, beyond fun and adventure, to dedicate their best efforts to the idea of raising up humanity. And there could easily have been a quarter-million or a half-million of them by now, if precious tax dollars had not so often been squandered on programs of violence, vengeance, and vituperation.

The Peace Corps is unique among American institutions. Though it is an agency of government, it is profoundly nonpolitical. That does not mean the Peace Corps is indifferent to the national interests of the United States. But it was conceived to reach beyond domestic political goals, and beyond international rivalries, to touch the deepest hopes of man. Without trumpets, banners, or weapons, the Peace Corps serves America abroad. It renders this service to our country by promoting an idea of an America that is caring and humane.

I remember an Asian prime minister many years ago summing up the vision of the Peace Corps for me, after reminding me that the arrival of the first twenty-one volunteers in his country had provoked Communist protests. A bit impudently, I asked him whether the protesters thought the volunteers were spreading germs. "In a certain sense, yes," he told me. "If these volunteers were simply twenty-one more Americans, there would be no interest in them at all. But these volunteers come representing an idea, the Peace Corps idea. That is why there is opposition." Those twenty-one Americans were a microcosm. They represented a working model of the kind of world—a world of commitment to freedom, to human well-being, to personal dignity—that we wanted our own children, and children everywhere, to live in. That is the message the Peace Corps has carried to foreign lands.

Knowing what we wanted to convey, we made some deliberate choices in 1961 about the composition of the body of volunteers. What we envisioned was a microcosm not so much of what America was as what we thought it should be. These choices, I am glad to note, have since become the norm of our society. But back then, if I may say so, making those choices took a bit of audacity. We knew that most of our volunteers would be young college graduates with liberal educations. But we also encouraged people who were older, more mature, and more experienced to join us, and we enlisted superb volunteers in their fifties, their sixties, and even in their seventies. More controversial was the decision to give women the same opportunity as men to serve. The conventional wisdom held that the Peace Corps inevitably had to be a man's world. We said it would not be, and since the first days, nearly one out of three volunteers has been a woman. The role of the two genders has been exactly the same throughout the Peace Corps' history.

We also chose to take a positive position on the race issue, which in the 1960s was a powder keg, threatening the cohesion of our society. We considered it vital not simply to *accept* blacks and other minorities into the Peace Corps, but actively to recruit them. And blacks responded to the call. I recall being told the story of four volunteers, living and working together at a small college in Nepal, visited one evening by a young Marxist who was prepared to denounce the Peace Corps for its American-style racism. The Marxist, however, could not reconcile his beliefs with the fact that he found one of the four to be black, and a graduate of one of America's best universities. The volunteers never denied that racism existed in America, but after several visits, the Marxist was persuaded that a change in our country was under way.

To me, that story illustrates the new politics which the Peace Corps was meant to represent. The foreign minister of Thailand once told me he considered the Peace Corps "the most powerful new force in the world today." In this age when nuclear stalemate and the danger of total devastation limit the use of military power, he said, we must rediscover and use a power that often seems to have atrophied from disuse. "The secret of your greatness," the foreign minister said, "is the power of American ideas and ideals." It is a secret which, he said, the United States has not adequately shared with the world. I agree with him. In every country, we are famous for our bombs, our high-powered technology, our capacity for organization, our wealth. "How many of us in foreign lands," the foreign minister said, "know that in the United States ideas and ideals are also powerful?"

I suspect the reason so few people appreciate our ideas and ideals is that we ourselves fail to understand our potential in this area. As a result, we consistently sell ourselves short. When we hear of a "secret" American power, our minds seem to turn automatically to killer devices. It is true that our weapons and our wealth are what is most clearly visible to the majority of the world. But our real "secret" power, I believe, is the vitality of our democratic life. I would like to quote David Crozier, who lost his life in an air accident while serving as a Peace Corps volunteer in Colombia. In a sadly prophetic letter to his parents, he said, "Should it come to it, I would rather give my life trying to help someone than to give my life looking down a gun barrel at him."

How much does the world know not just of the Peace Corps but of the great network of our private voluntary agencies, community organizations, labor unions, service clubs, or philanthropies? Do we not fail to convey our real pride in such federal programs as the TVA, VISTA, the National Institutes of Health, Social Security, and Head Start, in our individual liberty, free speech, and free elections? In fact, I think we take them for granted, leaving the world too intimidated by the power of our weapons and insufficiently aware of the power of our democracy. It is the humanity and concern of our system that the Peace Corps represents.

But let me assert the Peace Corps is no naive organization, aiming to do good while indifferent to the existence of evil in the world. We know the United States is involved in a contest of ideologies being waged in many arenas, not the least of them the underdeveloped nations. The Peace Corps plays a role in this struggle. But let us be clear that its role lies not in its solicitation of these nations' support for America's political positions, much less our alliances. The role lies in the contribution the Peace Corps makes to *their* success. If these countries succeed in their plans for economic, social, and political progress, it will not matter much whether they agree with us on a given issue, or even whether they like us. If they become healthy, democratic societies, they will not be a threat to world peace. That is what matters.

The arena in which the Peace Corps makes its stand for America is in the nations where a peaceful outcome to the world's ideological struggle remains possible. Most of the African continent meets that test, as do Latin America and East Asia. But I exclude no region of the world. We must not let our preoccupation with the Cold War and military confrontation blind us to the opportunities waiting for us throughout the globe. Though the Peace Corps volunteers carry no rifles to battle, they serve their country on fronts that are vital to the peace of the world. They serve in the Third World, home for hundreds of millions of people whose only ideology is to create a decent life for themselves, a life that measures richness with dignity, that is free of fear and instability. The time to reach them is not when military action becomes necessary, when war or violent revolution is impending. Peace Corps volunteers are not trained to deal with enemies bearing arms. Their enemies are hunger, ignorance, and disease. By forcing these enemies into retreat, the Peace Corps serves humanity's interests, and America's.

It seems a paradox to say that Peace Corps volunteers make their contribution to American foreign policy by staying out of the foreign policy establishment, but it is true. Peace Corps volunteers are not trained diplomats, not propagandists. For the most part, they are not even technical experts. They represent our society by what they are, what they do, and the spirit in which they do it. They scrupulously steer clear of intelligence activities and local politics. The Peace Corps' strict adherence to these principles has been a crucial factor in the decision of politically uncommitted countries to invite American volunteers into their homes, and even into their classrooms to teach future generations of national leadership. In an era of sabotage and espionage, Peace Corps volunteers have earned a priceless but simple renown: they are *trustworthy*.

When the Peace Corps goes abroad, it spreads the ideal of a free and democratic society. Its strategic premise is the sense of concern that every member has shown by the act of volunteering. The Peace Corps' secret weapon is example. This example proclaims that in America, the color of a volunteer's skin, or a human's religious or political beliefs, do not determine personal dignity and worth. We have sent black Americans to white men's countries, white Americans to black men's countries. We were told that we could not send Protestants to certain parts of Catholic countries in Latin America, and that we could not send Jews to Arab countries. But we sent them. Rarely have these decisions spawned discontent. Far more often, they have elicited admiration and, if I may say so, even envy. On a practical level, what a volunteer has left behind may be a well, or a proficiency among a few students in English, or a better way to raise corn. But he or she has also left behind the germ of the Peace Corps vision, and it is a germ that inevitably spreads. I believe there are few more important contributions to be made.

We never meant for Peace Corps volunteers to go abroad as promoters of a particular political theory or economic system, much less a religious creed. But that did not mean they were without a mission. The volunteer goes overseas as a willing and skilled worker. He also goes as a representative of the ideals that America, with all its imperfections, embodies better than any society in our time. It is the idea that free and committed men and women can cross, even transcend, boundaries of culture and language, of foreign tradition, and great disparities of wealth and culture, to work in harmony with one another. The Peace Corps has a commitment to overcome old hostilities and entrenched nationalisms, to bring knowledge where ignorance has dominated, to challenge traditions that may enslave, even as it respects the societies from which they emerge. The Peace Corps was designed for different cultures to meet on the common ground of service to human welfare and personal worth, so that men and women might share what is valuable in the spirit of each.

Those of us who were around at the beginning conspired in sending volunteers off on assignment as free men and women. I say "conspired" because what they secretly carried in their baggage, along with the books and clean socks, was the Peace Corps ideal. As Americans, they were free to travel, to write, to read, and to speak as they chose. They were surrounded by no wall of censorship, nor constrained by any authoritarian code of discipline. They were trained to work with people, and not to employ them, or use them, or give them orders. Volunteers from the start were instructed to do what the country in which they served wanted them to do, not what they, out of some sense of cultural superiority, thought was best for their hosts. That does not mean volunteers did not often have to rely on their own initiative to make best use of their time and talent. The Peace Corps encouraged their initiative. The staff provided the framework and then relied on the creative energies of dedicated individuals to fill in the spaces.

Let me quote a few lines of a letter I sent to President Kennedy in December of 1961, shortly after we dispatched the first contingent of Peace Corps volunteers to their destinations. I wanted to make clear to him that we were serious about the objective of showing that Americans were not soft. "Volunteers are expected to live simply and unostentatiously," the letter said. "We believe it will make their work more productive and effective. They have a twenty-four-hour-a-day job. They receive little or no pay and accept substantial hazards to their health and even to their safety. . . . The Peace Corps is not just a job. There are no 9:00 to 5:00 days in our operation. There will be little tolerance of a 'tomorrow' philosophy or an 'it can't be done because it hasn't been done before' attitude. We know the American people are behind us."

For a quarter-century the Peace Corps has remained faithful to this vision. Very early, the Peace Corps perceived the trap of neocolonialism, and volunteers understood that they must, if necessary, go out of their way to avoid it. They have lived not in some figurative house on the hill, not in isolated compounds or chic neighborhoods, but physically among the people they have served, in intimate contact with them. A visiting Ghanaian once said to me, "Peace Corps teachers in my country don't live so badly. After all, they live as well as we do." We did not inflict discomfort on the volunteer for discomfort's sake. Rather, by their way of life volunteers have shown that material privilege has not become the central and indispensable ingredient in American life.

From the beginning, Peace Corps volunteers have not only lived sparely but have eaten the food and talked the language of rural villagers, of dwellers of the barrios, of communities of seaside fishermen. They shopped for bargains in the marketplace and rode in buses or on bicycles. They enjoyed no diplomatic immunity and observed the same local laws as everyone else. They received modest living allowances in the field, sums fixed to match local conditions, far from conventional American salaries. They sweated in hot climates without air-conditioning and made their own fires in wood stoves when the weather was cold.

One of my favorite letters was from a volunteer who said, "For the last four months I lived with a Filipino family who were my friends and my companions. I soon forgot that I was an American and they were Filipinos. They treated me as one of the family. All of us, as human beings, have the same basic needs and desires and a common yearning to be understood and respected." I doubt that any young officer of a colonial administration ever wrote a letter back home like that. What it reflected, I think, was the volunteer's understanding that his service in the Peace Corps was not a one-way channel of communication, not a mission to a lesser people. He knew he had something important to contribute, but he also knew that the land and the people he was assigned to serve had something important to give him.

Living in the developing world, the Peace Corps volunteers have learned new facts of life. They have escaped from what is all too often a kind of cultural imprisonment, brought on by American affluence, and exposed themselves to the reality of life in much of the world. This is a world which, for all of its richness of culture, often still lives on the edge of survival. I could feel the suffering of the Peace Corps volunteer who wrote to me from East Africa, "People die here for want of so little." How many Americans have the painful privilege of learning that lesson?

The volunteers who brought back from their experience abroad a revised sense of the human condition also acquired an appreciation of the fact that answers to its problems are generally much more complex than they appear at first glance. Those who think there are panaceas for the ills of emerging nations, who believe all that is needed is more money or more schools or a few more dams, or even more democracy or more private enterprise, never served in the Peace Corps. The wisdom that volunteers brought back with them has added to the reservoir of compassion and understanding in America. It has provided our nation with insight into the thinking of the great majority with whom we share the globe. But Peace Corps volunteers, because they were toilers and not just observers, also learned that they need not sit by impotently while others suffer. That, too, is an important lesson for America.

So, in 1986, we look back across a quarter-century of soul-filled history. We have known the summer heat of the Sahara, the biting cold of the Alte Plano of Peru, the endless rain of the Asian monsoons. We have often overcome the obstacles of the federal bureaucracy, only to stumble over our own mistakes. But we have survived, and precious gifts have been bestowed upon us. We have seen the smile on the face of a child whom a volunteer has taught to read. We have been grateful that a volunteer has had a hand in building a feeder road, establishing a credit union, forming a cooperative for buying a tractor or marketing fish. We have marveled at the energy of a people in a dusty village after a volunteer has persuaded them to lift the dead hand of hopelessness.

In twenty-five years, the Peace Corps has made a start. The idea is in the air, a seed being carried on the breeze of human contact to people and institutions throughout the world. I do not know how many converts the Peace Corps has made, but I would like to think it has dealt a solid blow to ignorance and hunger. I want to believe it has moved human dignity to a higher plane. I pray it has moved peace a trifle closer, while chasing the shadow of nuclear war to a more distant reach.

Regretfully, I acknowledge it will require more time and still greater effort for the vision of the Peace Corps to win the world. That a pugnacious nationalism seems once again to be sweeping over our country does not so much mean that the Peace Corps has failed as that it has not tried hard enough. I know that, even in its brief life, the Peace Corps has emitted a glow, faint though it may be, that has helped light the way to a better and more peaceful life over a great area of the earth's surface. I take its triumphs, however, not as a cause for congratulation, but as a challenge. After twenty-five years, the task ahead is clear: to bring the Peace Corps and its ideals back to the top of America's agenda.

Passing the Torch

by Alan Guskin

When my wife, Judith, and I think about the letter we wrote that began the student Peace Corps movement, it still surprises us. We were not letter writers, nor were we even student activists on the University of Michigan campus. But there we were in the basement of a greasy-spoon restaurant, composing on a napkin a letter to the editor of the *Michigan Daily* that expressed our personal commitment to serve and that urged others to do the same.

As we began to write the letter, we thought about what John Kennedy had said and what Chester Bowles (Kennedy's foreign policy adviser and, later, his undersecretary of state) had more or less repeated on our campus. We had been only two out of the ten thousand students who had heard Kennedy at 2:00 A.M. on that chilly fall night of October 14, 1960, and had joined five hundred students who had heard Bowles a few days later. We wrote the letter wondering whether others felt as excited as we did about the idea. We ourselves had not seriously thought of serving abroad before that week, and we did not know anyone who had done so. Yet Kennedy had inspired us, and we were ready to make a commitment. Perhaps others were, too. Still, we never expected what was about to happen.

John Kennedy had come to the Michigan Union to get a good night's sleep, not to propose the Peace Corps. He had just concluded the third debate with Richard Nixon and was about to begin a hectic whistle-stop tour of the state the next day. He was said to have been surprised by the crowd and did not have a prepared speech. The press, having been told nothing was going to happen, had gone to bed. No major newspaper or wire service reported his remarks. Yet what he said touched deeply many of the students who waited for him, and especially the two of us.

Alan Guskin is president of Antioch University.

Why would ten thousand students wait until two in the morning to hear a few words from a presidential candidate? Curiosity has its limit, usually about midnight on a cold night. To understand why we waited to hear Kennedy, and the response that followed his talk, it is important to look at the world of twenty-five years ago through student eyes.

There was excitement surrounding the presidential campaign of 1960. It was not so much the issues discussed—proposals on the Cold War and the arms race conveyed little excitement—as a feeling that students had a role to play, that the torch was, indeed, being passed to a new generation. Change was in the air, and students at Michigan and elsewhere sensed that they were to play an increasing role in making it happen. The civil rights movement, begun in the South, was advancing to campuses in the North. Students were organizing politically to influence their own education. In Ann Arbor, students were collecting canned food to send to a tent city, picketing local stores of national chains that didn't serve blacks, creating a student political party called Voice, and planning a major conference on the state of the university.

Most significantly, John Kennedy's words that early morning seemed to present to students on our campus a way to live our idealism, an opportunity to commit ourselves to the service of others. When Chester Bowles, probably unaware of what Kennedy had said a few days earlier, described how his son and daughter-in-law were serving in an African village, he inadvertently triggered a ground swell of enthusiasm among his restless listeners. What he described was much like what would later be the Peace Corps.

Bowles had given substance to the idea that Kennedy introduced. There were, indeed, people in their twenties living and working in Africa. If they could do this, why couldn't we? Maybe we could make a difference, not only by contributing to economic development but also by helping to create world conditions that could lead to peace and disarmament. After exciting discussions with some of the students in the room where Bowles had just spoken, Judith and I sat down to write our letter. It appeared in the *Michigan Daily* on October 21, 1960:

> . . . Representative Chester Bowles and Senator Kennedy in speeches to the students of the University of Michigan both emphasized that disarmament and peace lie to a very great extent in our hands and requested our participation throughout the world as necessary for the realization of these goals.
>
> In reply to this urgent request, we both hereby state that we would devote a number of years to work in countries where our help is needed. . . .
>
> We also would like to request that all students who feel that they would like to help the cause of world peace by direct participation send a letter to this paper and/or our address. These letters will be forwarded to Ken-

> nedy and Bowles as an answer of the students of the University of Michigan to their plea for help. If it is at all possible, we would like students to start asking others in their classes, dorms, sororities, fraternities, houses, etc. to send letters expressing their desire to work toward these goals. We also request that those who have friends at other universities write to them asking them to start similar action on their campuses.
>
> With this request we express our faith that those of us who have been fortunate enough to receive an education will want to apply their knowledge through direct participation in the underdeveloped communities of the world.

The campus was energized overnight. The phone in our apartment rang constantly, spontaneous discussions dominated the campus, and we did what we could to organize response. We founded a group called Americans Committed to World Responsibility. In less than two weeks, eight hundred students had signed petitions committing themselves to spend several years of their lives serving in developing countries, most of them students who had never previously been involved in campus activism of any kind.

The organizing group sensed that this was a rare moment in which students could have a considerable impact on the formation of a major governmental program. We were right. Millie Jeffrey, a union official who was Kennedy's campaign director in Michigan, heard about the enthusiasm of the students and contacted Ted Sorensen, Kennedy's chief aide and speech writer. Sorensen talked to Kennedy, and a few days before the election, the candidate—describing the response on the Michigan campus—proposed the Peace Corps in a major speech in San Francisco's Cow Palace.

The next day, we were part of a small group that met with Kennedy at the Toledo airport. When Kennedy was challenged about his intentions on the Peace Corps, he answered, "Until Tuesday [Election Day] let us be concerned with this country. After Tuesday, the world."

For us, it was an intoxicating three weeks from Kennedy's speech on campus to the promise of the Peace Corps. Meanwhile, information was pouring into Michigan—and Washington—about student excitement elsewhere. We received petitions from students at Antioch, heard of activity at Princeton and Harvard. The two of us gave speeches on other campuses. On December 9th and 10th, our group in Ann Arbor held what would later be called a teach-in, in which students and faculty members discussed the potential work of the Peace Corps. The conference organized ongoing seminars to prepare papers on the Corps' potential requirements. Their work became a report that later shaped the agenda of a national conference.

Still, we worried that Kennedy might renege on his promise, so we decided to go to Washington for a conference on economic development. We met with Phil Hart, a sympathetic senator from Michigan, who disappointed us by saying he could not publicly support the Peace Corps without Kennedy's endorsement. The next day, however, *The Washington Post* reported that Hart was urging creation of a Peace Corps. Our disappointment turned to elation!

At the conference itself, we found skepticism about the willingness of American youth to serve in the Peace Corps. Convinced that the passivity of college students that had characterized the 1950s was still with us, the panelists urged a small, limited, experimental effort. I challenged those present with the evidence of the previous two months. Students were willing to serve, I argued, and were committed to aiding the developing world. Mrs. Chester Bowles came up to us after the session and spoke fondly of the work done by her son and daughter-in-law in Africa.

In Washington, we also learned of a group at American University that wanted to run a national conference on the Peace Corps. Here was an opportunity to have collaborators, resources, and a Washington site. The conference took place in March 1961, a few days after Kennedy created the Peace Corps by Executive Order 10924. Its sponsors were our Michigan group, the students at American University, and the National Student Association. Representatives from some four hundred universities attended.

Senator Hubert Humphrey, generally considered the father of Peace Corps legislation, delivered a forty-five-minute extemporaneous talk. Sargent Shriver gave his first public speech as Peace Corps director.

The conference, originally planned to lobby the President and Congress to establish the Peace Corps, became a major national meeting to demonstrate the depth of student commitment to Peace Corps service. The Washington meeting was followed by many others like it around the country. In the months that followed, the Kennedy administration was deluged with offers from tens of thousands of young people who wanted to serve in the Peace Corps.

Why did this happen? The 1960s was a time in which students like us were consumed with concern for social values, as well as strategies for change. We were determined not just to participate, but to have an impact on the events that affected our lives. When Kennedy came to Michigan on that night in 1960, the message he left behind was that young people could make a difference in helping to create a better and more peaceful world. He told us we had skills that were useful and ideals that could serve the future of our country. We responded.

Kennedy was forty-two at the time, and many of his advisers, including those involved in planning the Peace Corps, were even younger.

Around the world, young leaders, having fought for independence, were taking on the responsibilities of government in more than forty new nations. At home, young men and women were leading the confrontation with racial discrimination, the most critical domestic issue of our time. The older generation in America had not done very well on this issue, and on others related to questions of war and peace. Kennedy wanted a new beginning for the United States, and we wanted to help him.

That was twenty-five years ago, and in retrospect we are said to have been a generation that was uniquely idealistic, self-sacrificing, active. Today's young Americans are often described as materialistic, asking not what they can contribute to society but what they can get from it. Judith and I sometimes have to remind ourselves that in the 1950s, on the eve of the Kennedy era, our generation, too, was described as passive and self-centered. What explains the fact that the Peace Corps is still alive and well, that thousands of Americans continue to volunteer for service every year? How bad, how indifferent to others and to their countries can this generation be? Has it lost all sense of service? Perhaps, like ours, it is waiting only to be asked.

In the summer of 1961, the two of us were invited to serve as Peace Corps selection officers in the headquarters in Washington. Shortly thereafter, we volunteered to serve in Thailand and entered a training program. On January 18, 1962, we left with the first group of volunteers for Thailand. We served for two and one-half years as teachers at Chulalongkorn University in Bangkok. These were among the most gratifying years of our lives.

LBJ and the Bureaucrats

by Bill Moyers

When the Peace Corps was about to be enacted back in 1961, the old-line employees of State and AID coveted it greatly. It was a natural instinct: established bureaucracies do not like competition from new people. There was another, slightly more idealistic, if still myopic reason: folks who had been presiding over foreign aid all those years simply thought they knew best how to do it, and they pooh-poohed the idea that volunteers could contribute to a field which had been dominated by professionals.

This was, of course, the fundamental fallacy in their perception of the Peace Corps. It was not to be economic assistance in the traditional sense. Money and goods were not to change hands. The Peace Corps wasn't even to be "technical assistance" in the way the term was used by the experts. It was to be a sharing of people. Their experiences, talents, personalities, and eventual contributions were so diverse that to shoehorn them into the existing job descriptions—which the bureaucracy wanted to do—would be to diminish, tame, and finally extinguish the purpose and enduring value of the program.

The very idea of the Peace Corps thus scared the traditional managers of the foreign assistance sector of government. But they couldn't oppose the Peace Corps outright because it had such high visibility with the new President. So they did the next best thing: they sought to absorb it. The result, we knew, would be anonymity for an organization that needed to be publicly conspicuous to attract and excite volunteers, and stifling regulation of an idea whose great virtue was that it was by the government but not for the government. We could not, or so it seemed to us, pour new wine into an old bottle.

By "we," I mean Sargent Shriver, myself, and our colleagues. I was

---

Bill Moyers is a commentator for CBS News in New York.

then working with them in establishing the Peace Corps, having left the service of my mentor and friend, Lyndon B. Johnson. It occurred to me that we should seek the counsel of the new Vice President, who had not only had long experience combating the Washington bureaucracy, but as a young man had been a director of a program not unlike the Peace Corps—the New Deal's youth corps. Shriver and I called upon him. His argument went like this:

"Boys, this town is full of folks who believe the only way to do something is their way. That's especially true in diplomacy and things like that, because they work with foreign governments and protocol is oh-so-mighty-important to them, with guidebooks and rulebooks and do's-and-don'ts to keep you from offending someone. You put the Peace Corps into the foreign service and they'll put striped pants on your people when all you want them to have is a knapsack and a tool kit and a lot of imagination. And they'll give you a hundred and one reasons why it won't work every time you want to do something different or they'll try to pair it with some program that's already working and you'll get associated with operations that already have provoked a suspicious reputation, and the people you want to work with abroad will raise their eyebrows and wonder if you're trying to spy on them or convert them. Besides, you don't have money to give out and all these other programs do, so you'll get treated like the orphan in a big family where your prestige depends upon your budget. And to top it off, they'll take your volunteers and make them GS ones and twos and you'll send little government employees marching off into the villages over there when you want those countries to accept you as American citizens and not employees of the secretary of state. And most important of all if you want to recruit the kind of people I think you want, you're going to have to ask them to do something for their country and not for AID or State.

"This boy here"—he was referring to me—"cajoled and begged and pleaded and connived and threatened and politicked to leave me to go to work for the Peace Corps. For the life of me I can't imagine him doing that to go to work for the foreign aid program. And I don't think your folks are going to write home and tell their mom and dad that they're giving up two years of their lives for the Agency for International Development.

"Earl Rudder [then president of Texas A&M] commanded the Rangers at Normandy—toughest little fightin' bunch in the war. He took a mess of gangly little country boys and turned 'em into the damnedest crowd Eisenhower let loose that day. Now, there had been a big argument in training over whether they were part of the regular forces or not, but ol' Earl told 'em they were an army unto themselves and they believed it. And I'll tell you this—when they went up those cliffs and through those hedgerows like Indians after my grandpa Baines' scalp, it wasn't for Eisenhower and it wasn't for Marshall and it wasn't for the Joint Chiefs of Staff—it was for Earl Rudder and glory.

"And if you want the Peace Corps to work, friends, you'll keep it away from the folks downtown who want it to be just another box in an organizational chart, reportin' to a third assistant director of personnel for the State Department. Who's your boss in this town is important, and as much as I like Dean Rusk, do you think he's going to have time to give to Shriver here when he has a problem that has to be worked out? Hell, he has to worry about the Russians and the Chinese and Charles de Gaulle. You'll wind up seeing his deputy's deputy. And who the hell is going to volunteer to go to Nigeria for the second deputy secretary of state? Who the hell is the second deputy secretary of state, anyway?"

Well, LBJ loved hyperbole, but his point was not lost on us. And he felt so keenly about it that he later personally called JFK and implored him to keep the Peace Corps separate and apart, with a life and identity of its own. The rest is history.

By all of this, I do not mean to disparage our foreign assistance program or our diplomatic force. At its best, foreign aid has also expressed the magnanimity of the American people. But the Peace Corps is to the American government what the Franciscans in their prime were to the Roman Catholic Church—a remarkable manifestation of a spirit too particular and personal to be contained by an ecclesiastic (read: bureaucratic) organization. It is not like anything else.

The Mystique

by Harris Wofford

From the beginning, America has been a sort of comic hero—young, idealistic, friendly, full of curiosity, ready for adventure, ripe for disappointment, never daunted. With self-government their self-proclaimed purpose and pioneering their way of life, the first Americans took the world by surprise. So did the first Peace Corps volunteers.

From Pocahontas and the presentation of the first pipe of tobacco to Queen Elizabeth I to Lindbergh's solo flight to Paris, the Old World has been fascinated by the bold ambitions, naive enthusiasm, and brash innocence of the new Americans. When Cornwallis surrendered at Yorktown, the band played, "The World Turned Upside Down." So America again intrigued the world by founding the Peace Corps.

At the beginning, however, President Kennedy took heat from critics of the new venture. It hurt politically to have his immensely popular predecessor, Dwight Eisenhower, ridicule it as a "Kiddie Corps." A respected career diplomat, Ellis O. Briggs, called the Peace Corps a movement "wrapped in a pinafore of publicity, whose team cry is: 'Yoo-hoo, yoo-hoo! Let's go out and wreak some good on some natives!' " One can be armed with a comic spirit and still not enjoy being laughed at. Yet Kennedy went ahead with the plan, and the President's presumption proved to be prophetic. As one of the first volunteers put it: "I'd never done anything political, patriotic, or unselfish because nobody ever asked me to. Kennedy asked."

To present the Peace Corps as "comic" is not to demean it. The category in which the Peace Corps experience falls is neither farce nor is it at the level of Dante's high comedy about man's spiritual destiny. It is comedy of the human kind, from which one laughs and learns. A comic

---

Harris Wofford is counsel at Schnader, Harrison, Segal and Lewis in Philadelphia and the author of Of Kennedys and Kings: Making Sense of the Sixties.

hero may fall on his face, but the complications and contradictions that trip him can be both entertaining and instructive.

The Peace Corps is "comic" in the spirit of Mark Twain, and just as American. Like Huck Finn and Jim rafting down the Mississippi, Peace Corps volunteers were being sent down larger rivers to deal with dangers more complicated than rattlesnakes.

On March 1, 1961, the President signed an executive order establishing the Peace Corps on a trial basis, a bold step in the absence of any congressional authorization. More than 25,000 people had already asked for applications. Congressional hearings on the proposed new program were soon to begin. But no clear-cut requests for volunteers had yet come from any country. Shriver and the President would surely fall on their faces if volunteers were ready with no place to go.

So Shriver went to talk with some heads of state. As President Kennedy's special assistant for civil rights, I was lucky enough to go along on an expedition to Ghana, Nigeria, Pakistan, India, Burma, Thailand, and the Philippines. The most crucial moments of that seven-country "fishing trip" were Shriver's meetings with Kwame Nkrumah of Ghana and Jawaharlal Nehru of India, two leaders of the Third World whose reaction could open or close the doors in many countries.

"We've come to listen and learn," Shriver said upon landing in Accra. This was a good note to strike with Nkrumah, a graduate of Lincoln University in Pennsylvania, who wanted to lecture Shriver on American shortcomings, some of which he had experienced firsthand in the days when Jim Crow practices prevailed in much of our country.

After some suspense, Nkrumah's response to the Peace Corps was affirmative, with qualifications. In more or less these words, he said:

> Powerful radiation is going out from America to all the world, much of it harmful, some of it innocuous, some beneficial. Africans have to be careful and make the right distinctions, so as to refuse the bad rays and welcome the good. The CIA is a dangerous beam that should be resisted. From what you have said, Mr. Shriver, the Peace Corps sounds good. We are ready to try it, and will invite a small number of teachers. We could use some plumbers and electricians, too. Can you get them here by August?

The Peace Corps had at last been invited, in person, by a head of state! Shriver vowed that he would break the bureaucratic bottlenecks that had slowed transmission in most U.S. aid programs and left expectant countries waiting for a year or more. The volunteers would be there by August.

Then Nkrumah teased Shriver: Why just one-way traffic? Didn't he want some young Ghanaians to volunteer for service to America? In the same half-serious spirit, Shriver said yes, he would welcome and find worthwhile assignments for some volunteers from Ghana. That pitch for reciprocity was repeated by others we met on the trip, and planted the seed for a small experiment a few years later, a reverse Peace Corps of volunteers to America. But that is another story, as is the fall of Nkrumah, who was overthrown in 1966 by a military coup that he charged was aided and abetted by the CIA.

In New Delhi, with his customary red rose in his lapel, Nehru created a different kind of suspense: he seemed almost to fall asleep while Shriver talked. But then he roused himself and said:

> For thousands of years outsiders have been coming to India, some of them as invaders, sweeping down the plains of the Punjab to the Ganges. Many of them stayed and were assimilated. Others went home, leaving India more or less the same as it was before they came. India has usually been hospitable to these strangers, having confidence that its culture would survive, and that it had much to teach the newcomers.
>
> In matters of the spirit, I am sure young Americans would learn a good deal in this country and it could be an important experience for them. We will be happy to receive a few of them—perhaps twenty to twenty-five. But I hope you and they will not be too disappointed if the Punjab, when they leave, is more or less the same as it was before they came.

Though the words were patronizing, this was the green light the Peace Corps needed. Even more significantly, Nehru's approval was an encouraging signal to countries of the nonaligned Third World.

In the fall of 1962, when 225 volunteers stepped out of three planes at the Addis Ababa airport, the Ethiopian minister of education said, "I haven't seen anything like this since the Italian invasion." The volunteers were the first of 500 invited by Emperor Haile Selassie to teach in all the high schools of that spectacularly stark and beautiful mountain country.

They were the largest contingent to go to one country at one time. In a single swoop they doubled the number of college-educated high school teachers in Ethiopia and enabled thousands of additional students to be admitted to studies in the fall. Having resigned from the White House a few months earlier to become the Peace Corps' special representative to Africa and director of the Ethiopian program, I was there to welcome them.

I was also drawn by the unique challenge of the Peace Corps. After the adventure of organizing the Peace Corps' African programs in Togo and Nyasaland (now Malawi), my desk in the old Executive Office Building never seemed quite the same. President Kennedy appeared to appreciate my work in the White House, where I served both as advocate for civil rights and buffer against some of the pressure of the civil rights movement, but I wanted to work on the larger frontier of world integration. Though he had sired the Peace Corps, Kennedy seemed puzzled by its peculiar appeal. Even in giving permission for me to accept the Peace Corps post, he asked, "Wouldn't you rather go out as an ambassador?"

We staff members *were* ambassadors of sorts, as were the volunteers. Open sewers openly arrived at were the first sight to strike the new Peace Corps contingent in Ethiopia as we were bused to the Imperial Palace. The second was the gorgeous mountain scenery.

Fortunately, no one described the scene on a postcard. By now, every volunteer knew what had befallen Margery Michelmore, the *magna cum laude* graduate of Smith College who was expelled from Nigeria for writing an indiscreet postcard home. (When President Kennedy bid goodbye to me, he said, "Keep in touch—but not by postcard!") A somber section of the *Peace Corps Handbook,* entitled "Living in a Goldfish Bowl," had warned volunteers: "You never will have real privacy. . . . Your every action will be watched, weighed and considered representative of the entire Peace Corps." One earnest volunteer teacher, sensing her full ambassadorial responsibility, took as her cautious motto: "Don't smile till Christmas."

Most volunteers, however, smiled soon and often—including at Christmas, when they were invited to visit the emperor to sing carols. During the visit, Haile Selassie told them he had favorable reports on their work from every province and said he had visited the classrooms of a number of Peace Corps teachers. He seemed to enjoy the informality of the volunteers, and at the Christmas party he got a taste of the rambunctiousness of the children of Peace Corps staff. As our own three-year-old son chased a tiny imperial Pekingese between the aging autocrat's legs, the amused emperor said, "If you help us to do away with some of our unnecessary protocol, that will be another of your contributions to my country."

Indeed, the volunteers' contributions were many, in the classrooms and in their communities, though in the schools, ironically, their friendly informality was not as well received as in the Imperial Palace. Teachers complained that the Peace Corps style undermined traditional authority, and students, too, were at first disconcerted. Headmasters warned volunteers to wear ties, not sit on desks, and keep their distance from the students after school. "We want to bring the young up to our standards, not lower ourselves to theirs," was one frequent refrain from Ethiopian educators. Ethiopians, as well as the many Indians in the teaching force, envied the freedom of the volunteers, who were not dependent upon their jobs for their future livelihood. Within limits, the Americans could say what they wanted to say and do more than the career teachers dared to do—or wanted to do. Moreover, with only two years to serve, the volunteers had more reason than lifelong career teachers to exert themselves and try to make their marks in a hurry.

Some of these marks were, of course, intangible, while others could be observed and measured. Ethiopia's choice of English as its language for all higher education made it essential to have teachers whose mother tongue was English. The Peace Corps provided a massive infusion of such teachers, and the students' level of proficiency in English, as measured in both tests and conversation, soared.

Another bottleneck to Ethiopian educational development that volunteers helped break was the centralization of teaching resources. The best schools were located in Addis Ababa, the capital, and Ethiopian and Indian teachers generally considered provincial assignments a purgatory from which they hoped to escape. Peace Corps volunteers, on the other hand, usually sought to go to the most arduous outlying posts. With more than three-fourths of the volunteers teaching in provincial schools, where they often constituted about half the staff, they brought about a rapid broadening of Ethiopia's educational base. This conveyed prestige to the provincial schools, which in turn made them more attractive to Ethiopian teachers.

Outside the classroom, the volunteers were no less audacious in shaking up the traditional school system. Before long, in schools that had previously had almost no extracurricular life, student newspapers, forums, debating societies, drama clubs, glee clubs, handicrafts, scouting, and many kinds of sports were under way. Volunteers taught night courses for adults, especially English for the elementary school teachers. In one town, volunteers advertised courses by beating drums in the marketplace.

In the provincial capital of Dese, U.S./AID had sent the school violins, cellos, clarinets, saxophones, trumpets, trombones, and drums, along with a piano and a record player, but before the Peace Corps, there were no music books and no music teacher. Two volunteers organized a music program for hundreds of students. Soon, amidst excitement in the school and town, the forty-member Dese marching band, with uniforms donated from the United States, was called to play before the emperor on his birthday. The school's pop orchestra, featuring Ethiopian songs, was called to Addis Ababa for national holidays. Soon, a Peace Corps volunteer far to the south at Harar entered the competition, organizing the loudest student band that side of the Nile.

In another provincial capital, volunteers forcibly broke a logjam in the distribution of textbooks, which a custodian kept hidden in the school warehouse "to keep down wear and tear." Each year, the custodian proudly reported that not a single book had been lost, damaged, or destroyed. Almost everywhere, in fact, local school librarians made their lives easier by refusing to lend books, or by keeping the libraries closed most of the time. In most provinces, volunteers fought the "battle of the books" diplomatically, but in Debre Markos, they actually stormed through the warehouse door and seized the books for distribution.

In the little town of Ghion, an independent-minded volunteer named Paul Tsongas—who was later to become a U.S. senator—rented an Ethiopian-style house and invited some of his students to move in. Coming from villages miles away from the town, from which they had commuted every day on foot, many did. Later, Tsongas enlisted a brigade of students to work with him in building a hostel—a one-story dormitory with electric lights that allowed the students to do their homework at night. It became a showpiece of the town and of the Peace Corps, and in due course received a visit and an enthusiastic blessing from the emperor.

The presence of women among the volunteers—more than one out of three of the original contingent—provided an even greater challenge to local traditions. Before the Peace Corps came, virtually no women taught in provincial schools, and Ethiopians could not understand why a young woman would come so far from home to live in a foreign land. They suspected the worst. Faced for the first time with female teachers, boys would grumble that a woman's place was in the home, and then (sometimes) flock to their classes. When a particularly attractive volunteer offered an additional course in French, she was overwhelmed by three hundred eager male applicants. Some Ethiopian male teachers found it difficult to maintain a friendship with Peace Corps women that did not include sex, and unpleasant incidents occurred more than once. But the volunteers held their own, and not one woman quit because of these difficulties.

In fact, after the early problems of adjustment, women volunteers usually earned the respect of their Ethiopian colleagues and students. They took special satisfaction in the influence they had on female Ethiopians, many of whom had never imagined, much less seen, independent women.

Often the triumphs were as simple as that. In fact, what most irked volunteers was the overblown publicity in the United States about their hardships and "sacrifices," as well as the exaggerated accounts that were published about their allegedly exotic experiences and dramatic successes. The story that ought to be told about them, one volunteer wrote, was "not of high adventure *à la* Conrad or Saint-Exupéry—but of dullness." He said volunteers needed a "philosophy which will satisfy our craving for accomplishment and a certain nobility, while we are faced with tedium, fatigue and the desire to sit down and dream."

Yet there were exotic—and comic—moments:

• A volunteer who taught school in the port of Mesewa on the Red Sea lived on a houseboat and was awakened every night by the mullahs calling the faithful to prayer. During the day, he endured the camels that poked into his classroom their not-very-intellectual noses, which he would push out the window with a broom.

• Far to the south, at the opposite end of the empire, a volunteer and staff member were driving a jeep that hit and killed a female camel, forcing them to flee angry Somali nomads who chased them with spears. Later, they settled their liability for $100.

• As Washington headquarters cut down the number of Peace Corps jeeps, in response to Congressman Otto Passman's goading of Shriver about "those blue jeeps roaming the roads of Africa," volunteers turned to other modes of transportation. Once Shriver told this fabled congressional penny-pincher: "I'm happy to report, Congressman, that the donkeys are up and the jeeps are down."

• Five volunteers in the northern province of Eritrea nearly died when they drove a Peace Corps jeep down to the sea for a three-day vacation. After a wrong turn and two flat tires, they found themselves marooned, fifty miles from the nearest village. With a pint of water, a peanut butter sandwich, and jovial recollections of Lawrence of Arabia, two of them set out for help. After walking all day and most of the night, they collapsed in the next day's noon sun. A Bedouin finally came to the rescue, with some sour milk from his goatskin bag.

• One volunteer got caught up in a dubious project started as a semi-jocular proposal when he was driving Shriver around Addis Ababa. Pointing out the confusion caused by the lack of street signs, he boasted to his VIP visitor, "We could make and put up signs in a week." Hearing about the boast, the mayor assigned the volunteer a crew of city workers and told him to go ahead. It took longer than expected, since they had to wait until the city named some of the streets.

• A more presumptuous project—my own—took the Peace Corps to the edge of the politically permissible in that feudal society. We knew the emperor was being pulled in two opposite directions. Younger Ethiopians were urging him to move faster with reform; the old guard was warning him to go slow. The Peace Corps itself was a point at issue. Several of the largest provincial landholders were arguing that the volunteers, by both word and example, were making students dangerously restive. Haile Selassie's better judgment pointed toward reform, and so did many of his statements, but his actions were ambiguous.

After an attempted coup in 1961, the emperor had approved a five-year plan to secure "the advance of our Nation at the fastest possible rate." The programs in that plan—such as universal public education—"are in themselves revolutionary," he said. When the volunteers arrived, they were given the five-year plan, which they considered an eloquent document. But they soon discovered that almost no Ethiopians had ever read it.

The problem was that it had been printed in very limited numbers. When we proposed to the Ministry of Education that it be adopted as a text in English classes, the Ministry approved, on the condition that the Peace Corps reproduce and distribute it. We did, and soon thousands of copies were being read and discussed by students in nearly every province.

Later, Ethiopian friends—some of them in very high places—urged me to exploit the special non-diplomatic status of the Peace Corps to reach the emperor and encourage him to move faster with reform. So, as our two-year term was coming to an end, I included in my formal report on the experience a section entitled "The Emergency," which I wrote with the emperor very much in mind.

A "state of Emergency . . . exists in any country where there is one child without a school or without a teacher or without a textbook," I wrote. The report then went on:

> The Peace Corps was created as an instrument to help interested countries meet this Emergency. It was not designed as a token for countries wishing to give merely the appearance of progress—for countries not prepared to move at the emergency pace required. . . . With millions of children requiring education, a few hundred teachers is a drop in the bucket of Ethiopia's needs. But if the dropping of several hundred American teachers out of the sky becomes the occasion for a far better and massive training and utilization of Ethiopia's own manpower, if the coming of the Peace Corps causes or encourages Ethiopia to double and triple the number of teachers and students each year, then we will have contributed to meeting the greatest need of Ethiopia.

Later, without comment, the emperor thanked me for the report, but on only one front did he take any new action that could be viewed as a response. He endorsed the idea of organizing a domestic counterpart of the Peace Corps to work in the Ethiopian provinces. "If Americans can come all this way to teach and work in our most difficult areas," Haile Selassie remarked to me in one of our last meetings, "how can Ethiopians not do so?" Soon the university was to require Ethiopian students, as a condition for a degree, to serve for a year as teachers in provincial schools. For many of us, the formation of the Ethiopian University Service was the high point in the saga, to paraphrase Mark Twain, of the volunteer Yankees in Haile Selassie's court.

It should be added, though, that these Ethiopian students, radicalized in the countryside, were to play a significant part in the emperor's overthrow a decade later. As I flew out of Ethiopia in 1964, I knew that the students whom Peace Corps volunteers had taught, and the student-teachers in the countryside, were impatient and restless. But no one foresaw the kind of revolution that was to come in the next decade.

The Peace Corps survived and even thrived in Ethiopia for a few years after we left. New volunteers came to add to the group, and to replace departing members. Each new arrival was invited to the Imperial Palace and personally welcomed by Haile Selassie.

But the day came when Haile Selassie, by then almost alone in his palace with his tame lions and his tiny Pekingese, was driven away to a dungeon and to death. Thousands of the students whom our volunteers had taught were also to die. So did other friends and colleagues, including the minister of education, the mayor of Addis Ababa and the president of the university, who launched the program to send students to work in the countryside.

That was a long time ago and in another country. Years later, Senator Paul Tsongas revisited Ethiopia to talk with the head of the revolutionary military government. When he returned to the town where he had taught and had built a hostel, he found few traces of his work. Late at night in his hotel in Addis Ababa, however, there was a knock on the door. Two of his former students were there to tell him how much he had meant to them.

By 1977, when the Peace Corps was forced to withdraw, more than three thousand volunteers had served in Ethiopia. When the former volunteers meet, as they do, they remember small lessons learned and large hopes. But no one can measure how much their teaching and friendship meant to a half-million or more young Ethiopians—or when the seeds of self-government that they planted will mature and flower. There is no telling what Americans will discover through the Peace Corps. But through the men and women who have served, the world has been rediscovering the mystique of America.

An Exchange Between President Kennedy and Tom Scanlon

President Kennedy, in a speech, June 20, 1962:

Recently I heard a story of a young Peace Corpsman named Tom Scanlon, who is working in Chile. He works in a village about forty miles from an Indian village which prides itself on being Communist. The village is up a long, winding road which Scanlon has taken on many occasions to see the chief. Each time the chief avoided seeing him. Finally he saw him and said, "You are not going to talk us out of being Communists." Scanlon said, "I am not trying to do that, only to talk to you about how I can help." The chief looked at him and replied, "In a few weeks the snow will come. Then you will have to park your jeep twenty miles from here and come through five feet of snow on foot. The Communists are willing to do that. Are you?" When a friend saw Scanlon recently and asked him what he was doing, he said, "I am waiting for the snow."

Scanlon, in a letter dated July 14, 1962:

It was a great surprise for me to hear that you had singled me out for my spirit of dedication. I am certain that in many parts of the ever-increasing sphere which the Peace Corps encompasses there are many who have had their dedication tested more than I. I have yet to be sick, whereas one-fourth of our group has had hepatitis. My living conditions are clean and comfortable, and I am sure that in other continents, such as Africa, the daily circumstances of life are much more difficult than they are in Chile.

Your mention was an undeserved honor involving a flash of kind for-

---

Tom Scanlon is president of Benchmarks, Inc., in Washington, D.C.

tune which brought my name to your attention from among the many who could just as easily have been cited. Now it is my duty to respond, and I can think of no better way than to tell you more about the people and place you spoke of. Forgive my presumption in assuming you might have time to glance through the story. The main reason for telling it to you is that it has taught me something about Communism and the role of my country in the world. . . . I have been accused by the socialist press in the most widely circulated newspaper in Chile of deluding you. Here is my translation of excerpts from the article.

BEATNIK YANKEE SCARES KENNEDY WITH HIS STORIES OF INDIANS IN CHILE

> Tom Scanlon is a Yankee youth of twenty-three years. He ought to have hair the color of carrots, freckled skin, drink a lot of milk, a shot of whiskey now and then, and chew one Chicklet after another. In his ranch, he never missed a television program. He likes the ones with lots of redskins.
>
> Now Tom is in Chile. They sent him with the Peace Corps, telling him that they were modern Boy Scouts, young kids who had to act among the Indians and the Communists in Latin America. Tom told President Kennedy about his adventures. They're the same as he saw in the television programs. The grave thing is that a President of one of the largest nations in the world has believed the story of Indians and villages buried in the snow. In what television program did Tom see all this? . . .

The conclusions to the story have to do with the rivalry which now exists between the United States and Communism in these Latin American countries. My experience tells me that Latin America has more to gain by working with us. The Communist solution is a political one, and it must be presented as the political system to end all systems to a people whose natural propensity is to make one political experiment after another. Ours is more social and economic—going directly to the real problems of the people. Our solution is not a political theory which must wait to be applied, but a stimulus to processes which should begin without delay.

I am jealous, Mr. President, of our country's right to be considered a leader in the world's struggle for development. Perhaps it is a youthful idealism to imagine that our whole nation would act in a humanitarian way even if the fear of Communism were not prompting it to do so. I believe it is no more impossible than democracy or human compassion themselves. It could be that this is our most important responsibility as Peace Corpsmen—the education of our people in their possibilities for doing great things in the world.

If this is our responsibility, we have not begun well in fulfilling it. The press reports on the Peace Corps have stressed our early successes rather than the problems that required our presence here. They make it seem we've already made a great contribution when, in fact, we are struggling toward a beginning. I fear the ballyhoo, Mr. President, the self-congratulation of the American people when they praise their own Peace Corps.

When I am working with the *campesinos* and Indians, I regard myself as the extension of the interest of the American people in my involvement in their problems, and when I return to the United States, I hope to hear more questions about their health than my own. Then I will know that my country, of which I am overwhelmingly proud, is ready to take the place of leadership in the world which belongs to it.

THE PEOPLE

The Volunteer

by Jody Olsen

The car was covered with mud as we pulled into the African village. We had driven for three hours over unpaved roads from the Atlantic coast, passing through countless groves of palm trees and neat family compounds, past roadside markets and lovingly tended gardens and farming plots. The young woman beside me was a Peace Corps volunteer, tense but consumed by a sense of anticipation. Since she had learned nine months earlier that she would be assigned to Togo, she had imagined this moment. In this village of five hundred, she would spend the next two years teaching health in the local primary school.

When we brought the car to a stop in the village center, a few people came near, smiled a welcome, and pointed to her new home, a two-room mud-brick hut with a thatched roof, surrounded by a neat fence of dried grass. Children peered shyly at her from behind the fences of their own houses as she moved in her baggage. Thus another Peace Corps adventure began.

I recalled at that moment, and I think often of it still, the start of my own Peace Corps adventure, when, nearly twenty years ago, I first saw my town in Tunisia. It was night, and I was confronted with high walls and veiled women. Since that day, part of my identity has been fixed to that town, and to the Peace Corps. Not far away from my sight, a group of Americans from the Agency for International Development worked as agricultural specialists, retreating each evening into large houses to resume their American ways. It was apparent to me that their technical competence far exceeded my own. My own self-esteem was to come from being part of the town itself, and of its caring people.

One of my responsibilities was to teach child nutrition, using Dr. Spock's *Baby and Child Care,* as it was the only book I had available. I remember

---

Jody Olsen is vice president of programs, Youth for Understanding, Washington, D.C.

an early lecture that I had worked so hard to prepare, on what to do for diarrhea. After I had proudly presented my lesson, an older mother raised her hand and said succinctly, "Give the child rice." I realized that there was a basic wisdom in that community, unsophisticated as it may have been, which I would have to learn to appreciate before I could really teach and be useful.

I am still not sure what I brought to my Tunisian community in the two years I lived there, though I did my best to teach English and family planning, and convey some modern notions of child nutrition. But I have a pretty good idea of what my town brought to me. Twelve years after I left, I went back for a visit, and the family I lived with embraced me as if we had never been separated. My own love for this family even today is as strong as for my family in the United States. In seeing my Tunisian family again, I understood and appreciated how I had grown, and how much I had learned from them, while I was a part of a very special people.

So I knew what the young volunteer was feeling as she reached her village in Togo, where I was then the Peace Corps' country director. I wondered what I could tell her to make her task easier. How could I share my own experiences with her? She had done well in training, but I knew formal training could only help her begin. The Peace Corps adventure is such a personal thing that each volunteer must handle it with the resources of a private, internal spiritual reservoir. It eludes generalizations, textbooks, even words.

I knew from my own experience that the Peace Corps was an adventure based not just on exposure to unfamiliar geography and cultures. That was the easy part. In my own case, the more important exposure was to a segment of my own psyche that I had not previously known. What excited me most as a new volunteer was the challenge of keeping an open mind, of trying out what I had never tried, of resisting the temptation to measure my experiences against what I had done before and was comfortable with, and of adjusting to a psychological insecurity brought on by the requirement to respond to a constant intrusion of the unfamiliar.

In time, the pride I took in myself as a volunteer was in knowing I had the ability and the self-confidence to cope not just with the different, but with the unusual, knowing I could survive. At one point during my first year I wanted to stay in bed to keep away from all the differences, and I got up at six every morning in the cold and did exercises just to force myself to get going. But I made it, and life became better and better. I knew I could give the young volunteer in Togo a few technical tips. But in joining into the life of her village, she was on her own. That is the experience that makes the Peace Corps special.

People in the Peace Corps have given a great deal of thought to the question of what makes a good volunteer, without ever settling on an answer. Aside from self-confidence, the volunteer must have common sense and a feeling for what is practical. I also think that a volunteer cannot succeed without being idealistic. As much as anything, volunteers must *want* to make things better in the community to which they are assigned. But, in equal measure, the volunteer must also have patience, a commodity often in short supply among Americans, especially the young ones.

In most communities in the developing world, the same work patterns have been in place for generations, and volunteers are likely to be dismayed at the desultory pace of change. Peace Corps volunteers usually arrive feeling that two years is all the time they have to make a difference, and that every day counts. Characteristically, they go through a low period, after the initial exhilaration but before they have really mastered either the local language or the customs, when they wonder whether what they do really matters. After that, they begin building friendships, while acquiring a sense of what is possible and what is not. Finally, they feel a part of the community and its reality, and stop worrying about what they cannot do. The best of the volunteers know how to make time pass in a positive way, while they are waiting for events to happen. They are dogged, without being impatient.

But volunteers must also know how to communicate their care and concern. They must know how to establish a trust between themselves and their community. In practice, they must know how to listen and how to detect differences between their own values and those of the community. Furthermore, they must be tolerant of these differences, accepting them as a base from which they may then introduce new ideas to make the community's life better. The volunteer who sees virtue in introducing oxen for farming, new vegetables for family gardens, or inoculations for child health must frame the proposal in a way the community understands and can accept. The success rate is low for new ideas that offend old values. Volunteers must be able to put aside their own cultural system to work in another. In its twenty-five years of experience, the Peace Corps has learned that this is not a capacity given to every volunteer.

Ever since its beginning, the Peace Corps has been trying to determine what makes a successful volunteer. There was apprehension in the beginning years that, unless some more or less scientific method was established to predict success, the Peace Corps would suffer from an excessive proportion of failures among volunteers. The early period was famous—and to some degree infamous—for stories of trainees taking standardized personality tests and drawing sociograms while being counseled and assessed by professional psychologists. This led to "deselection" of those whose inadequacy was predicted, with furtive departures from training that were embarrassing and often damaging. Furthermore, there was never much evidence that the psychological tests were particularly valid. So when pre-service training was moved from the United States to host country sites in the late 1960s, the tests were abandoned.

Now most candidates, having been selected on the basis of academic or professional record, more or less screen themselves out in the course of "in-country" pre-service training. The system is geared to those who *want* to become volunteers, and, empirically, that desire has proved as valid a psychological test as any. When the Peace Corps has had a failure, it has as often been the result of the inadequacy of a project as of the inability of a volunteer to adapt (on an average, about 28 percent of volunteers do not complete their two-year assignments).

There is surely no single reason that Americans decide they want to become Peace Corps volunteers. There has always been a mixture of motives, fusing idealism and practicality. It seems fair to say that a good volunteer must have this combination. It is hard to imagine a successful volunteer who is totally visionary, any more than one who is completely self-serving. In the early 1960s, idealism seemed to be the key, reflecting the mood of the Kennedy years. Recruitment emphasized service over technical skills. In fact, the Peace Corps has from the beginning been quite successful in imparting to generalists in its training programs the basic technical skills needed to provide useful service. On the whole, volunteers have responded ingeniously in adapting the skills taught in training to the needs of the communities in which they have served. Thus, from the start, the Peace Corps felt confident in adhering to the principle that a volunteer's most important attribute was commitment.

Nonetheless, by the beginning of the 1970s, there was a shift in the design of Peace Corps programming, which led to a heavier emphasis on technical skills in the recruitment of volunteers. The Peace Corps began to think of itself as a more conventional development agency and shifted away from volunteers with capacities for improvisation to accommodate volunteers with existing technical training. This, as it turned out, was probably the least successful era in the Peace Corps' history.

The end of the 1970s saw a shift back to an interest in generalists, and in volunteers with high levels of motivation who could be trained in the field. At the same time, the host countries of the Third World—a little older now, and with citizens of their own with advanced levels of training—were requesting volunteers with greater specialization, particularly in the areas of mathematics, science, forestry, engineering, and agriculture. The result, relative to earlier periods, has been an effort to recruit volunteers with "practical idealism," a combination of generalist background with some technical specialty, but more important, an ability to acquire the needed technical skills in the three months of training without ever losing the desire to make a difference. As it happens, the Peace Corps does not seem to have difficulty recruiting volunteers with these attributes.

What explains why an American will volunteer to serve two years away from family and home, often in some physical discomfort, at no pay, frequently in conditions of considerable loneliness? It is a question routinely asked by the Third World people among whom Peace Corps volunteers serve. In some cases, the question reflects suspicion. Some local people simply cannot believe that volunteers would willingly give up American comforts for their more basic way of life. But more often, the question emerges out of the bewilderment of people who may love the Peace Corps volunteers who have come to their community, but who consider estrangement from family and home the worst imaginable punishment.

I specifically remember wanting to join the Peace Corps long before I could give it a rationale. I wanted to go to another country, live in a new environment, test myself on the unfamiliar terms that I knew I would encounter. I knew I wanted to "make a difference," a notion that seems to be a recurring theme among Peace Corps recruits. Who knows where this motivation comes from? In one way or another almost every volunteer has it, combining a fundamental idealism with a practical objective.

For some, the motivation is simple curiosity, the desire to discover another country, experience its food, dress, customs, language. The Peace Corps is, after all, an exposure to the unfamiliar and, to a degree, the unpredictable. The presence of this objective seems to explain why the more exotic countries that the Peace Corps serves, those whose cultures are most far removed from our own—Nepal, for instance—are traditionally those most sought after by volunteers for assignment.

The practical counterpart of this idealism is the prospect, apparently entertained by increasing numbers of volunteers, of using the Peace Corps experience as a springboard into an international career. Twenty-five years ago, this prospect was absent, because there was no precedent, but international organizations have since learned to appreciate the attributes that Peace Corps volunteers possess. Returned volunteers are recognized as having a unique sensitivity to other ways of life and other cultures, and they rate high marks compared with other Americans for their language ability. Peace Corps volunteers, after all, are trained and work in some two hundred languages. It is no exaggeration, furthermore, to say that the energy and adaptability of the volunteer working abroad have become legendary.

Over the past twenty-five years, returning volunteers have become involved in every kind of international work—banking, charity, business, education, and, of course, diplomacy. Currently the Peace Corps is the chief recruiting ground for the State Department and the Agency for International Development, which have on their rolls more than a thousand former volunteers. The World Bank, CARE, and Chase Manhattan Bank provide similar reports. Increasingly, international organizations have revised their job requirements to recruit returned Peace Corps volunteers.

Prospective volunteers also see the Peace Corps as the opening to careers other than international. Graduates of the social sciences and the humanities often consider the Peace Corps a way to spend two useful years while they define their life goals. The Peace Corps is virtually unsurpassed in teaching the use of a foreign language. It has proven important to volunteers in learning or sharpening skills in agriculture, forestry, public health, architecture, and engineering. Many returned volunteers build upon their foreign experience to go into higher education, government service, and even electoral politics. Getting away, having time to think, serving while making personal decisions, and absorbing the meaning of new experiences have all become reasons for joining the Peace Corps.

The rising age of volunteers in recent years suggests that more and more recruits are motivated by divorce, retirement, the loss of a job or the death of a spouse. The 120,000 Americans who have served in the Peace Corps clearly represent a reservoir of information, upon which applicants from every sector of the nation's life feel free to draw. Peace Corps service is becoming familiar—and surely less intimidating—to increasing numbers. The recruiting forecasts of the Peace Corps itself are based upon a belief that, in the coming years, volunteers will be drawn from an ever wider circle, chronologically, geographically, socially.

Still, though every American over the age of eighteen is eligible to join the Peace Corps, it is clear that the pool of available recruits is much narrower. Those wanting to volunteer, for example, must be able to set aside personal and professional activities for a minimum of two years. They must be able to support themselves without compensation other than a stringent monthly allowance averaging $325, and a $4,000 "readjustment" payment after successful completion of the two-year term of service. The financial costs thus tend to exclude the poor, as well as those with family or professional responsibilities.

There is further exclusion in the requirement that all Peace Corps volunteers have a four-year college degree. The only exception is for a few technical posts, but even for these assignments, preference goes to degree holders. Volunteers, furthermore, cannot take children with them, and spouses can go only if there is a position for both husband and wife. Since the Peace Corps currently accepts only about one applicant out of four, the preference inevitably goes to those with the highest levels of education, substantial previous travel experience, a proficiency in languages, and specific technical skills.

The built-in bias in favor of Americans from prosperous origins explains the relative failure of the Peace Corps to bring in minority volunteers. Members of minority groups are less likely to be able to afford the luxury of volunteering. The number of Hispanics who have applied has increased in the last four years, while the percentage of applications from blacks has remained steady. The percentage of blacks who are accepted, however, is less than 3 percent, a fourth the ratio in America.

In fact, the Peace Corps made special efforts to recruit minorities long before the practice was adopted in the United States generally, and it continues the effort. Yet, despite its many recruitment programs, the representation of minorities actually dropped to less than 6 percent in 1985. From the ethnic perspective, the Peace Corps has failed to represent the United States in its full diversity. It is probably the Peace Corps' misfortune that service in its ranks is a privilege of the relatively rich in our society.

In respect to gender, however, the Peace Corps has done substantially better. When the Peace Corps began, 63 percent of the volunteers were men, that figure rising to 69 percent by 1970. Since then, the ratio has dropped to almost fifty-fifty. These numbers come close to representing not only the balance in society but, more pertinently, the balance among college graduates.

Traditionally, the Peace Corps has tended to typecast women in their assignments. Men were generally given jobs in agriculture or construction; women were assigned to teaching or social work. In recent years, however, this has begun to change. It is true that most Third World communities expect men to do the work in forestry or fisheries or in building water systems, but it seems likely that the involvement of women in this work has had a positive impact, not only on women in the Third World but on development itself.

The growing role of women, besides reflecting an important change in our own society, is the product of deliberate Peace Corps policy. Despite the reluctance of individual countries to accept women on certain projects, the Peace Corps has encouraged them to compete for any assignment. I remember the looks of amazement when one of the first female volunteers showed up in a village in Togo on a motorcycle with tools and seeds in hand, ready to work. The Peace Corps assigned a woman as its country director in Oman, a very conservative Islamic nation, and women have become part of a range of projects in many Arab countries. Such women have become important role models in developing societies.

The shift in roles has exacted its price from women in the Peace Corps, as it has in some cases at home. A woman who performs what has traditionally been a man's work has characteristically had to do it better, and with significant community surveillance and harassment. In my own case, working in an Arab country, I waited months before I felt that my contributions were recognized. At that point, I was made to feel I had become the "third sex," playing neither the traditional male nor the traditional female role. The success of one woman usually makes it easier to place other women in "male" jobs, though the sense of unease often remains. But the Peace Corps has committed itself to a principle, and in projects from Liberia to Tonga it has encouraged female volunteers to take the lead in promoting a position of equality for women in development.

"Senior" volunteers are also becoming more common. A husband and wife who had run a restaurant for twenty-five years transferred their experience to an entirely new setting to become food co-op leaders in Fiji. Though a smaller percentage of older volunteers has completed college, they offer years of professional experience in its place. Older volunteers are usually well received in communities in host countries and, in fact, often become community leaders. One recent widower, who became a boat builder and educator on a small Pacific island, so engaged the concern of his neighbors that they regularly offered him candidates for marriage. Another older volunteer told me she had sat around despondently for a year after her husband's death, finally responded to a Peace Corps recruiting advertisement, then left her children and former life to find happiness as a nutrition educator in the Philippines.

When I went back a year later to the village where I had left the young health education volunteer, I found her in her hut with two Togolese "sisters" by her side, playing a flute sonata. She was waiting for me with a special Togolese meal, jointly prepared with her family. Afterward, she excitedly took me on a tour of her village, calling to each person by name. She also described to me the special village rituals and traditions, achieved only by knowing the language. She talked of health issues and of the new well she and the village had just found the money to build. It would be completed before she left.

In her first year she had struggled, had questioned her purpose, had wondered why things moved so slowly. She had received some discouraging letters from home and had cried a little. But now she was happy, was learning, and, more important to her, knew she was making a difference, at least to the families near her. After completing her tour in Togo, she came home to make new decisions about what really mattered in her life. She typified the Peace Corps experience, one we all share. It ties all of us together, no matter when or where we have served.

Letter from India (1962)

I am sure that in some ways my experience differs from that of other volunteers because I am one of two Negroes serving in south India. Few people here have any idea what a Negro is or looks like, and even fewer have ever seen one. Thanks to the movie industry, the common belief is that all Americans are fair-skinned, rich, and polygamous. Fortunately or unfortunately, I don't fall into any of those categories. Whenever someone asks, "Where is your native place?" and I answer, "The United States of America," I encounter undisguised expressions of disbelief. As the conversation progresses, I am again asked the same question, followed by, "And your father's native place?" The same answer again serves to convince my inquirers that I am the world's greatest liar.

My first experience at the village barber angered me until I remembered my uniqueness, and then the situation became comical. As soon as I sat down in the chair, runners were sent out in all directions. When most of the villagers had touched and inspected my head—as the barber stood aside, beaming with pride—my haircut proceeded. I'm sure the first strands never hit the floor, as there was a mad scramble for souvenirs.

At present, I am lecturing in English, world civilization, health, and sanitation, and supervising a physical training program at a rural institute. Two or three nights a week I spend in villages showing educational films in the local language.

So far, my life here has been without any unfortunate incident pertaining to race and color. Hardly a week passes when I don't receive an invitation to attend some social function or to visit someone's home. I feel somewhat of a hypocrite when I speak of the glorious and wonderful life of an American, the free and advanced educational system, job opportunities, politics, and social life. I praise these institutions knowing that this life is not enjoyed by all Americans. I often wonder what thoughts occur in the minds of volunteers who, in the U.S., live in places where to extend similar hospitality to a Negro would mean sure social ostracism and possibly economic reprisal.

Words fail me when I try to express the feeling I get of living in a country where I am free to come and go as I choose, without that nauseating feeling that occurs when you sense you will be denied service in a restaurant. In some ways, it is ironic: I am enjoying, in a country thousands of miles from my own, a way of life that every male in my family has served in the U.S. armed forces to protect. It is an ordeal to explain how the black man came to be an American. Describing the Civil War in a new and strange language is no easy feat. Even with thoughts of this and of life in the southern U.S., when I am asked to name the country I would prefer to live in, I do not hesitate to say America. With all its faults, I sincerely believe that I can one day share in the wealth and glory of what I think is the world's greatest government and people.

Letter from Iran to the Peace Corps Director (1965)

This letter concerns something which I have strongly come to believe. If I didn't feel a sense of responsibility for the work of Peace Corps everywhere, but especially in Iran, I wouldn't bother to write you. I've been here a little over nine months, and it is my conviction that unmarried girls shouldn't be included in a Peace Corps project in Iran. I write this not as a volunteer serving in a small provincial town, but as one who teaches in a university in a large provincial city. One would think, therefore, that we have had a chance to meet many Iranians, relate with them, discuss ideas with them, and in general get beyond the scope of "teaching English." This is not true. All of our colleagues are older men who couldn't speak with us other than good-day pleasantries for fear of breaking social customs. Never could we have been invited into their homes. The only exception was a young Irishman hired to teach English with us and who formed our sole basis for intellectual and social activities at the university.

We attempted to make up for this lack by starting an English club for our students, getting to know those Iranians who make an effort to be friendly, and meeting other Westerners in town. Our English club was the one thing that the students had which resembled a group working situation—not for grades but for fun and pleasure. But this evidently upset some of the other professors and our dean, who saw a breakdown of the traditional teacher-student relationship. It also caused unfavorable comment about our conduct.

We've received no reaction whatsoever from our teaching activities, except an unfavorable one from the fact that we spoke pleasantly in the halls to our students or answered their questions between classes in the school commons. As for meeting Iranians who were largely educated abroad, we've found out now that these fellows haven't a respectable reputation in town. That we were seen talking to them (not dating, mind you) caused comment enough for us to be censured by the dean.

We never considered the consequences from our meeting and associating with other Westerners, who turned out to be our *only* social contacts. This isn't particularly desirable in light of the Peace Corps ideal of living with the people. It also classes us with other Westerners who live and work here, and that may be bad. I don't know yet.

Every action we've taken has been scrutinized. We bother Iranians who can't fathom why unmarried girls would leave their homes to come here and live alone. Their conclusion is that such girls are up to no good. No one bothers to understand our motives, least of all the average man in the street, who takes advantage of an un-*chadored* girl to say dirty phrases to her, brush up against or bump her, or even actually deliberately run into her on a crowded street. All these actions, without exaggertion, have happened to me *every day.* In addition, the taxi drivers make unpleasant comments. Why? Obviously, we've given them cause to think they can be familiar—we come and go at will to our classes, some of which are at night, are seen visiting the homes of our friends later than nine-thirty or ten in the evening, make business trips to Tehran alone, and give parties in our home.

It is my contention that our mere presence here is hurting Peace Corps' image. True, we aren't here to be like other Americans. But I don't think it's necessary to become "just like an Iranian." Men are allowed much freedom in this double-standard country. As far as Peace Corps is concerned, this means a male volunteer is freer to be himself, to relate with other men, to get to know them and their country. I feel hampered, though I shouldn't be, for I feel I was told what would happen by many, including two earlier volunteers in Iran who were at our training site. All of it just didn't sink in. Much has happened to me that has been wonderful. I wouldn't trade places with anyone. I didn't expect it to be easy. But I didn't understand what it means to be a second-class human—a female.

Letter from Mauritania (1985)

As an American, I can never really forget that I'm in a developing part of the world. Nothing could illustrate that better than my life here in my village, N'Gawle. At the same time, because I am so immersed in the culture, in the timelessness of this life, for the most part it has come to feel very natural. Yesterday, for the first time when I demonstrated my skill, women actually told me I *could* pound rice! What an accomplishment.

There's a fatalistic, *Allah jebbi* (If God wills it), things-take-time attitude here. It really permeates the whole country. Partly due to Islam and the absolute omnipotence of Allah, but also I think related to the different perspective of Africans. The concept of progress is so ingrained in us as Americans—your children should do better than you. That drive is pretty absent here. It's more of an honor for the kids to be Koranic students, and beg for money and food for themselves and their teacher, than to go to school and learn French. It really gets me crazy when I think about the fact that none of these kids ever reads books—maybe they have one school book but, beyond that, nothing. Things are oriented much more toward the land, the status of the rice harvest, where the money for oil for that day's lunch will come from. Life here on the banks of the river is the life they've lived for centuries. A Yale education didn't prepare me for a lot of the challenges I face here.

At times, identifying and clarifying my role in the village presents the toughest obstacle. There will always be resistance to me, perceptions of me as a *tubok* (foreign, white person), as a patron (source of money, gifts), even as I eat what they eat, live as they live, dress as they dress, speak their language. Similar constraints hamper my work. I'm working on opening a health center, where I can give lessons, weigh babies, dispense the village medications. But they have no real reason to listen to me—they have done things the same way forever. If I don't have any medicine or shots to hand out, what possible good am I? The people here welcome me into their homes, but the health education I try to dispense is too foreign an approach. Every day I have to remind myself that change takes a long time. And they'll tease me about not being married and pester me to pray to Allah five times a day until I leave.

Although I am a bit low now, and thus aware of the loneliness and isolation that goes along with all this, I continue to marvel at the experience. But if I enjoy it so, and feel so myself here, why do I choose to cram into that bush taxi and, every few months, ride away from it all? I long and long for the escape to Nouakchott [the capital], for that submersion into Americana. Shouldn't that yearning tell me something? In Nouakchott I feel dispirited about my work, but I get into that taxi, and after, onto the sacks of powdered milk in the back of a pickup truck that takes me the windy last three hours to N'Gawle, because I expect it of myself. It's what I came here to do. And the joy of it is that after the initial readjustment, I am *so* happy to be here. I know that I have come home.

Reports and Letters on Life, Work, and Love in the Peace Corps

MALAWI

This afternoon I got out our trusty dull hatchet and killed a chicken—mmm! We cooked a fried chicken, hot-water cornbread, tomatoes, other vegetables such as eggplant and squash. Well, after we finished eating, here came the chief's daughter with plates of food. So we ate a bit, bursting at the seams all the while. After we had eaten that, we sat around and groaned and wished for milk of magnesia when here came Modesta's son (Modesta is one of the chief's daughters, who is married and has about six children)—with a big bowl of bean soup! It was delicious, but I was too sick to appreciate it.

Last night we went to Mwanje, about two miles away, to a Youth League dance. The League is the compulsory organization that all Malawi young people must belong to who are not in school—which is most of them. It is a political organization. They march for three hours four days a week. I don't know why, but they do—girls and boys. They march and run and sing political songs. They are organized by the Young Pioneers, a tough young bunch of men, and not to be fooled with since they have been declared as a legal police force with the power to arrest and even shoot anyone suspected of plotting against the government. A great responsibility for young men with little or no education and only some training in marching and military maneuvers. These Youth League dances are held every Wednesday night and Saturday in each district, and no dances can be held in the villages when a Youth League dance takes place. You see, the admission fees go to the party organization.

When we entered the dark hall, lit by a kerosene lantern at one end, the crowd parted before us, and we were led to the front of the hall, where chairs had been placed for us as guests of honor. I was so embarrassed! They were trying to be very kind to us, but I would rather they had just gone ahead as if we weren't there. But it was not possible. The dance was enjoyable, and we danced much. Around midnight we left. The two-mile walk home in the moonlight was beautiful, although as were descending one hill, on the gravel, I slipped and fell and cut my leg a little. Nothing serious, though.

We are really beginning to feel a part of the village now, because the babies don't cry anymore when they see us—in fact, miraculously enough, a couple of them will even let us hold them without screaming, although they do keep an eagle eye on their mothers to make sure they are not being abandoned to these bleached persons. We are slowly getting to know the names of some of the children. They are beginning to become personalities, and are nearly all little characters and show-offs. They've taught us some Nyanja songs, and we've taught them some American ones.

TUNISIA

Endurance, patience, and determination are necessary for a volunteer placed in an ill-defined job that he is all too often technically ill-qualified for. He needs these characteristics to stick it out until he can get across to the strangers around him who and what he is and what he is trying to do. This can be a discouraging task, and sometimes, when his and the Peace Corps' concept of the job is out of kilter with local reality, it is an impossible task. In the latter case, he needs these qualities to avoid defeatism as he either modifies his concept of the job or seeks a different one.

Take Marilyn, a girl whose humility keeps her from standing out in a group. When she arrived at Hammam Lif to take up her physical education assignment, she related, "They asked me what I was and why I was there. It was depressing to get such a reception." When she explained her assignment, they put her to work right away, but mostly at making beds and keeping the kids quiet during endless idle hours. "I was overburdened," she said, "but with things any moron could do." She worked with two shifts of girls at the Bourguiba Village, four hours with each shift. The girls got their physical education at the school they were taken to in town. Marilyn's job was to occupy their spare time. She supervised games outdoors in good weather and organized projects like puppet shows indoors in bad weather.

Marilyn's problems were made harder because the directress of the village was indifferent and stayed away from it as much as possible, and because troublemakers from other villages were transferred there. The directress never bothered to get equipment, not even shorts, which Marilyn finally bought out of her own pocket.

Inevitably, she said, "I ran out of things to do, and the novelty wore off for them. By the end of the school year, I was really fed up." But she met many Tunisians, and these friendships, she said, were what made life bearable. In her second year, she doggedly diversified her mission. She persuaded the directress that four hours a day of spare-time minding was too much for the village girls as well as for herself. So she works at the village only in the mornings now. Four evenings a week she teaches English at the Bourguiba Institute in Tunis, commuting by train and bus. Saturdays she spends teaching at a school for the blind. Weekday afternoons she prepares for her night classes.

"I'm really enjoying this year," she says. "All three projects are challenging. But I believe the change from last year is more in me than in the situation. I've grown up a lot and learned a lot about myself."

PERU

Kitty and Sue have developed their programs within urban Arequipa. Kitty, an arts and crafts worker, has established contact with local producers of small articles and is working, particularly with ceramics producers, to help them improve the quality and design of their products. Sue has organized a local choral group which recently won second prize in an area competition. She has found there is a great deal of interest in music within the *barriadas.* She discovered her own counterpart in a music teacher who is assigned to the general Arequipa area. She is now forming a boys' choir in an orphanage. Out of 100 boys she got 100 percent turnout. Her own vitality and interest serve as a spark to her activities. She is well-received in the communities, and is well-liked by the young children with whom she works.

Jim and David are interested in the small-industry approach to manual arts. In addition to their classes, which have reached 250 persons, they have been holding meetings with local artisans and encouraging discussion of their problems of production and marketing. The manual arts group has high hopes of being successful, and I believe this project can contribute greatly to the development of the community, if its members are content to settle on one or two activities and keep the project within the local context.

SIERRA LEONE

Barbara, Jack, and Eleanor have taken the town and the school by storm. Barbara runs the library; Eleanor operates what amounts to an outpatient clinic; Jack took over the training of the school track team. Jack does carpentry with the villagers; Barbara gave a huge party for her cook's wife (featuring dancers from the women's secret society); the three have started raising chickens and vegetables. But their splashiest project was the library for the primary school.

During the Christmas vacation, the group invited a large number of Peace Corps volunteers to Jimmi to build a library. Volunteers swarmed to Jimmi. Without much Sierra Leonean help, they made the blocks for the building and began to put up the walls, leaving it unfinished to return to their jobs. The volunteers, doing something different and tangible, were most enthusiastic about it. The paramount chief and the principal were gratified and impressed. Jimmi Bagbo had never seen anything like it.

After the volunteers left, local people slowly began to work on the unfinished building, which will soon be opened and dedicated. The project was spectacular but would have been worthless if the villagers had not finished it. Why they did hasn't been fully explained. The only explanation I can offer is that after two years, the town has come to identify with the volunteers, as the volunteers have identified with the town. If the same project had been started when the Peace Corps arrived, the building would still be unfinished.

NEPAL

I think I may have solved, or at least partially solved, the problem of students making disruptive noise while I teach. The other teachers told me how to do it. "*Tapaille le bademas haru lie pitnu parcha,*" they said, which roughly translates as "You have to hit the bastards."

The mere mention of corporal punishment prompted in me the proper amount of Northeastern-white-liberal-public-school-educator reaction, as I informed my colleagues that I *never* hit students. It's just not necessary, I said. Boy, was I a stooge. It *is* necessary. People respond here only to punishments they've been conditioned to expect—and to view fear *as* punishment. Just as corporal punishment wouldn't work in Montgomery County, Maryland, noncorporal punishment doesn't work in Pythan, Rapati. I've also found that you have to give a kid a fairly good punch to make the punishment effective. They've been struck by parents, older siblings, and teachers throughout their lives, so a light shove won't do more than elicit laughter.

I hit my first kid early last week and have since struck two more. Not really hard blows (he wrote defensively, betraying the fact that he hardly feels as comfortable with the new method of discipline as he'd like to), but hard enough to keep the noise down—or at least to keep them quiet enough to run a class. It wasn't easy hitting that first kid. I actually didn't hit him, but threw him to the ground. But it was interesting how quickly I got over it. Immediately afterward, I felt like a complete schmuck. I was the guy friends have said makes Mahatma Gandhi look like Caspar Weinberger, and here I was betraying everything I believed in. Or so I thought. But as soon as I resumed the lesson and hit my stride, I forgot about it.

Adaptation isn't a matter of choice out here. You simply have to do it, and this includes the adaptation (adulteration?) of your most strongly held principles. A lot of the Peace Corps literature they send you before you join is bullshit, but the part about doing things that surprise yourself isn't. It's fact.

CAMEROON

Tony, who came here to teach English, explored the warm beer circuit in the village bars for awhile. He took walks on the beach, talked with fishermen. The picturesque coastline in both directions from Kribi is peppered with fishing villages, some of them populated by Nigerians or Togolese. The fishermen make big catches, but a very small percentage satisfies the local food demand. Although some of the balance is crudely smoked and lasts awhile longer, the bulk is left to rot on the beach.

Tony went to the prefect of Kribi. Why not organize a cooperative and transport the surplus catch to inland towns for sale? The prefect was agreeable, but pointed out that it had been tried once before and failed, mostly because the guy who ran the co-op absconded with the receipts.

"The prefect doesn't want to risk his political position on a project that might fail," said Tony. "He won't do anything about arranging transport until I can prove the project will be sure-fire. I want to start small and take a few chances but I can't until I can get some transport. It's a delicate chicken-and-egg sort of thing."

At this point it is hard to tell which will come first, but Tony has been moving steadily toward success.

First, he got himself invited out on the ocean to fish in pirogues. Next, for $8, he had his own dugout built—a *moustique* about twelve inches wide and ten inches deep. But handling it in the surf is tricky, and he gets dumped into the sea with considerable regularity. Under construction while I was there was a bigger and less tippy pirogue, which Tony had built for a flat $16. The fishermen weren't sure at first why Nutty Tony wanted to dump himself in the drink and learn about fishing, but they are all for him. They listen now, when he explains his plans for marketing their fish.

Tony has walked several miles north and south along the coastline, talked chiefs into calling meetings, proposed his scheme to fifty or sixty at first. Soon, new fishermen came around looking for him. He's made his pitch to more than two hundred, and they want to give it a go.

"I have had money offered, but won't take it until I am sure it will get back with a profit," says Tony. "Between school terms this Christmas, I'll go to Ebolowa and Yaoundé to try to get merchants there to agree to pay for fresh fish. If I can bring that assurance back to the prefect, I think I can get him to arrange the transport."

Tony had been at Kribi a little over three months when I saw him. He says he has only two years and wants to start something that will carry on after he leaves.

"For hundreds of these people on the coast, this could be an economic transfusion," he says. "For people in the interior, a whole new source of protein in their diet."

His project faces many pitfalls, but even if it fails, the Africans around Kribi won't soon forget the American Peace Corps English teacher. He's the first white man they've ever seen taking on the ocean on their own terms, walking the beach with an idea about their rotting surplus.

MALAYSIA

Are married couples more effective in community development than single volunteers? For rural Malay society, the answer to this question seems to be yes. Malay society is built around the family as social unit. The pervasive values in the rural areas are social ones. These values underlie all activities in a *kampong* [village], so in order to function naturally and effectively in the rural Malay setting, one must be accepted as a social unit, that is, a married couple. Without this social status, acceptance into the community in which one lives becomes more difficult, because the people do not know what position to assign you.

The single community development volunteer can work on the periphery of society, not necessarily becoming emotionally entangled.

However, the inherent advantage of a married couple's involvement in society carries along with it the pressures of continual social demands. The problems of acceptance and involvement are the first steps to beginning community development work. After, the question of what the man does and what the woman does arises. The inferior role is extremely difficult for an American woman to accept; yet the Malay social context places her in this position.

The wife often has periods of depression, seeing her husband go off to dig ditches, pour cement, or split bamboo. She wishes her part of the job could be so easy! By physical labor willingly given, a man can earn the immediate respect of the *kampong*. His advice is thereafter sought on various community problems.

A woman cannot easily play an influential role in *kampong* affairs. Negotiations are considered more serious when undertaken by a man. A wife can be more effective by being a good cook, housekeeper, or gardener. Her peers, the other *kampong* wives, will be curious at first about her activities, but will soon identify with her and offer their friendship. A wife in community development can also carry new ideas—family planning, sanitary housekeeping, children's education, handiwork opportunities—directly to the member of the family who can use and benefit by them the most.

To look separately at the jobs of a husband and wife in community development is to see only half of the situation. The people of a *kampong* look upon them as a unit. They complement each other in many respects, so that their work cannot be broken down into male-female categories. The husband gives his wife support by providing an authority figure for some of her ideas and projects. Married, the female volunteer has a needed identity as wife. *Kampong* women become aware of an additional aspect of her life, that of the wife actively supporting her husband's endeavors and participating with him as a unit, a couple, in community affairs. Rather than letting the world pass them by, *kampong* women may be encouraged out of their complacency to extend themselves beyond their mundane daily activities.

TOGO

The problem of sex might just as well be raised here as anywhere else. It is a problem for a variety of reasons, and the country doctor is struggling manfully to cope with it, but there is really little he can do, humans being what they are.

There is an impending marriage between a reluctant fishing volunteer and the daughter of a chief. There is also ample indication of affairs involving female volunteers and Togolese men. There are affairs involving female volunteers and volunteer men. There are affairs involving volunteer men and Togolese women. And there is a bit of VD.

The Togolese, I am told, take these things rather lightly. But the question of paternity suits, already noted in one African country, may well seem chronic in the course of time, and the Peace Corps may be forced to give the question of sex greater attention during training.

PAKISTAN

A few things some volunteers brought or were sorry they did not:

Food: canned meats, popcorn, candy
Film: very expensive here
Camera, radio, typewriter, raincoat
Injector blades: impossible to get here
Toothbrushes, shaving lotion
Knapsack: excellent for traveling and trekking
Iron: international model, 220V
Sears catalog, pictures of family, home, etc. Very important!
Clothing: Many of you will have clothes made here, so don't spend your whole clothing allowance before departing. Men should have a good supply of underwear, T-shirts, socks, and work shoes. I can't help the women on this topic.

RECIPE FOR HOME BREW

10 lbs sugar
3 lbs. malt (bring this from States)
1 pkg. yeast
19 gal. H_20

Set in crock until no bubbles rise (ten to fifteen days). Bottle and let it set two weeks before sampling.

GHANA

Example of making students think: one day he took a math class out to the athletic field, divided it into groups of eight, and had each group elect a leader. He gave each group a one-foot ruler, and then handed one group an old tire, another a board, a third a crooked branch, told the fourth to find its own implement, and told them their assignment was to measure the track—and to start doing it by some method within two minutes. There were excited conferences. The kids with the tire started by measuring its diameter and flopping it end over end; then someone figured out that they could measure its circumference and count the rolls around the track. The students to whom he had given no implement decided to use a girl student's belt as their measuring rod. Each group completed the task with reasonable accuracy in short order and with a great feeling of accomplishment.

A challenge never to do himself what he can get the students to do themselves. "The Ghanaians have a clock that runs about an hour behind ours, a calendar that runs a day behind. Time and again I have to choose between letting them complete a task behind schedule or doing it myself. I force myself to let them finish it—late."

The Benefits

by Warren W. Wiggins

Once upon a time, two social philosophers named Burdick and Lederer wrote a book. They had a notion that America was sending abroad beauty-contest winners as the people's representatives: good-looking, well-barbered, handsomely dressed "cookie pushers," who stayed in the big cities, didn't travel to the boondocks, and could always be found not too far from their spacious air-conditioned houses, swimming pools, well-stocked commissaries, and chauffeured limousines. Lots of ordinary Americans read this book and agreed things abroad were a sorry mess.

The social philosophers also described a man who wasn't pretty, who lived in the boondocks and helped people build water pumps and dig roads. His trousers were striped with grease and dirt. He was devoted to helping poor rural people, so he learned their language, ate their food, and wore clothes appropriate to his work. Although he was not blessed by good looks, to the poor people he was helping, he was beautiful.

Burdick and Lederer named their book after this central character, calling it *The Ugly American.*

And the ordinary Americans who read the book said: "We need more ugly Americans overseas."

Twenty-five years and 120,000 ugly Americans later, we are faced with the question: "What has it all meant?"

We know that the Peace Corps expressed the tenor of the times. President Kennedy then symbolized a philosophy of optimism, a belief in the role of leadership, a sense of new beginnings, and an assertion that youth was to be valued for its vigor and freshness. Kennedy went further and challenged Americans to "Ask not . . ." He expected the youth of America to be participants in a revitalized, personalized, optimistic approach to overseas involvement.

Warren W. Wiggins, president of The New Transcentury Foundation in Washington, D.C., is one of the founders of the Peace Corps.

The assessment of the Peace Corps' achievements begins with the three original purposes enunciated early in 1961, though they were but one part of the new President's broad program.

The first purpose was to provide skilled manpower for some of the jobs that needed doing in the Third World. As a large-scale employment/placement agency, the Peace Corps has done a creditable job. However, as Peace Corps director *ad interim,* I was also painfully aware of French speakers assigned to Latin America, trained science teachers raising chickens, and medical technicians teaching English. Worse memories, of course, are about thousands of volunteers who never found *any* meaningful job in the course of their overseas tour.

Nonetheless, the Corps' record as a provider of skilled manpower remains good. Most volunteers attest to this, and the host countries continue to ask for these people. It is still true that all Peace Corps accomplishments begin with a solid job that needs doing, and by and large volunteers have done it well.

The second purpose was to enable people in the Third World to learn more about Americans. To the extent that the poor of the villages and rural areas had *any* prior perception of Americans, it came from the propaganda mills of the West and East via rumor and grapevine, and via odd bits of scattered images, nearly always by word of mouth.

And the one word that dominated these images of Americans was "rich." Of course, by any standard, it was a highly accurate word. But the people in Third World villages knew that "rich" always meant a blend of uncaring, overbearing, insolent, and untrustworthy. In their experience the rich were the hated landowners and employers, the tyrants and the oppressors. Rich people were different, strange, and their behavior was bad news.

But this new American arrived on a jitney, mammy wagon, lorry, or bush taxi. Sometimes the volunteer arrived on foot or bicycle, and half the time it was a young woman! Though these Americans told stories of the prosperous land of their birth, the actual volunteer came to *stay,* to live, to work, to wear the same clothes, to eat the local food, to speak the language. But most important, they came to help do the usual, regular work of the town: teach in a classroom, help build a feeder road, raise chickens and ducks, and try to market vegetables for a piddling amount of cash.

And it still remains a mystery to thousands of the world's poor *why* this young American, this *rich* young person, would want to be poor for a couple of years and would want to do one of the menial jobs so abundant in their towns.

But what happened was not a mystery. For two years their kids were taught; they daily saw this American at work on the road that would lead to a market, and they sang and played together, became friends, and above all, shared lives in an atmosphere of growing mutual understanding and admiration.

The third purpose of the Peace Corps was to increase American understanding of Third World peoples. There is little doubt that our national perceptions of the Third World, both positive and negative, have been greatly enhanced by this people-to-people program. Peace Corps volunteers not only grow enormously in their understanding of the developing world during their years of service, they also become more effective people. After the Peace Corps service, they have often ended up in positions where their increased knowledge is communicated to fairly large numbers. Many of them have substantial responsibility for influencing great American institutions.

But this understanding was not just an encyclopedic addition of the Third World's social, political, and economic features. What was learned also had to do with a growing appreciation that other peoples have different life goals, different sets of values, different dilemmas in their national and individual lives. Peace Corps volunteers grew in recognizing that *effective* help from one nation (usually rich) to another (usually poor) must truly start with understanding. And as this appreciation grew, the volunteer changed. His or her own value system was altered, his or her own framework for evaluating approaches to fundamental life issues was enlarged.

This learning process was quite remarkable. Young Americans went abroad, leaving at home the elaborate support systems that had enveloped them. Graduating college seniors came out of one of the most protective human environments ever devised. And the product of this protective environment was not considered especially susceptible to new kinds of learning, particularly the kind of learning that required a reassessment of one's value systems.

The Peace Corps "took" this graduating senior and with appropriate transitional training sent him or her overseas *without* any of these usual supports, and often without defined regular activity. The volunteer was then confronted with new customs, different food, and a goal: *to live as if he were poor*. He was to behave as if wealth, career enhancement, fame, or fortune were not motivating features. She was stripped of nearly all the trappings of American civilization. The volunteer was asked to stand naked in a strange land: somewhat embarrassed, insecure, misunderstood, without technology, and, above all, he or she was asked to be the quintessential American. On top of all this, it was abundantly clear to the volunteer that he or she had a real, ever-present responsibility to both his or her hosts and his or her own country to be effective on the job and in personal relationships.

As we assess the Peace Corps' accomplishments, it becomes clear that the purposes proclaimed twenty-five years ago have not essentially changed. What *have* changed are the times. Thomas L. Hughes, president of the Carnegie Endowment for International Peace, recently noted a shift in America's position on international involvement. "Traditional internationalist themes are no longer significant outlets for political idealism in the United States," he remarked. "Instead, they are the objects of derision and contempt." Hughes' perspective suggests that there is a clash between the Peace Corps' ideals of service and mutual learning on the one hand and "exhausted internationalist impulses" on the other.

Yet it remains manifestly clear that there is a continuing need for skilled people to fill jobs in the Third World. Further, the need for mutual understanding remains, whatever the shift in the overall national mood.

We also need to consider the developments in Third World thought that have coincided with the change in America's stance. The Third World is now telling us:

> Yes, we need your help, your dollars, your wheat, your technicians, your Peace Corps volunteers, but we don't like the way you insist on managing the whole show. Your programs are awfully slow, terribly bureaucratic, and you are so afraid of a little waste, a little personal "take" in public programs, and a little political influence in economic development issues. Because you are the "donor," you behave as if you have divine rights to manage our so-called "cooperative arrangements" with *your* people, *your* accounting systems, *your* formulations of the good economic development planning process. We prefer to be more in charge; we prefer to apply our value systems even if we achieve "less development" by your computerized standards. Please don't tell us how to balance minority rights or race relations with economic theory. Please don't tell us how women in our country are held back by our antiquated cultural perspective. Even when you come to our country as foreign AID managers or as Peace Corps representatives, remember your primary identification in our mind is as an invited guest. And don't think that because we understand you better, or because we have known volunteers, that indeed we will vote with you, adopt your values, or even like you better—though we might.

On reflection, those of us who were involved in the original design of the Peace Corps must now recognize how "American" it all was: the designers, the implementers, the leaders, the selectors, the trainers, and, most important, the volunteers—all American.

The Peace Corps was one of many forces that helped Third World peoples to change and grow, so that from their viewpoint, the greater the success, the less relevance the Peace Corps has to their lives and to their countries. Moreover, the history of the Peace Corps and its accomplishments, as measured against its initial purpose, is of such high order that we can take heart in having launched a new enterprise that sustained itself. There is no reason that we should not be able to come up with other approaches, reconciling the new mood in the United States with new goals overseas.

In considering our future needs for new forms, a different retrospective evaluation of Peace Corps accomplishments is useful. Having rolled the dice in 1960 and 1961 and come up with a winner that has stood the test of decades, we now need to ask: how was it possible for the federal government to initiate a new, daring, even bold experiment that was well received by U.S. citizenry and the overseas developing peoples? What were the elements that enabled the U.S. government to successfully launch this new tool, this new approach? What were the significant factors that enabled the Peace Corps to be born, and to survive, when it was designed to be anti-bureaucratic; when many of its goals ran counter to civil service tradition; when many of its pronouncements indicated pride in its renunciation of some hallowed aspects of its parent agency, the Department of State?

The innovative birth of the Peace Corps is important to America as a retrospective case study, particularly now that America asks itself what will replace the old internationalism. It was not a freak occurrence; maybe there are more where it came from.

Central to this—and no doubt any future—creation was the belief of everyone involved that risk was an essential ingredient that was *not* to be avoided; minimized, yes, but not avoided. Significant risk was thought to be a positive feature. The Peace Corps was not *crucial* to anything; therefore it—and all associated with it—could be, and should be, at risk. It was valuable if it worked, but it sought only participants who could risk failure. The volunteers and staff risked their time and, to some extent, their reputations in something that might well have flopped. But while they were doing it, they were proud of the risk—it was a *positive* element of their service. With risk as an ingredient, the right kind of human resources were assembled to enhance the chances for success of the institutional innovation.

In some future time, a Third World social philosopher might say: "Since the Peace Corps happened here, not in America, I will write the sequel to *The Ugly American.*" In the closing chapter of his book, he will seek an answer to the perennial question "What has the Peace Corps meant?"

He will rely first on an exchange recorded by Gerard T. Rice in his fine study *The Bold Experiment*:

> In El Salvador (which at the time of the Peace Corps was an independent nation-state) there took place the following encounter between a Peace Corps "official" and a Peace Corps volunteer:
>
> Official: How will you describe your Peace Corps experience?
> Volunteer: Well, I won't sell it. (Pause)
> Official: What will you say?
> Volunteer: I'll tell them what it was like. (Pause)
> Official: Such as?
> Volunteer: The best goddam experience a young man can have. Worth four years of college.

His second story will concern a couple. The wife decides that they—husband and wife—will do what *she* wants to do for the first time in their long married life. They are an older couple living in California, and they have always made life's big decisions based on the husband's career. He is a conservative corporate gentleman who sees no reason ever to "volunteer" his services. He wants to start his own business at age sixty-five, improve corporate management practices, and make more money. So his wife fills out *his* Peace Corps application as well as her own. She then engineers a time and place to force him to sign the application or face family embarrassment.

To avoid embarrassment, he signs the application with a hostile display of silent disdain, sure that he will *never* be invited by the Peace Corps. Then his wife takes his signed application and in front of the family announces to her husband: "I'm now going to put your Peace Corps application in the mailbox along with mine. Speak now, or *forever* hold your peace!" He remains glumly silent. She mails the applications, they are both invited to training: they serve successfully abroad as Peace Corps volunteers. Many years later, there is the following exchange with the husband:

> Family Member: Now that you can look backward on having been a Peace Corps volunteer in Peru, what is your advice for other people your age about joining the Peace Corps?
> Husband: Do it!
> Family Member: Knowing now what you know about the Peace Corps, its problems and inefficiencies, would you again join the Peace Corps as a volunteer?
> Husband: Damn right!

The couple were my mother and father. The questions were mine.

The writer will conclude his sequel to *The Ugly American* by saying that in his travels in his country, in other industrial nations, and throughout the developing world, he has found a nearly universal affirmative evaluation of the Peace Corps. In answer to his often repeated question "Was the Peace Corps worthwhile?" in a multitude of languages with many variations, he received the same response: "*Damn right!*"

Reminiscence: The Dominican Republic

by Christopher J. Dodd

Dozens of times, in interviews and conversations with friends, I've been asked how my service in the Peace Corps affected me. I'm sometimes reluctant to answer because I know I can never fully explain how profoundly the experience shaped my life and career—the truth sounds too altruistic, even corny.

President Kennedy asked, "How many [of you] are willing to spend two years in Africa or Latin America or Asia working for the U.S. and working for freedom?" When he asked that question, it was like getting a genie out of a bottle.

The original idea hasn't changed all that much. The Peace Corps was meant to help the people of disadvantaged countries learn the skills they need for economic advancement, and at the same time spread the ideals of America and expose some Americans to the culture and outlook of Third World nations.

There is now, perhaps, a greater expectation that the volunteers will create something substantial in their host countries. There is a sense that the standard of success can be measured in the number of water projects or schools that get built.

No doubt the schools and pumping stations and bridges are welcome, but I'm sure the real value of the Peace Corps is more intangible. The communities that have accepted Peace Corps volunteers have been enriched by the vitality of young people who were inspired by the challenge of creating a new and better world. In my case, the experience was pivotal.

The Peace Corps took a nice kid from suburban Connecticut, whose

---

Christopher J. Dodd is United States senator from Connecticut.

father was a United States senator, and sent him to a remote part of the Dominican Republic to "do something good."

I may have done some good, but mostly I learned. I learned about the complexity of a culture that is close to us geographically, but far, far away from our understanding. I learned to speak Spanish, the language of our neighbors. I learned to teach others some of the skills most of us take for granted. I learned to organize people to help themselves. Most important, I learned that one person can make a telling difference in the lives of those around him.

When I arrived in Moncion in 1966, the United States, despite the brewing turmoil of the Vietnam War, was riding the crest of its economic, military, and cultural authority in the world. It is difficult to remember how myopic we Americans were in our relations with the rest of the world.

I was told to expect hard conditions, but I was unprepared for the personal and cultural shock of arriving in a place where people had next to nothing. Nothing of any material value, at least.

I learned more than how to recognize the face of poverty: I learned about the anger and danger that poverty creates. On my first trip into the capital, Santo Domingo, the van I was riding in was pelted with fruit by youngsters yelling "*el Americano feo*" ("Ugly American"). I realized that I had never known blacks or Hispanics or even poor people. I grew up to the world.

The Dominican Republic was a hot blast of reality. Living in a tin-roofed shack without running water was not especially romantic. It was, however, an unforgettable lesson in the results of substandard public sanitation.

Dysentery is not a laughing matter, and it drives home immediately the importance of medicines we Americans take for granted. Living with the threat of diarrhea and dehydration, and watching what it does to tiny children, was a constant reminder of how the basic amenities of society protect us and bind us together. The saddening vision of children needlessly ill with diseases that can be easily treated or avoided prompted me to embark on the central project of my stay in the Dominican Republic. Shortly after settling in, I began organizing an effort to build a hospital for expectant mothers.

The response was so overwhelming that we were able to build the area's first maternity hospital in a matter of months. Almost nothing in life has satisfied me more than working on that hospital.

Our mission in the Peace Corps was not especially well defined, which may have been a fortunate thing. We were there to help, but also to exchange values and to make person-to-person contact. We were there to dispel the image, all too frequently deserved, of "*el Americano feo.*"

The Peace Corps was intentionally designed to be the positive expression of the American spirit. It taught me to reject cynicism and embrace idealism. It taught me that our personal choices cannot be separated from the political decisions of nations.

Every day each one of us faces dilemmas and frequent decisions about what to do with his or her life. When we choose to help others, and when we do so as representatives of our country, we make the world a better place and we make our own lives better, too. The Peace Corps provides people with a unique opportunity to help the less fortunate of the world, and in doing so they help America. That they also gain so much for themselves is a blessing for us all.

Reminiscence: Malawi

by Paul Theroux

My record was so bad (they sent the FBI to check up on you then) that I was first rejected by the Peace Corps as a poor risk and possible troublemaker, and was only accepted as a volunteer after a great deal of explaining and arguing. The alternative was Vietnam—this was 1963, and President Kennedy was still muddling dangerously along. I was sent to Nyasaland; soon it became Malawi. And then a month before my two-year stint was over, I was "terminated"—kicked out—fined arbitrarily for three months' "unsatisfactory service," and given hell by the Peace Corps officials in Washington. Of course they believed the truth—that I had been framed in an assassination plot against Doctor Hastings Banda, the President-for-Life ("Messiah," "Conquerer," and "Great Lion" were some of his lesser titles). But the case against me looked bad. I was debriefed. There was a session at the State Department. The Peace Corps deducted my Central Africa-to-Washington air fare from my earnings, and I ended up with $200. Out I went—it was now 1965. I still had the draft to contend with.

It was a mess, and for a long while afterward I hated the Peace Corps and laughed at the posters they put up in the subway. I hated the bureaucracy, the silliness, the patronizing attitudes, the jargon, the sanctimony. I remembered all the official freeloaders who came out from Washington on so-called inspection tours, and how they tried to ingratiate themselves. "You're doing wonderful work here. . . . It's a great little country," they said; but for most of them it was merely an African safari. They hadn't the slightest idea of what we were doing, and our revenge was to take them on long, bumpy rides through the bush. "Sensational," they said. They went away. We stayed. Most Peace Corps volunteers know that feeling: the smug visitor leaving in the jeep and the

---

Paul Theroux is a travel writer and novelist.

dust flying up; and then the dust drifting slowly down and the silence taking hold.

On the subject of Vietnam, these Peace Corps bureaucrats were surprisingly hawkish and belligerent. Most of them, including the reps, believed Vietnam to be a necessary war. The volunteers were divided. This was an important issue to me, because I had joined the Peace Corps specifically to avoid being drafted, and I was dismayed to find so many Peace Corps officials advocating the bombing of Hanoi or the mining of Haiphong harbor. As a meddlesome and contentious twenty-two-year-old, I made a point of asking everyone his views on Vietnam. I believed the war was monstrous from the very beginning, and I have not changed my views. What astonishes me today is how few people remember the ridiculous things they said about Vietnam in the sixties.

But we are a country of revisionists, and the chief quality of the revisionist is a bad memory. No one now remembers how confused Kennedy's Vietnam policy was or how isolated the student movement was. I had been involved in student protests from 1959 until 1963—first against ROTC, then against nuclear testing, and then against our involvement in Vietnam. How could I have been inspired by Kennedy to join the Peace Corps? I had spent years picketing the White House—and in doing so had made myself very unpopular. When I applied to join the Peace Corps, this career as an agitator was held against me. It was all a diabolical plot, I felt. And there was the President with such style—money, power, glamor. He even had culture! I had to fight my feelings of distrust and alienation in order to join. There were many like me—anti-authoritarian, hating the dazzle and the equivocation. And when the President was shot—we learned about it halfway through a lecture in Peace Corps training (something about land tenure in the Nyasaland Protectorate)—we were all properly put in our place. More revisionism, more guilt, and I thought: get me out of here.

Nyasaland—soon to become the independent republic of Malawi—was the perfect country for a Peace Corps volunteer. It was both friendly and destitute; it was small and out-of-the-way. It had all of Africa's problems—poverty, ignorance, and disease. It had only a handful of university graduates. It had lepers, it had Mister Kurtzes, it had Horatio Alger stories by the score. It had a fascinating history that was bound up not only with early African exploration—Livingstone himself—but also one of the first African rebellions, Chilembwe's uprising. It was the setting for Laurence van der Post's *Venture to the Interior.* The people were generous and extremely willing, and as they had not been persecuted or bullied, and had been ignored rather than exploited, they were not prickly and color-conscious like the Kenyans and Zambians. There was a pleasant atmosphere of hope in the country—very little cynicism and plenty of goodwill. The prevailing feeling was that the education we were providing would lead to prosperity, honest government, and good health.

An added thrill was that many settlers were still in residence. Some of these were old-timers—"wog bashers," as they sometimes called themselves—who remembered the place when it was even wilder and more wooded. They had little contact with Africans—the place had never been a colony in the strict sense, only a backwater—and yet they resented us. Most of us hated them and mocked them, and we had a special loathing for the few volunteers who began moving in settler society. These pompous little creeps—so we said—went to gymkhanas and cocktail parties at the local club and dated the settler children when they returned from their Rhodesian boarding schools. We saw them as social climbers and traitors, and feelings were very strong on the issue. It was not uncommon for a Peace Corps volunteer in town for supplies to approach a group of settlers in a bar and say something crudely provocative, such as "The Queen's a whore" (her portrait always hung over the bottles); nearly always a fight would start. To Africans these antagonisms were very exciting.

We had arrived in the country speaking Chinyanja fairly well, and we had plunged in—made friends, taught school, run literacy programs, coached sports, and generally made ourselves useful. We were, as the English say, "at the sharp end"—on our own and exposed, and doing the toughest jobs. The Africans were eager. Afterward it occurred to me that over the years of British rule the Africans had become extremely lonely and curious—always seeing whites at a distance and wondering what the hell they were like. The Peace Corps volunteers were the first foreigners to offer them a drink. They were amazed that we were interested in them, and they repaid our interest with hospitality.

In addition to my teaching, I collaborated with a man at the Ministry of Education on writing two English textbooks to replace the miserable ones that had been standard. *Foundation Secondary English,* Book One and Book Two, is still being used in Malawi twenty years after it appeared, and I am still receiving royalties on it.

We were pestered by Israeli soldiers, who had been taken on to train our students to become single-minded cadets in a goon squad, but apart from them the school ran well. I planted trees, and we put a road through. I was proud of the place; I liked my students, I enjoyed working with my colleagues. And the country affected me as no other country has, before or since. I felt I belonged there, I was happy, I was committed. I was having a good time as well as doing something worthwhile—what could have been better?

Now and then I remembered that I was in the Peace Corps. That gave me an odd feeling. I disliked the idea that I was with an outfit, and I rejected the suggestion that I was an American official working abroad. I had never been easy with the concept of the Peace Corps as an example to spineless Marxists, and the implications of fresh-faced youngsters wooing Third Worlders away from Communism. I was well aware that American officialdom used us to deflect criticism of Vietnam and of more robust and spread-eagled diplomacy.

I wanted the Peace Corps to be something very vague and unorganized, and to a large extent it was. It did not run smoothly. The consequence was that we were left alone. I was glad to be able to call my soul my own. The Peace Corps was only proprietorial when it suited them, and generally speaking, they took an interest in volunteers only when an official visitor arrived in the country. Then we were visited or invited to parties. "You're doing wonderful work. . . . They're saying great things about you." But I didn't want attention. I didn't want help. I wanted to be self-sufficient. Anyway, most of our jobs were too simple to require any backup, and we seldom wrote reports.

We were not trusted by the embassy personnel or the State Department hacks—all those whispering middle-aged aunties who couldn't speak the language. The feeling was mutual. We felt embassy people were overpaid and ignorant, always being fussed over by spoiled African servants. We were, we felt, independent spirits—English teachers, health workers, answerable only to our students and patients. I regarded the Peace Corps as a sort of sponsoring organization and myself as an individual who had only the most tenuous link with it.

I had met many Peace Corps officials, and it seemed that the higher you went in the Peace Corps, the less you knew, the less you accomplished. The officials were ambitious and political, and it often seemed to me that they hardly knew us and had little idea of what we were doing in the country. I think I am typical in believing that the Peace Corps trained us brilliantly and then did little more except send us into the bush. It was not a bad way of running things. After all, we were supposed to use our initiative. And I think we were never more effective as volunteers than when we were convinced that we were operating alone, at the sharp end, putting our own ideas into practice, far away from the bureaucrats.

Because we were on our own, the Peace Corps officials regarded our situation as delicate. The Peace Corps did not want us to be too visible, too friendly, or too involved. "Keep a low profile" was the advice we were always offered; I did not follow it, and so eventually I got the boot. I was insulted when I was sent out of the country. It seemed like the act of an absent parent, someone I hardly knew asserting his authority over me.

That is why I do not associate my years in the Peace Corps with group photographs, horseplay, heart-to-heart talks with the rep, images of President Kennedy showing me the way, softball games with the other volunteers, and the sort of hands-across-the-sea camaraderie that you see on the posters. It was not "the dream—the vision." It was much more interesting.

It was to me most of all the reality of being very far from home and yet feeling completely at home in this distant place. It was a slight sense of danger; the smell of woodsmoke; hearing the Beatles for the first time in a bar in the town of Limbe. In the States there was a sort of revolution in progress, but it had started partly as a result of the first Peace Corps group that had gone to Nepal. Those volunteers returning from Kathmandu had blazed the hippie trail.

In Malawi we had all of that, too—good people, wilderness, music, ganja, dusty roads, hard-working students, and a feeling of liberation. Things were on the move, it seemed. In Malawi I saw my first hyena, smoked my first hashish, witnessed my first murder, caught my first dose of gonorrhea. One of my neighbors, an African teacher, had two wives. My gardener had a gardener. Another neighbor and friend was Sir Martin Roseveare, who liked the bush. He was principal at the nearby teachers' college, and he died only last year, in Malawi, at the age of eighty-six. (He was knighted in 1946 for designing the foolproof and fraud-proof ration book in wartime Britain.) After I lived awhile in a cozy bungalow with two servants, I moved into an African township, where I lived in a semi-slum, in a two-room hut—cold water, cracks in the walls, tin roof, music blasting all day from the other huts, shrieks, dogs, chickens. It was just the thing. The experience greatly shaped my life.

When I think about those years, I don't think much about the Peace Corps, though Malawi is always on my mind. That is surely a tribute to the Peace Corps. I do not believe that Africa is a very different place for having played host to the Peace Corps—in fact, Africa is in a much worse state than it was twenty years ago. But America is quite a different place for having had so many returned Peace Corps volunteers, and when they began joining the State Department and working in the embassies, these institutions were the better for it and had a better-informed and less truculent tone. The experience was an enlightening one for most volunteers. I still do not understand who was running the show, or what they did, or even what the Peace Corps actually was, apart from an enlightened excuse for sending us to poor countries. Those countries are still poor. We were the ones who were enriched, and sometimes I think that we reminded these people—as if they needed such a thing—that they were left out. We stayed awhile, and then we left them. And yet I think I would do it again. At an uncertain time in my life, I joined. And up to a point—they gave me a lot of rope—the Peace Corps allowed me to be myself. I realized that it was much better to be neglected than manipulated, and I learned that you make your own life.

The Veterans

by Roger Landrum

The first 800 veterans of the Peace Corps returned home in 1963. Every year since, several thousand others have come back from service in Africa, Asia, and Latin America. Counting both volunteers and staff, they now number roughly 120,000. They have served in more than ninety Third World countries, under vastly diverse circumstances, having carried out a wide range of different tasks.

Yet a singular image surrounds Peace Corps veterans: the image of a common experience, which they have a mission to share with the nation. And the image holds. In the words of one returned volunteer, "The thing about the Peace Corps is that it doesn't end after two years, it lasts a lifetime." I suppose I am testimony to the truth in the image. Having returned from service in Nigeria in 1963, I have been involved with the Peace Corps—sometimes professionally, nearly always in spirit—ever since.

Addressing departing volunteers in 1961, President Kennedy said, "Come back and educate us." And earlier that year he noted that, "Our own young men and women will return better able to assume the responsibilities of American citizenship and with a greater understanding of our global responsibilities."

Hubert Humphrey, who probably did as much as John Kennedy to make the Peace Corps possible, went even further. "I foresee a new day," he stated, "when hundreds of thousands of Peace Corps alumni will be decision-makers in American industry, our leaders in government, and the teachers of our young." And President Reagan's Peace Corps director, Loret Ruppe, testified at her 1981 confirmation hearings, "Returned Peace Corps volunteers should be exploited in the best sense of the word."

Gerard T. Rice, author of *The Bold Experiment,* reports that between

---

Roger Landrum is a consultant for the Ford Foundation and president of the Returned Peace Corps Volunteers of Washington, D.C.

them, Peace Corps veterans have a "deep knowledge and understanding of a thousand different cultures, a facility to speak nearly 200 languages, and personal bonds with people in 93 countries." And former AID administrator Douglas Bennet said in 1980, "We have an asset that no other country has. Instead of a bunch of retired colonial officers or international businessmen who come home to settle, we've got almost 100,000 people who've been through the Peace Corps experience and who can share their experience with others."

Clearly, Peace Corps veterans are viewed by others as a choice minority. They bring back to this country an intense, grass-roots experience on the frontiers of global development. They are selected for the independence of spirit that initially impelled them beyond conventional careers and wisdom into the Peace Corps. Their separate experiences overseas seem to have hammered and refined an attachment to common Peace Corps ideals.

Peace Corps veterans themselves feel a particular kind of bonding. Former Senator Paul Tsongas, among the most famous of the veterans, cites the Peace Corps as "the formative experience of my life. If I have a meeting with someone and I find he's a former Peace Corps volunteer, there's an instant sort of attachment."

Tsongas has further endeared himself to his fellow veterans by saying, "You can always be a senator, I suppose, by title, but in terms of what made you what you are emotionally and psychologically, clearly the Peace Corps was that experience."

Many former volunteers inevitably ask themselves how seriously to take all this rhetoric. The dictionary defines a corps as a "body of persons acting together or associated under common direction." Perhaps they achieved the cohesion of a corps overseas, despite the fact that they did not serve elbow to elbow, but do they remain in any sense a "corps" back home? What impact are they having on American institutions? Do they remain associated in any organized fashion?

The first organized effort to rally former volunteers came in March 1965. Only 3,000 had returned by this date, but 1,000 came to a conference convened in Washington by Vice President Humphrey at the request of President Lyndon Johnson. Reporting in *The New Yorker,* Richard Rovere called this conference "the most informal as well as the liveliest gathering ever to have taken place in that ungainly pile of concrete [the State Department] in the heart of Foggy Bottom."

The idea was to bring former volunteers together with 250 leaders of American institutions, and to explore the roles that the veterans might play in education, business and labor, community programs, and government. What resulted, however, was more a collision than a conference. Many of the former volunteers reported finding American institutions distressingly rigid and called for sweeping changes, but they had few specific suggestions to offer and detested being called "special people." On the contrary, many declared, they had just had the most humbling experience of their lives.

Bill Moyers chided the former volunteers for their reticence about being called "special." He had helped organize the Peace Corps and was now special assistant to the President. "You are special," Moyers said, "and when you come back from abroad, if you don't think yourself special, you will simply disappear into the bog of affluent living."

The institutional leaders seemed eager to embrace the virtues and talents of the veterans as a tonic for American society, but they were surprised by what seemed to be the volunteers' uncertainty, and even timidity, about how to proceed. Many urged the former volunteers to get proper credentials to make the reforms they desired. Secretary of State Dean Rusk told the veterans, "I can assure you, if you apply for the Foreign Service, that your experience in the Peace Corps will be a plus with respect to others who may be applying for that Service." Yet a report prepared for the conference revealed that 865 former volunteers had already applied for the Foreign Service. Of the 579 who actually took the exam, 110 passed the written exam, 14 passed the oral exam, and only 3 had been appointed.

Chief Justice Earl Warren, Vice President Humphrey, Secretary of State Rusk, and Defense Secretary Robert McNamara all sang the praises of the Peace Corps at the conference. They urged former volunteers to give to America what they had contributed overseas. But even as they spoke, former volunteers were circulating petitions in support of stronger civil rights legislation, action against the Republic of South Africa, and opposition to American policy in Vietnam. State Department guards were given an order to enforce a building regulation against distribution of "outside literature." The Vice President had said: "If you think things are not as they ought to be, right in this State Department, tell us," and higher officials waived the regulation in favor of the right of free speech.

Later, a special session was called to consider proposals by some veterans to form alumni organizations locally and nationally. The large majority opposed the formation of a national organization, as well as any use by returned volunteers of the Peace Corps name. "I didn't join the Peace Corps to have forty-five or twenty-two or any number of people express my views," said one veteran. "If I want to express them, I'd just as soon express them myself." Another veteran echoed this anti-organizational sentiment with the words, "Lord, not another American Legion!"

The worst fears expressed at the conference about abuse of the views of veterans and the name of the Peace Corps were soon realized. A national organization was formed under the name Committee of Returned Volunteers. A radical wing within the group soon drove out all moderating and dissenting voices, moving the organization from support for civil rights and opposition to the war in Vietnam to actions and positions to the left of Mao Tse-tung. At one point, members attempted to blockade the entrances to Peace Corps headquarters. And they threw red paint on the Chinese embassy to protest revisionist tendencies.

The Committee of Returned Volunteers soon burned itself out. It would be many years before efforts were again made to establish a national organization of Peace Corps veterans.

In preparation for the 1965 conference, a questionnaire had been mailed to the 3,000 former volunteers, and, astonishingly, 2,300 were returned. The results showed that more than half were back in school. Forty-one percent were employed, with 14 percent working in government, 14 percent in teaching, and the rest distributed in a wide variety of jobs. Very few were unemployed.

Eighty-eight percent reported they had decided upon lifetime careers, most of them acknowledging that they had changed direction during Peace Corps service. According to the survey, many were planning careers in various types of international work, but only six wanted to enter politics.

The survey also disclosed that many volunteers were troubled by an indifference they perceived in America's attitude toward the Third World, and by the problems of communicating the subtle meanings of the Peace Corps experience to others. Many complained about a lack of sufficient challenge in their present jobs or education.

The pattern of former volunteers has changed dramatically since those days. Recent State Department figures show that at least 10 percent of each new class of Foreign Service officers are former volunteers. A thousand or more are currently employed by the State Department and the Agency for International Development, in Washington and in embassies around the world. By 1980, 15 percent of nearly 100,000 Peace Corps veterans had taken positions with government organizations at home or abroad. At AID, 12.5 percent of its staff were returned volunteers. In Costa Rica, 53 percent of the AID mission were Peace Corps veterans, with 40 percent in Cameroon and 28 percent in Jamaica. Not one of the fifty-five AID country missions was without a former volunteer. Douglas Bennet, then AID administrator, said, "The Peace Corps has changed the face of AID substantially."

By 1985, roughly 540 of AID's 4,000 professional staffers were Peace

Corps veterans. They constituted 40 percent of AID's intern classes and 25 percent of its newest professional staff members.

To take another case, by 1985, half of the Peace Corps' own staff were veterans. For many years they have routinely been appointed directors of country programs, though none has ever been named Peace Corps director. In fact, of the twelve senior positions at the agency, only one is currently filled by a former volunteer.

It is also estimated that over 100 former volunteers currently work on congressional staffs. Two rose all the way to the top: Paul Tsongas, who recently retired from the Senate but remains a leading figure in the Democratic Party, and Christopher Dodd, a Connecticut Democrat who served in the Dominican Republic and has become one of the Senate's experts on Central and South America. Four former volunteers have been elected to the House of Representatives: James Courter of New Jersey (Venezuela), Thomas Petri of Wisconsin (Somalia), Paul Henry of Michigan (Liberia and Ethiopia), and Tony Hall of Ohio (Thailand).

Peace Corps veterans have had enormous impact on private voluntary organizations working with Third World nations. They constitute 50 percent of the staff of the Experiment in International Living, 40 percent of CARE's staff, 25 percent of Catholic Relief Services' staff, 30 percent of staff at Volunteers in Technical Assistance, and 75 percent of staff at International Voluntary Service.

Leonard Robinson, who was among the 5 percent of black volunteers during the 1960s, having worked in poultry-raising in India, was appointed head of the African Development Foundation in 1984. Timothy Carroll, a former Nigeria volunteer, heads Eye Care, Inc. (a private organization that raises money for rural eye services in Haiti). Thomas Scanlon is president of Benchmarks, Inc., a highly successful international development consulting firm. Many others have started innovative private programs and services.

Even at the World Bank, layered with bureaucratic red tape and careful not to hire too many Americans, some 5 percent of the professional staff are Peace Corps veterans. Walter Price, a former Morocco volunteer and an agricultural consultant to the World Bank said, "If I had to choose between the Peace Corps experience and graduate school preparation for a career in international development, I would definitely choose the Peace Corps. I could never have conducted an appraisal of a multimillion-dollar project for the World Bank had I not known how it would affect the grass-roots level." And in the business world, many multinational corporations employ former volunteers on their staffs. It seems likely that these veterans will play a significant role in expanding trade between American businesses and Third World countries into the year 2000 and beyond.

Peace Corps veterans are opening up intellectual horizons as well. Former Malawi volunteer Paul Theroux has written classic travel accounts and, with *The Mosquito Coast,* has become a major American novelist. John Coyne and Richard Lipez, who both served in Ethiopia, are successful novelists. Charles Murray's *Losing Ground* has been called the publishing event of 1985 for the conservative movement. *Impulse to Revolution,* an account of cycles of revolution in South and Central America, was written by former Peru volunteer Jeffrey Barrett. Galen Hall, who served in Malawi, has written *A Small Business Agenda: Trends in a Global Economy.* Several scholarly works have been published by former volunteers, including Kenneth Wylie's *The Political Kingdoms of the Temne.* Large numbers of former volunteers—an estimated 27 percent—have also gone into teaching in American schools and universities. To give a few examples, University of Michigan anthropologist Susan Schaefer Davis has become a leading authority on Moroccan culture. Thomas Gouttiere directs the Center for Afghanistan Studies at the University of Nebraska. One of the country's leading scholars of African art, Yale's Robert Farris Thompson, calls the Peace Corps "a proto-fellowship in African studies." Donna Shalala, who served in Iran, is president of Hunter College; Alan Guskin, who served in Thailand, is president of Antioch University.

There are other signs of impact. A 1979 survey indicated that 75 percent of former volunteers discuss their overseas experiences with community, social, and religious organizations; 16 percent have taught formal classes on the developing nations; and some 66 percent of former volunteers maintain direct contact with their host communities overseas, either by correspondence or by visits.

Gerard Rice argues plausibly that the third goal of the Peace Corps—education at home—has been realized entirely through informal means. No division of the Peace Corps headquarters or senior agency official has ever been given responsibility for implementing this goal. No significant share of the agency budget has ever been devoted to it. There has never really been a plan for carrying it out. What "home education" there has been has come about through the initiative of returned volunteers.

During the late 1970s, the veterans' antipathy to forming alumni organizations gradually dissipated. Local organizations of former volunteers have emerged in at least twenty-five states and cities. Various nongeographical, wild-card groups have also been created.

Paradoxically, this was not a good period for the Peace Corps. Both the organization and its ideals had faded from view during the Nixon

Presidency. Perhaps the obscurity generated a need among Peace Corps veterans to reaffirm their collective sense of identity. Perhaps the fierce individualism abated as large numbers of former volunteers approached middle age. June Gertig, who is a partner in a large Washington law firm, recently said, "I've become middle-aged and well-off, and I want to do something again for the values I worked for in the Peace Corps." She proceeded to become membership chairman of the Returned Peace Corps Volunteers of Washington, D.C.

Many of the local alumni organizations started as social gatherings. The larger, more dynamic groups—in San Francisco, Boston, Atlanta, the Washington area, New York City, and Madison, Wisconsin—prospered with effective fund-raising and educational and social activities. As membership grew and a more formal structure developed, conflicts were resolved between political activists and others who did not want to be pushed into the support of a single political position. Generally, the resolution has been a policy acceptable to both sides: political advocacy is carried out by subgroups under separate names, though often with financial support from the main organization.

In 1979, a core group of former volunteers invited veterans from around the country to attend a conference on the Third World. Over 150 came. They met in a special session and agreed in principle to form a national organization to carry out the "third goal." And in 1981, 46 former volunteers signed a charter establishing a National Council of Returned Peace Corps Volunteers. It operates through a board of 21 members elected by the national membership, and has grown steadily to 1,400 members in early 1986.

Other organizations of Peace Corps veterans include Friends of Togo, Peace Corps Alumni Foundation for Philippine Development, Friends of Ethiopia, Ploughshares (Returned Volunteers Working for Peace), and the Peace Corps Institute. The latter is not a membership organization, but has a board composed primarily of former Peace Corps staff and is headed by William Josephson, a founder of the Corps who was known as its "legal sword." The network of organizations boasts some impressive achievements.

In 1982, attorney Thomas McGrew, a member of the Returned Volunteers organization of Washington, D.C., launched a Committee on the Peace Corps Budget. At that time, the agency was one of the few in the federal government with a budget that had declined in real dollars through the Nixon, Ford, and Carter administrations. During this period, the number of volunteers in service overseas had fallen from a peak of 15,000 in 1966 to less than 5,000 in 1981. If the Peace Corps itself could not lobby for a budget outside White House guidelines, the McGrew Committee could. It identified the level of funding the Peace Corps really needed to be more effective and located allies among congressional staffers (many of them former volunteers). It relayed timely information to the National Council and local groups so that senators and congressmen could be approached and pushed the Peace Corps hearings to the forefront of the congressional appropriations process.

This got results. For the first time in over a decade, Congress in 1983 and 1984 increased the Peace Corps budget beyond White House requests, enabling the agency to reverse its decline. In 1985, the line was held against substantial cuts proposed by the White House.

Feeding on this initial success, the Washington group established a Task Force on Peace Corps Recommendations. Its aim was to identify major policy reforms that could pass Congress and contribute to the Peace Corps' impact. Five consensus reforms were proposed in a widely circulated publication entitled *The Peace Corps in 1985: Meeting the Challenge*. The publication called for (1) an increase in volunteers in service to 10,000, with stronger representation in South America and Asia; (2) removal of political patronage considerations in the hiring of Peace Corps staff, particularly country directors; (3) establishment of a new advisory council of former volunteers; (4) elevation of the third goal to a central mission of the agency with generous funding; and (5) at the end of Loret Ruppe's tenure, appointment of a former volunteer as director.

Senators Cranston, Kassebaum, Lugar, and Dodd skillfully turned the second and third proposed reforms into bills and orchestrated Senate passage. Congressman Jim Leach, who had originated the first 10,000 volunteer goal, got that bill through the House. All three reforms were then passed by both houses and signed into law by President Reagan in 1985.

Meanwhile, local organizations of former volunteers have established a record of fund-raising for selected overseas development programs. Peace Corps Partnership Programs—small-scale village projects identified by volunteers currently in service—have been financed by veterans' groups throughout the United States. Several groups have raised substantial sums for Oxfam America and the Ashoka Society.

Many of the groups have sponsored education activities on Third World topics. A group in Washington conducts bimonthly issue forums. In 1985, the National Council received grants from AID and the Carnegie Corporation totalling $90,000 to plan and implement a national development education program, using Peace Corps veterans. A group in New York City—with support from Mayor Koch and the Board of Education—is sponsoring an essay contest on global development in sixteen high schools. The winners will spend three weeks living with Peace Corps volunteers in Africa and Latin America.

The dilemma currently faced by former volunteers is not only whether some kind of unified national association should be formed, but to what purpose. The National Council and the existing local organizations are only loosely affiliated at this point. They have no paid staff to work on the development of common purposes and programs, or even to keep in touch with each other. They lack a collective agenda. They do not have the means of reaching 120,000 former volunteers and staff—or even as many as can be found—in the absence of good records. In fact, there is not yet a clear commitment on the part of those who have been active in local associations, much less on the part of the many who have not, to shape a wider, unified national association that can reach agreement on strategies and goals. Yet the rapid development in the past few years of an organizational network suggests that such a commitment may be growing nearer.

Through the local organizations, Peace Corps veterans have also demonstrated a willingness to support the kinds of development programs—small-scale, people-to-people projects—on which they themselves worked in the Third World. So far their efforts have been on an *ad hoc* basis, distant from the kind of cohesive undertaking that can mobilize enough funds and energy to have a strong impact on development policy. What seems more imminent is the mobilization of a larger number of Peace Corps veterans to support carefully selected development projects, especially for the countries in which they served. But even this goal requires the establishment of regular communication channels.

Even further from the current agenda of active veterans are larger questions of American foreign policy. Despite their identity as veterans of a *Peace* Corps, former volunteers have not much considered the traditional issues of "peace." Apart from scattered efforts, active veterans have not been inclined to take unified positions on trouble spots in the Third World, on East-West relations, or on disarmament.

Perhaps the fact that volunteers have been drawn from a wide national spectrum precludes their taking collective positions on major foreign policy issues. These are highly divisive matters within that spectrum, and it is no surprise that Peace Corps veterans do not necessarily agree on them. But it is also possible that consensus, or near-consensus, can be reached on a few, carefully selected issues to which Peace Corps veterans have had a virtually unique grass-roots exposure. It is worth noting, however, that even if such consensus is achieved, organizational means will still be needed to bring it to the attention of Congress and the American people.

What is harder to understand than the silence on foreign policy questions is why Peace Corps veterans have said so little in the domestic debate over national service, precisely the kind of issue that touches them.

On the West Coast, for example, Peace Corps veteran Robert Burkhardt directs the San Francisco Conservation Corps. This kind of program—small domestic service corps engaged in community projects—is taking shape in some thirty-five states and localities. It seems to be a growing, and promising, movement. Yet former Peace Corps volunteers have done precious little to build support for it.

One thing by now is clear: if the Peace Corps veterans do not build that kind of support themselves, the Peace Corps headquarters will not do it for them. The Peace Corps, as a federal agency, has obviously decided to keep the organizations of veterans at arm's length. Whatever assistance returned volunteers can give—whether in promoting the Peace Corps' institutional interests or in advancing the "third goal" of educating Americans—it is accompanied by a risk to the agency in making common cause with associations whose purposes and activities it cannot control. The Peace Corps director is, after all, politically appointed and responsible to the President. Similarly, the returned volunteers have made clear an aversion to limiting their freedom for the sake of formal association with the Peace Corps. The consequence is that veterans—beyond some informal help from headquarters—are on their own in developing their organizations and purposes.

Whatever the obstacles, a movement toward some form of collective identification among the veterans has been established, and some 8,000 of them are involved. The form it will take, and its goals and programs, are now being hammered out in debates among groups of Peace Corps veterans all over the country. Together, they represent an enormous potential for translating Peace Corps ideals into a positive force, and they are clearly gathering momentum.

THE JOB

As a Development Agency

by M. Peter McPherson

In 1963, when the blush of early Peace Corps success had subsided a little and the volunteers had begun returning to the United States, several returnees suggested to Peace Corps Director Sargent Shriver that he tone down the ballyhoo and describe a little more realistically what a Peace Corps volunteer could expect to accomplish in two short years.

Shriver and his staff came up with a new series of recruitment ads stressing that change in developing countries is often painfully slow. One ad displayed a single inch of a ruler with the caption, "This is how the Peace Corps measures progress." Another advertised sixteen-hour workdays and hordes of mosquitoes. One poster I remember particularly well showed two identical pictures of a squalid village, side by side. The caption on the left was "Before the Peace Corps"; on the right, "After the Peace Corps." Prospective volunteers were warned that the world couldn't be changed overnight.

It hasn't been overnight, but twenty-five years. The question today is whether the development picture has changed for the better and, if so, how the Peace Corps has contributed to that change.

From the start, it is essential to acknowledge that the Corps has two other purposes besides development: to help promote a better understanding of Americans on the part of the peoples served and to help increase America's knowledge of other cultures.

The explicit, essential tasks Peace Corps volunteers undertake—the development tasks—constitute the vehicle through which the second and third goals are realized. Like Ben Franklin's vision of the thirteen colonies in revolt, the Peace Corps' three goals must stand together—or each will assuredly fall separately.

M. Peter McPherson is administrator of the Agency for International Development in Washington, D.C.

Nonetheless, it is my belief that the Peace Corps has never reached its full potential as a development institution. Each Peace Corps volunteer represents an investment of some $20,000 per year on the part of the American public in the developing world. Though these costs are small when compared with those of other development institutions, they still are real. They are generally justified to the Congress in terms of the impact that the volunteers make in the developing countries. Yet I do not believe the Peace Corps has ever fully committed itself to development as its central, driving mission. The time to do so is now.

The Peace Corps is an important development institution, one of the few that operate at the level where the world's neediest live. It has a record in which it can take pride. And it concerns me when some suggest that its development mission is solely symbolic, or that the Peace Corps can be justified merely on the basis of its role in cross-cultural understanding.

Some point out that it is neither possible nor desirable to describe the Peace Corps' development impact in measurable terms. The journalist Eric Sevareid, in the early years, expected "some spot benefits in a few isolated places," but maintained that "the Peace Corps had little to do with the fundamental investments and reforms on which long-term development of countries depend." Others have charged that the Peace Corps has had virtually no impact on development at all. Recently, one critic said the Peace Corps "survives now largely because its hosts are still too polite to suggest that we may be wasting our energy and their patience." I strongly disagree. I feel that the Peace Corps can be one of the most effective American organizations operating in the Third World.

As a former Peace Corps volunteer in Peru, writing from the vantage point of a quarter-century of experience with the agency, and from my current perspective as administrator of the Agency for International Development, I am convinced that the Peace Corps has contributed to development both directly and indirectly, both concretely and conceptually. I also believe that it can do much more in the years ahead.

The task of measuring the Peace Corps' direct developmental impact is difficult. The very nature of the Peace Corps militates against effective and sustained measurement of progress—two-year volunteer tours, in-country assignments negotiated yearly with host governments, work with institutions that are disorganized, and, most important, the intangibility of the Peace Corps' service to the disenfranchised and the disengaged.

The transfer of skills and knowledge is extraordinarily difficult to quantify. Success is measured by most volunteers at a personal level—the sudden recognition in the eyes of a school child, the pride of a community in its self-built schoolhouse, or the sense of competence of workers who have formed their own cooperative.

The Peace Corps operates at the micro level of development, in one-to-one relationships with individuals or local villages. It would be virtually impossible—and certainly uneconomical—even to attempt to track the impact that an individual volunteer or group of volunteers makes on a country's development. How can one quantify the short-term (let alone long-term) effects on three farmers learning how to raise more crops on their land? Or the development consequence of twelve mothers who understand that they must boil water before giving it to their babies to drink? Or the cost-benefit impact of immunizing twenty children? Yet these tasks are at the very heart of development and, indeed, echo priorities AID has set for itself on a wider scale. Although development is more than simply the sum of these incremental changes, these changes are necessary if development is to take place at all.

The Peace Corps reminds us that peace and development—like war and destruction—are waged in the trenches, even if planned in the staff rooms. One of the great deficiencies of both international and national development efforts, in fact, is that there are so few people with skills and commitment who are willing to carry on the struggle at the village level, where most volunteers are stationed.

Still, there have been some attempts to quantify the impact of the volunteers. In 1966, the Social Research Institute of the University of Hawaii found evidence of a strong positive impact of volunteers on the educational system of the Philippines. A sophisticated statistical analysis by Cornell University concluded that communities in Peru with volunteers made more progress than communities without. Recently, an evaluation of Peace Corps projects to which AID had contributed small cash sums revealed that the projects had met their development objectives in nine out of ten cases.

What is lacking, to the best of my knowledge, are long-term, longitudinal looks at what Peace Corps volunteers did and what effect they have had over the span of years. The ads were right: you cannot change the world overnight. But it is helpful to know, and the Peace Corps needs to determine, whether the cumulative changes made over five or ten or fifteen years have yielded any substantial results at all. Such knowledge will be even more essential in the years ahead, as competition increases for scarce federal budget dollars.

Unfortunately, the institutional obstacles to development may be difficult to resolve. There are several reasons for this.

First, the Peace Corps since its inception has focused on the recruitment, training, and placement of volunteers—a placement bureau rather than a mission-driven agency. Coupled with that has been the enormous logistical task of supporting thousands of volunteers in every part of the world. Measurement has focused on the movement of people—numbers sent out, brought back, trained, debriefed, and so on. These numbers tell us nothing about the achievement of the first goal—helping Third World people to develop their countries.

Second, the Peace Corps has functioned without a vital component: institutional memory. With volunteers leaving after two years, and staff members required to go after five years at most, there is no real mechanism for it. Reinventing the wheel becomes not a popular pastime but a method of operation. And without institutional memory, there is no incentive for evaluation and documentation of achievements over the long term. The early emphasis on evaluation clearly subsided as the volunteer turnover and the "five-year rule" on staff tenure began to take effect.

But perhaps most important, development simply is not at the center of the Peace Corps' agenda. My experience with government management tells me that once the leadership and the institution really adopt an agenda, much can be accomplished, and the required decisions become clear. Accordingly, I feel that if the Peace Corps accepts its development agenda as the primary, driving mission of the organization, certain essential and critical changes in the way it has been been conducting its business over the past twenty-five years will become necessary and, indeed, will be put into place. For example:

• The Peace Corps should change its present method of programming volunteers. Present policies call for volunteer assignments to be based strictly on host country requests. This policy is too reactive, in that it does not allow enough room for creative programming. It results in volunteers being assigned to such a diversity of program sectors that it makes it difficult even to describe the overall program—much less measure its impact.

• The Peace Corps should, in my opinion, consult host countries and adopt a few principal program sectors (such as forestry, child survival, agricultural development, and education), and focus volunteer efforts in these areas. Focused efforts would improve programming, make technical training as well as technical support to volunteers more effective, and help the Peace Corps compete more effectively for federal dollars.

• The current Peace Corps director, Loret Ruppe, has made specific commitments to action on two major development issues: the food problems of Africa and the education needs of Central America. By adopting these problems as Peace Corps goals over the next ten years, Ruppe is pioneering the kind of focused programming that will make the Peace Corps a more vital development institution in the years ahead.

• The Peace Corps also needs to recruit as overseas staff individuals who are more experienced and better trained in development work. Congress recently prohibited the application of political criteria in the selection of "in-country" staff for the Peace Corps. This is as it should be. The Peace Corps must go beyond this, however, and recruit individuals with extensive experience—hopefully including Peace Corps experience—in development assistance.

• The five-year rule should be reexamined and possibly relaxed, even beyond the recent changes made by Congress. This requirement, which prohibits any staff person from working continuously with the agency for more than five years, has kept the Peace Corps dynamic, energetic, and free of bureaucratic inertia. At the same time, many highly qualified Peace Corps staff members are forced to leave when they are most able to make their best contribution.

• Finally, more focused programming and a stronger commitment by the Peace Corps to its development role will mean that measuring direct impact on developing countries will be more feasible in the future. A focusing of efforts will mean that more is done for poor people, and what better reason could there be to follow that path?

But even in urging change in the Peace Corps' orientation, I should add that I believe the agency is already moving in the right direction. The trend in recent years has been to move toward development as the central focus of the Peace Corps.

It is also true that the Peace Corps has had at least one sure focus almost from the beginning, that of education. In the early days of the Peace Corps, the host countries wanted teachers. Happily, it was precisely teachers—or generalists who could be trained as teachers—who tended to volunteer.

Yet, in spite of its successes, the Peace Corps' role in education has always been controversial. In the early days, critics charged that it was inappropriate to emphasize formal education for young people in developing countries who were for the most part destined to return to subsistence farming. Development economists did not regard education as a form of capital investment.

Fortunately, Sargent Shriver, the first director, was a staunch supporter of a strong Peace Corps role in education. A former chairman of the Chicago Board of Education, he was convinced, whatever the experts maintained, that basic education was crucial for a country's long-term development. And in the long term, development economists and other sages came around to Shriver's view.

The impact of Peace Corps teachers over the past twenty-five years has been astounding. As of 1981, Peace Corps teachers had taught nearly five million students and could take credit for a long list of accomplishments.

In recent years, the emphasis has shifted from expanding school availability and enrollment to improving the quality of education. Fewer Peace Corps volunteers are now being placed as teachers, and more are being asked to develop curricula, write texts, and train teachers. Nevertheless, a need for teachers still exists. In Sierra Leone, for example, colleges still produce only twenty graduates a year in science and math—not nearly enough to fill teacher needs in those important fields.

The same story, year after year, in country after country, is not the sort of thing that attracts the attention of the Congress or the media. It is, however, a story of great importance, when one considers the implications of the numbers and the cumulative effect of the Peace Corps in classrooms throughout the developing world.

One of the most rewarding developments during my tenure as administrator of AID has been the growing cooperation between my agency and the Peace Corps. We have come a long way from the constant bickering that characterized our relationship during the early 1960s.

Much of this animosity, as reported by people familiar with both sides, certainly stemmed from a basic mistrust, or perhaps a misunderstanding, of each other's policies and purposes. At its creation, the Peace Corps was seen as a refutation of traditional foreign aid programs.

In 1960, presidential candidate John Kennedy decried the "lack of compassion" of then-current foreign aid administrators and urged that "Our aid now should be concentrated not on large-scale monuments to American engineering, but on the village and the farm." It is not surprising that AID wanted little to do with the Peace Corps, this neophyte competitor whose very existence seemed to be a reflection of AID's limitations.

Many AID officials of that generation harbored resentment of the Peace Corps' insistence upon independence and its refusal to be taken under AID's bureaucratic wing. Many were skeptical of the ability of the young volunteers, whose role was often overglamorized, to make any meaningful contribution to foreign assistance.

On the other side, the Peace Corps took pains to set itself apart from AID. The Peace Corps set policies to keep the volunteers from being identified with AID money and decreed that "Separateness from other overseas operations of the U.S. is important to achieving the desired image."

Since those days, our agencies have grown closer together in approach and attitudes. We are both mandated by Congress to assist in the end goal of meeting basic human needs. This common goal underpins complementary programs and policies, and provides a common ground for sharing ideas and strategies. Also on the staff of AID there are now five hundred former Peace Corps volunteers, myself included, and their presence clearly promotes mutual understanding.

Over the past five years, we have made a special effort to build upon cooperation between AID and the Peace Corps to achieve a better foreign assistance program. The Peace Corps director and I have attempted to coordinate our development strategies wherever possible, so that the unique resources and strengths of each agency are used to their fullest. Each agency helps the other and gains in the process. And the people we assist reap the benefit.

For AID, cooperation has meant direct access to the communities and people most in need of assistance, important feedback from volunteers on how development projects function in the field, and skilled volunteer assistance with critical programs in fifty-six countries around the globe. For the Peace Corps, cooperation has meant that volunteers and their coworkers in the host countries can benefit from the technical and financial support that AID can provide. The positive results are unmistakable. Cooperation between our two agencies has meant vital joint endeavors, both at headquarters and in the field.

With AID support, the Peace Corps has more than doubled the number of specially trained volunteers working in forestry programs. Our joint child survival programs have trained hundreds of volunteers and local health workers in all regions of the world in oral rehydration therapy to reduce illness and death from diarrhea, and in techniques to assist local governments in improving primary health care for young children. The Small Projects Assistance program, one of our most successful cooperative enterprises, provides modest grants for development projects to communities where volunteers are stationed. The program has overwhelming support from both AID and the Peace Corps because it reaches the really needy in communities that have access to no other resources.

Our efforts have helped the poor of these countries to enjoy a better quality of life by bringing about improvements in food production, health, education, housing, energy, and income. In example after example, AID and the Peace Corps reinforce each other by reaching toward shared development goals. Here are only a few of them:

- We are helping to raise incomes and improve nutrition among the rural population of Cameroon by developing inland fisheries. The Peace Corps has been involved in this effort since 1969; AID assistance in 1980 expanded the project in the northwestern and western provinces.

• AID and the Peace Corps have been working together on a large project to bring safe drinking water to rural communities in Malawi. AID has financed the construction of gravity-fed piped water systems. Peace Corps volunteers organized community residents to help build the systems and taught them how to maintain and protect them. More than thirty-five systems have been constructed, providing water to 800,000 people.

• In Senegal, we have designed a project to save energy by promoting improved, fuel-efficient cookstoves in both rural and urban areas, so that fewer trees will be cut down. AID has provided salaries, equipment, and materials over the four-year life of the project. Six Peace Corps volunteers coordinate Senegalese teams that build stoves (largely from scrap materials) which save 35 to 50 percent of scarce wood and charcoal resources.

• Our two agencies have been cooperating to help small-scale farmers in Paraguay. Approximately thirty-five volunteers complement the efforts of AID and the Paraguayan government by teaching improved production techniques and promoting self-sufficiency among farm families through crop diversification, beekeeping, and other income-generating activities.

One of the most significant contributions of the Peace Corps to development has been its impact, both through its institutional experience and its cadre of former volunteers, on the way in which the United States perceives and practices development in the Third World.

The Peace Corps' approach has remained consistent for twenty-five years—local, low-cost solutions to local problems, direct assistance to the neediest, and direct service in the field. That methodology, through example, has dramatically affected the way in which development has been re-evaluated and development strategy reformulated. It has come to be recognized as having elements of success lacking in earlier development philosophies.

As the Peace Corps moves into its second twenty-five years, I believe it is time for the organization to recognize that it has become an important development agency and that it must focus more attention on achieving specific development objectives. Clearly, the Peace Corps achieves its impact working with and through people. But while mutual understanding is important, it is more a means than an end.

The seriousness of the problems of poverty and underdevelopment demands that volunteers be focused on contributing, in some measurable way, to improving the lives of the people with whom they are working. In many cases, this can best be achieved through an institutional commitment by the Peace Corps to support specific programs and objectives on a multiyear basis.

I believe that the Peace Corps' first twenty-five years have been illustrious ones. And most important, they have provided the experience that will make possible an even greater direct impact on the problems of the poor in the years ahead.

The Experience: Africa

by C. Payne Lucas and Kevin Lowther

In his celebrated Arusha declaration of 1967, Tanzania's president Julius Nyerere articulated a doctrine of rigorous national self-reliance that was to guide the nation's future development. Tanzania would seek foreign assistance, he said, but no more than was absolutely required to advance toward an authentic African socialism. Education, too, was to be directed to this need. It was to foster national identity and encourage mass participation in national development.

If such was the case, Nyerere was asked, how does the role of the Peace Corps fit in with this ideal? By then, more than two hundred Peace Corps volunteers were serving in Tanzania, most of them teaching in the high schools. Nyerere, himself a teacher, appreciated their work. He often remarked that more Peace Corps volunteers than Chinese worked in Tanzania—though China was a Third World brother, a fellow socialist state, and was building an important railroad line into the heart of the country. How does the Peace Corps fit, he was asked, into Tanzania's ideal of self-reliance?

"It doesn't fit in anywhere at all," he replied. "We know our limitations. . . . I will continue recruiting teachers. . . . I can't close the schools in order to prove that we are self-reliant. The schools will have to go on. And I will teach teachers with borrowed teachers, and go on like that.

"But the emphasis all the time is on self-reliance. This is an indication of our limitations. . . . Borrowing must all the time be what it is: not the answer to our problems but a result of our problems."

The esteem in which Nyerere held the Peace Corps teachers was based more on their personal than on their professional qualities. "They come to Tanzania," he once told the local press, "and if you tell them to go

---

C. Payne Lucas is executive director of Africare. Kevin Lowther is Africare's regional development officer for Southern Africa.

anywhere, they go. They do not complain. If you tell them to go to Kogoma, they go; or to Masailand, they go. . . . The volunteers have a spirit I would like to see more of in Tanzania's teachers."

Nyerere recognized that the Peace Corps volunteers, in spreading their democratic values, had infected some Tanzanian students with an impatience toward his own one-party state. Having survived one coup attempt, he was not anxious for more. But he recognized that Peace Corps volunteers were different from the Englishmen who had ruled the country during the colonial era, and he acknowledged that the Peace Corps had an important—albeit transitional—role to play in Tanzania's development.

Indeed, many Africans were suspicious when the Peace Corps arrived. They liked these Americans, who seemed so earnest and sincere, but they wondered why these foreigners, most of them white, tried to speak their languages and live in villages in the bush. Were they spies? But they seemed too naive, too inexperienced to be spies.

They were certainly different from the old colonial administrators. Not only were they learning to communicate in Swahili and Mende and Twi, but they accepted African hospitality instinctively and readily passed over the cultural threshold that few of the old colonials had been willing to cross. On a continent where the spirit of reciprocity anchors human relations, they were prepared to receive as well as to give. Only gradually were the doubts of Africans dissipated and the volunteers accepted, for the service they were willing to perform and for what they actually were.

We first arrived in Africa with the Peace Corps in the early 1960s. Lucas directed volunteer programs in Togo and Niger for several years, then became African regional director. Lowther served as a volunteer teacher in Sierra Leone and, later, in staff positions at Peace Corps headquarters in Washington. We left the Peace Corps in 1971 to found Africare, a private development organization, and have since continued our work in Africa.

As we saw it, the Peace Corps experience in Africa contrasted sharply with that in Asia, Latin America, and the Near East, where early volunteers encountered nations and societies that were far more established, far more self-assured. By chance, the arrival of the first volunteer groups coincided with a changing order not only in Africa but in the United States as well. The American civil rights movement was forging new bonds between blacks and whites, and the Peace Corps was ready to take on the same struggle for equality in Africa. Perhaps sooner than the volunteers themselves, the Africans sensed that something important was happening and appreciated the broader social and political implications of the races' working together as equals.

Having largely achieved their independence by the early 1960s, African governments were responding to their people's next priority: educational opportunity, which not only promoted development but also, as colonial experience had shown, guaranteed the prestige and salary of a white-collar job. The advent of the Peace Corps coincided with this demand and gave many African nations the means to expand their school systems far beyond anything they—or early Peace Corps planners—could have imagined.

In America, unexpected thousands were applying for volunteer service, and the Peace Corps began sending as many of them as possible to teach in African schools. The Africans had very simple expectations of these young and mostly inexperienced American teachers. Their job was to stand in a classroom and teach, and the more of them who were available, the more classrooms would be filled, and the more parents would be satisfied that the government was meeting their needs.

The Peace Corps, however, soon began to suspect that it was encouraging expansion of school systems and curricula that were manifestly inappropriate to African conditions. Peace Corps volunteers and staff became concerned that they were engaged in mere slot-filling. The Peace Corps' own inspectors frequently confirmed these fears and thus stimulated an ongoing debate over the scope and purpose of the volunteers' role in African education, and the Peace Corps' commitment of teachers to individual countries.

There was a conceit among Peace Corps volunteers and staff that they had something special to offer African education, and it took many forms. It was assumed *a priori* that the British and French colonial emphasis on rote learning, Eurocentric textbooks, and irrelevant curricula ought to be reformed. While valid, this did not necessarily require thousands of Americans who, for the most part, were barely trained to teach, much less to help overhaul entire school systems. In fact, the Peace Corps may actually have slowed reform by enabling several African countries to concentrate instead on expanding their flawed educational models.

It was widely believed in Peace Corps circles that the volunteer teachers' major contribution to their students was not in the knowledge imparted, but in new attitudes transmitted, principally the concepts of individual achievement and responsibility, as well as the power of reasoning. The Peace Corps never asked its African hosts if they minded having their children's values changed. It did, however, seek—and find—empirical evidence that volunteer teachers were having a positive impact on student attitudes and presumably preparing them for the development process.

One major study reported in 1968 that Ethiopian secondary school students who had been taught over several years by Peace Corps teachers had superior skills to those who had not. They were more fluent in English, were better problem-solvers, had stronger achievement motivation, and generally had a more modern outlook on life.

The report asserted that the hundreds of volunteers teaching in Ethiopian schools were equipping their students with motives and attitudes that would promote the country's economic development. It did not, however, comment on the possible effect volunteers were having as "active catalysts in the ferment of Ethiopia's present age of change," to quote a Peace Corps staff member in 1963. In the mid-1970s, student strikes and violence—some directed at volunteer teachers—brought education to a halt for months. Change was fermenting much faster than expected.

Ironically, the Peace Corps had indeed played a critical role in sharpening student awareness of their world and of Emperor Haile Selassie's slow pace of modernization. Deliberately or not, volunteers encouraged student enthusiasm for a less autocratic political system, as well as for a government less dependent on American help. The Ethiopian Ministry of Education had even felt obliged at one point to remind the Peace Corps staff in Addis Ababa that it was not conducting a community development program. It pointed out politely that the government, in asking for volunteer teachers, considered *teaching* to be their most important responsibility.

Also ironically, Haile Selassie emulated the Peace Corps by requiring students at the national university in Addis Ababa to spend a year teaching at schools in the country's rugged interior. The students went, but they resented their enforced rustication. It was this diaspora of restless and articulate university students that began the indoctrination in the secondary schools of the ideas that ultimately toppled the imperial regime. Yet, well before the fall, the Ethiopian government had begun scaling down Peace Corps involvement in the country, aware perhaps that the volunteers had been all too successful as "agents of change."

The Peace Corps liked being a catalyst for orderly social and economic change throughout the Third World. This was a natural instinct for any organization established to improve the quality of people's lives. But the Peace Corps has since learned to appreciate the arrogance of consciously trying to bring about change and to concentrate on doing the job it has been asked to do. It has learned that change, in any event, is a constant process and that volunteers, by their mere presence as alien carriers of different ideas and values, are participants.

Africans soon understood this, too, and by 1966, governments had begun to have second thoughts about the Peace Corps teaching program. At that time, more than two thousand volunteer teachers were serving on the continent, the two largest contingents being in Ethiopia and Nigeria. Nigeria's fondness for the Peace Corps declined sharply at the time of its civil war in 1967, when many volunteers sided openly with breakaway Biafra. Ethiopia's love affair with the Peace Corps ended in the political turmoil that began shortly afterward. By the mid-1970s, there were no Peace Corps teachers at all left in these two countries.

In Tanzania the circumstances were different—though still enmeshed in domestic turmoil—but the results were exactly the same. Nyerere recognized that the large numbers of volunteer teachers presented the danger of subtly undermining the impetus toward self-reliance, and the volunteers did not necessarily disagree. For the most part, they applauded the ring of genuine independence in Nyerere's words, though it meant they might themselves have to leave. In late 1966, Tanzania imposed a moratorium on all new volunteers, forcing reassignment of more than one hundred who were preparing to take up posts in primary schools. Rising anti-American sentiment, provoked largely by the Vietnam War and the unsavory revelations about the CIA, hastened the disaffection, and by late 1969, the Peace Corps program had been phased out. It was clear that for the Africans, huge Peace Corps teaching programs had proved to be too much of a good thing.

The Peace Corps would return to Tanzania in 1979, again at Nyerere's invitation, to work in much smaller numbers and much more specialized pursuits. This was a different Peace Corps and a different time. The volunteers were no longer known in Tanzania as the "followers of Kennedy" (whom millions of Africans idolized). The charisma and novelty of the Peace Corps had long since faded. Instead of the highly visible, often dominant presence of teachers, the Peace Corps in Africa was now maintaining a lower profile and attempting to provide a broader range of skilled volunteers. In retrospect, the shift from an overwhelming emphasis on education to a more balanced portfolio of volunteer assignments, including food production and primary health care, was historically inevitable. In comparison to 1966, there are 1,500 fewer volunteers standing in front of African blackboards.

Just as dramatic is the overall shift in Peace Corps programming worldwide. Whereas Africa accounted twenty years ago for just over a quarter of all volunteers, today 45 percent work in twenty-three African countries. While much attention over the years has been paid to the steady "decline" of the Peace Corps, in Africa it has established a relevance to development that is far more substantial than the massive teacher programs of the 1960s.

Volunteer projects in Asia and Latin America are today a mere 30 percent of their previous numbers, while African programs are holding at 68 percent. The reason for this is that the Peace Corps, more than any international development agency, has overcome the racial legacy of five hundred years of slave trading, colonialism, and apartheid.

It was not the sometimes questionable skills that volunteers brought to the schools and villages of Africa that made them welcome. Africans usually knew more about growing food, finding water, keeping healthy and protecting the environment than most volunteers acknowledged. In fact, the African was often surprised at how little technical knowledge the average volunteer possessed. Had the Peace Corps at first sent mainly highly trained agronomists, engineers, and economists, however, its stay in Africa might have been far less enduring. Instead, the Peace Corps sent—and continues to send—the legendary "BA generalist," or liberal arts graduate.

These generalists have never had high-tech credentials, but they do have the desire to learn the language and comprehend the host culture. Though many volunteers have failed to master the local vernacular, and few have become as sensitive and knowing as a trained social anthropologist, most have managed to say something extremely important to the Africans. After centuries of dealing with merciless exploitation, Africans have found a new and more humane image of the white race in the guise of the Peace Corps volunteer.

Africans assumed initially that American "volunteers" would bring nothing more than variations on entrenched colonial themes. Given their long and bitter association with Europeans, Africans had no reason to believe that young, mostly white volunteers would be any more capable of respecting their traditions, values, and history than the average colonial civil servant or teacher had been.

Instead, one of the great revolutions of the twentieth century occurred the day the first Peace Corps volunteers set foot on African soil—in Accra, Ghana, in September 1961. Soon there were several hundred, then thousands, of volunteers responding to African hospitality. They ate African food. They rode the buses, lorries, and mammy wagons. They greeted passersby in halting Hausa, Wolof, and Swahili. They made the Africans feel that their languages, their food, their ways and culture had meaning and importance in a world that had seemed to exclude that possibility.

In 1961, when one trainee's postcard home—noting but not complaining about the dirty, smelly streets of Lagos—fell into Nigerian hands, it seemed to confirm the worst fears of American diplomats skeptical of the wisdom of sending naive American youth on such a mission. This would not be the last embarrassment for the Peace Corps in Africa, but after a brief venting of Nigerian outrage—and the voluntary departure of the unfortunate young woman—Africans typically forgave the incident. They did not, however, wipe it from history. Five years later, the Nigerian head of state, General Yakubu Gowon, unexpectedly raised the matter with visiting Peace Corps director Jack Vaughn, to reassure him that Nigerians were not bitter over the affair.

Gowon's gesture reflected Africans' desire to make strangers feel welcome, lest they be given reason to misbehave or become enemies. Perhaps more than anything else, it is this strain running through so many African cultures that has created such an enduring bond between Peace Corps volunteers and Africa—the twin traditions of hospitality and reciprocity. Volunteers have generally understood the importance of both. They have felt curiously at home in Africa, having instinctively understood how and why they could show their hosts that they did so. Volunteers' efforts to comprehend the African cultural and spiritual universe have overshadowed all else the Peace Corps may have contributed in terms of skills and concrete monuments to progress.

In the months following the arrival of the first volunteers, it became widely known among African leaders and villagers that President Kennedy had sent "a new white man." Africans had seldom witnessed white people waiting patiently to see a minister, a local doctor, or even a district police officer. They were delighted that volunteers loved to dance to African music. Villagers were impressed that "their" volunteer would drink palm wine with them, share the joy of their births and grief of their deaths, laugh at their jokes, and listen to their oral history.

While stressing the interracial dimension of the Peace Corps' work in Africa, we also have to cite its failure to attract black and other minority volunteers. Estimates vary, but blacks probably have accounted for no more than 2 to 3 percent of all volunteers. A recurring nightmare for Africa regional staff has been all-white groups of trainees and volunteers. It is sadly ironic that, during an era of black cultural and historical renaissance, the Peace Corps has been unable to represent America's multiethnic heritage to the world, and especially to Africa. If there is one item of unfinished business on the Peace Corps' agenda for the next quarter-century, it should be to rectify this imbalance.

In defining the Peace Corps' impact and effectiveness vis-à-vis Africa's enormous needs, it would be simple enough to produce statistics proving that volunteers, in their collective mass and individual genius, have left their mark on African education, food production, and community development. The Peace Corps has helped to improve the quality of African life.

We would argue, however, that its greatest contribution lies in African-American relations. Had the Peace Corps not been established, especially when it was, American interest in Africa and understanding of its problems would have remained abysmally low. Many volunteers and staff who have served in Africa with the Peace Corps have joined a growing cadre of informed Africanists working in academia, business, government, and private development agencies. Increasingly over the years, when Africans have had to relate to an American—whether a diplomat, US/AID official, educator, journalist, or aid worker—they have found themselves dealing with someone who shared experiences, language, and values drawn from years of working in the Peace Corps in Africa.

Although Africans have strongly opposed American policies in Vietnam, South Africa, and elsewhere; although one continues periodically to hear African charges that volunteers are spies; and although some African governments have closed Peace Corps operations for political reasons, Africans have always regarded the volunteer as an individual, to be accepted into their world or not on the basis of personal qualities. When a Tanzanian village chief was instructed in 1965 to make an anti-American speech to his people, he complained that he could not understand the order. "The only Americans I know are the missionary in our village and the two Peace Corps teachers," he said, "and they are nice people. I guess it is the South Americans I am to attack."

Being shrewd judges of human nature, Africans have long concluded that the typical volunteer comes as a good person and therefore may live among them—in peace.

From a Talk with Dr. Siaka Stevens

Things you take for granted in the United States, you don't get here. Some of our boys have gone to school in Russia, married Russian girls, and brought them here. I don't think we have two here now. It's the environment. Take a girl from Kiev and bring her here, and she'll see hell. But Peace Corps volunteers have a sense of dedication. I've met them in very remote areas, where our own people don't want to go. They have this motivating factor in the back of their minds. That is their driving spirit. When the Peace Corps started here, we didn't like them at first. Some said the volunteers were CIA agents. But they mingled with the people and got integrated. Recently, I told a volunteer when he finished his second year, "To watch you work is an education." Peace Corps volunteers have built feeder roads and other things. It is an education for my people to see them. "Hey, this is a white man who is digging the gutter! Maybe work isn't all that bad." I've seen them everywhere in the country. They teach us to be proud of two pigs and ten chickens: build it gradually, see it grow. Now we are doing fish farming. That is something out of this world. I didn't think it was possible. We need the thinking process. Seeing these volunteers work teaches us to decolonize our minds.

Dr. Siaka Stevens is president of Sierra Leone.

Letter from Kenya (1965)

It does not seem at all like Christmas here. The sun is hot, the corn and beans are growing quickly after several weeks of rain. We have not heard any Christmas carols, and no one is counting shopping days. The sounds at this moment are those of children, cows, some sheep, and bird calls. In the morning, we wake up to a rooster, donkeys make their humorous braying noise all day, and at 4:30 P.M., we are able to hear the beep of the intervillage bus.

Thanksgiving was spent at a coffee society working on their accounting books. It does not sound like a Peace Corps-type project, but the audit year ended last September, and the societies are behind, so we helped. We bicycled there with sleeping bags and a safari cooking set. In the evening we talked to the guard on duty and found we were well-protected. Private ownership of a gun is not permitted, so he had the next best thing, a set of bows and arrows. We slept in the cement-block storage room on sacks full of coffee. I only fell out of bed once. The next day we finished our work, and the secretary brought us milk and ten eggs. These are expensive items; the prices are the same here as in the States. We are often given eggs and are embarrassed to receive them. The children need them more than we. But the people want to give something they know we like, and we do not want to offend by refusing them.

On five out of seven days, we visit the coffee cooperatives to talk to general members. We speak in Swahili, and it is translated into Kikuyu. The topics are cooperative principles, characteristics of a good committee member, how a society spends the members' money, and coffee competition on the world market. Our talk lasts about two hours. We spend from two to four hours bicycling. We also visit primary schools and speak to the seventh grade classes. The first time, they are extremely curious because they rarely ever see a white person. So we talk a little in English about cash crops in Kenya and compare it to farming in the U.S. This gives us a chance to assess their understanding of English and general knowledge. Then the second trip, we discuss cooperative principles with them, and the kinds of cooperatives which have been developed in other places in the world.

A problem in working here is a sense of isolation. It is not the lack of news so much as the difficulty in sharing your thoughts and feelings with others. Part of the problem, of course, stems from the language. We have finally finished our Kikuyu-Swahili-English dictionary. I was surprised to discover what you can learn about a people just by studying the words they use. If we could master these words and the changes caused by adding tenses, we would be able to converse in Kikuyu in most situations. Our Swahili has taken a jump in the last couple of weeks, and we can understand most rapid conversation now. But the rest of the problem is one of culture. Man may share a common humanity but not common life experiences. The same simple words do not evoke the same responses in us and in them. The diversity of experiences enriches our life here, but we always feel isolated.

Report from Niger (1965)

"Your volunteers can show our young people that working with their hands is not shameful," President Diori said last fall in welcoming the Peace Corps to his nation.

Dr. Bana of the Ministry of Health said of the volunteers: "Their effect is primarily psychological, on our educated elites who are so alienated from our people."

When I asked him what the function was, Mark R. simply said: "We care."

Hardly anyone thought the first purpose of the Peace Corps was to bring technical skills, and in fact, many of their counterparts have more formal training than the volunteers.

In the short run, the real function of the volunteer is the policeman's role that some of them find distasteful: by their presence, they incite local officials to be more honest and conscientious. In the long run, the volunteers must have an effect on attitudes that are preventing the nation's development. Like all African countries, Niger is deeply divided between elite and masses. Most members of the elite appear interested in show, in imitating Europe, but little concerned with their people. For the masses, progress is a myth that belongs to foreigners; two of the Hausa terms for Europeans are "the lucky ones" and "the victors."

The volunteer finds himself caught between these two classes. All his instincts are to side with the masses, but the elite runs the government and controls the volunteer's job. Nowhere is this conflict clearer than in public health.

Look at the Maradi clinic, for instance: Long after opening time, Mme. B., the director, is sitting at her desk reading a magazine, while outside dozens of women are waiting silently in the hot sun with their sick babies. Two volunteers are also waiting, acutely and guiltily aware of the women outside. Time drags on, but Mme. B. goes on reading her magazine; the women and the volunteers wait. Inside the clinic is a shocking sight: sixteen dusty cases of powdered milk stacked in a corner. The cases are marked "Gift of UNICEF and the Swiss Confederation." After many months, no one has made a move to distribute their contents. A closet contains piles of unused medicines. Many have now expired; some have been in that closet for years. The women need the milk, and the hospital needs the medicine.

Why doesn't Mme. B. open the clinic, distribute the milk, and send the medicine to the hospital? "Lack of training," someone is sure to say, but this is sheer nonsense. With her three years of midwife studies in Germany, Mme. B. is far better trained for her job than the volunteers. But like so many of the women of her district, Mme. B. is all charm and sex appeal and lies. With a dazzling smile, she tells you that the volunteers are great, that their home visits will get rolling soon. But the milk doesn't move, and the clinic opens late, and a boy with a burned stomach is sent away because it is five minutes past closing time.

Mme. B. just doesn't care. It is as simple as that. Those peasant women standing in the sun and sand are not her people; her people are the fashionable women in that magazine she is reading while everyone waits.

In Bouza, a Saharan hill town to the north, two volunteers wanted to start a soccer game for the local kids. But the school kids refused to play with the kids who do not go to school; they called them "barbarians." In Firgoun, another pair of volunteers was in the market at lunchtime with their counterpart, who is with the Ministry of Agriculture. The volunteers wanted to eat in the market. That is "not done," the counterpart explained; members of the elite do not eat with the peasantry. He said they would have to go to a nearby home and send a servant to the market to get the food so they could eat indoors, away from the masses.

The examples are endless. In a dozen details of their daily lives, the volunteers are forced to choose sides for or against the elite. Each time a volunteer picks up a tool, he is commenting on the elite's view that manual labor is beneath an educated man. If he dresses in casual American-style working clothes, he is also choosing sides, for the elite's natty dress is a class uniform. The austerity (or lack of it) of the volunteer's housing and way of life is still another comment on the values of the elite.

What should the volunteers do? At one extreme, they can denounce the school director openly, tell off the school kids, and refuse to eat anyplace but in the market. In their daily lives, they can stake out firm positions against the elite. But this will alienate the local power structure and ultimately make the volunteers' position untenable, for it is the elite, not the volunteers, that holds the power of decision. At the other extreme, they can conform in their dress and manner, contenting themselves with doing their own jobs well without ever challenging the elite's behavior. This is likely to result in the volunteers going home without having had any effect on Niger at all.

The Experience: The Pacific

by Russell G. Davis

My country treated me to two long looks at the East Asia–Pacific region: one as a rifle scout in the Marine Corps, the other as regional director of the Peace Corps. Both times I was with brave young people in their magic years, when it seems possible to win at least one race in life, the run to change a little piece of the world before it changes a big piece of you. And we did some of it, and some people and things grew. The Marine Corps is remembered, but on the long scroll of Asia, is there even a brush stroke that says Peace Corps?

When I started as regional director, the East Asia–Pacific (EAP) was the largest of the four Peace Corps regions, both in area (though most of it was underwater) and in the number of volunteers. The working areas varied immensely in culture, level of development, and needs. But I knew that in contrast to the other regions the Peace Corps served, it contained a pervasive pride of civilization, a hunger for change, and a freedom from the worst hang-ups of religious and social tradition.

On the Pacific rim was Korea, a high and ancient culture, hard and war-tested. Thailand, richer and softer inland but tough at the east frontier, was looking into Vietnam and a war that threw a shadow all across the region. Peninsular Malaysia had squelched most of its insurgency, but rancor and division remained. Insurgency and massacre were just ended in Indonesia, a place still so riven that the Peace Corps had been forced to withdraw; often as I tried, I couldn't get us back in. The Philippines, with its many regions, languages, cultures, religions, and problems, was complex—except by comparison with American Micronesia. American Micronesia was little dots spread out in a continental-size area

---

Russell G. Davis is professor of education and development at Harvard University.

of water. Its island groups could have been separate country domains, and later were, but then it was treated as one, united only by a common lack of resources, bloody battles remembered, and an uncertain future built on political, economic, and strategic ambiguity.

At times, it seemed that EAP led all the other Peace Corps regions in one thing—problems—and chief among them was that there were too many inspired young Americans in too many uninspired jobs, or in no jobs at all. The solution was to reduce the number of volunteers, or to increase the number of real jobs to assign them. Both solutions were against certain Peace Corps traditions.

It baffled traditionalists that anyone would want to think "smaller." Moving on the alternative solution—increase jobs to match volunteer numbers—revealed that very few in the Peace Corps (or elsewhere, and to this day) know how to create jobs.

Many in the Peace Corps made no pretense of being development "pros." "AID types" was a term of scorn. The staff members saw themselves as "generalists," pursuing not so much development as the other Peace Corps goals: to win friends abroad, increase international understanding, and provide a rich intercultural experience for young Americans. Those more development-oriented responded to this by saying, if that's all they do out there, we ought to pay poor countries tuition for the learning experience. But despite the differences in outlook, there was one thing that joined both camps, and that was a common aim to help people who needed it, whatever the immediate cost in personal reward and comfort.

Both were right: the important thing *was* motivation and human concern, because that was what powered and unified all the efforts. But at the same time, to teach others how to do the job, you had first to know how to do it yourself. The problem was not solved either by cutting the number of volunteers or by vastly increasing the number of jobs. Attrition cut some numbers, and new volunteers were not assigned until programs were tested. Meaningful jobs became a major criterion for program approval, but a secret formula for programming good, developmental jobs was not found.

Programming jobs was easier in large development works, such as in the Muda region of Malaysia, which was an irrigation/area-development project with heavy capital investment. In this and similar programs, jobs with high development potential were created.

Nonetheless, the old standby Peace Corps jobs continued to be in education, especially English and secondary-school teaching. The demand for secondary education—above all, training in math, science, and English—was rising throughout East Asia and the Pacific. In Micronesia, the schools could never have expanded as they did without volunteers.

But educational expansion, especially at the secondary level, chiefly met what economists call "social demand," in contrast to "economic demand." General education met the social and cultural needs of people who craved it as a form of consumption, and as a "credentialing" device. It was less well calibrated with economic requirements, in the sense of training people for the enterprises and jobs that could realistically be developed in the island areas of Micronesia. And there was concern as to how it would be supported when the large human resource subsidy was withdrawn and the Peace Corps went home. What do such things matter to a bright, poor kid who has a chance for more schooling, whatever foreign experts think? The answer from my own experience—one of ten kids in a working-class family—is to get any schooling you can.

In education, the Peace Corps could deploy the one form of manpower it had in surplus supply, the generalist, and whatever the economists say, the generalist teachers were as welcome as the most precious of cargoes in the islands and on the mainland. In EAP, more than 60 percent of the volunteers were generalist teachers, and at times the proportion was higher. Another fact should be noted: many young Americans were vastly versatile. The diploma might say "History," but these could still be farm kids who knew gardening and poultry, swine and cattle rearing, beekeeping and fishing, and how to keep the machinery running to produce the food. From hobbies such as radio and electrical and electronic devices, communications experts were born, and some rural areas were linked by Peace Corps radio networks.

Health was another major service area in which AB generalists served well, usually supported by medical professionals but sometimes working with little close support in island areas or rural Korea. Malaria control, sanitation, and other environmental health activity led to strong programs early on. Later, the cutback came in Malaysia and the islands for the happiest of reasons: diminished need.

Korea seemed as hard a place to serve as any in the region, especially in the countryside. The language was hard, the hills were hard, the winter was hard; and I especially remember it was a hard place on marriage for the young couples who were sent there. Country staff caught most of the marriage counseling, but the problem was that male Americans were invited out for very permissive nightlife by male Koreans, while females were expected to stay home and be happy. Once the partnership became strained, young American wives had few family resources, and sometimes little work or cultural satisfaction, to fall back on.

Korea had another unique twist. A Korean official told me bluntly, when I commented on the difficulty of some of the assignments and low performance ratings: "We don't expect or care if the young Americans do a good job out there. The point of the project is that they are out there, and we can point them out to our people who don't want to serve out there, and say 'Look at the Americans! Do they complain?' " Yes, they did, mightily, but they still hung in and served.

Agriculture was the third main area, and it covered everything but large field crops like wheat and corn. Rice cultivation—paddy in the Philippines and hill rice in Asia—was the chief interest. Backed up by mature scientists and teachers, a strong volunteer-manned "rice program" took shape in the Philippines, then spread to Malaysia and Thailand. Apart from extension and production support, strong work was done in curriculum development (extension education) and instructional technology. Some volunteer curriculum work would impress veteran educators.

Pond and pool fish projects were a big Asian activity, and the Peace Corps served in that department, too. In Fiji and Micronesia, this included improving the technology and gear; installing refrigeration systems to preserve and enhance the catch; and helping in communications, boat repair, and maintenance. The Peace Corps was youth in East Asia–Pacific; it was no country for old men. But older volunteers, those great and exceptional few, were outstanding. One older fellow was a legend—the story had it he had been a World War I German machine gunner—who made a mighty contribution by setting up shops, systems, and procedures for repair and maintenance of motors and craft in Palau.

One of the most dramatic programs, though not large, was helping island free-form divers to go deeper and gather more sponges through improved breath-control techniques. The Peace Corps sent several kinds of divers to the Pacific, including professional salvage and deep-sea types who worked at the end of hose lines. But watching free-form divers, many of them volunteers from Hawaii, working with the islanders was dramatic.

In the Peace Corps, as in the Marines, the stories long remembered and often told are shaped by the exceptions. One young man served through several tours, working with the hill tribes in Thailand on such problems as the ravages of slash-and-burn agriculture in the face of a shrinking land base. A tough Thai soldier, who worked on the same problem using different methods, told me, "He not only taught those people up there, he taught me how to teach people." There were volunteers who performed great feats in setting up communications networks in Malaysia and the islands, some just as an adjunct hobby to their regular job assignments. Areas were linked that had never been linked before.

In development work, many pros find that the hardest thing to do is to aid the development of entrepreneurial activity, the kind that promotes small industries to produce goods and services, to make enough profit to survive, to create jobs and earnings for the entrepreneur and his family, his neighbors, and his landsmen. This is called EDP (entrepreneurial development programs), and it requires a combination of market study, technological analysis, marketing and training plans, credit arrangement, and much support and counseling. Entrepreneurial development is not hard to do in rich countries where family traditions and culture encourage it. The challenge was in the poverty-stricken Philippines and Micronesia. It is easy to teach the rich to take a chance that they might get richer, but to teach the poor to play in a lottery where they have never seen a winner, or even an honest drawing, requires entrepreneurs of great faith and missionary zeal.

East Asia–Pacific, as a region, started with 4,400 volunteers and ended with 3,300, less than two years later. We were not very "entrepreneurial," if that quality is measured in live body count, as some did. There were fewer volunteers in non-jobs or bad jobs at the end, but good jobs were always hard to find.

A few peculiar incidents come back to mind, such as trying to give an earnest young volunteer a sound reason why she should not be allowed to work bare-breasted on her island, when all the other women there did. Or trying to explain to an earnest young man that being a patriot did not require him to brief the CIA station chief on rural politics, and that Peace Corps policy was to keep the two apart. Or chasing a brig rat from Da Nang who wore a big .45 and rode a Honda with a girl attached to the saddle, claiming to be a Peace Corps member to get gas money.

But the memory that stands out above all is of watching a girl who ran extra-help sessions every day because the regular teacher caught an early boat home and some of the kids, stranded there until later boats came, were from remote areas with no schools.

The girl was using a cardboard clock face with numerals 1 to 12 and attached hands to teach time. A kid was having difficulty overcoming the illogic of it all, that the small hand indicated the big time period and the big hand the small. But he worked at it, and got it, and twitched with joy as he rattled back correct times to her.

Afterward she said, "They're really not dumb. I just didn't teach it well. They come from big, poor families, but give them a chance and they can learn anything. All they need is the opportunity." Not hearing anything from me, she got defensive: "Don't you believe that?"

I came to and said, "Yeah, sure I believe it. It's just that the kid reminded me of someone."

She said, "Me, too. He reminded me of me." She waited, then, but the only response she got was New England silence.

The young find it so easy to be honest! That's what the Peace Corps was founded on; that and the need to remember where you come from when you go where you have to go.

Remarks on the Decision to Withdraw from Indonesia (1965)

by Alex Shakow

May 30, 1965, would have marked the second anniversary here in Jakarta of our first group of volunteers. These seventeen were followed by an additional fourteen in January 1964, and the final group of fifteen that December. At one point, we had forty-five volunteers on duty in eighteen provinces and twenty cities, teaching and coaching sports and physical education. But we are not going to reach the second anniversary here, for by May 5th I hope to have all the current crop of volunteers out of the country. What happened?

We came here on an "experimental" basis in a flush of goodwill. Peace Corps Director Sargent Shriver and President Sukarno talked in Bogor in September 1962 and exchanged notes seven months later. At the time that our first volunteers arrived, relations with the U.S. were at a high point, for it looked as though the United States and its allies were going to lend Indonesia $400 million. Despite a barrage of Communist press attacks, the Indonesian government held firm to its commitment. In fact, the next six months were quiet politically. Our volunteers had trouble adjusting to the food, to the people, to the absence of scheduled work, to Indonesian family life. But they learned. Meanwhile, the pressure began to mount a bit as Malaysia became a significant issue here. The attacks on the Peace Corps very rarely had anything to do with the coaches' competence, but rather identified our volunteers with "imperialist"

Alex Shakow, who at the time of this essay was Peace Corps director in Indonesia, is now division chief for international economic affairs at the World Bank in Washington, D.C.

American actions, including the CIA. This was not a real problem until some of the Communist youth became violent.

Our most striking case was that of Semarang in Central Java, where a volunteer named Bob was dragged from his home by a mob of Communist youth and taken to the governor's office for expulsion from Indonesia as a spy. The group was received by the governor, who praised their revolutionary spirit and sent them home. The governor then told the volunteer not to be concerned and to continue his work. Two days later, a dozen of the mob were arrested and detained for a week. Although they were never brought to trial, there was no more trouble in Semarang. The mob neglected the fact that the volunteer lived with an army colonel. Nonetheless, the city was covered with anti-Peace Corps signs; one wall even bore the scrawled expression "Beware of Bob's smile."

In certain regions there has never been any trouble to speak of. In others, the trouble has come in spurts. But lately, political trouble has become our stock in trade in almost all regions, and has come in more difficult and significant ways. Whereas before, resolutions came from Communist groups, recently they have been coming from the local and regional governments. Several regional bodies have requested that the central government withdraw the Peace Corps from their region; other local parliaments did the same in response to the demands of Communist groups. In each case, we would scurry around here in Jakarta and have the sports minister or, more frequently, the foreign minister, take action. I began to feel more like a fireman putting out small blazes than anything else. We never had to withdraw a volunteer from an area where he had been placed, but we did some long, hard thinking on several cases.

Our volunteers are not politicians; they are physical education coaches. They are not paid Foreign Service officers hired to fight for the nation's cause at the conference table, nor are they soldiers trained to battle in guerrilla war. Yet the situation that they increasingly faced resembled something like this. Great struggles are going on in this country that are none of our business. The inner conflict has nothing to do with the Peace Corps, but we inevitably became involved. President Sukarno has of late been making clear Indonesia's opposition to many American policies. In the regions, this policy line is particularly clear, for there is little contact there with anything but official government policy.

I knew that President Sukarno had expressed his admiration and appreciation for the volunteers, as had the sports minister in various closed conversations. As I traveled around, I tried to portray the Jakarta feeling to leading regional officials. It felt very strange, to say the least, trying to explain President Sukarno's support for the Peace Corps to these officials, but if I did not, who would? Almost all these leaders were prepared to implement any decision that the central government presented to them. But it was quite clear that some, especially those not interested in sports, were scared at the injection of this essentially alien, international issue into the already troubled climate of their own political situation.

Under these circumstances, we concluded that the useful life of the Peace Corps here was nearing its close, for volunteers who in some places could coach basketball only under the protection of bayonets were not really Peace Corps volunteers. When our many friends in the regions found it dangerous to help us, then it was time to pack up. When work was hampered not only by the expected and usual technical problems, but also by political and security factors, it was time to withdraw, even though such a decision was made with the greatest reluctance.

The door is open to future Peace Corps programs in Indonesia if the Indonesian government should ever want them. The exchange of notes remains in force. Of course, all depends on future political developments. Although I have an obvious prejudice, I think that our experience here has been a positive one. Despite all the trouble they had, two-thirds of the volunteers who served out their terms said on going home that they would choose Indonesia again if they had the chance. Not a single one of our volunteers has gone home early or quit. They pulled their hair out at how disorganized the sports world is here. They complained bitterly because inflation made their rupiahs worthless and I would not raise their allowances. But all our volunteers will leave with regret at the loss of many close friends and disappointment that they could not do the job they wanted.

The Experience: South and West Asia

by John Chromy

The noonday south Indian sun seared down unmercifully as our train slowly carried us through this, the third day of our trans-India journey. It was June of 1963, and ten days before, we sixteen Peace Corps volunteers had left our homes all over America. Already we felt nostalgia for those lush green landscapes. We stared at the dry, eerily empty Indian countryside, which slid by at barely twenty miles an hour. The fixation of our eyes partly reflected our exhaustion, after thirty-three hours in the air and two days on the ground, where the temperature had not fallen below 100 degrees. But what concerned us more was the mission on which we had been sent in this vast subcontinent.

Here we were to assist village people in growing more food to improve their nutrition and bring new hope to their lives. But how were we to work such miracles in a land that, in three days of travel, revealed to us only dry, barren, dun-colored landscape and almost no people, except those gathered in the towns bordering the tracks? Where were those 380 million villagers we had read so much about? Where were the crops that fed them? Where were the sacred cows, the monkeys, the tigers, the elephants? Where had they all gone? How were we to help them?

This initial trip with its unanswered questions was my stunning introduction to the underbelly of Asia, which stretches from the shores of the Mediterranean to the Bay of Bengal. Later, as the Peace Corps' deputy regional director at the end of the 1970s, I saw more, but the lands remained a mystery. A panorama of ancient civilizations, vast numbers of people, dry, barren hills and plains, stunning scenery, exotic wildlife, millennia of brutal political strife, crossroads of world trade and in-

---

John Chromy is director of management and administration, Special Olympics International.

trigue, and to this day lands of stark contrast. These lands confronted us not only with proud and independent cultures, resistant enough to our assigned responsibility as agents of change, but with even more prideful and more stubbornly independent subcultures, like the Kurds of Turkey and Iran, the Pathans of Afghanistan and Pakistan, the Sikhs of India.

Within ten days of the end of our train ride, barely settled into our homes as brand new Peace Corps volunteers, we learned our first secret about this robe of contrasting colors, the saving grace of the lands of South Asia. The surprise was India's famous monsoons, which struck with their first gentle refreshing and life-giving gift. The rains had come, and now out of everywhere flowed people, animals, wildlife—out of homes, out of hiding places. But what also flowed out was hope.

The people rushed to ready the fields, to prepare the seedlings and sow their crops. And rush they must, for the monsoon season is always fickle and sometimes cruelly short. They must place their seeds in the ground quickly, so that they may drink up the monsoon moisture as greedily as possible. For too soon there would be no more. The crops which, in a warm tropical climate, leap toward the sky, will wither and die beneath the harsh skies of South Asia unless man moves quickly. Water feeds and water cools, and without it the crops die, and so does life.

If the seeds are planted promptly and the rains are good and gentle, at least when the crops near ripeness, then each and every village family will reap from its small plot enough food to eat well through the year and, possibly, to have some small amount left over to sell for cloth, meat, or plastics, and to save for a dowry to marry a daughter. But if something fails, if the showers loiter, the rains start falsely and then turn away, or the rains beat a heavy and crushing drumbeat near harvest time, then each of India's 380 million villagers knows that the family will face January, February, and March with only two meals a day. In April, May, and June many will have only one—mothers and daughters first, and then sons, and finally fathers eating only one meal of the rough, tasteless, ground-grain gruel, since those most able to sow and reap must be fed and kept the healthiest. Then the limited supplies will be stretched until the next harvest, and the cycle will start all over again.

And so this explosion of activity, this rush to till and plant, surprised the volunteers, strangers in this vast, unique, and overpowering land. This dependence on short, focused, seasonal rains is a phenomenon that engulfs and governs the life of nearly all of Asia's underbelly, and it had unique effects upon the assignment of volunteers. It demanded that Peace Corps volunteers work with Iranian farmers, for instance, to seek out and even to breed hardy strains of grain and trees, to find millet that could survive on little water, and to learn the ways of macadamia nuts, whose trees bore fruit with no water in sight. These were strange demands, indeed, for farm boys from Wisconsin and Pennsylvania.

For this, we had journeyed at a snail's pace nearly the entire length of the subcontinent, from the shadow of the perpetually snowcapped Himalayas, across the endless Deccan Plateau, nearly to Kanya Kumari, the beautiful land's end where the powerful Arabian Sea swirls into the flowing Indian Ocean. As we made our way across, the land had been in hibernation, waiting for these rains. For three months the heat of the Indian summer is so overpowering that it saps the mind, body, and soul of every creature. Ten thousand years of unrecorded history had taught these people that in this season the only sane response to the overpowering force of nature is to submit, to drink as much water as is available, to move about only from dusk until soon after dawn, to talk quietly to the young, to protect your precious animals, and to pray to the gods that in their goodness and wisdom they will soon send the rains and the life-giving nourishment they produce.

Hibernation and then a rush to plant, cultivate, and harvest was a cycle that most Peace Corps volunteers serving in South Asia came to know, work with, be frustrated by, and ultimately accept. For truly, it was not only the sane response to the environment, it was the rhythm of life's seasons.

Summer in India was what winter was in my native Minnesota. It gave the land, the farmers, and their animals a chance to rest, to replenish the spirit, and, most important, to pause and think—about man, god, animals, and nature, and their relation to each other. Metaphysics we called it when I was in college, but the philosophy and mythology of Buddhism, Hinduism, and Islam all urge man to focus on the questions of his relationship with his god and the use he is making of his time. And I began to realize that here, ten thousand miles from home, literally and figuratively on the other side of the world, East and West had that much in common, except that maybe East had learned it better. I remembered Ecclesiastes 3 speaking of the same phenomenon: "To every thing there is a season," including the season to die.

Though Peace Corps volunteers all across South Asia understood, in varying degrees, the villagers' need to accept the perils of the environment, to take what advantage they could of them, and, most important, not to fight them, nonetheless to the short-termers, the can-do spirited Americans, this was a source of enormous frustration. Peace Corps nurses fought it. They traveled by camel to remote valleys of Afghanistan to administer medicine and inoculations to people who had never seen modern medical care. These young women of Boston and Austin, Texas, would rather travel over vast, arid terrain on the back of a camel than be kept from their duty.

For those who worked in agricultural production, with only two rainy seasons before they had to go home, there was always impatience. They did not easily face the fact that in two growing seasons they had to help the farmers change, and that it took one season to learn about the setting and another to spread the word, and that was about two seasons too short. Adult learning moves more slowly, especially when the learning so deeply concerns each family's source of life. Two growing seasons were not enough, and by 1967, the Peace Corps had learned to place agriculture volunteers only where there was irrigation, or at least where there was enough moisture for two cropping seasons. Americans do not sit and wait for the gods to deliver the rains very well.

Wherever Peace Corps volunteers served in Southwest Asia and South Asia, they entered into ancient cultures, patterns of living that often evoked Biblical times, cities with names that hauntingly recalled tales of Alexander the Great, the Arabian Nights, the British wars of the Northwest Frontier, the travels of Marco Polo, Genghis Khan, and Shah Jahan. They found peoples who firmly believed in new and old gods that resembled more the ancient gods of Greek mythology than the Christian God we thought we knew so well. They found a hundred million people who believed in a god called Allah, for whom Jesus Christ was only a respected prophet.

These men and women of the Peace Corps went forth to change things among peoples who believed that the most noble thing was to die in Allah's service, while others among them were convinced that the most important thing was to live out your current lot in life just as it was, no matter how impoverished or bitter, because only by accepting one's fate in this life would a person be reborn into a better one in the next incarnation, which would surely come. Worse yet, not to accept graciously one's lot in life risked community censure, or the assurance of reincarnation to a lower form in the next life or, perhaps worse still, the possibility of being unable to find a husband for one's daughter.

Think of how enterprising Americans reacted to this enormous burden of history, culture, religion, and climate, as they worked for change. Then add a more formidable, more daunting foe: sheer numbers. In India alone, the more than 400 million people (now 720 million) outnumbered the populations of Africa and South America combined. If the Peace Corps had placed in South Asia the same proportion of volunteers it had in Micronesia, no less than 4 million Peace Corps volunteers would have gone to the subcontinent.

The sheer numbers of people involved in each problem gnawed away at even the best volunteer's will to go on.

Peace Corps nurses in Indian hospitals would treat two hundred people in a day and still find the line of those waiting to be seen as long as the sunset in the West. The wards in their hospitals contained two hundred beds where only seventy fit, and waiting in the hospital gardens were the families of the sick, cooking food for the patient and reinfecting him even before he was cured and able to be sent home.

Volunteers working in agriculture expended enormous effort to help twenty village farmers produce 25 percent more food in two years, and then noted that the families each had 20 percent more mouths to feed, so little ground was gained.

Peace Corps teachers pleaded with a state Ministry of Education to raise the salaries for elementary school teachers by $3 a month, only to be informed that in that Indian state, there were 33,000 schools and 102,000 teachers, and if each of them received a $3 raise, the funds needed would be more than the Ministry's entire nonteaching budget. Yet only 40 percent of the children in the villages of the state had any school to go to at all.

It was in the face of all this—this vast South Asian subcontinent with its seas and deserts and mountains and plains and heat and cold and wildness and ancient civilizations and multifarious religions—that energetic and enthusiastic Americans went to work. They did much. They helped build schools by the hundreds, raise chickens by the millions, teach people in schools and out, inoculate children, dig wells, build bridges, grow and lose and save crops, form cooperatives. Some were also married, and gave birth, and many nurtured and carefully cultivated friendships which were thriving two decades later.

Yet, in the end, as S. K. Dey, the Indian government's minister of planning, told one group of Peace Corps volunteers, "India has withstood and indeed absorbed many invasions over four thousand years. She often took the best of what the invaders had to offer and discarded the rest. I am confident India will do likewise with the American Peace Corps. So we are glad to have invited you to come and we are glad you are here. Please give us all that is good about America and please do not give us what is bad. And be patient with us, for life has been going on for a very long time in this part of the universe, and it will go on for a very long time after you have gone."

Minister Dey was right.

Letter from India (1964)

Six of us in the India program were trained to work in irrigation extension. We were to be stationed together in one district north of Calcutta to help develop the transmission systems and teach the cultivators how to use more efficiently the water pumped from dozens of government tube wells. More or less, we would act on the "county agent" job level in the States, advising cultivators on agriculture and irrigation. Sounds plain enough, doesn't it? Exactly what I thought, but now let me explain what really happened.

On arrival in Delhi, we six learned that only three would be going to the original destination, and one of these was transferred to work in beekeeping. Tom and I were transferred to Purulia, and the third was sent to a state poultry farm as a mechanic. Flexibility! The sooner the volunteers accept this word, the more they will enjoy India. In reality, Purulia district is like the Imperial Valley of California before the Colorado River was brought in . . . desert! Irrigation experts in a desert with no water. Laugh, but that is the way things stand now. On top of this, we had no actual job definition when we arrived, and still don't. Officially we are under the supervision of the district agricultural officer, but he isn't sure just how we are supposed to be used. We have done some work for the office—surveyed and mapped several new seed farms, helped erect the agricultural display at the state exhibition, advised on crops, etc., for private cultivators—but the most satisfying work we have had has just fallen into our laps.

An example: A family here in town had twenty-five chickens which weren't laying any eggs. One day while visiting them, I was asked to take a look at the flock. I had no training and very little practical knowledge of poultry, but I suggested more feed and a higher protein content. He tried it and two weeks later was getting twenty-two eggs per day. From this conversation a five-hundred-bird project has developed, along with some wheat cultivation that I also urged him to try. He plans to double his wheat acreage next year and has even bought himself a tractor.

An orphanage in town had a tomato patch that was dying. We checked it over and, for lack of anything else, suggested some ammonium sulfate. The idea worked, and they had tomatoes to sell. They also gave us all we could eat. We are also toying with the idea of starting a goat herd and selling sterilized, bottled milk. We are awaiting the O.K. signal from P.C. Delhi.

Letter from Iran (1965)

Z., like many small towns, is prone to gossip. In a Moslem society, there is strict separation of men and women, and people are very sensitive about any infringement on this. The schools, for example, are let out at different times so the boys and girls won't be on the street together. For several months I have been having my advanced English class, six girls about twenty, meet at my house, giving us a more informal atmosphere. Sometimes my husband's closest friend in town, an unmarried boy of twenty-three, comes to the house while my class is here, and usually he and my husband go off to the bazaar. But when the weather was bad, they sometimes sat talking in the other room of the house. Imagine my chagrin when the chief of education and several of the English teachers informed me that I had better move my class back to the school building, as it was a bad idea to have boys over when the girls were here. These men, realizing the extent of gossip that goes around town about us, primarily because we're the only foreigners here, wanted to tell us who we could have come to our house and when. They informed us that since my husband's friend was "only a bank clerk," we shouldn't associate with him at all. It was most uncomfortable, especially since he has been one of the kindest and most devoted people we have ever known, and aside from him we really have no close friends here. Now, if he happens to come when my class is meeting, my husband simply meets him at the door and they leave.

Letter from East Pakistan (1963)

I've been assigned as a communications technician to the East Pakistan nutrition survey team. The survey team goes out to a rural site about once a month, and I go along with them. I've made one trip, and it was quite an experience.

I was the big sideshow. In fact, I felt like the Pied Piper as droves of children and assorted adults followed me around. Then delegates from neighboring villages came to see the main attraction. One afternoon I was quietly minding my own business when I saw a long line of women and children coming across the rice paddy. I hid in my room until I got so hot that I had to come out. There were forty-eight women and children, and they just stood there and stared. When they finally left, another group of about twenty-five came over. The next afternoon, I was taking a nap and suddenly awoke to find about twenty women and children standing around my bed looking at me. Needless to say, I jumped up, rather shaken, and shooed them out. Everyone was quite surprised that the women would come out of the villages to see me, because the purdah tradition is very strong in the rural areas.

The Experience: Latin America

by Frank Mankiewicz

To understand what distinguished the Peace Corps program and philosophy in Latin America from those of other regions, I think you have to begin with Sargent Shriver, the first Peace Corps director. Then, as now, Shriver was an intellectually curious man, unwilling to accept any orthodoxy without a thorough testing and, if possible, a robust argument. It was Shriver who best exemplified for me the Peace Corps' emphasis on action and its disregard for bureaucratic formalities.

In late 1961, the Peace Corps already had volunteers in the field, but it was still unsure in what direction either they or the organization itself was going. So one day, Shriver called in John Kenneth Galbraith, then ambassador to India but also one of America's leading development economists, to talk with his senior staff. Galbraith was a man who combined a knowledge of international economics with an urgent sense of the political needs of emerging nations.

For two hours, Galbraith talked about development in the Third World (a new phrase, but a useful one) and the optimum way for American policy to emerge there. But instead of the then-current (and highly ethnocentric) theories of the wisdom of large-scale U.S. projects—dams, highways, infrastructure investment—Galbraith talked in terms of *barriers,* and what the Peace Corps could do to break them down. He spoke of "brakes" on development, continent by continent, region by region, culture by culture.

In India, Galbraith said, the great barrier was a lack of investment. No industrial fortunes had survived independence. The British had taken

---

Frank Mankiewicz, executive vice president of Gray and Company in Washington, D.C., served as the Peace Corps' regional director in Latin America.

their capital with them, and the Indian banks were unable to fill the gap. The United States, he said, could help most with substantial credits.

In Africa, the problem was not a lack of capital or resources but of educated and trained personnel. The colonial administrations had made no effort to leave an educated, trained bureaucracy behind, having preferred to run the countries through expatriates. The Peace Corps' best contribution could be a massive infusion of teachers to take the place of the colonials, without their preferred status.

In sharp contrast, the barriers to economic development in Latin America were neither resources, which the region had in abundance, nor capital, with which the government and governing classes were amply supplied. Nor was it a lack of trained personnel. In theory, at least, independence had come in the nineteenth century, and local bureaucracies were well trained and in place. The great obstacle to development in Latin America, Galbraith said, lay in a feudal social structure. So long as upward social mobility was strictly limited—as it had been since the Spanish arrived—no significant amount of wealth would reach the people. Thus, the goals of economic development would never be achieved.

Galbraith's words reminded us that, in Latin American countries—a difficult concept for many North Americans to grasp—the great majority of people despised and felt remote from the leadership that presumed to speak for them. As *el presidente* or *caudillo,* these leaders were regularly on the front pages of their newspapers in the company of the U.S. ambassador, starting a new "project" or announcing a new offensive against Communist guerrillas. In the eyes of the great majority of Latin Americans, that scarcely spoke well for the U.S.A.

Galbraith's words further reminded us that throughout most of the region, the rich effectively paid no taxes, and tiny fractions of the population owned virtually all of the arable land. In the United States, where homesteading and a progressive tax system was commonplace, land and tax reform may not have seemed a monumental change. But in Central and South America, this was truly a revolutionary doctrine—and was seen as such by the wealthy, land-owning class that began a savage attack on the Kennedy administration. In this effort, alas, they were often joined by the local administrators of U.S. foreign aid, who were unwilling to contemplate changes in traditional economic assistance, as change could mean termination of their programs and their jobs.

Past American failing thus imposed a very heavy responsibility on the Peace Corps in Latin America. We thought the Peace Corps had not just to teach, not just to build water or sewage systems, not just to introduce new methods of agriculture, but to bring enough awareness to an excluded majority so that they might reach for the levers of power. In

American foreign policy, characterized since World War II by resistance to social reform in friendly countries, by support for political dictators, and by a comfortable embrace for the local aristocracies, there were few models for young Peace Corps volunteers.

To put the Peace Corps' work in the context of its times, it is important to recall that in 1961 Latin America was undergoing one of its periodic pulsations of change. In Venezuela, Colombia, Peru, Honduras, Cuba, and the Dominican Republic, brutal military dictatorships had given or were giving way to progressive regimes pledged to a better life for the *campesinos* and the urban poor. These "revolutionaries"—Rómulo Betancourt of Venezuela, Juan Bosch of the Dominican Republic, Fidel Castro of Cuba, Alberto Lleras Camargo of Colombia, among others—talked openly of ending a century of privilege in which a handful of oligarchs owned virtually all the valuable land. In the case of Peru, they even owned the Indians who worked the land.

It is also important to remember that President Kennedy had explicitly put the United States on the side of change. For the first time since Franklin D. Roosevelt took the Marines out of Nicaragua and proclaimed the "Good Neighbor Policy," an American administration had rejected the repressive regimes of Latin America in favor of reform. Kennedy had announced the Alliance for Progress, and it is hard to remember just how revolutionary it appeared. We will give no foreign aid, we said, to countries where democratic governments are overthrown or where militarism reigns. Furthermore, we will tailor our aid precisely to those countries with broad programs of human rights, tax reform, and land redistribution programs, and we will extend technological help to those countries that need assistance in the effort to reform.

It is hard, even now, to measure President Kennedy's extraordinary impact on the ordinary people of Latin America, and even on some of its leaders. To this day, his picture (often on yellowed and fading newsprint) is taped and tacked to millions of adobe, tar-paper, and straw walls in the mountains and the *favelas*.

The memory is enshrined, to be sure, not because of any single tangible achievement. The Alliance for Progress soon dwindled down to just another technical assistance program, in which U.S. bureaucrats spent tours of duty shuffling papers with their local counterparts, reviewing countless feasibility studies and compiling mountains of meaningless statistics. Still, Latin Americans, with the exception of the rich and powerful, loved John Kennedy because they sensed he loved them. "If we cannot help the many who are poor," he told them in his inaugural address, "we cannot save the few who are rich." In that time, in that place, they knew he was talking about them.

At that moment, the Peace Corps arrived on the scene. This "other arm" of U.S. policy strengthened and reinforced the Alliance for Progress. It told the miserable of a continent, abused by their leaders for decades while the United States supported those leaders and reaped the economic benefits, that at last we had changed. Not only were we to alter the habit of a century and actively support reform and policies designed to bring economic and political power to the poor; we were even going to send our young people to live with them and help them change their lives.

Step by step, the peculiarly Latin American version of the Peace Corps emerged. It was not the almost mystic village-style Peace Corps of India, nor the technical-assistance programs of Southeast Asia, and surely not the teacher-dominated program of Africa. It was, as we all freely recognized, a "revolutionary force," and we called it "community development."

In truth, we hardly knew where to start, but our model was in the streets of Chicago. The community development movement began in Chicago's "Back of the Yards," founded by Saul Alinsky and his disciples, who forged an instrument by which the scorned and disenfranchised could reach for a share of power and participation. Alinsky believed in working by building organization, almost for the very sake of organization. He thought the poor should "rub raw the sores of discontent," and if that meant demonstrations, then his people would demonstrate. If it meant picket lines in residential neighborhoods, they would picket. Alinsky's community development groups were highly vocal and highly visible. They brought home to the "haves" the needs and deprivations of the "have-nots."

Any organizational tool would do, just to get people together who had never sensed a feeling of group power before. Sooner or later, the theory held, the establishment would take note, recoil in horror and sometimes in violence, and then, reluctantly, act, often too late and mostly with too little, but act. And then, as time went on, they would act some more. It was a time-honored principle of American governance—"the wheel that squeaks the loudest gets the grease." The trick was to get the poor to squeak at all.

At first formlessly, then with conscious direction, community development became the model for Peace Corps programs in Latin America. Later, under Sargent Shriver, "community action" became the technique adopted for the War on Poverty. The "maximum feasible participation" of the poor mandated by the anti-poverty law was an extension of the principle validated by the Peace Corps of Latin America, the principle which held that organizing the *outsiders* of society could bring them *inside.* Volunteers bound for Latin America were trained, at least for the first five years and sporadically thereafter, to believe their job was to bring the dispossessed into a society whose leaders did not want them in. That, for better or for worse, was a *revolutionary* mission, and it was not without its opponents. Even within the Peace Corps, a strong conservative tendency soon appeared, manifested in a bland "hands across the sea" missionary instinct, endemic to foreign policy bureaucracies.

To those of us in the day-to-day training and administration of community development, with its emphasis on projects to transform urban slums and remote Andean villages, it was often distracting and even irritating to find scarce Peace Corps resources diverted to soft, easy-to-publicize projects whereby, for example, an American school could build a counterpart school in a developing country, whether it was needed or not. But for the most part, the community development effort proceeded with high-level support and, best of all, some discernible success on the ground. Shriver was never less than wholly supportive and enthusiastic, and often cited communities of the poor who had forced their way, through the techniques of organization, into the mainstream.

The challenge faced by volunteers was aggravated by the remoteness in Latin America of the concept of cooperation that was central to community organization. De Tocqueville, in *Democracy in America,* had made much of the American genius for self-government and voluntary association, a quality scarcely apparent in Central or South America. The notion that people in a neighborhood could pool different skills to help build one another's houses was not to come naturally to Latin American culture.

This was hardly surprising in countries where the suspicion prevailing between insiders and outsiders was so harsh. From Guatemala south to Chile, all along the spine of the Andes, are countries where the Indian majority was regarded as not only inferior but hardly human at all. It was the white and *mestizo* elements that ran and decided everything in those countries.

In Peru, for example, Peace Corps volunteers questioned whether it would do any good to build a new school in an Indian village if the white teachers who would be sent there continued openly to regard the children as animals for speaking their native tongue, rather than Spanish. When a social worker ostentatiously wipes off the chair in the family home on which he or she is about to sit, the interview is not off to a good start. Peace Corps volunteers were appalled when Andean children, asked which animal they would most wish to emulate, offered the ant or a rat as a reply. When they were asked to draw themselves and their families, the figures often appeared without hands or feet—a classic self-portrayal of helplessness.

During the early years, a conscious effort was made to keep volunteers' living standards close to those of the people with whom they were working. That meant, in remote mountain villages and near-jungle settlements along the river, a lack not only of electricity and running water but of any source of reliable medical care. A Peace Corps doctor was on duty in every country, and kept fairly steadily on the road, but it still seems a miracle that more serious illness did not occur.

Such handicaps notwithstanding, conscientiously and imaginatively the volunteers plodded forward to apply the best community development training the Peace Corps knew how to provide. Usually they worked in pairs, to lessen the degree of cultural trauma. Characteristically, they took some time at the start to make an inventory of their community, ask questions, identify potential leaders, and seek organizing possibilities. If it turned out, for example, that one of the "sores of discontent" was a closed and locked playing field, then the appropriate organizing tactic might be to form two community teams and enlist the local priest, perhaps by a collective visit, to join in petitioning the authorities to unlock the field. Or perhaps it was simply a matter of climbing the fence and using the forbidden field for practice. Community development called for experimentation and improvisation. For each success, there were many failures.

Organization around credit unions and co-ops proved to be a useful tool in small towns and villages. The task was harder in the sprawling shantytowns, where agriculture was impossible and the daily gathering of food and water consumed almost all a family's time. These shantytowns—not really slums in the American sense of decaying urban environments—are a phenomenon of Latin development. With the exception of Cuba (where Castro put almost all available development funds into roads, health centers, markets, and schools in the countryside, while starving Havana), every large Latin city is ringed by squatter settlements containing perhaps twice the population of the city itself.

The settlers, classically, seize vacant land, usually under cover of darkness, carrying rudimentary straw or cardboard walls and roofs with them. By morning, a sizable new "suburb" is in place, complete with marked-off streets, a few small "stores" selling soft drinks and cigarettes, and perhaps a defiant flag or two. These invasions are highly organized and include, usually, people from a particular zone or village or of a single political persuasion—sometimes both. If the invasion is successful, and it nearly always is, then the settlement expands. Newcomers arrive, a rudimentary administration is set up, and the residents take their place as an urban interest, embarrassing to the government but a presence to deal with.

In the cities, the Peace Corps volunteers had a harder task than in the villages. Outside the city, the population is identifiable, origins are easily acknowledged, and a need around which a community can be organized is not too hard to locate. In the countryside, an organization formed to get a playing field, protest an inadequate farm-to-market road, or create a co-op can be held together when its members begin to sense their power. But in the city, allegiances shift, populations are far from stable and hard to track, and needs proliferate. Leadership there is very often plain old demagogy. The urban barrio dweller, ripped from familiar surroundings in the country and humbled to the point of scrounging for food, was a far harder target for the Peace Corps volunteer than the villager who came from a stable family structure.

Much has been made, some of it by the very Alliance for Progress bureaucrats who found Latin America's community development projects hard to "quantify," of the "failure" of urban community development volunteers. It is true that the work was difficult, and for a young American in a strange culture-within-a-culture, it was often easier to succumb to boredom and culture shock than to listen, observe, and organize around a community need, however dimly perceived. But for those who succeeded, the rewards were great. For many volunteers, a sense of success would not come until years later, and many have reported returning to their villages or settlements after a decade or more, to find the seeds of early community organization grown to the sturdy young branches of a co-op, credit union, playground league, or burgeoning political center. Nearly all have found stronger communities, which are more willing to speak up and try to influence the traditional sources of power. Community development seems, by and large, to have made an impact.

Since the peak days of the middle and late 1960s, the number of Peace Corps volunteers, as well as countries in which they serve, has declined significantly in Latin America. That may be a statement of the volunteers' effectiveness. Some of the traditional governments asked the volunteers to leave, no doubt, for the very reason that they were *too* successful. It was the same reason that made the mayors of many American cities glad when the War on Poverty ended and the community action organizers went home. As soon as the outcasts of society begin to claim the right to be involved in the process of government, the establishment resists. In many countries of Latin America, I believe it was an index of community development's progress that the Peace Corps was asked to leave.

In reviewing the Latin American experience, I recall that the first of the Peace Corps' objectives is to better people's lives. Cuba and Nicaragua, where no volunteers ever served, also had revolutions, accomplished by force of arms. While the lot of the ordinary citizen is far better than under the old military dictatorships, the immediate future, without strong institutions and under relentless American pressure, is not promising. I would contend that the Peace Corps' work in community development has produced results that, while surely less dramatic, perhaps stand on a sounder foundation.

Centers of power alternative to the traditional oligarchies continue to develop. The social structures today, in most countries, are not so feudal; the number of people excluded from meaningful participation in decision-making has declined. Governments—again, in most countries—seem somewhat more responsive to the ordinary citizen.

Perhaps more important, there is in Latin America today a clear trend back to democratic institutions. In Argentina, Guatemala, and Peru, freely elected presidents have taken over from military and oligarchic strongmen. Other democratic leaders are waiting in the wings, even in such rigid dictatorships as Chile and Paraguay. For the first time, furthermore, these new leaders seem to have behind them strong democratic organizations. It is not farfetched, I think, for the Peace Corps to claim some of the credit for this change. The generation rising to power in Latin America today was introduced to politics in the era of John Kennedy, when the Peace Corps arrived. The idealism the volunteers left behind—along with the concepts of participation and organization—may have had a more powerful impact than we will ever be able to measure.

The Peace Corps' second objective is to make the people of the host countries better acquainted with the United States. In Latin America, the record seems clear. For at least five years and to a remarkable degree thereafter, our "hosts" saw a different breed of American. They were neither rich nor arrogant, and they shared the hardships of the poor they had chosen to help. In a sense, most important of all may have been the independence Peace Corps volunteers showed from their own country's foreign policy, which for nearly two centuries most Latins have considered misguided, if not actually oppressive.

A dramatic example came in the Dominican Republic in 1965. A government proclaiming its commitment to constitutional rule was under attack by generals anxious to return to the military dominance of Trujillos' time. President Johnson, citing "Communist atrocities," airlifted American troops to "preserve neutrality," which meant to safeguard the military junta. When the U.S. troops arrived, the one hundred members of the Peace Corps in the country were unanimously on the other side. Indeed, when a U.N. observer team visited Santo Domingo, it was only Peace Corps volunteers and staff who could pass through the lines and enter the territory controlled by the constitutionalists. As power in the Dominican Republic continues to shift back and forth, the lesson of the Americans who cast their lot with the people has not been forgotten.

The impression in Latin America of the volunteer as being from a truly democratic society has persisted. The volunteer is a role model in a continent of societies by no means all committed to freedom. It is perhaps significant that the new reformist regimes in Latin America, while extremely jealous of their independence, seem to be less reflexively anti-American than the reformers in the past. The notion carried by the Peace Corps—that the United States can be on the side of democratic change—remains alive and well.

Finally, the Peace Corps experiment was intended to create in the United States a better understanding of life in the underdeveloped countries where volunteers had served. In this respect, the Peace Corps in Latin America has been an unqualified success. More than 37,000 volunteers—about a third of all who have enlisted in the Peace Corps—have served or are now serving in Latin America, and they will carry with them permanently a sense of what life is truly like for the underclass of a continent.

It makes them, in the majority, more skeptical of easy theories, and of the automatic fear of reform and freedom that has so often characterized U.S. policy in Latin America. As those volunteers come increasingly to assume the central places of leadership in our country, they will undoubtedly continue to work a change in our views and our policies. Then the Peace Corps will have proved to be, as Sargent Shriver once exuberantly called it, "the point of the lance," the instrument by which Americans will have come to understand the best part of our natures and to act, as a nation, on our best impulses. For so small an investment, that will have been a major return.

Peace Corps Bulletin #5, Guatemala (1965)

Last week, the government of Guatemala decreed a "State of Siege" condition throughout the entire country as a measure on behalf of public safety and against terrorism and sabotage. Because of this situation, we urge you to observe the following instructions:

1. In case of demonstration, riots, disturbances, or street disorders, stay in your household. These things don't last long. You are safer among the people who know you than anywhere else. If you are not at home when trouble of this nature arises, get away from the scene of disturbance and head for home or a well-known safe spot (church, prominent hotels, etc.).

2. During "State of Siege" periods, do not travel at night, except for emergencies that merit risking your life. Curfew restrictions might be imposed suddenly. If you do not hear about curfews, it then becomes dangerous to you in that roadblocks may legitimately try to stop you. You will have no way of knowing whether to stop or not. Both can be dangerous.

3. During a "State of Siege" or trouble times, listen to a radio frequently in order to keep abreast of news, announcements, or developments.

4. Stay away from areas that present dangers (example: Do not travel in zones of rumored or known guerrilla activity).

5. Touch base with the local authorities frequently. Let them know where you are and how you can be located. In case of emergencies, we usually must resort to calls to the police, military, and *alcaldias* in order to reach you.

6. Carry adequate identification at all times.

7. Do not carry or possess firearms or dynamite or anything that might subject you to suspicion of violation of Guatemalan laws. Furthermore, during troubled times, be wary of doing irregular favors. You may unwittingly be storing weapons, hiding wanted people, carrying unlawful messages, etc.

8. Refrain from voicing opinions relative to delicate local issues of the day. (If pressed to do so, merely state that you are not aware of all the facts on which to base an opinion.)

9. Contact some Peace Corps staff as expeditiously as possible whenever you or your property are threatened or whenever you are in any danger. If you can't reach us, try to contact U.S. consul or duty officer at embassy. Always contact local authorities (military, police, *alcaldia*) for immediate needs for protection.

Letter from Bolivia (1965)

The area in which I work with two other volunteers is an ambitious colonization project, to bring Bolivians down from the Alti Plano to the Alto Beni, where, hopefully, they can build a better life. When you first see the jungle that is presented to the new colonist, armed with only his machete and hatchet, you can't help thinking that his task is impossible. Yet in a few months he will have cleared 2½ acres, enough for 500 cocoa plants and space for his house. It has been a great feeling to see these houses go up—a sign the project may succeed. I became pretty discouraged at first, but now things are shaping up.

My life here is so different from what I had grown up in that perhaps this change will be the greatest one I will ever experience. Living in a small, dirt-floored room and eating low-quality food are things that anyone can adjust to. The big problem comes with the psychological adjustments necessary to let you do a good job.

Every volunteer shares the problem of the lack of privacy. Physically, my room affords no corner in which I can shut myself from the rest of the world. People always want to know what the volunteer is doing, where he is going, etc. As a result, my life is open to inspection at all times. This has been especially hard for me, for I treasure quiet and meditative periods. Even when I'm alone, the noisy sounds of the battery record player penetrates, so there is little chance for complete quiet.

Another problem which I had to overcome was the recollection of the things that we North Americans have in abundance. The thoughts of good food, opportunities to go places and do things, and other material joys must be put out of mind. This becomes easier to do as one becomes more involved in the life around him.

Due to isolation and lack of diversion, fiestas are popular. These people have a fiesta that could last a few hours or all night, and the day of the week doesn't matter, since work can always be put off. Birthday fiestas are perhaps the most grueling, because they commence at midnight. As a Peace Corps volunteer, I feel I must put in an appearance at these events, but I am one of the earliest quitters and lightest drinkers. We average two fiestas a week, but so far I have kept to my work schedule regardless of fiesta activities.

We have no church, and the nearest priest is fifteen miles away, downriver. There is no sign of religion here, either through symbols or religious observances. I had the opportunity to say the first table grace at Thanksgiving time, when the Peace Corps volunteers took over the dinner.

So you are wondering, no doubt, what I am doing here. Let me tell you about my work. The first month was difficult, but the one thing I did do was help put in an irrigation system for a nursery. I'm sorry to say that this project has not been completed and may never be. Basic tools are lacking, but in three or four days of searching, things like pipe wrenches can usually be found. The whole job ground to a halt when the pipe thread cutter broke. We have had pipe fittings on order in La Paz for two months now, and I don't know when the parts will arrive.

I spent the next six weeks after I was foiled on the irrigation project surveying farmers' property lines. This work was needed before the cocoa could be planted, and it should avoid disputes later on. The work allowed me to have a fixed program, but, most important, I got to know the colonists better as I worked on their land. I had a crew of three Bolivians with me every day, and one of the fellows was able to learn enough about simple surveying that he could probably do the next surveying job in the area. He still cannot lay out the work on paper, but once that is done, he can follow plans and construct the appropriate lines in the field. The surveying work allowed me to get exercise, since we estimate that we have walked seventy-five miles each week.

Now I am working with individual farmers and their cocoa, trying to be with each of them when he first plants. Most of the farmers have attended demonstrations on proper planting, but I have not encountered one who remembers the correct way. In the course of the work, many questions are raised about other crops which colonists want to plant. Through these questions and my study, I am learning about tropical agriculture.

Two months ago a naturalist passed through, and I had the good fortune to take a couple of hikes through the jungle with him. In the course of about four hours, I learned more about the jungle than I would have in two years on my own. He showed me a wild vanilla plant and mentioned that it might make a good food crop for the area. With the thought of a second cash crop for the farmers in mind, I initiated a study project on vanilla. The U.S. Department of Agriculture supplied some good material, but, considering the soils and the planning involved, I had to rule the vanilla plant out.

Now that I have become better acquainted with the farmers and their problems, projects pop up right and left. Though my time is so occupied with the cocoa, I have attempted a few side projects. Some problems have quick and easy solutions. For example, farmers in one particular area have to make a four-mile round trip to get water. I suggested that they make simple water catchments, using their roofs as a start. They did, and this alleviated the problem to some extent.

The Vocation

by Francis A. Luzzatto

The early days of the Peace Corps are still remembered for how they inspired a generation of Americans. It was a legendary burst of energy and creativity that carried the Peace Corps forward for its first twenty-five years and will likely carry it forward for many years to come. Few government programs began with such promise; even fewer have managed to retain such a spirit of idealism and success. Those of us who came later were conscious that we were guardians of a precious legacy.

The Peace Corps' mission was and remains "to promote world peace and friendship." How this rather lofty mission is to be pursued has been discussed continuously since the beginning. The development of Third World countries was an afterthought. As far as I know, none of the founders originally saw development as central to the Peace Corps' role. The shift was based largely upon early volunteers' experiences and the need to attract support from Congress and the executive branch. By 1963, the Peace Corps' leaders had begun to present the program, at least in part, as contributing to Third World development.

From the very beginning, the Peace Corps' three goals have been: (1) "to assign volunteers to interested countries to help them meet their needs for trained personnel"; (2) "to promote a better understanding of Americans among the people served"; and (3) "to promote better understanding of people of other countries among the American people."

With these three goals, the founders indicated that technical assistance was not the Peace Corps' *raison d'être.* They insisted that in order to make significant contributions to world peace, the Peace Corps would have to go beyond the more traditional, impersonal modes of "trickle down" development assistance. Likewise, they committed the Peace Corps to reaching beyond the scope of existing international educational and cul-

---

Francis A. Luzzatto is a consultant with NDPL and Associates in Washington, D.C.

tural exchange programs. What motivated them was a recognition of the intrinsic value of having people from diverse cultures living and, above all, working together for extended periods of time.

Thus the Peace Corps was to be an investment in the future, to be paid off by creating a cadre of Americans who would come to understand the beauty and strength of other cultures, while contributing to the development of Third World nations. The founders firmly believed that it was in this country's long-term interest to learn more about the rest of the world, just as it was in the interest of other nations to learn more about us. It was expected that the volunteers would share their insights with America and would ultimately help shape national policy. The founders understood, then, an idea that is only now beginning to be accepted and that is still not fully understood by most, namely, that we—rich nations and poor—truly live in an increasingly interdependent world.

From the outset, the emphasis was on structuring field assignments so that the volunteers would be living and working with their "counterparts" at the village level. Recruitment, selection, training, and field support were all designed to create an entirely new brand of international worker. It is now, perhaps, difficult to appreciate the extent to which new ground was being broken. Until then, no one really knew whether large numbers of predominantly young Americans could function effectively for extended periods of time in physical and cultural circumstances so alien to their own. No one knew whether the volunteers would be accepted by the people with whom they lived, much less be taken seriously by host government officials.

Reports on the success of the early volunteers came quickly. The first volunteers not only functioned effectively, they seemed to thrive. The personal rewards of working directly with people and becoming part of their community were incomparable. Physical difficulties appeared to be inconsequential and even lent mystique to the Peace Corps. In the public arena the Peace Corps was declared a success.

Within the development community, however, the volunteers were regarded as well-meaning amateurs, at best. The experts argued that serious development work could not be performed by "unskilled" volunteers, ignoring that our own country, not to mention every other industrialized country in the world, had been developed by its own ordinary citizens. It has been said that among the tragic legacies of colonialism is the attitude that advanced degrees are essential to all forms of development work. To some, one of the Peace Corps' greatest contributions has been to demonstrate through its volunteers that effective programming, intensive short-term technical training, and, above all, motivation can make ordinary people into effective development workers. This is a view, however, that is not universally held. Most development professionals, particularly in the early 1960s, argued that specialists alone were capable of having a substantive impact in development.

My own father, who by the early 1960s had spent many years of his career directing foreign assistance programs, had grave reservations about the Peace Corps on just those grounds. Having succeeded in Europe with the Marshall Plan, he and his fellow "development experts" turned their attention to the Third World, initially equating development with reconstruction. They did not then fully appreciate that while the process of *reconstruction* can be accelerated by massive amounts of external assistance, *development* is a far slower, more evolutionary undertaking, particularly in predominantly rural societies. Those early criticisms of the Peace Corps' approach to grass-roots development were taken seriously enough so that the stage was set for periodic examination of the Peace Corps' role in development.

Every Peace Corps director has, in fact, attempted to clarify the Peace Corps' contribution to development. There were those who used their tenure to make the Peace Corps into what they felt was a more serious development agency. Inevitably, their successors would try to reestablish a balance between the Peace Corps' three rather elusive goals, reemphasizing the experience of the individual volunteers and their relationships with the people with whom they lived and worked. No matter how important the Peace Corps' role in development was to become, goals two and three continued to be seen as essential to overall success.

Over the years, attempts have been made to reinterpret or otherwise alter the Peace Corps. And, while some of these attempts have left their mark, few substantive initiatives have survived. The Peace Corps remains essentially unchanged. It still sees itself almost exclusively as a "volunteer-sending" organization. Volunteers still serve two-year terms, are still assigned to work on development projects at the community level, and are still supported by a Peace Corps "in-country" staff. The Peace Corps' second and third goals, which stress mutual understanding, remain the Peace Corps' soul.

And yet, while these "bottom-line" tenets represent the Peace Corps' rather unique sense of purpose, they have served to isolate it from change. New ideas and challenges have all too often been treated as threats rather than seen as opportunities to expand the scope of the agency or to make it more effective. I say this as a strong believer in the program's success, but also as someone with strong convictions about what the Peace Corps could and *should* become.

Perhaps inevitably, and with few exceptions, Peace Corps directors have spent the bulk of their time administering the program as it was turned over to them. They spent their first six months learning about the program and the remainder trying to keep the program on track. The imperatives of day-to-day operations have dominated their tenures. I am in no way denigrating the past or present leaders of the Peace Corps. To the contrary, each of them has worked hard to sustain the program, at times against great odds. Yet, any review of how the Peace Corps has evolved must question whether over the years, the Peace Corps has become a little too self-satisfied, and too resistant to change.

In the late 1960s, battles were fought over the effectiveness of community development projects. Peace Corps volunteers were trained to spark development by first identifying and then addressing problems once they had been assigned to a specific village. In reality, and by necessity, programs were so loosely structured that training could not predict what technical skills would be needed. These programs served to strengthen the view that the Peace Corps was populated and run by well-meaning amateurs. Peace Corps loyalists responded that traditional foreign assistance strategies were bypassing the vast majority of the people at the community level and that the Peace Corps approach was on target.

Perhaps the most aggressive effort to redirect the Peace Corps began in 1969. Joseph Blatchford, appointed director by President Nixon, responded to the increasing criticism of unstructured programs by propelling the Peace Corps into what he called his "new directions." At the heart of these "new directions" was a commitment to professionalize the Peace Corps. He called upon the overseas staff to program for more highly skilled volunteers. He revamped the recruitment, selection, and placement systems to accommodate this new agenda. Countries began to see the Peace Corps in a different light. They now looked to it as a means of acquiring additional skilled technicians without having to expend scarce resources.

To the proponents of these "new directions," the Peace Corps was finally responding to what the Third World needed and wanted. But to many, Blatchford's approach upset the delicate balance between the agency's three goals. No longer were an applicant's personal qualities and motivation considered as important in the selection process as professional skills.

And whereas great emphasis had been placed on having volunteers become involved in community activities and in initiating projects on their own, more volunteers were now placed in ministries or research institutions in an effort to increase their impact. By necessity, many of these volunteers were assigned to urban areas, where the sustenance derived from becoming part of a community stopped being an inherent part of the experience. More and more volunteers viewed their assignments as a nine-to-five job, rather than as a twenty-four-hour-a-day commitment.

Trainee and volunteer attrition climbed, and within a short time requests for highly skilled recruits outstripped the agency's ability to deliver. But most of all, by sanctifying "higher skills," the Peace Corps demeaned the integrity of other volunteers. The term "generalist," which had been part of the Peace Corps' lexicon from the very beginning, took on a pejorative connotation. More people began to see the Peace Corps purely in development terms.

By 1974, the "new directions" approach had begun to give way, as the Peace Corps staff shifted back to making constructive use of its natural constituency, the recent liberal arts graduate. Only this time, greater emphasis was given to developing programs with more carefully defined goals and objectives, and to designing more comprehensive technical training. And while there was an attempt to rehabilitate the "generalists," the more self-conscious term "skill-trained volunteer" formally took its place. This was an indication that the Peace Corps could not go back. The theme emerged that, through more sophisticated programming and better training, "ordinary" volunteers can in fact become effective development workers. There is no doubt that the Peace Corps of today is in many ways stronger for having had to resolve some of the issues raised during Blatchford's time.

In 1971, Blatchford was appointed to head ACTION, a new federal volunteer agency that incorporated both the Peace Corps and VISTA, its domestic counterpart. VISTA (Volunteers in Service to America) was started by Shriver in 1965 as part of President Johnson's War on Poverty. In its early days, VISTA was virtually a carbon copy of the Peace Corps, recruiting predominantly middle-class Americans and assigning them to inner cities, Indian reservations, and rural pockets of poverty. By 1968, VISTA had made a radical departure from the Peace Corps by recruiting some of its volunteers from the "target populations" for service in their own communities.

Those of us who had worked with VISTA and who had been advocates of VISTA's move to enlist "locally recruited volunteers" first viewed the merger with the Peace Corps as an opportunity to conduct "joint programming." We even saw the potential for working with some of the emerging domestic volunteer programs in the Third World. From an administrative point of view, it was hoped that the two agencies could operate more efficiently by performing such functions as volunteer recruitment in common. From the start, however, the merger with AC-

TION did not work well. Both VISTA and the Peace Corps immediately felt under siege. The staff in both agencies, rankled by no longer being able to control their own destinies, worked hard to preserve as much independence as they could. Eventually, both the Peace Corps and VISTA went their separate ways.

Despite the failure, a number of initiatives taken during the first six years of the Peace Corps' uneasy relationship with ACTION should be noted as having had an impact. In making a departure from what had been done in the past, at least three innovations should be considered major factors in the Peace Corps' evolution.

One innovation focused on training: heretofore, volunteers had been trained either in the United States or at "regional" training centers in Puerto Rico, the Virgin Islands, and Hawaii. By 1973, most pre-service training had been transferred to "in-country" locations. This move had a positive effect on the entire Peace Corps: training was brought closer to programming, it incorporated more actual experience; language and cross-cultural training were redesigned to take advantage of new opportunities provided at the new sites. The decentralization of training contributed to the further decentralization of many administrative and programming decisions.

A second major innovation was the establishment of the Peace Corps' Information Collection and Exchange (ICE). ICE was begun on the premise that, in addition to providing volunteers to development projects, the Peace Corps could become a *source* of technical information about how development works at the micro level.

The theory behind ICE held that volunteers living and working at the local level learn to function within constraints as tangible as the lack of resources and as difficult to define as cultural attitudes. Volunteers are sent to their assignments with only limited access to the capital and materials associated with development programs. By necessity, they often have no choice but to approach problems in the field by making use of locally available materials. Furthermore, they are in a position to understand and take into account whatever inhibitions to development affect the people they live with. As individuals, they discover some of the most precious lessons in development, namely, what works, what doesn't work, why, and under what circumstances.

In 1973, Ernst Schumacher popularized an approach to development now known as "appropriate technology." Schumacher argued that all too frequently the more sophisticated technologies introduced by Western development agencies were not relevant, at least in the poorer areas of the Third World, where a vast majority of the population lives. Furthermore, the principles he promoted recognized the role culture plays in the acceptance of technology. He stressed the importance of putting people to work, instead of replacing them with a machine for the sake of modernity. He placed high priority on the use of local resources, so that development projects would not inadvertently cause communities to become even more dependent on outside sources of material and capital. But most of all, he underlined that appropriateness can only be judged in local terms. In a very real sense, the Peace Corps had become a unique primary source of field-tested "appropriate technologies."

By 1975, over 60,000 Peace Corps volunteers had served, covering a wide spectrum of community-level development programs. They had accepted, rejected, modified, and even invented countless tools, methods, and technologies. They had not only adapted technologies to a particular set of circumstances; in many cases they had even written or translated technical material into a local language. The possibilities of harnessing these experiences seemed limitless. But despite scores of reports, files, and even numerous technical papers and manuals written by volunteers on their own, there had never been a systematic search through the records in Washington and in field offices for descriptions of practical techniques and strategies that could be used by volunteers, not to mention by other development workers.

ICE set out to identify and collect these by-products, then gathering dust in closets and filing cabinets in Peace Corps offices throughout the world. The "take" was impressive, and in short order ICE had catalogued materials covering nearly the entire range of Peace Corps activities in the field.

ICE became a great success. For the first time, staff and volunteers alike could write to an office in Washington, asking for technical information. Inquiries were answered by sending a manual published by the Peace Corps, a technical publication purchased by the Peace Corps, or a copy of an unpublished technical paper selected from ICE's extensive files. In the years following its inception, ICE has continued to grow. It has published well over one hundred technical manuals and has greatly increased its collection of field-generated information, making it available as a technical information base.

Those of us who started ICE had also theorized that the information produced by the Peace Corps could be of use to development workers outside the agency, thus greatly multiplying the Peace Corps' overall impact. Almost immediately, individuals and organizations concerned with micro-level development projects, such as private voluntary organizations and international donor agencies, began asking for ICE publications. In some cases these requests came from ministry officials and other organizations in the Third World that had little or no association with the Peace Corps.

It is unfortunate that the Peace Corps does not present itself as an agency whose impact could go well beyond the direct work of its volunteers. There are just too many villages and too few effective development workers of any kind to be satisfied with the work several thousand volunteers perform each year. To put it bluntly, in terms of actual development, its five thousand or so volunteers each year are hardly making a dent. However, the systematic dissemination of technical information derived from the work of the volunteers could greatly enhance the Peace Corps' effectiveness, but it would take a major step, which thus far has been resisted. It has been argued that such a move would detract from the public's perception of the Peace Corps and would be rejected out of hand by the Congress as not being within the purview of the Peace Corps. I am not convinced. Presenting the dissemination of field-generated technical information as a natural function *co-equal* with the assignment of volunteers in no way diminishes the volunteers. On the contrary, it lends greater dignity to their work. What I have just described is a familiar concept to the business community, where the marketing of by-products often becomes as important and as profitable as the primary product itself.

A third innovation of this period actually had roots back in the early sixties, when the Peace Corps was instrumental in organizing an international conference on voluntarism, held in Puerto Rico. The purpose of this conference was to determine whether the Peace Corps and the other bilateral volunteer-sending programs should band together to help other nations start their own international and domestic programs. The result was the formation of the Peace Corps Secretariat (later the International Secretariat for Voluntary Service).

Yet within a few years, in part due to tighter budgets, the Peace Corps' interest in promoting domestic voluntarism in the Third World had waned. In retrospect, I would attribute this lack of interest, once again, to the Peace Corps' single-minded concern with its "main-line" function of deploying volunteers in the field.

In the late 1970s, the Peace Corps negotiated its first interagency agreement with the U.S. Agency for International Development (AID). Heretofore, there had been little or no collaboration at the agency level, although in many countries, informal arrangements were made locally. It had taken more than fifteen years for the two agencies to recognize that each had something to offer the other. AID, under pressure to support more programs at the local level, sought to take advantage of the Peace Corps' special ability to sustain small projects in rural areas. Meanwhile, the Peace Corps saw AID as a source of money to support additional volunteer technical training, short-term technical consultants, and programming and training conferences, particularly for its staff.

The marriage of convenience worked. Several additional interagency agreements have been negotiated under directors Richard Celeste and Loret Ruppe. In each case the interagency agreement allowed the Peace Corps to expand its technical support to its field staff and volunteers in specific program areas such as agriculture, energy, forestry, and health. One of the most recent agreements with AID created the Small Projects Assistance fund (SPA). SPA allows Peace Corps country directors to fund small community projects identified by volunteers, while providing AID with the administrative ability to support a wide range of small community projects. For the first time, volunteers had direct access to project funds specifically set aside for their use by the agency. And while reserving money for volunteer use may appear to violate one of the Peace Corps' original principles, in practice, ambassadors in several countries had for some time been setting aside portions of their self-help funds for the volunteers. They, too, had concluded that volunteers were in the best possible position to identify worthwhile projects at the community level. The SPA program has met with the almost unanimous approval of volunteers and staff alike.

The Peace Corps' relationship with AID has come so far that, today, there is a standing AID/Peace Corps Coordinating Committee chaired by the director, Loret Ruppe, and Peter McPherson, the AID head, who is himself a former Peace Corps volunteer.

To many, the Carter election of 1976 seemed to herald the "restoration," after the Nixon/Ford years, when "new directions" were foisted upon the Peace Corps and the agency was administratively subsumed under ACTION. And yet the Carter years would prove to be among the Peace Corps' most trying.

The reasons for the antagonism between the ACTION and the Peace Corps directors were complex. Part of the problem can be attributed to the continued resentment on the part of the new Peace Corps leadership of ACTION's role in determining its policies. After all, didn't restoration imply independence? In retrospect, other disagreements can be attributed to stylistic differences between the leaders. But the most significant disagreements between Sam Brown, the ACTION director, and Carolyn Payton, the newly appointed director of the Peace Corps, stemmed from a rather fundamental disparity in the vision of what the Peace Corps had become and what it could be.

The first such disagreement erupted over the role of the "education" volunteer. Prior to this time, it had always been assumed that assigning volunteers to teaching was one of Peace Corps' strongest programs. From the very beginning teachers were assigned to primary schools, secondary schools, universities, and teacher training institutions. Also from the beginning, a significant number of education volunteers taught English, primarily at the secondary school level. Education volunteers were relatively easy to recruit, train, and support, and by all accounts derived great job satisfaction from their work. Most of all, some host governments had made it clear that their highest priority was to have the Peace Corps teach English.

But shortly after his arrival at ACTION, Sam Brown began to ask some difficult questions. Should the Peace Corps expend its scarce resources on teaching English when so many in the Third World did not have such bare essentials as food, potable water, or adequate medical care? Why were Peace Corps volunteers teaching English to the elite of a country, giving them an even greater advantage? Why, after so many years of teaching English, were volunteers still needed in some countries, and didn't this indicate a lack of effectiveness? At the very least, did it not suggest an unhealthy dependency? Maybe the Peace Corps had gone on too long on its own momentum without rethinking some of its program assumptions. Maybe there were other roles in education that volunteers could perform.

The leadership of ACTION charged ideological impurity, contending that the Peace Corps was out of touch with progressive forces in the Third World. ACTION wanted the Peace Corps to perform as a "true" anti-poverty effort or, in development jargon, as technical assistance to the poorest of the Third World's poor. The Peace Corps, on the other hand, charged the leadership of ACTION with failing to understand the realities of programming in the Third World and of trying to impose its own American anti-poverty rhetoric on host countries. It argued that legitimacy lay in pursuing all three of its goals and that it took seriously its commitment to be responsive to the requests of host governments.

Earlier, a group of experienced programming and training specialists had been hired to analyze the Peace Corps' work, from recruitment to impact, and to recommend improved models. A later group developed additional models, published a comprehensive set of "core curriculum" training manuals, redesigned the programming system, and upgraded the skills of the field staff through a series of workshops. They also responded to a series of questions now raised as to whether Peace Corps projects were designed to meet "basic human needs." By and large they found that much of what the volunteers were doing met this standard. Nevertheless, the questions posed during this process did force the Peace Corps staff to engage in a rather tough self-evaluation. Policies were rewritten, and priority was given in the allocation of resources to projects that appeared to meet the "basic human needs" strategy. In some cases new projects were developed that might not otherwise have been considered.

ACTION's leadership also tried to get the Peace Corps to update its vision of how the program would operate in the future. From ACTION's point of view, while the world had significantly changed since the 1960s, the Peace Corps was relying on a watered-down version of how it had operated in the past. From ACTION's perspective, the Peace Corps gave an unacceptable response: to a large degree, the Peace Corps is defined by its host countries; what the Peace Corps is, and what the Peace Corps will be, is the sum of what our host countries ask of us; we will tell you where the Peace Corps is going when we add up the sixty-odd country management plans at the end of the year. It was not long before relations between the two agencies broke down. When the dust settled, ACTION was forced to give the Peace Corps a greater degree of autonomy, and the Peace Corps had a new director.

The new director was Richard Celeste, whose first goal was to ensure that the Peace Corps had the authority to set its own policies. Having accomplished this, he took a step that set him apart from most of his predecessors. To educate Americans about the development needs of the Third World, Celeste appointed an associate director for development education. Of the Peace Corps' three goals, development education aims at the third. In the past, implementation of the third goal, by and large, had been seen solely as the responsibility of returned volunteers. The only effort to explore an institutional response had been taken under the leadership of Blatchford. Under his direction, the Peace Corps experimented with "transition centers" for returning volunteers, but the program was soon discontinued for failing to meet the test of contributing to the Peace Corps' overseas operations. Celeste's effort was to be more comprehensive, stressing the responsibility of the Peace Corps as an institution to assist its former volunteers in sharing with the American people what they had learned.

In 1981, Celeste's replacement, Loret Ruppe, endorsed his proposal, but more important, she presided over the restoration of the Peace Corps' full statutory independence. Henceforth, the agency would report directly to the President. Universally, Peace Corps supporters are grateful to Ruppe for providing the agency with stable leadership and strong public advocacy. The African Food Systems Initiative recently established under her direction is a case in point. The enthusiastic response to her public appeal by individuals willing to work on agricultural projects in Africa once again proved that the Peace Corps can excite the imagination and idealism of the American people.

During her five years as director, Ruppe has taken a number of other initiatives that should be noted. The first, and possibly the most significant, is the rapprochement with AID. Under her leadership and Peter McPherson's, the two agencies have encouraged efforts to collaborate at all levels. Among a series of other steps they have taken was the decision to develop a joint strategy for how the Peace Corps and AID will support the work of the many private voluntary organizations that have become an integral part of this country's foreign assistance program.

This effort on the Peace Corps' part has a precedent. In the early 1960s, the Peace Corps relied heavily on the expertise of the major organizations that had preceded it in the Third World. A separate division of Peace Corps headquarters coordinated agency relations with private voluntary agencies, universities, and other non-governmental organizations. But rather quickly, two camps formed. There were those who favored assigning volunteers to private agencies because they were relatively less bureaucratic, and those who favored assigning the volunteers directly to host country ministries as a way of instilling confidence and gaining support from the leaders of these countries. The latter position prevailed, and the Peace Corps' formal relationships with the private agencies gradually diminished. Only recently, in fact, has the Peace Corps reestablished formal ties with the private community.

In the past several years, at least three countries have let it be known that they are interested in hosting a group of Peace Corps volunteers, but not if it means accepting a Peace Corps *staff* responsible to the U.S. embassy. A departure from the Peace Corps' standard approach is a recent program that places a group of volunteers in the Sudan without staff. Its support is furnished by AID, and its program is conducted under an agreement between Transcentury, a private development organization, and Georgia Tech. This model eliminates the need for a government-to-government agreement, as well as the need for an "in-country" Peace Corps office. While this approach has been applied to only one country and for a limited number of volunteers, it is one of the very few times the Peace Corps has experimented with an alternative model for fielding volunteers.

Over the past several years, the Peace Corps has left, among other countries, Korea, Malaysia, Colombia, the Ivory Coast, Venezuela, and Brazil. In all these cases, the departures were amicable. In each case, the point was made, either by the country itself or by the Peace Corps, that the country had "graduated," that it did not *need* the Peace Corps anymore. Objectively, this argument may be correct. Such "middle-income" countries often do not require the type of technical assistance the Peace Corps usually provides. But such a narrow interpretation of the word "need" misses two points: no country, including our own, is ever so developed that there is no work left to be done; and the world we live in is so interdependent that we do *need* each other.

If these assertions are correct, technical assistance cannot be the primary justification for the Peace Corps. No matter how difficult it is to accept, and no matter how much we believe our own mythology, we must face the fact that over the years we have come to rely more and more on technical assistance arguments to sell ourselves to our host countries and to justify ourselves to the Congress. We must also take into account that most countries see us principally as a source of technical assistance. But inevitably, fewer and fewer nations will find it acceptable to host a Peace Corps that has come to symbolize their dependence on external assistance. Unless we begin developing an alternative rationale for placing our volunteers in someone else's country, and unless we design new program models that embody that rationale, we may wake up someday to discover that the Peace Corps has been bypassed by history.

The seeds for such a rejuvenation already exist. Those of us who worked in VISTA know firsthand that no country ever graduates from developing itself. We may have thought otherwise in the early 1960s, but by the mid-1970s we knew better. If there will always be a need for development work in our own country, it is likely that this will be true in every other country as well. The issue, then, is whether other nations will accept having Peace Corps volunteers working side by side with their own citizens, only this time *not* in a "giver-receiver" relationship. The standards we should apply for providing our volunteers are not so dissimilar from the past: the volunteers must be productive, but they must also have a positive "volunteer experience."

Depending on the country, this may mean not insisting on having an "in-country" Peace Corps office with American staff members, but assigning the volunteers directly to a host-country institution or domestic development service. With some other countries, particularly those now referred to as "middle-income," we may well have to work toward a reciprocal Peace Corps as the price of admission. Not only would we benefit, but it is a price we should pay willingly. No single step would more convincingly change how the Peace Corps is perceived than to be able to bring host country "volunteers" to work on "development" problems in our own country. Ironically, such a pilot program existed in the late 1960s but was eliminated after two years because a senior congressman stated that "we don't *need* them"—the very argument now being used to exclude the Peace Corps from numerous countries.

The problems the Peace Corps will face are real. And while the solutions are more elusive, I am convinced that the Peace Corps should experiment with alternative models, particularly models involving cooperation with private agencies and those better suited to "middle-income" countries and countries with strong volunteer programs of their own. The models should emphasize "equal" rather than the "giver-receiver" relationships that the Peace Corps has adopted over the years. While there is no question that the present model for how the Peace Corps supports its volunteers is effective, and is likely to be so for many countries for the foreseeable future, it is also evident that it is no longer relevant to a growing number of others. Unless we solve this problem by developing a variety of program models, the Peace Corps is destined to become increasingly marginal.

For the Peace Corps to survive for another twenty-five years and to continue to excite future generations of Americans, it may well have to make some rather fundamental changes. It must, first of all, recognize that we do *not* want to "work ourselves out of a job," as one of the Peace Corps' most popular slogans asserts. This and other similar phrases may make eminent sense at the volunteer level, or even at the project level. They most certainly do not, however, make sense at the country level, where they are a direct contradiction of the second and third goals. Without volunteers, there are no opportunities to learn about one another. The challenge ahead is to make sure that the Peace Corps is as relevant and important to the United States and to the Third World as it has been in years past. Our children and grandchildren who may want to serve deserve nothing less.

Reminiscence: the Philippines and Mali

by Parker W. Borg

The traditional "naming" ceremony was one of the first contacts I had as ambassador to Mali with the new group of Peace Corps trainees. This is the occasion when all the trainees are given an African name by the Malian families with whom they have been living for the "in-country" training.

We had no trouble finding the site: an open area, brightly lit with a string of bulbs connected to a whirring generator and surrounded by a large circle of chairs. The trainees bubbled with excitement as they spoke of how their families had arrived at the names they would receive. Without any announcement, groups of women began dancing to the beat of drums in a circle in front of us. The beat moved from one frenzied tempo to another while women of all ages entered and left the circle, sometimes waving their scarves, but always stomping their feet and stirring up a fog of dust. Occasionally, one or two of the men, usually older ones, would enter and execute a few fancy steps. On invitation, the trainees and some of the guests joined the group. The dancing continued until, finally, a notable went to the microphone to announce solemnly the names of the new members of the village community.

Through the din, dust, and excitement, I thought back twenty years to my own initiation into the Peace Corps. It was the spring of 1961; the Peace Corps had just been announced. When I visited the new headquarters in Washington, I was told the organization was not looking for liberal arts graduates like me, but people with experience, or graduates

---

Parker W. Borg is deputy director of the Department of State's Office for Counter-Terrorism and a former United States ambassador to Mali.

from agricultural and technical schools. This negative reaction plus the opposition of my parents to such an outrageous post-graduate plan made me even more determined to join. I looked over the first programs, directed at Ghana, Tanganyika (now Tanzania), Colombia, and the Philippines. I made out my application to look as if I would be a good prospective English teacher in the Philippines, and I was selected for training.

Our training at Penn State was intense but jumbled. Psychological testing was an important part of the process. Of the 150 of us who arrived, only 128 would be selected, and we were never sure of the criteria. I was not "selected out," a fate which all of us were convinced would blacken the rest of our lives. We finished our six weeks at Penn State about the same day Congress made the Peace Corps official.

"In-country" training in the Philippines consisted of six additional weeks of living in a Boy Scout dormitory on the campus of the University of the Philippines. We studied the national language, Tagalog (though not more than a dozen of us went to Tagalog communities), heard lectures about Philippine culture and institutions, got to know some Filipino students and faculty members, and observed Filipino life from our pleasant mountaintop. Although we studied something called "culture shock," few of us were prepared for the realities of the rural Third World, where we found ourselves a few weeks later.

A hand from a Malian woman beckoning me into the dusty dancing circle brought me back to the present. I thought to myself, how much better prepared volunteers are now, at least in Mali. This cultural introduction was less artificial. From the beginning, the Malian Peace Corps volunteers had learned to live among people like those they would find in their villages. Whenever they returned to the capital, they would look upon their village, rather than some academic dormitory, as their home. If the training program in Mali was the norm, the Peace Corps had come a long way in twenty years.

Like all the volunteers in the Philippines, I was supposed to work as a teacher's aide in the elementary schools in the fields of English, math, and science. Since the Philippines already had a surplus of teachers, we were not permitted to displace Filipino teachers. I was told we might assist teachers in classes, offer special courses, or run seminars for them. Since the Filipino school officials had no idea what a teacher's aide might do, the project was seriously flawed. We were each left to work out whatever role we liked. As long as we did not cause any problems, the Peace Corps staff did not seem to care what we did. The priority of the Peace Corps at that time was to get as many volunteers placed as quickly as possible in this, the biggest of its early efforts. By June 30, 1962, nine months after we went to our villages, there were already 272 volunteers working in the Philippines and another 282 in training. If we did not like the school, we were encouraged to build toilets or piggeries or take on any project we wanted as long as we seemed busy and did not complain.

I chose to stick with the school. During the first months, I wandered between classrooms as an observer, and it was agreed I would substitute for certain teachers on a regular basis to give them time for administrative activities. Soon I had four days a week at a local elementary school, teaching English to first graders, math to third graders, and science to sixth graders. On Fridays, I taught American literature and current events at a high school. As rote memorization was the standard, I attempted to find special techniques to make learning enjoyable: games to learn multiplication tables, science experiments, and dramatic presentations. I also coached the elementary school soccer team, emphasizing drills, passing the ball, and not drinking or smoking. Largely because there were so many overaged sixth graders, we won the provincial championship. I never learned whether the Peace Corps considered me a success, but I kept myself productively occupied.

I did not think too highly of the Peace Corps' efforts to encourage frustrated teachers to become organizers of community development projects. The Philippines already had plenty of trained cadres working throughout the country. If Americans built sanitation projects or promoted piggeries, it not only undermined existing development programs, but, more important, it seemed to reinforce the Filipinio rural mentality that Americans, by their very nature alone, could accomplish things that were beyond their own capacities.

Several years later, my previous Southeast Asian experience made me a natural candidate to fill the State Department's Vietnam quota, and after one year of language training, I found myself doing rural development work with a thirty-man army unit in a small Vietnamese town. My counterpart was a Vietnamese lieutenant who was responsible for all civil operations in this district of about one hundred hamlets. A development skeptic, I was transformed suddenly into a community development officer. Our job was to help restore the government's civilian presence through the construction of roads, bridges, schools, or whatever seemed necessary. We asked village officials to select priority projects for their communities—and if the villagers agreed to provide the labor, AID would supply the funds to buy materials.

The program proved that the initiative of the villagers could be harnessed if the resources were available, but the funds necessary from the United States for the effort were staggering. It was war relief on the cheap through self-help, and we never learned whether the principles of community organization could make a difference in the absence of seemingly unlimited money.

When I arrived in Mali in 1981, I found that community development projects had been a central part of the Peace Corps program for several years. I attempted to travel outside the capital as often as possible, setting for myself a goal of one trip per month to a different part of the country. I liked escaping the unending rounds of official ceremonies and diplomatic receptions I was otherwise forced by protocol to attend. After selecting the place I wanted to visit, I would assemble a list of local development projects, and the names of volunteers in the area.

I never worried about knowing where a volunteer lived. Upon pulling into any community, I could ask in the market area and find somebody willing to guide me to the American's house. At first I was appalled by the living conditions. Most volunteers lived in quarters made of mud with thatched roofs and an adjacent outside toilet area. I remember one volunteer living on the ground in an eight-by-ten foot mud hut—just room enough for his mattress and mosquito net—with a solitary window opening on the pen where the owner kept a flock of bleating goats. Inevitably, I would be asked to compare these conditions with my own experiences twenty years earlier, when the Peace Corps was just beginning. With some embarrassment I talked about our large house with electricity and running water.

The differences between Mali and the Philippines—and all other countries where I have lived—are striking. I avoided comparisons whenever possible, explaining that geographic, climatic, cultural, and historical conditions made every development situation unique. Each country was different, I would explain, but common to all Third World communities was the ongoing process of change which twentieth-century technology and communications had forced upon the traditional societies. I recalled arguments we had as volunteers about the merits of the development process. Rather than act as agents for change, wouldn't it be better to let traditional societies decide for themselves whether they wanted change? One volunteer in our Philippines group resigned over this question. Even at the time I argued that such change was inevitable and that the outsider's role should be to introduce the many beneficial elements of technology appropriate to the problem.

Peace Corps projects in Mali were varied, and demonstrated that the Peace Corps had come a long way from the early days when we were dumped in villages. There were teachers running the English department of Mali's teacher training institute, math volunteers in secondary schools, health workers at dispensaries and maternity clinics. There were also community development projects, some related to water and others devoted to building more fuel-efficient earthen stoves.

Some of the projects were better than others, but the Peace Corps staff was regularly evaluating the effectiveness of each program. For example, the staff abandoned a program to monitor the weight of babies with a view to reducing infant mortality through nutrition awareness, largely because mothers considered it a foolish exercise and instantly questioned the qualifications of the volunteers.

Fortunately for everyone, the Peace Corps had a strong staff, and the management formula was a good one: establish well-defined projects, but permit each volunteer flexibility in the implementation; bring problems promptly to the attention of responsible officials; provide staff support that is technically competent and sympathetic but capable of firm action. On my part, I met frequently with the Peace Corps staff to discuss plans and difficulties, participated in special events, invited volunteers to the house on occasion, and attempted to visit as many of them as possible in their villages.

Americans are known around the world for always being in a hurry. In the United States, our technology, communications, and system of government provide quick fixes for situations and quick solutions to problems. As Americans working overseas, we think about what we might accomplish in terms of the length of our assignment. We are willing to devote two or three years to a particular activity, but we expect to see concrete results.

While working as head of the U.S. consulate in Lubumbashi, Zaire, in 1976–78, I asked a Belgian Jesuit who ran one of the country's teacher training institutes how he could put up with the corruption all around him. He responded by noting that there had not been much change since he arrived fifteen years earlier, but he always tried to set a good example for the students and teachers. "We have to look ahead," he added, "not five or ten years, but to the difference our collective effort will make in a hundred years."

The American effort to provide development assistance to countries around the world is full of half-completed, canceled, and forgotten projects. Not only do we as individuals want to see rapid progress, but our institutions also frequently demand it. When traveling around West Africa in 1979 and hearing AID officials talk about current and future projects, I often asked about the past. If Congress required you to prepare a report about projects completed here through the American assistance effort since it began, what projects would you list? It was surprising, in country after country, how few specific past projects they could name.

Too many projects are canceled because there is a change in available funds, the transfer of the project's promoter, the arrival of a new project officer with a different perspective, or a change in priorities directed from Washington. Sometimes corruption is also a factor, but rather than recognize the inevitability of this type of problem and take steps to minimize it, we are too quick to halt U.S. participation. We prefer to plan new projects, rather than sort out the problems of the past. For too many of us, by the time we move our projects from the approval process into implementation, our tours have ended and our replacement has arrived, only to start the cycle again.

One such failed project, in a desert community of Mali, started with a promising cooperation program between AID and the Peace Corps. AID had supplied the villagers with motorized pumps to permit the cultivation of three times more wheat than could be grown by the traditional system of irrigation. But the project floundered because the villagers could not maintain the pumps, while corrupt officials lined their pockets with project funds. Unfortunately, such scandals attract more publicity for development efforts, including the Peace Corps, than dramatic successes in food production or in the adoption of other changes.

In this case, however, the AID mission agreed to fund a Peace Corps program to repair the pumps. Since there were no mechanics in Mali, volunteers were recruited for three months of temporary duty from Peace Corps programs in neighboring countries. About eighteen volunteers spent the planting season traveling between villages putting the pumps back in order. The experiment, on the second go-around, was more productive, and motorized irrigation based on this project may yet become a part of the landscape in Mali. Only time will tell. If the project had been dropped at the initial setback, which many in Washington urged, the villagers would have been even more resistant the next time outsiders brought in proposals for change.

When the history of the development effort is finally written, there are two ways that the Peace Corps should be remembered. First, there is the direct legacy: the thousands of volunteers and their projects, which have brought education and technology, and perhaps some self-sustaining activities, to hundreds of Third World communities. The second Peace Corps legacy is even less tangible. Each year since 1963, hundreds of volunteers who have finished their Peace Corps tours have found ways to continue participating in the process of economic development. Some stay on to work on specific projects, others find similar jobs in neighboring countries, join government organizations, or go to graduate school to develop special technical skills that will permit them to pursue careers in the Third World. This is true throughout Africa, Asia, and Latin America, where the Peace Corps doggedly has made important contributions to the long-term development effort during the past twenty-five years.

Reminiscence: Thailand

by Judith Guskin

When my husband, Alan, and I arrived in Bangkok in January 1962 with the first group of Peace Corps volunteers, we were met at the airport by Thai officials, who seemed pleased to have us respond in our hesitant but accurate Thai to their speeches of welcome. The picture in the Bangkok *World* the next day showed a newly arrived volunteer properly making a *waj*, the traditional Thai greeting with the palms of the hands placed together, while one of the Thais held out his hand for a handshake. We were all a bit embarrassed, as we would frequently be over the next two and a half years. But when Alan and I said good-bye in 1964, we were genuinely sad at leaving so many close friends.

From time to time we have looked at the pictures of our farewell at the airport. I look young in my bright blue Thai silk suit (which I later gave to Sharon, our daughter). Al was gracefully returning a respectful *waj* when the camera snapped him. We kept in touch with a few of them, but in the ensuing years, we wondered often what had happened to all our former students, colleagues, and friends.

Like most volunteers, we kept in our lives something of the country in which we had served. We cooked Thai food and displayed our friend Chumpon's wedding picture and the silver bowl our faculty colleagues gave us. We shared stories about our experiences with friends and other Peace Corps volunteers. A few of our Thai students and colleagues visited us in the United States, bringing us much joy.

Finally, sixteen years later, we returned, and as we approached for the landing, we searched for the once familiar emerald green rice fields, thumbed one last time through the torn and stained copy of the Thai language text we had saved, and wondered if anyone would remember

---

Judith Guskin is an independent television producer in Yellow Springs, Ohio, and is on the staff of Antioch University.

us. In a way, we wanted to see things unchanged, but we also wanted to see positive change. Like many former Peace Corps volunteers, we had considerable anxiety about this return visit.

Once we were out of the plane, the airport seemed big and unfamiliar. We gathered our suitcases and made our way to customs. Suddenly, we saw a sign with our name. Someone had come to meet us. Our Thai friend Sippanon Ketudat, who had married Emily, a Peace Corps volunteer in our group, had sent a car to get us. He was then minister of education, and as we were whisked through customs, we smiled to ourselves at the strange feeling of being (as Thais would say) *phu jaj,* or "big shots," in Thailand, rather than volunteers.

Then, through the window, outside the customs area, we saw a familiar smiling face. Dirake! He had received a message from us. A student who had lived with us for two and a half years, Dirake had helped see me through the ordeal of Al's serious illness and Kennedy's assassination. We had shared meals and dreams together. Dirake had taken vacation days to be with us during the visit and wanted to take us to the hotel. After a moment of embarrassed negotiation with the ministry official, we were off with Dirake to a fancy new hotel, a place we would not have felt comfortable entering as volunteers sixteen years before.

As volunteers, we had been university teachers, teachers of teachers. We were not community development volunteers. We did not dig wells, breed chickens, or create fish ponds. We did not live in a thatched-roof hut in a small, rural village. We lived in Bangkok, a major city. We taught at Chulalongkorn, then as now Thailand's most prestigious university and one of the best in Southeast Asia. In the early days, we struggled with our assignment. Were we really Peace Corps volunteers, as many people had come to imagine the volunteer to be? In a moment of humor, we thought that to be effective volunteers at the university, we should dig a ditch through the center of the campus. This would be a real Peace Corps assignment!

One of my sharpest memories is of a field visit by Sargent Shriver, for whom all the Peace Corps volunteers we knew had love-hate feelings. We liked him because in spirit he was one of us. Yet we were determined to criticize what we regarded as his tendency to oversell us. On his first visit, the Thailand volunteers met him at the American embassy. Many had traveled considerable distances to see him, no doubt complaining about him all the way. We met in the large living room in the ambassador's residence. The volunteers sat on the floor and on couches; some stood. For hours we grilled him as to why he didn't stop telling all those glamorous stories about us. He pretended to be shocked, but he was unrelenting in his enthusiasm for our work, and he berated us for being too self-effacing. He said we had trouble looking beyond our work to the large picture. Shriver understood the Peace Corps as a social movement, and, in retrospect, after twenty-five years, I think maybe he was right.

While we were in Thailand, we struggled with the image of the volunteer created by the Peace Corps staff and supported by an adoring press. We thought the reality of our role as teachers was quite different. Like other volunteers, we were involved in a people-to-people program. Our success, like theirs, could not be judged by major economic and social changes, but by small increments, through the individuals we taught and befriended. Al and I resolved our personal concern only when we saw our students develop and grow. Finally, we took heart in thinking that some day they would be teaching the courses we taught, doing the research we did, and preparing their own students to teach teachers.

We even recognized our potential to have a long-term impact, but we did not like to indulge ourselves with it. While some of our students were from wealthy families, others were children of working people. Some were poor. But all had been admitted to Thailand's best university, and all were intelligent. We reasoned that we might be exercising an influence on a generation that one day would be running the country. An early evaluation report of the Peace Corps in Thailand seemed to emphasize this point when it recommended expansion of university teaching assignments. But on a day-to-day basis, we did not have such grand ideas. Our real work was with relatively few people.

It was to them—a circle of former students and friends—that we returned. Like us, they had grown to maturity. We knew from correspondence that many had become successful in their professions and had children. How did they remember us? Had we made a difference? Was it important to them that there had been Peace Corps volunteers teaching at the university?

The first evening, we had dinner with a group of our most intimate old friends. The restaurant, which we remembered as a modest place in the shabby neighborhood where we once lived, was now large and elegant. Sippanon, the minister of education, greeted us warmly at the door, and when Al and I sat down, we all began exchanging news. Somsak had married Nisa and they had a child, and Nitya had married Emily's colleague at the Institute of Asian Technology and had two children. The former Peace Corps volunteers who had remained in Bangkok were doing very well. The biggest surprise was that half the people invited had recently been appointed to high government positions and had just come from their first cabinet meetings. Two were ministers, one was a deputy minister, another an assistant to a minister, but they were still the same warm, bright, funny, wonderful men and women we remembered. As the conversation switched from English to Thai and back again, we found ourselves rapidly picking up words we had not heard for so long. We felt at home with our friends.

The next day we returned to the university to visit the Faculty of Education, where Al and I had taught. We loved seeing familiar faces and receiving the warm greetings that accompanied them. The tree under which my students and I had read *The New York Times*—I remember our talking together about the civil rights movement in Alabama and Mississippi—had grown larger. Al's glass-topped desk was being used by a former student, who was teaching some of the same psychology courses he had taught, and the two of them discussed Al's ongoing influence in legitimizing research at the Faculty. I was thrilled to see Sumitra, who had been one of my brightest and most intense students and who, having gone on to obtain a Ph.D., now headed the graduate program. That evening, we had dinner with a former student of Al's, now a well-known author, and as we parted, she gave him a very low and respectful *waj*. When Al returned the gesture, she placed her head on his outstretched hands. Tears welled up in his eyes. To have placed her head on Al's hands was the highest form of respect a Thai can show.

I should note that we did not like everything we saw in Bangkok, like the huge building downtown with a sign in English and Thai that said "Central Plaza." It was a large shopping mall, not different from those at home, where Thai families shop in clean, air-conditioned comfort. I went to the food section and tried to remember the names of the strange and wonderful fruits with prickly skins that I had not seen in so many years. In the mall, Thais have a wide selection not just of food and clothing, and books in all languages, but snacks at Mr. Donut and Kentucky Fried Chicken. I couldn't help but compare it with the dark, damp, fly-infected markets I remembered. This was economic development, central to the Peace Corps' mission, and Thais were now able to afford the items that were for sale. But I was nostalgic for an earlier day and regretted that Thai boys and girls now meet each other at fast-food stands rather than at temple fairs.

Our visits with our friends were intimate and intense, and full of the laughter and teasing that we remembered from our Peace Corps days. We talked about the pains of development, and of the transformation that had taken place in Bangkok as it grew from two to five million people. We understood the tension, and the personal struggle, as they pursued their careers and raised their children while trying to change Thailand and at the same time preserve its essential culture and traditions.

In some ways, our conversation was more candid than it had been in our Peace Corps days, when Thailand was under a military dictatorship. Students and faculty avoided talking about politics then, out of fear. There was very little sense of the importance of freedom of speech. Al and I took some satisfaction in learning how the people at the university had played a major role in the revolution that led in 1973 to Thailand's adoption of democracy, with free speech and political parties. Unfortunately, there was a painful regression shortly afterward, which our friends called the "dark ages," when people were shot and books were burned. But then another change took place. A new and democratic prime minister was appointed, and it was he who asked our friends to serve in the government.

Our return to Thailand and our visits with old students and friends filled both of us with a sense of pride. It is possible to count the number of wells dug or acres sown by Peace Corps volunteers, but how do you measure the results of teaching? It's hard to measure the impact of a teacher anywhere, and Peace Corps teachers are no exception. What matters for teachers is not only that students learn, but that they learn to love learning, to have faith in their own abilities, to want to give themselves fully to whatever they do. A teacher feels a sense of accomplishment through the achievement of his or her students. I think Al and I can say, like most Peace Corps volunteers, that we affected the lives of a few individuals. For them, we thought, we had somehow made a difference. Our Thai students, colleagues, and friends are different as a result of our being in Thailand.

But then, so are we.

In the Developing World

by Abdou Diouf

On the occasion of the celebration of the twenty-fifth anniversary of the creation of the American Peace Corps, I want to pay tribute to an organization which, in my judgment, is among the most exciting experiments of the latter part of the twentieth century.

In 1963, three years after the resounding appeal of President John Kennedy and the attainment of our own national independence, Senegal received its first contingent of Peace Corps volunteers. They were fifteen teachers, and they came to teach English in secondary schools throughout our country. Then others arrived to train our athletes for the first International Friendship Games, and our teams comported themselves brilliantly. Since then, nearly 1,500 volunteers have served in our country, working chiefly in the fields of rural development, public health, and education.

Today, twenty-five years after the Peace Corps' founding, there are more than one hundred volunteers in service in Senegal, contributing to a wide diversity of programs, such as rural development, fish farming, appropriate technology, health education, teacher training, and assistance to young farmers. These are the sectors that enlarge the capacity of our people to take the initiative for self-help. They are the foundation stones of our economic, social, and cultural development. They are the stages on which Peace Corps volunteers have played and are still playing a key role in building our society.

The results produced by the Peace Corps between 1979 and 1981 prove—as if proof were needed—just how diverse and how important its work has been. They are evident in "grass-roots" projects responding to the needs and hopes of our population, of a value totaling nearly $90 million. Specific projects have included the boring and repairing of wells;

Abdou Diouf is president of Senegal and of the Organization of African Unity.

the construction of classrooms, day-care centers, and health clinics; the erection of individual and family latrines; the raising of livestock; the organization of a motor repair center; and the assembly of flour mills.

Even this list, however, reveals only a fraction of the human impact, felt by Americans and Senegalese alike, as they worked together as real partners in the Peace Corps mission.

Each Peace Corps volunteer lives and works in a Senegalese village, with an adopted family, and before long considers himself, and is considered, a true member of that family, a son among other sons of the village, doing his share of the work of the community. Day by day, he conveys to the village what Americans already know so well: that a man can achieve almost anything by calculating his needs wisely and managing realistically the means at his disposal.

To reach the goals established in the Peace Corps Act of September 22, 1961, the volunteer's first task is to assimilate the culture of Senegal. He learns and talks one of our local languages. The ways and customs of the community in which he lives become his own, and each day he works shoulder to shoulder with his hosts. The personal determination, discipline in organization, and modern methodology that he demonstrates are the richest elements of his culture, which the culture of the village in time absorbs.

Another benefit emerging from the Peace Corps presence comes from the experience acquired by the agencies of the Senegalese government that supervise the work of the volunteers. This experience emerges from the intimate collaboration between these agencies and the Peace Corps. Allow me to attest here that this collaboration has become progressively closer over the years, particularly the relationship between the Peace Corps staff in Senegal and the Ministry of Social Development, which is directly responsible for utilizing the services of 60 percent of the volunteers stationed in the country.

This collaboration is most dramatic in two types of programs, separate but largely overlapping.

They are, first, the Peace Corps programs directed at the recruitment and preparation of volunteers for specific tasks proposed by Senegal; the maintenance of these volunteers during their stay in our country; the collection of useful information to improve their training, including the evaluation of the Peace Corps program and of the volunteer's effectiveness; and the assistance to the volunteers, within the framework of the agreed rules, in the exercise of their tasks.

And second, our own programs directed at organization and selection of programs, and the priorities attached to them; the definition of the projects and conditions of work; the support of the volunteer at all times in the accomplishment of his tasks, including the improvement of his selection, welcome, and integration in Senegalese society. In the accomplishment of these tasks, I point with pride to the important training center situated in the city of Thiès. This center, built at a cost of several million francs, has been donated for Peace Corps use by the Ministry of Social Development and is operated efficiently by the Peace Corps staff.

Thus the integration into village life, as well as into useful work, provides the volunteer with an opportunity to be a bridge between two cultures, engaged in a dialogue in the interest of peace.

For Senegal's part, in the interest of furthering even more the cooperation between our two peoples, the government, working directly with the leadership of the Peace Corps, has committed itself to specific responsibilities in long- and short-term planning. They include the selection of sites for the deployment of volunteers, based on geographic, socioeconomic, and work criteria, and the readying of living and working conditions through programs of training to promote understanding at the level of the Senegalese village and family. At the same time, the government provides Peace Corps volunteers during the in-country preparation period with a village to serve as a training site, as well as a place in which to study the life they will be living for the ensuing two years. Thus, before being taken to "their own" village, the volunteers will be exposed to the real rural life of our country.

After this preparation, the last but essential preparatory phase is to provide each volunteer with a base of operations. At that moment, national, local, and village authorities combine to prepare an annual work plan to permit efficient and cooperative administration of the Peace Corps program. To achieve this objective, management committees are created to supervise and evaluate designated projects in agriculture, the development of water resources, and health and nutrition programs to improve the condition of women, and others.

On the national level, a committee under the direction of the Ministry of Planning and Cooperation provides the guidelines for the activities of the Peace Corps in Senegal. Each year, all of the government agencies that use volunteer services meet with the Peace Corps staff to determine logistical needs and provide for their being met. The committee has been in existence, doing this work, for more than ten years.

We are delighted that the volunteer, having selflessly and devotedly served the needy population of a developing country like our own, does not forget us. The volunteer will bring a vital mission home with him, a readiness to explain to his own compatriots the economic, social, and cultural realities of a nation that he will know from the inside out. From the time that he leaves us, his role will be to clarify the vision; to combat the prejudice and confusion he encounters; to permit two peoples so distant from each other in their character to come closer together, to respect each other, to grow fond and confident of each other. Can we ask for more in the hope that peace will reign?

The Peace Corps represents a special moment, coming none too soon, which permits committed young Americans to work for the cause of world peace and human understanding. What I am saying would be no more than a pious wish if, in spite of all kinds of obstacles, the Peace Corps did not confirm it with hard evidence.

In making volunteers welcome in their land, many African countries send the message that they share the same peaceful ideal as the United States. We are today nearly twenty-six countries, all members of the Organization of African Unity, having established relations of cooperation among ourselves. Nearly 120,000 volunteers have followed the first Peace Corps pioneers in performing service in eighty-eight countries of the world, each volunteer mobilized for the same noble cause. I salute these young men and women, and their willingness to make personal sacrifices for peace.

We commemorate this year the twenty-fifth anniversary of the Peace Corps, at the same time we celebrate the Year of Peace, which the United Nations has declared 1986 to be. We pray that God will in 1986 bring to the combatants in this army of peace the satisfaction and energy needed to continue their work, and to win new and dramatic victories.

Excerpts from Interviews with Foreign Leaders (1981)

From the very beginning, I had direct contact with the volunteers who arrived in Costa Rica, and during the past twenty years I've seen really extraordinary things. To donate a piece of machinery or to provide financial resources is to give something away, but the period which a young person of the Peace Corps gives to our country is a synonym of giving of himself. It is the closest possible joining together in human relationships. I could tell you I've seen a volunteer putting together a fishing net. I've seen a volunteer driving a jeep he helped a farmer repair. But what he really brought was understanding, and that is fundamental. We're establishing the basis of a relationship that is different from that which we've had before. I'm sure that in a country like the Dominican Republic, the Peace Corps volunteer helps present another face of the American people from the Marine who also arrived there. Almost all of the members of the Peace Corps that I have known are Anglo-Saxons, but they're learning to live with Latins. We're cultivating mutual understanding.

—PRESIDENT RODRIGO CARAZO ODIO OF COSTA RICA

When we obtained our independence, there was an exodus of Europeans, technicians, and teachers. Among those who came to help us were the Peace Corps volunteers. This was important to West Cameroon, because it is an English-speaking area, so we had volunteers in our schools. I was prime minister of West Cameroon then, and was always in touch with Peace Corps leaders and with the volunteers when I made my tours. Right in my village there is the fish farm which is being run by the Peace Corps volunteer. Not only that, I have a personal fish pond which is a demonstration project. Apart from these activities, they took part in cooperative societies, getting people to work together. Sometimes we would see a single young lady in a village, alone, in a small house, spending her time with people. Or a young man on a motorbike going through very rugged roads. I think they have done a great deal to contribute to our development, particularly among the peasant families.

—SOLOMON MUNA, PRESIDENT OF THE NATIONAL ASSEMBLY OF CAMEROON

As a student here in the 1960s, when President Kennedy announced the Peace Corps program, I was aware of the charisma and appeal it had. As a young man at that time, I shared that dream and vision. Soon thereafter, I went back to Nepal and was instrumental in signing the Peace Corps agreement. My first role in the government was as a central planner. I was chief coordinator for all foreign technical cooperation. I visited Peace Corps people in the field, including in the village where I was born.

The overall effect of the Peace Corps begins with a dialogue at the people's level, independent of both our governments. Both governments facilitated the Peace Corps' work, but once the volunteers were there, they were with the Nepalese people. One of the first groups that went to Nepal was a group of English teachers. We were short of manpower. There were not enough Nepalese who knew English or who could teach English, so the Peace Corps volunteers filled an important gap. But on another level, in the community, Peace Corps volunteers were winning friends, really winning friends. They came from afar to live within the community as one of our people, not beyond the means of the local community, sharing the level of poverty of the Nepalese village people.

What the Peace Corps volunteer did was extraordinary. For the average Nepalese, Americans were cut down to human size. Such a rich country, with GIs throwing dollars all over, a country which can afford almost everything, competing with the Russians to go to the moon—you know all the euphoric and highfalutin things. The impact the Peace Corps volunteers left was not only on children who learned English, but on others at the local level who witnessed their lives and behavior.

One volunteer who I went to visit, for example, was living in a hut with two Nepalese school teachers. Inside the hut he had changed the living arrangement, the living environment. He had used essentially the same things that Nepalese use but had created more hygienic living conditions. The teachers picked up these habits and, in turn, taught them to the rest of the village. If we were to take the same problem to the World Health Organization or another interested agency, the first thing they would do is send a $40,000 consultant to look at village sanitation.

By the time they write the reports, thousands of dollars flow into documents, and then bureaucrats at both ends go and organize a health team. They take months to prepare a report. But the Peace Corps is different. Things like these may be very small, but how profound an impact they make. They cannot be measured in economic terms.

—BHEKH BAHADUR THAPA, AMBASSADOR TO THE UNITED STATES AND FORMER FINANCE MINISTER, NEPAL

In a Changing World

by John W. Sewell

Development progress throughout much of the Third World is threatened in the 1980s and 1990s by a combination of natural disasters, slow growth, rising protectionist pressures in the industrialized countries, and poor policy choices by donor and recipient countries alike. The critical issue for those concerned with development is how social and economic progress can be resumed in the remainder of this century.

The Peace Corps has a special role to play in meeting this challenge. For the past twenty-five years, Peace Corps volunteers have been a symbol to Third World peoples that America does care—and cares deeply—about development. The role that Peace Corps volunteers have played in American public diplomacy may be their single greatest and most enduring contribution to American policy toward the Third World. The organization has much more than a symbolic function, however. It is a well-managed, innovative, and effective organization that can have a significant positive impact on the lives of those it touches.

In the period ahead, the Peace Corps' effectiveness will be strongly challenged by adverse trends in the international economy. To an extent, this is nothing new. The organization has always had to work within boundaries set by host countries and the U.S. government, and by cultural, economic, and technical limitations. But as the problems of the 1980s persist, the context within which Peace Corps volunteers operate will become increasingly difficult and complex. For the organization, and for the development community as a whole, the central challenge will be how to use its always limited resources most effectively throughout the remainder of the century to pursue both economic growth and poverty alleviation.

John W. Sewell is president of the Overseas Development Council in Washington, D.C.

The relationship between the United States and developing countries, and the role these countries play in the international system, has changed radically since the idea of a Peace Corps was first proposed in 1960. In that year, there were 67 independent developing countries. Foreign aid comprised two-thirds of total financial flows from the North to the South. Today, the 141 independent developing countries of the world are of far greater importance to the U.S. economy. Developing countries purchase over one-third of all U.S. exports and comprise half of the top U.S. trading partners. Developing-country debt to U.S. commercial banks totaled over $125 billion in 1985. U.S. direct foreign investment in the Third World was $54 billion in 1984, 23 percent of total U.S. foreign investment worldwide.

The growing importance of Third World economies to our economic health is clearly illustrated by the impact of debt and recession in developing countries on the United States. Between 1980 and 1984, the United States lost 560,000 jobs as a result of the decline in exports to the Third World. In addition, 800,000 new jobs would have been created if the developing countries' growth rate of the 1970s had been maintained after 1980. The U.S. trade deficit with the Third World reached $53 billion in 1984, roughly 43 percent of the total U.S. trade deficit.

These changes in the economic relationship between the United States and the Third World mean that the success of the Peace Corps' efforts has become even more crucial. Development is not a purely altruistic endeavor; growth and progress in the Third World have considerable implications for America's own economic well-being.

Over the past twenty-five years, the number of volunteers has fluctuated from a high of 15,500 to a low of 5,200 in 1982. Happily, it is now being reinvigorated. Volunteers have increased steadily over the past four years, and the agency hopes to raise the number back to 10,000. But its small budget makes this difficult. Last winter, when the tragic impact of the drought and famine in Africa penetrated American awareness, Loret Ruppe made a public appeal for volunteers to fill six hundred posts in Africa. Ten thousand Americans responded to her call. Routinely, the organization can accept only one in four qualified applicants for volunteer positions. At a time when there seems to be much "aid fatigue" among policymakers, it is heartening to know that so many Americans are still willing to contribute their skills and their time to the development effort.

The Peace Corps' popularity is not restricted to potential volunteers. At their own invitation, sixty countries now host volunteers, and they request at least 50 percent more volunteers than can be provided. In addition, several countries are on a "waiting list" to receive volunteers. The success of the Peace Corps is also illustrated by the fact that several other countries, such as France, Germany, and Britain, have initiated similar programs.

Despite the Peace Corps' special strengths and the talents at its disposal, the fact remains that it is a very small actor on a very large and complex stage. The organization has proved time and again that a single talented volunteer and a little bit of money can successfully mobilize indigenous resources for significant local impact. But, over the long term, the success or failure of many if not most Peace Corps projects is determined by forces beyond the control of the agency, the volunteers, and the project participants. These forces include:

The slow growth rate of developing countries. The world is slowly emerging from one of the most serious global recessions of this century, and most Third World economies remain sluggish. The International Monetary Fund estimates that GNP growth in Latin America in 1985 was only around 2.5 percent. The record of the last eighteen months indicates that resumed growth in developed countries—even with sharp reductions in the price of oil—will not automatically trickle down. The economic prospects for low-income countries are poor.

The foreign debt crisis. Total developing country debt was $686 billion in 1984. In an effort to meet debt obligations, developing countries have adopted radical policy responses, cutting government spending and slashing import levels to save scarce foreign exchange for debt service. While adjustment policies have been intended to eliminate waste or correct structural economic problems, the impact on development progress has been severe. Import limits have affected not only consumption but production, as access to imported spare parts, fuel, and machinery has become limited. Development projects have been halted due to a lack of local counterpart funding. Per capita income levels have clearly declined in many countries. While empirical evidence is lacking, it seems clear that poorer, disadvantaged groups have borne a large share of the adjustment burden.

Poor trade performance. Growth in the volume of world trade slowed from about 8.5 percent in 1984 to around 3.5 percent in 1985, as demand weakened and protectionist measures increased. The International Monetary Fund estimates that the exports of developing countries—oil exporters aside—grew by only 4 percent in volume in 1985, a third of the 1984 rise. Prices for commodity products, which comprise approximately 70 percent of total developing country exports, have been generally falling for the past three decades. While international interest rates fell in 1985, for most developing countries the loss in export earnings has been greater than the benefits of lower interest rates.

Uneven pattern of development. The past two and a half decades have been a period of tremendous growth and progress for most of the developing world. Perhaps the recent global recession and the tragedy of African drought and famine have contributed to a now-popular perception in the United States that development has failed. Placed in the perspective of development history, however, this conclusion is not persuasive. From 1960 to 1982, the low- and middle-income countries grew at an average annual real rate of 4.8 percent, a growth rate well in excess of any sizable group of countries over any equally long period prior to World War II. Their share of gross world product increased from 15 percent in 1960 to 20 percent in 1979. Even in the poorest countries, indicators of quality of life—health, life expectancy, literacy, infant mortality—have improved.

While the development experiment has been a success in general, the pattern of development has been uneven. There is a growing differentiation within the Third World. The newly industrialized countries are now not only major markets for American products, but are also new competitors, providing the United States with relatively sophisticated goods. Brazilian commuter airplanes are shuttling passengers between American cities, and Korean passenger cars have recently entered the U.S. market. The middle-income countries have also done well, taking advantage of a relatively open trading system and expanding capital markets. The low-income countries, however, particularly those in sub-Saharan Africa, have lagged far behind in development progress.

Africa's development crisis. Nowhere are the failures of the development experience more clear than in sub-Saharan Africa. With limited access to commercial capital, these countries continue to rely heavily on foreign aid for investment. Average per capita incomes in the region are actually lower than they were fifteen years ago and will continue to decline for the next decade. Increases in African food production continue to be outpaced by population growth rates. Because many African countries remain largely exporters of commodities, low commodity prices have severely cut into export earnings. While the region's debt of $100 billion receives little attention from the international community, since it represents only about 10 percent of the total developing country debt, it places a staggering burden on African countries.

Poor policy choices. Many developing country governments have pursued unwise policies that have stalled or reversed development progress. These policies differ in each country, but among them are inadequate investment in agriculture, poor incentives for small-scale farmers, concentration of resources in large, inefficient public projects, overvalued exchange rates that prevent exports from competing on the world market, and inflationary fiscal and monetary policies.

Aid donors have also pursued ill-conceived policies. Changes in donors' preferred strategies—from large-scale infrastructure projects, to an emphasis on providing basic human needs, to the current private-sector focus—have provided little continuity to the development effort. In a similiar vein, fluctuating aid levels and uncoordinated efforts have occasionally distorted priorities as recipients are encouraged to take advantage of whatever funding is currently available.

Inadequate resources for development. In the immediate future, scarce resources will be a significant constraint to development efforts. Alarmed at the deteriorating quality of their assets in the Third World, commercial banks have cut back on lending. U.S. direct foreign investment in most developing countries is unlikely to expand significantly, as long as these countries continue to be plagued with slow growth, debt, and general economic uncertainty. Lower demand and rising protectionist sentiment in the United States and other industrial countries threaten the efforts of developing countries to boost export earnings needed for debt repayments and for investments for growth.

Since development resources are not likely to expand commensurate with need, new strategies and approaches are required to improve development progress. How can the Peace Corps respond to the harsh international economic conditions of the 1980s and 1990s?

Concentration of resources. Resources must be concentrated in those regions and countries most in need of assistance, and most likely to profit from development cooperation.

Africa must be given high priority. The Peace Corps currently has programs in twenty-five African states. Of the 2,700 volunteers in the region, 1,200 are involved in agricultural efforts. The Peace Corps has also launched the Africa Food Systems Initiative, a ten-year campaign to help up to twelve African countries reverse their decline in food production. Under the initiative, volunteer teams, in collaboration with other agencies, will work with small-scale farmers on activities such as irrigation, local fertilizer production, and preservation of food crops. These efforts deserve further support so they can be continued and expanded.

The Peace Corps could also play a significant role in assisting African states to meet their short-term need for skilled personnel as training for Africans expands. Peace Corps volunteers with specialized skills could be recruited selectively from American management schools and from the pool of retired Americans to help fill the gap in areas such as economic planning and forecasting, program evaluation, and computer programming, while local personnel are trained to assume these responsibilities.

Increased coordination for maximum impact. There are dozens of official aid agencies and hundreds of private agencies operating in developing countries today. In order to maximize the impact of resources, better coordination among agencies and between agencies and host countries is essential. The Peace Corps has already made significant progress in this direction. Under the Small Projects Assistance program established in 1983, the Peace Corps works with the Agency for International Development in community-level projects. And volunteers often work with private voluntary organizations, such as CARE, Catholic Relief Services, Africare, and others. In 1985, the Peace Corps had over 250 ongoing projects with private voluntary organizations worldwide. These efforts must be sustained and expanded.

Growth. Short-term budgetary constraints are severe, and the likely possibility is for cutbacks in all programs, including the Peace Corps. But over the longer term, expansion of the Peace Corps should be a prime goal for those concerned with U.S. development policy. It is hard to claim that six thousand volunteers are adequate for the challenging task ahead. The current level of volunteers is less than half that of the mid-1960s, while the need for volunteers is greater. Further, the cost per volunteer—roughly $40,000 for the two years—is not high when measured against the impact a single volunteer can have. In Botswana, for example, one volunteer working with host-country nationals constructed fifty dams, which benefited sixty-five villages, bringing potable water to thousands of people. This is not an isolated example. Peace Corps projects have a high payoff at minimal cost. In the long term, the number of volunteers should be constrained only by the number of qualified applicants, the requests received for volunteers, and by issues of volunteer safety.

In a recent statement before Congress, the Peace Corps director said, "Only at the village level, where incentive and technology must fuse with social, cultural, and economic realities, will the final battle against hunger be won." But in order for progress against hunger, poverty, and disease to be achieved and sustained, even on the village level, both national and international economic and political conditions must be conducive to growth. The Peace Corps can change one life at a time—no small task. But the challenge of creating open, progressive, and equitable national and international systems is a global responsibility.

THE PLACE

In a Changing America

by Loret Miller Ruppe

Like most twenty-five-year-olds, the Peace Corps strides toward the next quarter-century with the boundless energy for which it is famous and with a heart full of hopes for an ever more influential future, armed with the confidence that it makes an everlasting contribution to both the United States and the world. Peace will come through development, through partnerships, and the Peace Corps has set free the American spirit of voluntarism in pursuit of it.

Reaching this point has required fortitude and character. While we had an easy birth, our childhood was difficult, and I think it's fair to say our adolescence was troubled. Observers look at our history, at the current conservative bent in the country's political profile, at a strife-torn world in nuclear jeopardy, and wonder how we've been able to survive. I tell them it's because we have a strong, absolutely bipartisan family that has sustained us throughout, has been an unending source of ideas and counsel, and is united in its motivation to pursue world peace and friendship.

Like most families, we have had disagreements from time to time, but we have managed to remain focused on our mission and its universal importance. The family comprises all who have played a role in the evolving Peace Corps story, from the first director, Sargent Shriver; through the nine directors who have followed, the thousands of returned volunteers, and the members of Congress who have supported us; to leaders and villagers in countries where we've served. All of them are still an integral part of the Peace Corps.

The Peace Corps' maturation has relied on flexible, rather than rigid, nurturing. Each person who has assumed the agency's helm has brought to it a particular vision and has applied whatever special skills he or she

---

Loret Miller Ruppe is currently director of the Peace Corps.

could muster to the challenge of the moment. Sometimes the conditions were extraordinarily difficult. But the deep conviction that what the Peace Corps does is valuable has kept us all on track.

In 1961, Sargent Shriver sent the first group of volunteers off from the Rose Garden with the willing assistance of the President. Part of America's first foray into grass-roots development, these young men and women left with much fanfare and the abiding hope of all concerned that they would do well. Products of an idealistic era in our national history, each volunteer had signed on in response to President Kennedy's challenge to find out what they could do for their country. It was a long time before another group of volunteers got a Rose Garden send-off.

During the Vietnam War, Peace Corps directors had to grapple with volunteers' protests against American foreign policy. A mirror of domestic ferment over national values and policies, the Peace Corps as an official government agency had to balance its concerns over bad publicity against the volunteers' rights of free speech as Americans. They were, after all, volunteers, and they were carrying the flag of American ideals—free speech among them—to foreign lands. Some at home worried that Third World citizens, unaccustomed to protests and generally inexperienced in the ways of democracy, would be unable to understand the volunteers' behavior as a legitimate exercise of their citizenship. Looking back on it, we can celebrate the fact that we have such a society and that it has survived transitory periods of painful and dramatic polarization. Such challenges were all part of our growing up.

Then there was the period when the Peace Corps, combined with all the voluntary agencies under an umbrella called ACTION, had to struggle to keep its unique focus and identity. Though appreciated by the public and supported by the Congress, it had to spend precious energy advancing its case within a sometimes inflexible bureaucratic structure. This hurdle and others notwithstanding, volunteers continued to work at their posts, and requests continued to come in from one foreign capital after another for technical assistance. This period also saw the Peace Corps refine its capacity to deliver increasingly specialized services, particularly in agriculture.

The product of what was forged during all those trials and tribulations has now begun to emerge. We make our contribution to bettering the lives of Third World people without *imposing* American values on them. We do not hold ourselves out as their saviors or even as wise men, nor do we stand on soapboxes. Instead, we place our values in the hearts of villages, in schools and fisheries and forests, and let our example speak for itself. American values, for many people in the Third World, *are* the volunteer they get to know and live with for two years. On this, our silver anniversary, we can take pride in the worldwide recognition we have earned as a genuine grass-roots development organization.

When my own term as Peace Corps director was launched in 1981, some harbored doubts that a housewife from Houghton, Michigan, could master the Peace Corps' administrative intricacies or keep it safely distant from the mire of partisan politics. The Peace Corps at that time was still struggling to overcome its 1970s image as a haven for hippies, and like so many valuable programs, was so busy doing its job that it didn't have time to stop to talk with the very people on whom its continuation depended—from members of Congress to key people in the executive branch. There were growing misperceptions about what we did or did not do, and how we went about it. Frequent changes in leadership had led many people to think there wasn't either a program worth leading or a leader capable of handling it. Morale was low. Somehow, the Peace Corps machine chugged ahead, but with an extremely low profile and an aloofness from the political process on which it was dependent. There were those who had concluded that the Peace Corps wasn't or shouldn't be functioning.

I was convinced that I was equal to the challenge. I possessed political connections through years of Republican organizing and had sharpened my political skills during the years my husband served in Congress. People whose judgment I respected most, including my husband, Phil, encouraged me. What an honor to be appointed to such an important post by President Reagan, and what hopes I carried to the consuming task before me! As a deep believer in the necessity of the Peace Corps, I was determined to meet the challenge vociferously.

It was during my initial visit to the White House that my hopes hit the first snag of political reality. I had been told that a certain man would be my contact there, and I was eager to discuss the Peace Corps with him. I sat in his office for nearly an hour while he rearranged furniture and even took a few phone calls. Finally he sat down long enough to tell me that he believed in candor, and candidly, he thought the Peace Corps ought to be abolished. He went on to report that he'd recommended as much during the campaign. In his mind, the Peace Corps was an anomaly in the Reagan administration, falling into the category of a "mushrooming federal agency" that was breaking the national treasury. He did allow, however, that "The President must not agree with me, since he appointed you." For my part, I promised to change his mind, and to find another White House contact.

I refused to agree that the Peace Corps was an anomaly. When the whole land is swept with conservatism, what could be more conservative than thousands of Americans willing to sacrifice two years of their lives for the betterment of people in the remotest areas of the world? Could there be a more conservative call to action than Kennedy's "Ask not . . ."? And if liberal Senator Hubert Humphrey was the Peace Corps' founder and congressional mainstay at the outset, it was his pairing with the conservatives' own Senator Barry Goldwater that sealed passage of the Peace Corps legislation. The Peace Corps, I told my White House contact, had actually shrunk in size over the years, so it didn't even qualify as one of those "mushrooming federal agencies." I vowed to stand in the way of its extinction.

Everyone in the Washington power structure needed an update on the Peace Corps. It has a mission of self-help that American volunteers perform with an almost religious fervor. Day in and day out, for the past twenty-five years, anywhere from 6,000 to 15,000 volunteers have been at work making valuable contributions to other countries, all of which are important to us. The Peace Corps illuminates the tenets of democracy for all who participate, whether they're doers or receivers. It is pro-American and pro-world. It is anti-poverty and anti-hunger. It is humanitarian. It is educational, for both the developing world and the United States.

It also responds to changes in America, and not just political ones. Over the years, the United States has moved from being a youth-oriented society to one that is older and more conservative, and the Peace Corps has had to adjust accordingly. Volunteers are older now, which is not surprising in a nation slated to grow "grayer" as we near the turn of the century. As the volunteer corps has grown more mature, our approaches to training and placement have had to change. We are learning to prepare older volunteers, to look for creative ways to maximize their skills, to open programs for them to be contributors in host countries. We're already discovering that the Peace Corps is now a second and third career, rather than the first step it has been for so many years.

Women, furthermore, are growing to be a greater part of the Peace Corps, which parallels another change in our society. We've gone from 32 percent women in 1962 to nearly 50 percent in 1985. Women are also emerging in nontraditional professions—as foresters, agricultural workers, engineers. My own daughter is presently an engineer helping to design rural bridges in Nepal, certainly neither the place nor the occupation I would have imagined for her twenty years ago. But how proud I am of her and each of our six thousand volunteers!

At the same time, a decrease in America's stock of certain skills has forced the Peace Corps to make adjustments accordingly. In 1961, the fifteen million family farms across the country fed us a supply of agricultural workers. With only one-third or so of those farms still in existence today, we have to look harder for our agricultural volunteers. Fewer young Americans are majoring in math and science these days, robbing us of prepared teachers still much in demand in Peace Corps countries. All of these changes, and more, have required adjustments—and the Peace Corps has responded.

As the new director, I knew that if we were going to flourish, we must take the success story of the Peace Corps in the 1980s to Congress, the executive branch, the diplomatic corps. We made it a policy to keep track of congressional and executive delegations planning trips to sections of the world where there were Peace Corps sites. We provided briefing papers on the region and followed up with personal visits whenever we could.

Once, I went with some trepidation to see conservative Republican Representative Gerald Solomon just after he had returned from a much-publicized trip to Africa. During the trip, he and his Democratic counterpart had had public disagreements over the role American aid could play, and I was apprehensive about his opinions of Peace Corps volunteers. But I was barely inside his office when he declared, "I've seen them. They've convinced me. Any time you want me to speak on their behalf, let me know."

Former House Foreign Affairs Committee member Representative Edwin Derwinsky admitted to me in a talk that he had not been a Peace Corps supporter—"You probably think I'm a Neanderthal . . ."—but once he had had a chance to see it firsthand on a visit, he was converted. He has been helping the Peace Corps ever since.

When I first came aboard, the Peace Corps budget was so undernourished that it was hardly noticed by anyone. By sheer chance, I discovered this budget had been sent over to the State Department and then to the Office of Management and Budget without my ever being invited to defend it, much less to try to get some of the drastic $10 million cut reinstated. A $10 million reduction without a day in court! I insisted on a review, and I marched on the White House armed with facts enough to smite any cuts, drown any dissent. I discovered opponents who could not comprehend why we needed staff in each country where we had volunteers. I don't think the people in charge of cuts had ever traveled to a developing country, or even heard of the Peace Corps prior to meeting me, so my persuasive tactics were sorely tested. I did return with a small triumph, though; I managed to get $2 million restored.

That the Peace Corps has *not* mushroomed into a massive federal agency has, in a sense, been our undoing. In terms of purchasing power after inflation, our current year's budget is far below earlier levels. We're so small that we are in constant danger of being traded away in budget negotiations, despite any of our arguments to the contrary. Our volunteer commitments run on a two-year cycle, but our budget allocations are on an annual basis. Thus, to grow, we must have an assured commitment that lasts for *at least* a two-year congressional term.

Meanwhile, the Peace Corps has received an increasing number of requests for volunteers, from countries of every size and description. I advise each country to make a formal request through diplomatic and executive channels, and I have worked with their embassies here to assist when possible. I also encourage their leaders to visit Peace Corps headquarters when they come to Washington. It often takes years now, and plenty of bureaucratic effort, before we can finally open a new program.

Not long ago, we received a boost from Prime Minister Ratu Sir Kamisese Mara of Fiji. Since he was the first head of state from the Pacific Islands to be invited to Washington for a state visit, a Cabinet meeting was called to welcome him. I had had the honor of visiting with him on a Peace Corps inspection trip earlier in the year. At the oval table in the Cabinet Room, I positioned myself near the Fijian delegation. After a discussion of nuclear-free zones and sugar quotas, there was suddenly a moment of silence. The prime minister, speaking with great intensity, then said, "Mr. President, I want to bring my people's appreciation for the men and women of the United States Peace Corps, who for so many years have served the needs of Fijians throughout the countryside." Every eye in the room turned to me.

Few could imagine the weight of this endorsement, however, until several weeks later, when I learned about a meeting that the budget review team had had with the President. The conservative Heritage Foundation had just issued a highly critical report about us, and many feared that this session would mean the end of the Peace Corps. The Peace Corps' turn on the agenda came, and whose voice rose to speak first? The President's! "We can't cut the Peace Corps," he reportedly said. "The prime minister of Fiji was just here saying how important their work is."

Sensing that the greater our constituency the more compelling our recognition, the Peace Corps has enlisted, in addition to the President, legions of others in our extended family. Families of Peace Corps volunteers themselves are now included in preparations for their children's missions. Promoting small business development throughout the world, chambers of commerce have become partners with us. Universities are offering attractive graduate packages, some subsidized by major corporations, to returning volunteers, in recognition of the valuable contributions they make to campuses. When the Reagan administration launched the Caribbean Basin Initiative, they turned to the Peace Corps as a natural partner, since we have had volunteers in that region since 1961 and could provide the necessary linkage to farmers and small businessmen targeted by the Initiative's programs.

Our crusade to put the Peace Corps on the registry of permanent American institutions, I believe, has left few stones unturned. Friends of the Peace Corps testified before both the Democratic and Republican platform committees in 1984, ensuring an endorsement in both platforms. White House speechwriters are provided with material about relevant Peace Corps programs in advance of every major speech the President gives, and in the 1985 State of the Union address, President Reagan mentioned the Peace Corps' unrelenting efforts to relieve famine in Africa.

Whenever we get a chance, we call attention to the fact that Peace Corps volunteers don't stop serving their country when they come home. They return to the United States and serve fellow Americans on development issues and community activities, and in a wide range of other ways. We hear back from congressmen that when they hold town meetings in their home districts, they often encounter returned volunteers and find them extremely knowledgeable and increasingly active constituents.

I think we have overcome the skepticism of a few years ago. Most of our leaders now recognize that the Peace Corps is important in providing plenty of bang for the foreign aid dollar. So I say it's time to turn to all of our "stockholders"—the citizens of this changing America—and suggest a doubling of their investment. We've proved ourselves to be cost-effective, prudent, and popular, and now we're ready for the next step. We need to be too big to trade away. The Peace Corps has enabled America to see what a few people can accomplish. I now propose that we enable the Peace Corps to show what an *army* of volunteers could do.

Recently we sent another group of volunteers off to their posts, with President Reagan present. It was my pleasure to say to them, "The Peace Corps is back in the Rose Garden, where it has always belonged."

The President had these words for the volunteers that day:

> When Loret Ruppe announced a recruitment drive for agricultural volunteers for Africa, the Peace Corps was besieged by responses from people rushing to volunteer, willing to interrupt their lives and devote two years to meeting the emergency. You are a cross section of America. Some of you are first-generation Americans; some of you are naturalized citizens. You come from all across the country, and you represent a wide variety of people. Soon you will be in Africa, where you'll be a vital part of the relief aid to help millions suffering from malnutrition and starvation. You'll be living in some of the most impoverished nations of the world, working for

food production, soil conservation, fisheries production, forest preservation, and water supply development.

By bringing your training and skills to bear on the underlying problems of agricultural and economic development, you can help your host nations make the difficult but vital journey from dependence on short-term aid to self-sufficiency. Last month, when Vice President Bush returned from his trip to the famine-struck regions of Africa, he gave me a personal account of the heartbreaking conditions in the land, and he told me of the outstanding work of the Peace Corps volunteers."

In a period when we are dedicating so much of our national might and wealth to building up security systems, I cannot help making a comparison with the few dollars it takes to do the current Peace Corps job. Look at the mammoth pie left to defense, and the relatively small slice it would take to reach our potential. When I look at the endless parade of missiles, tanks, and warships being procured, I have to ask myself, where are the battalions of teachers, agricultural workers, and health personnel who can personally deliver assaults for peace in the world? I look at the debt we continue to incur and wonder if this is a fair legacy for the generations we hope will follow us. I read that the most gifted and talented young Americans graduating from our universities are being attracted to jobs in the defense industry, and I wonder what they might be able to wreak should they be handed the challenge of developing interdependence on this planet.

What really is the true measure of America as a world leader? We don't want to be the only rich ones in a sea of raging discontent. Wouldn't it be the most magnificent boast of all if we were able to field tens of thousands of our youth, our mid-level technicians, our newly retired, and our elderly, around the world, a mobile Pentagon of ploughshares? Our example would be the mightiest of deterrents, a powerful sight to behold. I am mindful of the tribal chief in Sierra Leone who said he'd heard of America before the Peace Corps volunteers came, but "Now we know what it means."

In a belt-tightening, more conservative, older America, the Peace Corps must rekindle its torch, lighting the way to a reordering of our priorities in the pursuit of peace. That is the challenge before us. We must continue to raise the flag of an interdependent world and let it wave over us. We have a covenant with the people of the world's developing countries to help them help themselves, so we all might live in peace together.

A Conservative Institution

by James A. McClure

It's been twelve years since my daughter, Marilyn, six months after graduating from William and Mary College, told my wife, Louise, and me that she was going to join the Peace Corps after she graduated.

Like many of her fellow volunteers, she was motivated in large part by a "What-can-I-do-to-make-the-world-better?" idealism.

Although Louise and I didn't relish the thought of our only daughter—born and raised in our small hometown of Payette, Idaho—living in a mud hut in the jungles of Africa, Asia, or South America, we supported Marilyn's decision wholeheartedly. The call to serve is admirable and necessary if hunger, disease, and squalor are to be wiped out.

As a strong believer in traditional American values, I was much in sympathy with the Peace Corps notion of having the individual give a hand to other individuals to create a better life. I was attached to the pioneer spirit, in which folks did things for themselves and helped others, without waiting for government to step in. People did not call that "conservative" when I was growing up; it wasn't even political. We just did it. And I was proud that my daughter, following in that tradition, wanted to do it, too.

Several months later, we saw her off as she began a 3,500-mile trek to the Ivory Coast.

In retrospect, what stands out most in my mind is the irony of it all. For years I had considered the Peace Corps a good idea gone awry. Much happened in those years to change my opinion of the Corps, but I still considered Marilyn's decision an interesting twist of fate.

The Corps' stated purpose, at its inception, was to help the uneducated, malnourished, and impoverished people of the Third World help themselves to a better life. Nonpartisan, philanthropic, relatively inex-

---

James A. McClure, a Republican, is a United States senator from Idaho.

pensive, and largely independent of government influence, it had the makings of greatness.

But during the 1960s—particularly the middle and latter part of the decade—there were many instances in which that lofty goal was cast aside. Altruism, unfortunately, was sometimes supplanted by politics.

In Latin America, for example, Peace Corps volunteers engaged in public demonstrations against the regimes of several nations. As a former volunteer put it, "The Peace Corps was selling America," and not imparting skills to the poor people it was supposed to be helping. Not surprisingly, some countries asked the Corps to leave.

Other problems beset the Corps as well. During the Vietnam War, the Corps was an easy escape for young men who didn't want to serve in the military. Others joined because—to use the vernacular of the day—they wanted to "find themselves." That's not what the Corps, its founders, or the people it was intended to aid needed. Some volunteers who protested U.S. involvement in Vietnam made their views known in anti-war demonstrations abroad.

The Corps, it appeared, was a noble experiment on the brink of failure—a victim of the political and social turmoil of the era.

Fortunately, the pending demise didn't come to pass. Public outrage and internal criticisms pinpointed the problems, and the program was put back on its intended course.

Ultimately, this catharsis transformed the Peace Corps into a thriving agency. To look at it now, at age twenty-five, is to look at a different organization from the one I cast a critical eye upon twenty years ago.

Programs have been streamlined to focus on problems unique to a particular country or village. There are no longer stories like the one about Peace Corps-built grain silos in Ghana being used as bedrooms because they weren't needed.

Foresters, engineers, agronomists, accountants, nurses, and nutritionists are sent to regions where there's a need for their services and where they'll do the most good.

The volunteer selection process is more stringent, with increased emphasis on skills and language, and greater participation among people over forty. Idealism is no less prevalent now than it was during the sixties, but it's more refined, aimed at community assistance instead of political reform, career development instead of career postponement.

The beauty of the Corps is seen in the void it fills between the military and economic aid the United States provides to other countries.

Military aid, while important, is difficult to keep in balance. Too much can exhaust a country's economic resources. Too little can mean the difference between freedom and oppression.

Economic aid often comes in the form of a gift, such as money to build a school. Unfortunately, there is no guarantee that those most in need will benefit. The haves get richer in some countries, while the have-nots continue to suffer.

The Peace Corps can often transcend these kinds of problems. It gives people on the bottom rung of society the kind of instruction and information they can use to improve themselves and their environment.

It's a people-to-people fight for improved economic and living conditions. Stable nations are based on a large, stable middle class—people who have a stake in society. They have something they want to protect and improve. The Peace Corps is a means to that end, helping the poor, sick, and uneducated to become active participants in their countries. What's more, it's not coercive in nature. The Peace Corps goes only where it is invited.

"By and large, volunteers are received warmly. People are anxious to get projects under way," Marilyn said recently. "They want schools and clinics, and the Corps is there to lead the way. That kind of acceptance fosters teamwork—and teamwork fosters success, which they hopefully will continue after the Corps is gone."

Some triumphs are big—eliminating tuberculosis in Bolivia or helping alleviate famine in Ethiopia. Most are small, like digging a well in Niger so villagers can drink fresh water, or planting cash crops for the first time in Botswana.

The impact of some efforts lasts forever. Others die the day a particular volunteer goes home. But it all contributes, in one way or another, to a more peaceful, neighborly world.

When Marilyn returned from the Ivory Coast, she said that if nothing else was gained, she and the villagers she lived with had had the chance to meet.

Being immersed in another culture, having the opportunity to partake of unfamiliar customs are rewards that can't be measured in dollars or any other form of commerce.

Marilyn said she was one of the few white women the villagers had ever seen. They wanted to braid her hair and touch her skin because the textures were so different from theirs. She learned much about herself, her country, and the world from her Corps experiences. Similarly, the Corps has learned much about itself in the last twenty-five years.

I liken the development of the Corps to the natural maturing process of a human being. There are the uncertain early days of living in an unfamiliar world. There are the preteen and teenage years of growth, sometimes rebellion, and, inescapably, mistakes. But we learn from it all. By the time we're in our late twenties, we have a clear focus of where we've been, where we're going, and how we're going to get there.

The Corps has matured nicely. Its future is bright. With emphasis on cost-conscious voluntarism and minimal government interference, it is one of the few programs embraced by politicians of every persuasion. It puts charity where it belongs—in the hands of individuals. The Corps knows where it's going and how it's going to get there.

Henry David Thoreau once wrote, "To affect the quality of the day is the highest of the arts." Twenty years ago, I wouldn't have drawn the parallel between those words and the Peace Corps. But his words do justice today to the Corps' mission and direction.

A Liberal Institution

by Hubert H. Humphrey III

"Peace is not passive, it is active. Peace is not appeasement, it is strength. Peace does not 'happen,' it requires work."

These words, spoken by my father, summarize the overarching premise of the Peace Corps. Whether by planting in the fields of a distant country or teaching in a classroom in Africa, Hubert Humphrey's dream was to work at peace by working with the citizens of our world. The Peace Corps idea was truly a "people helping people" program.

I can remember hearing about the idea from my father in the late fifties. He told me how he had talked to some missionaries who mentioned an idea roughly the same as the Peace Corps. Although their concept was smaller and contained within the church, my father understood the great benefit a national Peace Corps program would bring to our country's foreign relations. The United States could supply developing countries with the knowledge, ideas, techniques, and teachers to help maintain their people. From increased agricultural productivity to increased literacy, a Peace Corps would be the model to supply the resources. My father once said, "Critics ask what visible, lasting effects there are, as if care, concern, love, and help can be measured in concrete and steel or dollars or ergs. Education, whether in mathematics, language, health, nutrition, farm techniques, or peaceful coexistence, may not always be visible, but the effects endure."

It was no small endeavor to promote and pass into law this plan whose idea was enigmatic and whose benefits were so intangible to decision-makers, more accustomed as they were to facts and figures, dollars and cents.

My father's other objective was to provide our young people with options to their education and work plans. He hoped to appeal to the al-

---

Hubert H. Humphrey III, a Democrat, is attorney general of Minnesota.

truistic vision of thousands of young people. When my father started to examine this issue seriously, he found more and more that young adults did not want to travel the traditional "four years and out into the world of work with a college education" route. The Peace Corps would be an attractive alternative to those not ready to don a suit and tie.

There was no political ideology in the Peace Corps notion of allowing young people to learn through experience. It took just good common sense to see that Peace Corps volunteers would gain as much, or more, from their experience as the countries in which they served. I doubt if anyone would dispute that this has happened. We can all point to a situation where we've said, "I had to work hard, but I learned a lot, too." This attracted many volunteers to the Peace Corps. They knew they would be sent to foreign surroundings, and they knew up front they wouldn't be paid for their service. Yet many volunteered because of their commitment to their country and also, I believe, because they thought they were making a significant and valuable contribution to world peace.

My father had an especially keen interest in agriculture. He said, "A hungry man knows no reason. Democracy or totalitarianism, peace or violence—they make little difference to starving men with nothing to lose." What Dad most wanted was to feed people. He thought that if a person had a full stomach, he had little need to ponder revolution. With our surplus of food and our great knowledge of optimum production, our nation, he felt, could export our ideas and experience to developing countries of the world. Although much work needs to be done, our programs to communicate our own farm technology have been a success—almost to the point of our losing abundant agricultural markets because countries have become more self-sufficient in food production.

My father had a great deal of respect for and confidence in young people. I am sad that this respect wasn't always reciprocated. He surrounded himself with young people who either worked on his staff or advised him on policy considerations. Hubert Humphrey admired their youthful spirit. The Peace Corps was one program intended to enrich the experience of young Americans. Like his confidence in the judgment of young people, Dad believed no one person had a monopoly on the concept of peace. If thousands of young Americans could scatter to all ends of the earth, we might find a thousand unique experiments in peace. This is why he lobbied hard for flexibility in the Peace Corps. He did not want the countries to fit into the Peace Corps model; he wanted the Peace Corps to adapt to the countries and their cultures.

Many fine people collaborated with my father to promote and refine the concept of a Peace Corps. One person was U.S. Representative Henry Reuss, from Wisconsin. He put a great deal of time and effort into convincing his colleagues in the House to support the Peace Corps. As hard as it was for some to accept, Hubert Humphrey and Henry Reuss demonstrated that even folks from the Midwest know a thing or two about the peacemaking process. You can see the Midwestern flavor in the Peace Corps in many aspects, not the least of them being its strong emphasis on agriculture and public education.

Although the word "liberal" has become a dirty word used to label anyone advocating government intervention, the traditional and practical elements of liberalism espoused by my father are still as relevant today as they were during Franklin Roosevelt's Presidency. My father said that the true liberal "looks upon the state as an instrument of society and servant of its members. The responsible state is held strictly to account for serving the common end of its citizens by means which are freely chosen and which may be freely changed." In this sense, the Peace Corps, instrument of a society serving the common needs of all people, is a liberal institution.

The opportunity to obtain a useful education, work, live in a decent home, and have access to health care and adequate public protection is a basic need of all citizens. These are the implicit concerns in our ideology. In the clearest definition, we, as liberals, feel government can help solve certain ills of society. We don't view government as the problem.

I have always been committed to the idea of providing service to a community. In this, I am an attentive student of my father. In Minnesota, I have been a strong proponent of a Youth Service Corps, which contains many attributes of the Peace Corps. A Governor's Task Force is now examining the issue and will decide how to implement such a program. Many young people today have to wait too long before they can do anything that we adults feel has any importance to society. A Peace Corps and a domestic Youth Service Corps are two ways our young people can move beyond the often rigid line between childhood and adulthood.

It is hard to measure the progress and achievements of an operation like the Peace Corps. But one would have to conduct an extensive search to find an individual who believes it has been a failure. I believe its acceptance among both liberals and conservatives serves as the testimonial to its continued relevance in our global relations.

I can remember the difficulty Dad had in the infancy stage of the Peace Corps. When he first introduced the idea in 1957, it did not meet with much enthusiasm. Traditional diplomats quaked at the thought of thousands of young Americans scattered across their world. Many thought it a silly and unworkable idea. It really wasn't until after the 1960 presidential primaries that the Peace Corps received serious discussion. John

F. Kennedy had recognized the merits of this idea and began advocating a Peace Corps during his campaign. With Kennedy in the White house, the Peace Corps was almost surely going to be implemented in some form. Dad felt that if the idea could ever be implemented, the Peace Corps would take on a life and character of its own. What is unique about the Peace Corps twenty-five years later is that it is not an idea, a law, a legal structure, or a bureaucracy that has outlived its useful purpose. Instead, just as Dad envisioned it would be, the Peace Corps today is action-filled, and flexible enough to meet the most practical needs of the diverse people it serves, bringing to them the real tools of life and peace.

I think if my father had a chance to speak out on this anniversary of the Peace Corps, he would say it is the best example of what the peace process must really be. Peace is not a passive condition. It is not just an intellectual concept. Rather, it is an active and practical application of constructive works by people dealing with real problems affecting individuals at the most essential level.

As our nation and others consider how to bring peace to the world, I hope our leaders remember that beyond political, military, and economic considerations, the action of peacemaking must take place with the people, in the villages, on the farms, in the factories, and at home. The Peace Corps is one of only a few programs to endure the recent budgetary retrenchment. I suspect the reason for this lies within its mission. No one can debate the issue of providing American aid to the less fortunate—not in the form of massive economic expenditures, but, rather, in personal training and education. The Peace Corps credo is simple yet enigmatic; its greatest benefits are not concrete but are certainly visible.

The Future

by John R. Dellenback

At twenty-five, the Peace Corps stands on the brink of a bright future, born of a distinguished past, bred with constant care, deep relationships, and commitment to service. Will the next twenty-five years be the same as the last? Does the Peace Corps have an expanded role to play in the world? Should the Peace Corps be cutting back or surging ahead? Can the Peace Corps maintain its reliance on the human factor in a world grown increasingly dependent on technology?

Tens of thousands of Peace Corps volunteers have done much good in assisting the people of developing countries to learn technical skills and acquire capacities that help raise the physical standards of living. But even more important in the long run have been the hopes and visions that have come alive in individuals, the relationships created, the exciting symbols and catalysts that have influenced so many. It's been estimated that in any given month, Peace Corps volunteers have an impact on more than one million people.

Indeed, the Peace Corps can lay solid claim to fitting within the old dictum of letting actions speak louder than words, for the volunteers have done much of their work without benefit of fanfare, financial reward, or fancy support structures. They have changed the definition of development in the Third World from one that is *thing*-centered to one that is *people*-centered. The bold mission which, initially, many doubted could even last a year has forged friendships between haves and have-nots in the world that I believe have led and will continue to lead to fundamental changes. The Peace Corps created a ripple that has developed the power of a still-rising wave.

A wise man in Thailand saw this clearly. A Buddhist priest, he kept an

---

John R. Dellenback is chairman of the Peace Corps' 25th Anniversary Foundation, Inc., and president of the Christian College Coalition.

eye on a Peace Corps volunteer's work teaching English to the village children. When asked if he thought the children had learned much English, he replied that he was sure they had. But he added that the most important part of the process was how much he and the volunteer were learning about each other, their new understanding of each other's cultures, and the commitment they had to each other's work. All of that, he said, would far outlast the volunteer's tour.

The Peace Corps' influence does reach far beyond the confines of the villages or countries where we've worked. The deeds of our volunteers, their spirit and commitment, have established a worldwide reputation. The Peace Corps is recognized as a voluntary agency that is an effective, well-managed motor in the complex machinery of development. It has taken its legislative mandate literally to foster world peace and friendship.

The legacy of the Peace Corps volunteers continues to grow even after they return home. In their jobs, their communities, their places of worship, and their families, they remain an important part of our nation's capacity to behave responsibly in a world grown increasingly interdependent. Just as they *became* the United States for the villagers with whom they worked side by side, so they now *are* Ethiopia, Korea, or Ecuador for the legions of Americans with whom they interact and whom they influence on a daily basis.

My own association with the Peace Corps began during my years in Congress, when, as a member of the House Committee on Education and Labor, I helped write the legislation that created ACTION, our super-volunteer agency, of which the Peace Corps was to be one part. With all the volunteer opportunities we offer as a government, it seemed logical that ACTION would be an effective way to consolidate some of the housekeeping machinery in activities common to voluntary agencies, such as recruitment and training.

In 1975, when I became Peace Corps director, I changed my mind and concluded that we of the Congress had made a legislative mistake, which we of the Peace Corps were forced to live with. I saw that the Peace Corps was aimed at promoting international relationships and world peace, using volunteers as a brilliant instrument to achieve that purpose, while the domestic programs in ACTION were aimed at involving volunteers, using whatever worthwhile domestic programs could be identified. Because the kinds of volunteers needed for the two types of programs differed considerably, recruiting for both suffered. During my two years as director, I became absolutely convinced of the uniqueness of the Peace Corps mission and the impossibility of getting the best out of either the international or the domestic volunteer efforts by lumping them together. Not long after I left the Peace Corps in 1977, I worked with former colleagues in the Congress and many others to undo what we had originally seen as a fine idea. Out of that effort, the Peace Corps reemerged as an independent entity.

The result is that the Peace Corps has regained its flexibility and openness, an American hallmark that has enabled it to shift and change its worldwide programs in much the same way that Congress goes about mending flawed legislation. In the beginning, many feared that we were setting out to Americanize the world—that we felt we knew what needed to be done and were sending forth a corps of do-gooders to save the world from itself. To the contrary, one of the Peace Corps' underlying strengths has been the commitment to working with each country in response to its own perceived needs rather than dictating an American agenda. Thus, if it is teachers the Indian government wants, that is what we send them. If it is planning assistance in Togo, that is what we try to deliver there. The Peace Corps is in some sense a broker for voluntary assistance, and as such it must constantly be aware of changing needs in each country.

The Peace Corps must also keep its eye on change in the world. Cliché or not, the world is much smaller today than it was twenty-five years ago. Technology has reduced the time it takes to communicate or to travel. Most of the remote corners of the world are now within satellite reach, which reduces the sense of isolation felt by individual volunteers. Fifty new nations have emerged during the first generation of the Peace Corps, nearly all of them struggling to survive in increasingly complex circumstances. Positioned in the midst of older and more established countries, involved with them in international trade, bombarded by their television, and rubbing elbows with their tourists, citizens of these countries see the contrast between haves and have-nots more sharply than ever before. Misunderstandings abound on both sides. A sense of interdependence with the rest of the world abides in the countries of the Third World, but their frail and underdeveloped economic systems create barriers and estrangement.

Seeking ways in which we can play an effective helping role in this changed and changing world is a priority of many Americans. With our energy, determination, and creativity; our nation's great blessings; and our demonstrated concern for others, we have solid credentials as agents of change. As seekers of goodwill, we do, however, have to face the fact that in the minds of people in many sections of this world, we are lumped together with the U.S.S.R. in a vat of distrust. However extraordinary the aid given by the United States to a defeated Germany and Japan after World War II, and however considerable our worldwide assistance since then, it is too often correctly perceived that much of our recent foreign aid is military. It does not go unnoticed that, measured by gross national product, more than a dozen countries poorer than we are giving away a larger percentage abroad. It is also widely perceived that much of what America does in the way of assisting developing nations is not out of international goodwill as much as it is to serve our own interests. Against such a backdrop, the Peace Corps stands out sharp and clear as a very special and genuine effort to give and to serve.

So what of the Peace Corps in the next five, ten, twenty-five years? With institutions, as with individuals, there is no point in change for the sake of change. At the same time, unless we remain ready and willing to make indicated, forward-looking transformations, we run the risk of the buggy-whip manufacturer in an age of automobiles and airplanes. However efficiently run and ably staffed his operation may be, the buggy-whip maker should hang it up and quit. The great impact of the Peace Corps has been and will continue to be based on its combining committed volunteers with identified areas of need. Initially the physical needs of underdeveloped nations were the targets upon which the Peace Corps was brought to bear. But its real magic was not in the physical things accomplished, however welcome and helpful they were. The real magic was in the influence of the service itself—both upon the served and the servers.

The served saw volunteers who were willing to perform hard, often unpleasant tasks that needed to be done, tasks from which they did not gain personally. The servers grew as people in what they did and learned much, obtaining great inner rewards from giving help to others. Relationships flourished, attitudes changed, and walls of distrust were leveled. The servers returned home changed people, ready and equipped to make a difference in America.

The deft knitting of volunteers into areas and pockets of need all over the world that has characterized the Peace Corps must continue. In one sense, the Peace Corps is a single organization headquartered in Washington with arms reaching around the globe. But in another, deeper sense, the Peace Corps is some sixty organizations, situated in separate countries and involving some six thousand individuals with different sets of mind, heart, and hands. Naturally, there should always be similarities throughout these organizations and those individuals, but let's be sure that they will never be expected to be identical, or all performing the same service. If something works well in one country, build on it and strengthen it; but if the same thing doesn't work well in another, we must be prepared to try another tack. The Peace Corps experience has proved so successful at its root that I believe, whatever else is changed, that we must hold firmly to those aspects which constitute the Peace Corps' uniqueness. We must also stand ready to welcome any new challenges brought about by our experience or the march of time.

I include the following in this:

1. The Peace Corps must continue to be essentially an organization of volunteers, organized and coordinated by professional staff who are servant leaders rather than masters. In this structure, with the idealism and commitment it demands and produces, lies much of the essential genius of the Peace Corps. To remain a credible advocate for the grass roots of the developing world, we must remain fundamentally a grass-roots organization.

2. The Peace Corps must resist all the logical, understandable arguments to shift its emphasis to highly skilled and eventually highly paid technicians in the field. The latter alternative runs the risk that the skill itself—provided free—will be more in demand than the presence of volunteers with their special capacity to motivate and build relationships.

3. The Peace Corps must also resist arguments for making it into a desirable haven for those who would have its service be a lifetime career. The current mandate for most of the staff limits employment to five years. This mandate is meant to ensure a continuous supply of new ideas, fresh approaches, and the limitless energy that is the trademark of the Peace Corps. It should not be changed.

4. The Peace Corps must resist the subtle, steady encroachment of the concept of turning the volunteer's readjustment allowance into a fair and reasonable salary. The message of the willingness of thousands of Americans to give two years of their lives to assist in the world's development will lose tremendous weight if the job of the volunteer becomes just that—a job. "Adequate remuneration" will threaten to corrupt one of the Peace Corps' most basic tenets, our willingness to give of ourselves voluntarily, out of a spirit of idealism.

5. The Peace Corps must continue to look for ways to cooperate with other agencies, both governmental and voluntary, and continue to promote cooperative interrelationships. Over the last five years, the Agency for International Development and the Peace Corps have expanded their ties, and this bodes well for the future. The Peace Corps should expand its Partnership Program, which directs funds from private American sources to specific projects in the Third World. The Peace Corps has also worked side by side with its counterparts from other countries in the "developed" world, adding another dimension to the enrichment of worldwide relationships. This type of partnership can be expanded to produce team approaches, with valuable results for all.

6. Within the United States, the Peace Corps has left returned Peace Corps volunteers and former staff members largely on their own. Until recently, little effort has been made to know where returned volunteers live, or what they are doing, what their special needs may be, or how effectively they could be strengthened in their role as ambassadors. While they are largely individualistic, and though they abhor the idea of being "used," we should not waste this solid core of expertise and wisdom as an important form of ongoing assistance in our joint mission.

7. Over the full twenty-five years of its life, the Peace Corps has had the great benefit of including in its ranks many older volunteers. Some of the very finest volunteers have, in fact, been older men and women, often at retirement age and well beyond, who have combined maturity and experience with commitment and idealism, and have been extraordinarily effective. The years ahead are going to bring into our society an increasing number of older Americans, many of whom could well serve as Peace Corps volunteers. They collectively represent a great resource for the nation. The Peace Corps should make renewed efforts to recruit from this growing supply for use in fields where their expertise can prove particularly valuable.

Beyond these administrative concerns, the Peace Corps of the future should expand its vision to encompass more and more countries. It has established a record of serving as a bridge between the United States and sixty developing nations. We are already profiting from our investment as leaders emerge, from among both the served and server, committed to a world at peace. Now we should move on to serve in every developing nation in the world.

We have been in many countries and left. We must find out why—and show our willingness to return. The needs in those developing countries are endless, and we cannot possibly meet them all. But there is a great reservoir of willing talent here, and we must reach more deeply into it. We know the benefit to ourselves. We must make a persuasive case to potential new countries.

Political ideology and differences may block our entry into some, but if so, let it be a blockade the other country erects, not one of our own. China, for example, the home of one-fifth of the world's population, is a prime candidate for Peace Corps involvement, regardless of its Communist orientation. I am convinced that our efforts in this realm will serve both America and world peace.

A final goal for the Peace Corps should be to establish a presence in every developed country in the world as well. The objective of the Peace Corps is to promote relationships that encourage peace, and rich nations need such bonds as much as poor ones. Every so-called developed nation—France, Japan, Australia, and all the others—has its own set of deep and acute needs. Whether it is in the area of health care, or urban problems such as race relations and street crime, the United States has developed capacities that could prove useful to those now experiencing them. Or, we could provide English teachers in areas where there is a need to build fluency in what is nearly a universal language.

At the heart of this new thrust will be the typical Peace Corps volunteer, whose presence and work will help dispel any fears of spying or hidden agendas. With the addition to our program of opportunities for reciprocal activities, in some countries our new linkages may shift from the concept of donor-donee to one of partnership. This new thrust will not come with the explosiveness that marked the beginning of the Peace Corps. Rather, it may come slowly, country by country. It will demand vision, leadership, top-level support from Congress and the executive branch, and large amounts of patience. But the contribution to world peace will be infectious and highly significant.

The world's capacity to feed, clothe, and house its rapidly increasing population can still be expanded. The human potential is limitless, though our supply of raw materials is finite. Strains between rich and poor are sharpening. To a substantial degree, those strains coincide with national and racial divisions. Avoiding an eventual violent confrontation between large blocs of the world's haves and have-nots demands thorough international understanding and demonstrated reciprocal concern.

From my perspective, the Peace Corps comes as close as a government agency can to living out genuine concern for others. It conducts the United States' most effective foreign relations. It is our nation's best instrument for giving to some of our brightest and best the opportunity to put their lives on the line in meaningful service to others.

As Americans, we can be grateful to the more than 120,000 volunteers and staff who have served the cause of world peace and friendship through the Peace Corps during its first twenty-five years. I am personally persuaded, however, that Shakespeare was correct when he said, "The past is prologue." Indeed, the best is yet to come.

Afterword

Making a Difference was commissioned as part of the commemoration of the Peace Corps' twenty-fifth anniversary. Only after I was invited to become its editor was I reminded that I had actually started working on it twenty-five years earlier.

One day last year, while visiting with James Mayer, head of the office in charge of the commemoration, I ran into Judy Guskin, who had been a member of the first group of volunteers in Thailand. Our recognition of each other was almost instantaneous. Judy and her husband, Alan, had led a group from the University of Michigan to Washington in January 1961 to lobby for the establishment of the Peace Corps. Then a city reporter for *The Washington Post,* I was assigned to cover their activities. I have a warm recollection of following them around town, sharing with them the euphoria that, for many of our generation, accompanied those early days of the Kennedy administration. This early involvement did not qualify me as a member of the band of brothers that clustered around Sargent Shriver to found the Peace Corps—a band I have long envied and admired—but perhaps it gave me a claim, as a distant relative, to edit this book.

I recruited Judy Guskin on the spot to write an article on the sowing of the seeds of the Peace Corps at Michigan while she and Alan were students. I then proposed they do another on the meaning of their experience in Thailand. Without even asking Alan, she said they would. I did not know it yet, but that was the kind of response I would receive from almost everyone whom I asked to contribute. Some howled that they were too busy. Many insisted their memories were too dim. All screamed about the deadline. But nearly everyone came through—sometimes with two, three, or even four drafts. All, in a sense, wrote autobiographically, but more than a few did prodigious amounts of research. I could not believe how willingly—nay, enthusiastically—they gave of their time and their services to this book. As an editor, I could not have asked for, I could not even have imagined, a more wonderful body of writers. They made my work a pleasure.

There were a few obstacles, however, not the least of which was that over the years, a very substantial portion of the Peace Corps' records has vanished. Some day they may turn up in an obscure archive. Meanwhile, instead of having twenty-five years' worth of letters, diaries, evaluations, and other documents on which to draw, I had only a seemingly random collection that had somehow survived.

As it turns out, it probably made little difference that I did not have more. When, for example, I examined letters from the early 1960s, I found they possessed nearly the same tone and content as the letters I obtained from the 1980s. Much as young Americans are said to have changed in the last quarter-century, I discovered a consistency in the sense of excitement, the feeling of commitment, the elation of self-discovery, and the good-natured innocence that volunteers, and staff members no less, brought to their work. Even as I sat poring over documents at a desk in the National Archives, where many of the files are stored, the words conveyed to me the special electricity that has characterized the experience of the Peace Corps throughout its history.

In addition to those who wrote the essays for *Making a Difference,* I would like to acknowledge the invaluable help of Ailene Goodman, who did much of the initial research; James Mayer, who was patient and proficient as liaison to the Peace Corps headquarters, and his stalwart office associates Sharon Statham and Margaret Pollack; Audrey Wolf, who was indefatigable in organizing the project; Deedie Runkel and Tom Scanlon, who labored behind the scenes; Harris Wofford and Francis Luzzatto, who tendered not only essays but advice; Perdita Huston, who conducted the interviews with foreign officials; Kerry Pelzman and John Zimmerman, who shared their letters; and others too numerous to name, who searched files, offered suggestions, prepared papers, and translated documents. It was amazing to me to see what so many people were willing to do for the love of the Peace Corps.

Milton Viorst
February 1986

About the Editor

Milton Viorst has been a reporter at *The Washington Post* and *The New York Post,* and has written for *Esquire, The New York Times Magazine,* and other periodicals. His many books include *Hostile Allies: FDR and Charles de Gaulle; Fall from Grace: The Republican Party and the Puritan Ethic; Hustlers and Heroes: An American Political Panorama;* and *Fire in the Streets: America in the 1960s.* Mr. Viorst lives in Washington with his wife, Judith, who is also a writer, and their three sons.